Hillcrest Edition

THE WRITINGS OF
MARK TWAIN
Volume XXI

This is the authorized
Uniform Edition of all
my books.
                    Mark Twain

Colonel Sellers introduces Sally to Lord Berkeley

THE

AMERICAN CLAIMANT

AND

OTHER STORIES AND SKETCHES

BY

MARK TWAIN
(Samuel L. Clemens)

NEW YORK AND LONDON
HARPER & BROTHERS PUBLISHERS

ILLUSTRATIONS

PHOTOGRAVURE

CONTENTS

Contents

THE WEATHER IN THIS BOOK

No weather will be found in this book. This is an attempt to pull a book through without weather. It being the first attempt of the kind in fictitious literature, it may prove a failure, but it seemed worth the while of some dare-devil person to try it, and the author was in just the mood.

Many a reader who wanted to read a tale through was not able to do it because of delays on account of the weather. Nothing breaks up an author's progress like having to stop every few pages to fuss-up the weather. Thus it is plain that persistent intrusions of weather are bad for both reader and author.

Of course weather is necessary to a narrative of human experience. That is conceded. But it ought to be put where it will not be in the way; where it will not interrupt the flow of the narrative. And it ought to be the ablest weather than can be had, not ignorant, poor-quality, amateur weather. Weather is a literary specialty, and no untrained hand can turn out a good article of it. The present author can do only a few trifling ordinary kinds of weather, and he cannot do those very good. So it has seemed wisest to borrow such weather as is necessary for the book from qualified and recognized experts — giving credit, of course. This weather will be found over in the back part of the book, out of the way. *See Appendix*. The reader is requested to turn over and help himself from time to time as he goes along.

THE AMERICAN CLAIMANT

EXPLANATORY

THE Colonel Mulberry Sellers here reintroduced to the public is the same person who appeared as *Eschol* Sellers in the first edition of the tale entitled *The Gilded Age*, years ago, and as *Beriah* Sellers in the subsequent editions of the same book, and finally as *Mulberry* Sellers in the drama played afterwards by John T. Raymond.

The name was changed from Eschol to Beriah to accommodate an Eschol Sellers who rose up out of the vasty deeps of uncharted space and preferred his request — backed by threat of a libel suit — then went his way appeased, and came no more. In the play Beriah had to be dropped to satisfy another member of the race, and Mulberry was substituted in the hope that the objectors would be tired by that time and let it pass unchallenged. So far it has occupied the field in peace; therefore we chance it again, feeling reasonably safe, this time, under shelter of the statute of limitations.   MARK TWAIN,

Hartford, 1891

THE AMERICAN CLAIMANT

CHAPTER I.

IT is a matchless morning in rural England. On a fair hill we see a majestic pile, the ivied walls and towers of Cholmondeley Castle, huge relic and witness of the baronial grandeurs of the Middle Ages. This is one of the seats of the Earl of Rossmore, K.G., G.C. B., K.C.M.G., etc., etc., etc., etc., etc., who possesses twenty-two thousand acres of English land, owns a parish in London with two thousand houses on its lease-roll, and struggles comfortably along on an income of two hundred thousand pounds a year. The father and founder of this proud old line was William the Conqueror his very self; the mother of it was not inventoried in history by name, she being merely a random episode and inconsequential, like the tanner's daughter of Falaise.

In a breakfast-room of the castle on this breezy fine morning there are two persons and the cooling remains of a deserted meal. One of these persons is the old lord, tall, erect, square-shouldered, white-haired, stern-browed, a man who shows character in every feature, attitude, and movement, and carries his seventy years as easily as most men carry fifty. The other person is his only son and heir, a dreamy-eyed young fellow, who looks about twenty-six but is nearer thirty. Candor, kindliness, honesty, sincerity, simplicity, mod-

land or institute suit.   The Fairfaxes kept their lordship alive, and so they have never lost it to this day,
although they live in Maryland;   their friend lost his
by his own neglect   You perceive now that the facts
in this case bring us to precisely this result: morally
the American tramp *is* rightful earl of Rossmore;
legally he has no more right than his dog.   There
now — are you satisfied?"

There was a pause;   then the son glanced at the
crest carved in the great oaken mantel, and said, with
a regretful note in his voice:

"Since the introduction of heraldic symbols, the
motto of this house has been *Suum cuique* — to every
man his own.   By your own intrepidly frank confession, my lord, it is become a sarcasm.   If Simon
Lathers —"

"Keep that exasperating name to yourself!   For
ten years it has pestered my eye and tortured my ear;
till at last my very footfalls time themselves to the
brain-racking rhythm of *Simon Lathers! — Simon
Lathers! — Simon Lathers!*   And now, to make its
presence in my soul eternal, immortal, imperishable,
you have resolved to — to — what is it you have resolved to do?"

"To go to Simon Lathers in America and change
places with him."

"What?   Deliver the reversion of the earldom into
his hands?"

"That is my purpose."

"Make this tremendous surrender without even trying the fantastic case in the Lords?"

"Ye — s —" with hesitation and some embarrassment.

"By all that is amazing, I believe you are insane,
my son.   See here — have you been training with that
ass again — that radical, if you prefer the term, though

the words are synonymous — Lord Tanzy of Toll-
mache?"

The son did not reply, and the old lord continued:

"Yes, you confess. That puppy, that shame to his
birth and caste, who holds all hereditary lordships and
privilege to be usurpation, all nobility a tinsel sham,
all aristocratic institutions a fraud, all inequalities in
rank a legalized crime and an infamy, and no bread
honest bread that a man doesn't earn by his own work
— *work*, pah!"— and the old patrician brushed imaginary labor-dirt from his white hands. "You have
come to hold just those opinions yourself, I suppose,"
he added, with a sneer.

A faint flush in the young man's cheek told that the
shot had hit and hurt, but he answered with dignity:

. "I have. I say it without shame — I feel none.
And now my reason for resolving to renounce my
heirship without resistance is explained. I wish to
retire from what to me is a false existence, a false
position, and begin my life over again — begin it right
— begin it on the level of mere manhood, unassisted
by factitious aids, and succeed or fail by pure merit or
the want of it. I will go to America, where all men
are equal and all have an equal chance; I will live or die,
sink or swim, win or lose as just a man — that alone,
and not a single helping gaud or fiction back of it."

"Hear, hear!" The two men looked each other
steadily in the eye a moment or two; then the elder
one added, musingly, "Ab-so-lutely cra-zy — ab-so-
lutely!" After another silence, he said, as one who,
long troubled by clouds, detects a ray of sunshine,
"Well, there will be one satisfaction — Simon Lathers
will come here to enter into his own, and I will drown
him in the horse-pond. The poor devil — always so
humble in his letters, so pitiful, so deferential; so
steeped in reverence for our great line and lofty

2A

station; so anxious to placate us, so prayerful for recognition as a relative, a bearer in his veins of our sacred blood — and withal so poor, so needy, so threadbare and pauper-shod as to raiment, so despised, so laughed at for his silly claimantship by the lewd American scum around him — ach, the vulgar, crawling, insufferable tramp! To read one of his cringing, nauseating letters — Well?"

This to a splendid flunky, all in inflamed plush and buttons and knee-breeches as to his trunk, and a glinting white frost-work of ground-glass paste as to his head, who stood with his heels together and the upper half of him bent forward, a salver in his hands.

" The letters, my lord."

My lord took them, and the servant disappeared.

" Among the rest, an American letter. From the tramp, of course. Jove, but here's a change! No brown-paper envelope this time, filched from a shop and carrying the shop's advertisement in the corner. Oh, no; a proper enough envelope — with a most ostentatiously broad mourning border — for his cat, perhaps, since he was a bachelor — and fastened with red wax — a batch of it as big as a half-crown — and — and — our crest for a seal! — motto and all. And the ignorant, sprawling hand is gone; he sports a secretary, evidently — a secretary with a most confident swing and flourish to his pen. Oh, indeed, our fortunes are improving over there — our meek tramp has undergone a metamorphosis."

" Read it, my lord, please."

" Yes, this time I will. For the sake of the cat:

14,042 SIXTEENTH STREET,
WASHINGTON, May 2.

My Lord—

It is my painful duty to announce to you that the head of our illustrious house is no more — The Right Honorable, The Most Noble, The Most

Puissant Simon Lathers Lord Rossmore having departed this life (" Gone at last — this is unspeakably precious news, my son,") at his seat in the environs of the hamlet of Duffy's Corners in the grand old State of Arkansas — and his twin brother with him, both being crushed by a log at a smoke-house raising, owing to carelessness on the part of all present, referable to over-confidence and gaiety induced by overplus of sour-mash — (" Extolled be sour-mash, whatever that may be, eh, Berkeley? ") five days ago, with no scion of our ancient race present to close his eyes and inter him with the honors due his historic name and lofty rank — in fact, he is on the ice yet, him and his brother — friends took up a collection for it. But I shall take immediate occasion to have their noble remains shipped to you (" Great heavens! ") for interment, with due ceremonies and solemnities, in the family vault or mausoleum of our house. Meantime I shall put up a pair of hatchments on my house-front, and you will of course do the same at your several seats.

I have also to remind you that by this sad disaster I, as sole heir, inherit and become seized of all the titles, honors, lands, and goods of our lamented relative, and must of necessity, painful as the duty is, shortly require at the bar of the Lords restitution of these dignities and properties now illegally enjoyed by your titular lordship.

With assurance of my distinguished consideration and warm cousinly regard, I remain

> Your titular lordship's
> Most obedient servant,
> *Mulberry Sellers Earl Rossmore.*

" Im-mense! Come, this one's interesting. Why, Berkeley, his breezy impudence is — is — why, it's colossal, it's sublime."

" No, this one doesn't seem to cringe much."

" Cringe — why, he doesn't know the meaning of the word. Hatchments! To commemorate that sniveling tramp and his fraternal duplicate. And he is going to send me the remains. The late Claimant was a fool, but plainly this new one's a maniac. What a name! *Mulberry* Sellers — there's music for you. Simon Lathers — Mulberry Sellers — Mulberry Sellers — Simon Lathers. Sounds like machinery working and churning.   Simon Lathers, Mulberry Sel — Are you going?''

" If I have your leave, father."

The old gentleman stood musing some time after his son was gone.   This was his thought:

" He is a good boy, and lovable.   Let him take his own course — as it would profit nothing to oppose him — make things worse, in fact.   My arguments and his aunt's persuasions have failed; let us see what America can do for us.   Let us see what equality and hard times can effect for the mental health of a brain-sick young British lord.   Going to renounce his lordship and be a man !   Yas!''

CHAPTER II.

COLONEL MULBERRY SELLERS — this was some days before he wrote his letter to Lord Rossmore — was seated in his "library," which was also his "drawing-room" and was also his "picture-gallery" and likewise his "workshop." Sometimes he called it by one of these names, sometimes by another, according to occasion and circumstance. He was constructing what seemed to be some kind of a frail mechanical toy, and was apparently very much interested in his work. He was a white-headed man now, but otherwise he was as young, alert, buoyant, visionary, and enterprising as ever. His loving old wife sat near by, contentedly knitting and thinking, with a cat asleep in her lap. The room was large, light, and had a comfortable look, in fact, a homelike look, though the furniture was of a humble sort and not overabundant, and the knickknacks and things that go to adorn a living-room not plenty and not costly. But there were natural flowers, and there was an abstract and unclassifiable something about the place which betrayed the presence in the house of somebody with a happy taste and an effective touch.

Even the deadly chromos on the walls were somehow without offense; in fact, they seemed to belong there and to add an attraction to the room — a fascination, anyway; for whoever got his eye on one of them was like to gaze and suffer till he died — you have seen

2***

that kind of pictures. Some of these terrors were
landscapes, and some libeled the sea, some were osten-
sible portraits, all were crimes. All the portraits were
recognizable as dead Americans of distinction, and
yet, through labeling added by a daring hand, they
were all doing duty here as " Earls of Rossmore."
The newest one had left the works as Andrew Jackson,
but was doing its best now as " Simon Lathers Lord
Rossmore, Present Earl." On one wall was a cheap
old railroad map of Warwickshire. This had been
newly labeled " The Rossmore Estates." On the opposite wall was another map, and this was the most imposing decoration of the establishment and the first to
catch a stranger's attention, because of its great size.
It had once borne simply the title SIBERIA: but now
the word " FUTURE " had been written in front of that
word. There were other additions in red ink — many
cities, with great populations set down, scattered over
the vast country at points where neither cities nor
populations exist to-day. One of these cities, with
population placed at 1,500,000, bore the name
" Libertyorloffskoizalinski," and there was a still more
populous one, centrally located and marked " Capital,"
which bore the name " Freedomolovnaivanovich."

The " mansion "— the Colonel's usual name for the
house — was a rickety old two-story frame of considerable size, which had been painted, some time or other,
but had nearly forgotten it. It was away out in the
ragged edge of Washington, and had once been somebody's country place. It had a neglected yard around
it, with a paling fence that needed straightening up in
places, and a gate that would stay shut. By the door-
post were several modest tin signs. " Col. Mulberry
Sellers, Attorney at Law and Claim Agent," was the
principal one. One learned from the others that the
Colonel was a Materializer, a Hypnotizer, a Mind-Cure

dabbler, and so on. For he was a man who could always find things to do.

A white-headed negro man, with spectacles and damaged white-cotton gloves, appeared in the presence, made a stately obeisance, and announced:

"Marse Washington Hawkins, suh."

"Great Scott! Show him in Dan'l, show him in."

The Colonel and his wife were on their feet in a moment, and the next moment were joyfully wringing the hands of a stoutish, discouraged-looking man whose general aspect suggested that he was fifty years old, but whose hair swore to a hundred.

"Well, well, well, Washington, my boy, it *is* good to look at you again. Sit down, sit down, and make yourself at home. There, now — why, you look perfectly natural; aging a little, just a little, but you'd have known him anywhere, wouldn't you, Polly?"

"Oh, yes, Berry, he's *just* like his pa would have looked if he'd lived. Dear, dear, where have you dropped from? Let me see, how long is it since —"

"I should say it's all of fifteen years, Mrs. Sellers."

"Well, well, how time does get away with us. Yes, and oh, the changes that —"

There was a sudden catch of her voice and a trembling of the lip, the men waiting reverently for her to get command of herself and go on; but after a little struggle she turned away, with her apron to her eyes, and softly disappeared.

"Seeing you made her think of the children, poor thing — dear, dear, they're all dead but the youngest. But banish care, it's no time for it now — on with the dance, let joy be unconfined is my motto, whether there's any dance to dance, or any joy to unconfine — you'll be the healthier for it every time — every time, Washington — it's my experience, and I've seen a good deal of this world. Come — where have you

B***

disappeared to all these years, and are you from there now, or where are you from?"

" I don't quite think you would ever guess, Colonel. Cherokee Strip."

" My land!"

" Sure as you live."

" You can't mean it. Actually *living* out there?"

" Well, yes, if a body may call it that; though it's a pretty strong term for 'dobies and jackass rabbits, boiled beans and slapjacks, depression, withered hopes, poverty in all its varieties —"

" Louise out there?"

" Yes, and the children."

" Out there now?"

" Yes, I couldn't afford to bring them with me."

" Oh, I see; you had to come — claim against the government. Make yourself perfectly easy — I'll take care of that."

" But it isn't a claim against the government."

" No? Want to be postmaster? *That's* all right. Leave it to me. I'll fix it."

" But it isn't postmaster — you're all astray yet."

" Well, good gracious, Washington, why don't you come out and tell me what it is? What do you want to be so reserved and distrustful with an old friend like me for? Don't you reckon I can keep a se —"

" There's no secret about it — you merely don't give me a chance to —"

" Now look here, old friend, I know the human race; and I know that when a man comes to Washington, I don't care if it's from heaven, let alone Cherokee Strip, it's because he *wants* something. And I know that as a rule he's not going to get it; that he'll stay and try for another thing and won't get that; the same luck with the next and the next and the next; and keeps on till he strikes bottom, and is too poor and ashamed to go back, even to Cherokee Strip; and at last his heart breaks and they take up a collection and bury him. There — don't interrupt me, I know what I'm talking about. Happy and prosperous in the Far West, wasn't I? *You* know that. Principal citizen of Hawkeye, looked up to by everybody, kind of an autocrat — actually a kind of an autocrat, Washington. Well, nothing would do but I must go Minister to St. James, the governor and everybody insisting, you know, and so at last I consented — no getting out of it, *had* to do it, so here I came. *A day too late*, Washington. Think of that — what little things change the world's history — yes, sir, the place had been filled. Well, there I was, you see. I offered to compromise and go to Paris. The President was very sorry and all that, but *that* place, you see, didn't belong to the West, so there I was again. There was no help for it, so I had to stoop a little — we all reach the day some time or other when we've got to do that, Washington, and it's not a bad thing for us, either, take it by and large and all around — I had to stoop a little and offer to take Constantinople. Washington, consider this — for it's perfectly true — within a month I *asked* for China; within another month I *begged* for Japan; one year later I was away down, down, down, supplicating with tears and anguish for the bottom office in the gift of the Government of the United States — Flint-Picker in the cellars of the War Department. And, by George, I didn't get it!"

"Flint-Picker?"

"Yes. Office established in the time of the Revolution, last century. The musket-flints for the military posts were supplied from the capital. They do it yet; for although the flint-arm has gone out and the forts have tumbled down, the decree hasn't been repealed — been overlooked and forgotten, you see — and so the vacancies where old Ticonderoga and others used to stand still get their six quarts of gun-flints a year just the same.''

Washington said, musingly, after a pause:

'' How strange it seems — to start for Minister to England at twenty thousand a year and fail for Flint-Picker at —''

'' Three dollars a week.   It's human life, Washington — just an epitome of human ambition, and struggle, and the outcome; you aim for the palace and get drowned in the sewer.''

There was another meditative silence.   Then Washington said, with earnest compassion in his voice:

'' And so, after coming here, against your inclination, to satisfy your sense of patriotic duty and appease a selfish public clamor, you get absolutely nothing for it.''

'' Nothing?''   The Colonel had to get up and stand to get room for his amazement to expand.   '' *Nothing*, Washington?   I ask you this: to be a Perpetual Member and the *only* Perpetual Member of a Diplomatic Body accredited to the greatest country on earth — do you call that nothing?''

It was Washington's turn to be amazed.   He was stricken dumb; but the wide-eyed wonder, the reverent admiration expressed in his face were more eloquent than any words could have been.   The Colonel's wounded spirit was healed, and he resumed his seat pleased and content.   He leaned forward and said, impressively:

'' What was due to a man who had become forever conspicuous by an experience without precedent in the history of the world? — a man made permanently and diplomatically sacred, so to speak, by having been connected, temporarily, through solicitation, with every single diplomatic post in the roster of this government, from Envoy Extraordinary and Minister Plenipotentiary to the Court of St. James, all the way down to Consul to a guano rock in the Straits of Sunda — salary payable in guano — which disappeared by volcanic convulsion the day before they got down to my name in the list of applicants. Certainly something august enough to be answerable to the size of this unique and memorable experience was my due, and I got it. By the common voice of this community, by acclamation of the people, that mighty utterance which brushes aside laws and legislation, and from whose decrees there is no appeal, I was named Perpetual Member of the Diplomatic Body representing the multifarious sovereignties and civilizations of the globe near the republican court of the United States of America. And they brought me home with a torchlight procession."

"It is wonderful, Colonel, simply wonderful."

"It's the loftiest official position in the whole earth."

"I should think so — and the most commanding."

"You have named the word. Think of it. I frown, and there is war; I smile, and contending nations lay down their arms."

"It is awful. The responsibility, I mean."

"It is nothing. Responsibility is no burden to me; I am used to it; have always been used to it."

"And the work — the work! Do you have to attend all the sittings?"

"Who, I? Does the Emperor of Russia attend the conclaves of the governors of the provinces? He sits at home and indicates his pleasure."

Washington was silent a moment, then a deep sigh escaped him.

"How proud I was an hour ago; how paltry seems my little promotion now! Colonel, the reason I came to Washington is — I am Congressional Delegate from Cherokee Strip!"

The Colonel sprang to his feet, and broke out, with prodigious enthusiasm:

"Give me your hand, my boy — this is immense news! I congratulate you with all my heart. My prophecies stand confirmed. I always said it was in you. I always said you were born for high distinction and would achieve it. You ask Polly if I didn't."

Washington was dazed by this most unexpected demonstration.

"Why, Colonel, there's nothing *to* it. That little, narrow, desolate, unpeopled, oblong streak of grass and gravel, lost in the remote wastes of the vast continent — why, it's like representing a billiard-table — a discarded one."

"Tut-tut, it's a great, it's a staving preferment, and just opulent with influence here."

"Shucks, Colonel, I haven't even a vote."

"That's nothing; you can make speeches."

"No, I can't. The population's only two hundred —"

"That's all right, that's all right —"

"And they hadn't any right to elect me; we're not even a Territory, there's no Organic Act, the government hasn't any official knowledge of us whatever."

"Never mind about that; I'll fix that. I'll rush the thing through; I'll get you organized in no time."

"*Will* you, Colonel? — it's *too* good of you; but it's just your old sterling self, the same old ever-faithful friend," and the grateful tears welled up in Washington's eyes.

"It's just as good as done, my boy, just as good as done. Shake hands. We'll hitch teams together, you and I, and we'll make things hum!"

CHAPTER III.

MRS. SELLERS returned now with her composure restored, and began to ask after Hawkins' wife, and about his children, and the number of them, and so on, and her examination of the witness resulted in a circumstantial history of the family's ups and downs and driftings to and fro in the Far West during the previous fifteen years. There was a message now from out back, and Colonel Sellers went out there in answer to it. Hawkins took this opportunity to ask how the world had been using the Colonel during the past half-generation.

"Oh, its been using him just the same; it couldn't change its way of using him if it wanted to, for he wouldn't let it."

"I can easily believe that, Mrs. Sellers."

"Yes, you see, he doesn't change, himself — not the least little bit in the world; he's always Mulberry Sellers."

"I can see *that* plain enough."

"Just the same old scheming, generous, good-hearted, moonshiny, hopeful, no-account failure he always was, and still everybody likes him just as well as if he was the shiningest success."

"They always did; and it was natural, because he was so obliging and accommodating, and had something about him that made it kind of easy to ask help of him, or favors — you didn't feel shy, you know, or have that wish-you-didn't-have-to-try feeling that you have with other people."

"It's just so yet; and a body wonders at it, too, because he's been shamefully treated, many times, by people that had used him for a ladder to climb up by, and then kicked him down when they didn't need him any more. For a time you can see he's hurt, his pride's wounded, because he shrinks away from that thing and don't want to talk about it — and so I used to think *now* he's learned something and he'll be more careful hereafter — but laws! in a couple of weeks he's forgotten all about it, and any selfish tramp out of nobody knows where can come and put up a poor mouth and walk right into his heart with his boots on."

"It must try your patience pretty sharply sometimes."

"Oh, no, I'm used to it; and I'd rather have him so than the other way. When I call him a failure, I mean to the world he's a failure; he isn't to me. I don't know as I want him different — much different, anyway. I have to scold him some, snarl at him, you might even call it, but I reckon I'd do that just the same if he was different — it's my make. But I'm a good deal less snarly and more contented when he's a failure than I am when he isn't."

"Then he isn't always a failure," said Hawkins, brightening.

"Him? Oh, bless you, no. He makes a strike, as he calls it, from time to time. Then's my time to fret and fuss. For the money just flies — first come first served. Straight off, he loads up the house with cripples and idiots and stray cats and all the different kinds of poor wrecks that other people don't want and he *does*, and then when the poverty comes again I've *got* to clear the most of them out or we'd starve; and that distresses him, and me the same, of course. Here's

old Dan'l and old Jinny, that the sheriff sold South
one of the times that we got bankrupted before the
war — they came wandering back after the peace, worn
out and used up on the cotton plantations, helpless, and
not another lick of work left in their old hides for the
rest of this earthly pilgrimage — and we so pinched,
oh, so pinched for the very crumbs to keep life in us,
and he just flung the door wide, and the way he
received them you'd have thought they had come
straight down from heaven in answer to prayer. I
took him one side and said, ' Mulberry, we can't have
them — we've nothing for ourselves — we can't feed
them.' He looked at me kind of hurt, and said,
' Turn them out? — and they've come to me just as
confid∂nt and trusting as — as — why, Polly, I must
have *bought* that confidence some time or other a long
time ago, and given my note, so to speak — you don't
get such things as a *gift* — and how am I going to go
back on a debt like that? And you see, they're so
poor, and old, and friendless, and —' But I was
ashamed by that time, and shut him off, and somehow
felt a new courage in me, and so I said, softly, ' We'll
keep them — the Lord will provide.' He was glad,
and started to blurt out one of those over-confident
speeches of his, but checked himself in time, and said
humbly, ' *I* will, anyway.' It was years and years and
years ago. Well, you see those old wrecks are here
yet.''

'' But don't they do your housework?''

'' Laws! The idea. They would if they could, poor
old things, and perhaps they think they *do* do some of
it. But it's a superstition. Dan'l waits on the front
door, and sometimes goes on an errand; and sometimes you'll see one or both of them letting on to dust
around in here — but that's because there's something
they want to hear about and mix their gabble into.

And they're always around at meals, for the same reason. But the fact is, we have to keep a young negro girl just to take care of *them*, and a negro woman to do the housework and *help* take care of them."

"Well, they ought to be tolerably happy, I should think."

"It's no name for it. They quarrel together pretty much all the time — most always about religion, because Dan'l's a Dunker Baptist and Jinny's a shouting Methodist, and Jinny believes in special Providences and Dan'l don't, because he thinks he's a kind of a free-thinker — and they play and sing plantation hymns together, and talk and chatter just eternally and forever, and are sincerely fond of each other and think the world of Mulberry, and he puts up patiently with all their spoiled ways and foolishness, and so — ah, well, they're happy enough if it comes to that. And I don't mind — I've got used to it. I can get used to anything, with Mulberry to help; and the fact is, I don't much care what happens, so long as he's spared to me."

"Well, here's to him, and hoping he'll make another strike soon."

"And rake in the lame, the halt, and the blind, and turn the house into a hospital again? It's what he would do. I've seen a plenty of that and more. No, Washington, I want his strikes to be mighty moderate ones the rest of the way down the vale."

"Well, then, big strike or little strike, or no strike at all, here's hoping he'll never lack for friends — and I don't reckon he ever will while there's people around who know enough to —"

"Him lack for friends!" and she tilted her head up with a frank pride —" why, Washington, you can't name a man that's anybody that isn't fond of him.

I'll tell you privately that I've had Satan's own time
to keep them from appointing him to some office or
other. They knew he'd no business with an office,
just as well as I did, but he's the hardest man to refuse
anything to a body ever saw. Mulberry Sellers with
an office! laws goodness, you know what that would
be like. Why, they'd come from the ends of the
earth to see a circus like that. I'd just as lieves be
married to Niagara Falls, and done with it." After a
reflective pause she added — having wandered back, in
the interval, to the remark that had been her text:
" Friends? — oh, indeed, no man ever had more; and
such friends: Grant, Sherman, Sheridan, Johnston,
Longstreet, Lee — many's the time they've sat in that
chair you're sitting in —" Hawkins was out of it
instantly, and contemplating it with a reverential surprise, and with the awed sense of having trodden shod
upon holy ground:
" *They !*" he said.
" Oh, indeed, yes, a many and a many a time."
He continued to gaze at the chair, fascinated, mag-
netized; and for once in his life that continental stretch
of dry prairie which stood for his imagination was afire,
and across it was marching a slanting flame-front that
joined its wide horizons together and smothered the
skies with smoke. He was experiencing what one or
another drowsing, geographically ignorant alien experiences every day in the year when he turns a dull and
indifferent eye out of the car window and it falls upon
a certain station-sign which reads, " Stratford-on-
Avon!" Mrs. Sellers went gossiping comfortably
along:
" Oh, they like to hear him talk, especially if their
load is getting rather heavy on one shoulder and they
want to shift it. He's all air, you know — breeze, you
may say — and he freshens them up; it's a trip to the

country, they say. Many a time he's made General Grant laugh — and that's a tidy job, I can tell you; and as for Sheridan, his eye lights up and he listens to Mulberry Sellers the same as if he was artillery. You see, the charm about Mulberry is, he is so catholic and unprejudiced that he fits in anywhere and everywhere. It makes him powerful good company, and as popular as scandal. You go to the White House when the President's holding a general reception — some time when Mulberry's there. Why, dear me, *you* can't tell which of them it is that's holding that reception.''

'' Well, he certainly is a remarkable man — and he always was. Is he religious?''

'' Clear to his marrow — does more thinking and reading on that subject than any other, except Russia and Siberia; thrashes around over the whole field, too; nothing bigoted about him.''

'' What is his religion?''

'' He —'' She stopped, and was lost for a moment or two in thinking; then she said, with simplicity, '' I think he was a Mohammedan or something last week.''

Washington started down town now to bring his trunk, for the hospitable Sellerses would listen to no excuses; their house must be his home during the session. The Colonel returned presently and resumed work upon his plaything. It was finished when Washington got back.

'' There it is,'' said the Colonel, '' all finished.''

'' What is it for, Colonel?''

'' Oh, it's just a trifle. Toy to amuse the children.''

Washington examined it.

'' It seems to be a puzzle.''

' Yes, that's what it is. I call it Pigs in the Clover. Put them in — see if you can put them in the pen.''

After many failures Washington succeeded, and was as pleased as a child.

" It's wonderfully ingenious, Colonel — it's ever so clever. And interesting — why, I could play with it all day. What are you going to do with it?''

" Oh, nothing. Patent it and throw it aside.''

" Don't you do anything of the kind. There's money in that thing.''

A compassionate look traveled over the Colonel's countenance, and he said :

" Money — yes; pin money; a couple of hundred thousand, perhaps. Not more.''

Washington's eyes blazed.

" A couple of hundred thousand dollars! Do you call that pin money?''

The Colonel rose and tiptoed his way across the room, closed a door that was slightly ajar, tiptoed his way to his seat again, and said, under his breath :

" You can keep a secret?''

Washington nodded his affirmative; he was too awed to speak.

" You have heard of materialization — materialization of departed spirits?''

Washington had heard of it.

" And probably didn't believe in it; and quite right, too. The thing as practiced by ignorant charlatans is unworthy of attention or respect — where there's a dim light and a dark cabinet, and a parcel of sentimental gulls gathered together, with their faith and their shudders and their tears all ready, and one and the same fatty degeneration of protoplasm and humbug comes out and materializes himself into anybody you want, grandmother, grandchild, brother-in-law, Witch of Endor, John Milton, Siamese Twins, Peter the Great, and all such frantic nonsense — no, that is all foolish and pitiful. But when a man that is competent brings the vast powers of *science* to bear, it's a different matter — a totally different matter, you see. The specter that

answers *that* call has come to stay. Do you note the
commercial value of that detail?"

"Well, I — the — the truth is, that I don't quite
know that I do. Do you mean that such, being permanent, not transitory, would give more general satisfaction, and so enhance the price of tickets to the
show —"

"Show? Folly — listen to me; and get a good grip
on your breath, for you are going to need it. Within
three days I shall have completed my method, and
then — let the world stand aghast, for it shall see marvels. Washington, within three days — ten at the outside — you shall see me call the dead of any century,
and they will arise and walk. Walk? — they shall
walk forever, and never die again. Walk with all the
muscle and spring of their pristine vigor."

"Colonel! Indeed, it does take one's breath away."

"*Now* do you see the money that's in it?"

"I'm — well, I'm — not really sure that I do."

"Great Scott, look here! I shall have a monopoly;
they'll all belong to me, won't they? Two thousand
policemen in the city of New York. Wages, four dollars a day. I'll replace them with dead ones at half
the money."

"Oh, prodigious! I never thought of that. F-o-u-r
thousand dollars a day. Now I do begin to see! But
will dead policemen answer?"

"Haven't they — up to this time?"

'Well, if you put it that way —"

"Put it any way you want to. Modify it to suit
yourself, and my lads shall still be superior. They
won't eat, they won't drink — don't need those things;
they won't wink for cash at gambling-dens and un-
licensed rum-holes, they won't spark the scullery
maids; and, moreover, the bands of toughs that ambuscade them on lonely beats and cowardly shoot and

knife them will only damage the uniforms, and not live long enough to get more than a momentary satisfaction out of that.''

'' Why, Colonel, if you can furnish policemen, then of course —''

'' Certainly — I can furnish any line of goods that's wanted. Take the army, for instance — now twenty-five thousand men; expense, twenty-two millions a year. I will dig up the Romans, I will resurrect the Greeks, I will furnish the government, for ten millions a year, ten thousand veterans drawn from the victorious legions of all the ages — soldiers that will chase Indians year in and year out on materialized horses, and cost never a cent for rations or repairs. The armies of Europe cost two billions a year now — I will replace them all for a billion. I will dig up the trained states-men of all ages and all climes, and furnish this country with a Congress that knows enough to come in out of the rain — a thing that's never happened yet since the Declaration of Independence, and never will happen till these practically dead people are replaced with the genuine article. I will re-stock the thrones of Europe with the best brains and the best morals that all the royal sepulchers of all the centuries can furnish — which isn't promising very much — and I'll divide the wages and the civil list, fair and square, merely taking my half and —''

'' Colonel, if the half of this is true, there's millions in it — millions.''

'' Billions in it — billions; that's what you mean. Why, look here; the thing is so close at hand, so imminent, so absolutely immediate, that if a man were to come to me now and say, Colonel, I am a little short, and if you could lend me a couple of billion dollars for — come in !''

This in answer to a knock. An energetic-looking
3***

man bustled in with a big pocket-book in his hand, took a paper from it and presented it, with the curt remark:

" Seventeenth and last call — you want to out with that three dollars and forty cents this time without fail, Colonel Mulberry Sellers.''

The Colonel began to slap this pocket and that one, and feel here and there and everywhere, muttering:

" What *have* I done with that wallet? — let me see — um — not here, not there — oh, I must have left it in the kitchen; I'll just run and —''

" No you won't — you'll stay right where you are. And you're going to disgorge, too — this time.''

Washington innocently offered to go and look. When he was gone the Colonel said:

" The fact is, I've got to throw myself on your in-dulgence just this once more, Suggs; you see, the remittances I was expecting —''

" Hang the remittances — it's too stale — it won't answer. Come !''

The Colonel glanced about him in despair. Then his face lighted; he ran to the wall and began to dust off a peculiarly atrocious chromo with his handker-chief. Then he brought it reverently, offered it to the collector, averted his face, and said:

" Take it, but don't let me see it go. It's the sole remaining Rembrandt that —''

" Rembrandt be damned; it's a chromo.''

" Oh, don't speak of it so, I beg you. It's the only really great original, the only supreme example, of that mighty school of art which —''

" Art ! It's the sickest looking thing I —''

The Colonel was already bringing another horror and tenderly dusting it.

" Take this one too — the gem of my collection — the only genuine Fra Angelico that —''

"Illuminated liver-pad, that's what it is. Give it here — good day — people will think I've robbed a nigger barber-shop."

As he slammed the door behind him the Colonel shouted, with an anguished accent:

"Do please cover them up — don't let the damp get at them. The delicate tints in the Angelico —"

But the man was gone.

Washington reappeared, and said he had looked everywhere, and so had Mrs. Sellers and the servants, but in vain; and went on to say he wished he could get his eye on a certain man about this time — no need to hunt up that pocket-book then. The Colonel's interest was awake at once.

"What man?"

"One-armed Pete they call him out there — out in the Cherokee country, I mean. Robbed the bank in Tahlequah."

"Do they have banks in Tahlequah?"

"Yes — *a* bank, anyway. He was suspected of robbing it. Whoever did it got away with more than twenty thousand dollars. They offered a reward of five thousand. I believe I saw that very man on my way east."

"No — is that so?"

"I certainly saw a man on the train the first day I struck the railroad that answered the description pretty exactly — at least, as to clothes and a lacking arm."

"Why didn't you get him arrested and claim the reward?"

"I couldn't. I had to get a requisition, of course. But I meant to stay by him till I got my chance."

"Well?"

"Well, he left the train during the night some time."

"Oh, hang it, that's too bad!"

"Not so very bad, either."

C***

" Why?"

" Because he came down to Baltimore in the very
train I was in, though I didn't know it in time. As
we moved out of the station I saw him going toward
the iron gate with a satchel in his hand."

" Good; we'll catch him. Let's lay a plan."

" Send description to the Baltimore police?"

" Why, what are you talking about? No. Do you
want them to get the reward?"

" What shall we do, then?"

The Colonel reflected.

" I'll tell you. Put a personal in the Baltimore
Sun. Word it like this:

A.   DROP ME A LINE, PETE —

" Hold on. Which arm has he lost?"

" The right."

" Good. Now then:

A.   DROP ME A LINE, PETE, EVEN IF YOU HAVE TO
      write with your left hand. Address X. Y. Z., General Post-
office, Washington. From YOU KNOW WHO.

There — that'll fetch him."

" But he *won't* know who — will he?"

" No, but he'll want to know, won't he?"

" Why, certainly — I didn't think of that. What
made you think of it?"

" Knowledge of human curiosity. Strong trait, very
strong trait."

" Now I'll go to my room and write it out and en-
close a dollar and tell them to print it to the worth of
that."

CHAPTER IV.

THE day wore itself out. After dinner the two friends put in a long and harassing evening trying to decide what to do with the five thousand dollars reward which they were going to get when they should find One-Armed Pete, and catch him, and prove him to be the right person, and extradite him, and ship him to Tahlequah in the Indian Territory. But there were so many dazzling openings for ready cash that they found it impossible to make up their minds and keep them made up. Finally, Mrs. Sellers grew very weary of it all, and said:

" What is the sense in cooking a rabbit before it's caught?"

Then the matter was dropped for the time being, and all went to bed. Next morning, being persuaded by Hawkins, the Colonel made drawings and specifications, and went down and applied for a patent for his toy puzzle, and Hawkins took the toy itself and started out to see what chance there might be to do something with it commercially. He did not have to go far. In a small old wooden shanty which had once been occupied as a dwelling by some humble negro family he found a keen-eyed Yankee engaged in repairing cheap chairs and other second-hand furniture. This man examined the toy indifferently; attempted to do the puzzle; found it not so easy as he had expected; grew more interested, and finally emphatically so; achieved a success at last, and asked:

" Is it patented?"

" Patent applied for."

" That will answer. What do you want for it?"

" What will it retail for?"

" Well, twenty-five cents, I should think."

" What will you give for the exclusive right?"

" I couldn't give twenty dollars if I had to pay cash down; but I'll tell you what I'll do. I'll make it and market it, and pay you five cents royalty on each one."

Washington sighed. Another dream disappeared; no money in the thing. So he said:

" All right; take it at that. Draw me a paper."

He went his way with the paper, and dropped the matter out of his mind — dropped it out to make room for further attempts to think out the most promising way to invest his half of the reward in case a partnership investment satisfactory to both beneficiaries could not be hit upon.

He had not been very long at home when Sellers arrived sodden with grief and booming with glad excitement — working both these emotions successfully, sometimes separately, sometimes together. He fell on Hawkins's neck sobbing, and said:

" Oh, mourn with me, my friend, mourn for my desolate house; death has smitten my last kinsman, and I am Earl of Rossmore — congratulate me!"

He turned to his wife, who had entered while this was going on, put his arms about her, and said: " You will bear up, for my sake, my lady — it had to happen, it was decreed."

She bore up very well, and said:

" It's no great loss. Simon Lathers was a poor, well-meaning, useless thing and no account, and his brother never was worth shucks."

The rightful earl continued:

" I am too much prostrated by these conflicting

griefs and joys to be able to concentrate my mind upon
affairs; I will ask our good friend here to break the
news by wire or post to the Lady Gwendolen, and
instruct her to —''

" *What* Lady Gwendolen?''

" Our poor daughter, who, alas! —''

" Sally Sellers? Mulberry Sellers, are you losing
your mind?''

" There — please do not forget who you are, and
who I am; remember your own dignity, be considerate
also of mine. It were best to cease from using my
family name now, Lady Rossmore.''

" Goodness gracious! well, I never! What *am* I to
call you, then?''

"In private, the ordinary terms of endearment will
still be admissible, to some degree; but in public it
will be more becoming if your ladyship will speak *to*
me as my lord, or your lordship, and *of* me as Rossmore, or the Earl, or his Lordship, and —''

" Oh, scat! I can't ever do it, Berry.''

" But, indeed, you must, my love — we must live up
to our altered position, and submit with what grace we
may to its requirements.''

" Well, all right, have it your own way; I've never
set my wishes against your commands yet, Mul — my
lord, and it's late to begin now, though to my mind
it's the rottenest foolishness that ever was.''

" Spoken like my own true wife! There, kiss and
be friends again.''

" But — Gwendolen! I don't know how I am ever
going to stand that name. Why, a body wouldn't
know Sally Sellers in it. It's too large for her; kind
of like a cherub in an ulster, and it's a most outlandish
sort of a name anyway, to my mind.''

" You'll not hear her find fault with it, my lady.''

" That's a true word. She takes to any kind of

romantic rubbish like she was born to it. She never got it from me, that's sure. And sending her to that silly college hasn't helped the matter any — just the other way."

"Now hear her, Hawkins! Rowena-Ivanhoe College is the selectest and most aristocratic seat of learning for young ladies in our country. Under no circumstances can a girl get in there unless she is either very rich and fashionable or can prove four generations of what may be called American nobility. Castellated college-buildings — towers and turrets and an imitation moat — and everything about the place named out of Sir Walter Scott's books and redolent of royalty and state and style; and all the richest girls keep phaetons, and coachmen in livery, and riding-horses, with English grooms in plug hats and tight-buttoned coats, and top-boots, and a whip-handle without any whip to it, to ride sixty-three feet behind them —"

"And they don't learn a blessed thing, Washington Hawkins, not a single blessed thing but showy rubbish and un-American pretentiousness. But send for the Lady Gwendolen — do; for I reckon the peerage regulations require that she must come home and let on to go into seclusion and mourn for those Arkansas blatherskites she's lost."

"My darling! Blatherskites? Remember — *noblesse oblige*."

"There, there — talk to me in your own tongue, Ross — you don't know any other, and you only botch it when you try. Oh, don't stare — it was a slip, and no crime; customs of a lifetime can't be dropped in a second. Ross*more* — there now, be appeased, and go along with you and attend to Gwendolen. Are you going to write, Washington? — or telegraph?"

"He will telegraph, dear."

"I thought as much," my lady muttered, as she

left the room. " Wants it so the address will have to appear on the envelope. It will just make a fool of that child. She'll get it, of course, for if there are any other Sellerses there they'll not be able to claim it. And just leave her alone to show it around and make the most of it. . . . . .Well, maybe she's forgivable for that. She's so poor and they're so rich, of course she's had her share of snubs from the livery-flunky sort, and I reckon it's only human to want to get even."

Uncle Dan'l was sent with the telegram; for although a conspicuous object in a corner of the drawing-room was a telephone hanging on a transmitter, Washington found all attempts to raise the central office vain. The Colonel grumbled something about its being " *always* out of order when you've got particular and especial use for it," but he didn't explain that one of the reasons for this was that the thing was only a dummy and hadn't any wire attached to it. And yet the Colonel often used it — when visitors were present — and seemed to get messages through it. Mourning-paper and a seal were ordered; then the friends took a rest.

Next afternoon, while Hawkins, by request, draped Andrew Jackson's portrait with crape, the rightful earl wrote off the family bereavement to the usurper in England — a letter which we have already read. He also, by letter to the village authorities at Duffy's Corners, Arkansas, gave order that the remains of the late twins be embalmed by some St. Louis expert and shipped at once to the usurper — with bill. Then he drafted out the Rossmore arms and motto on a great sheet of brown paper, and he and Hawkins took it to Hawkins's Yankee furniture-mender, and at the end of an hour came back with a couple of stunning hatchments, which they nailed up on the front of the house

— attractions calculated to draw, and they did; for it was mainly an idle and shiftless negro neighborhood, with plenty of ragged children and indolent dogs to spare for a point of interest like that, and keep on sparing them for it, days and days together.

The new earl found — without surprise — this society item in the evening paper, and cut it out and scrap-booked it:

By a recent bereavement our esteemed fellow-citizen, Colonel Mulberry Sellers, Perpetual Member-at-large of the Diplomatic Body, succeeds, as rightful lord, to the great earldom of Rossmore, third by order of precedence in the earldoms of Great Britain, and will take early measures, by suit in the House of Lords, to wrest the title and estates from the present usurping holder of them. Until the season of mourning is past, the usual Thursday evening receptions at Rossmore Towers will be discontinued.

Lady Rossmore's comment — to herself:

"Receptions! People who don't rightly know him may think he is commonplace, but to my mind he is one of the most unusual men I ever saw. As for sud-denness and capacity in imagining things, his beat don't exist, I reckon. As like as not it wouldn't have occurred to anybody else to name this poor old rat-trap Rossmore Towers, but it just comes natural to him. Well, no doubt it's a blessed thing to have an imagination that can always make you satisfied, no matter how you are fixed. Uncle Dave Hopkins used to always say, 'Turn me into John Calvin, and I want to know which place I'm going to; turn me into Mul-berry Sellers, and I don't care.'"

The rightful earl's comment — to himself:

"It's a beautiful name, beautiful. Pity I didn't think of it before I wrote the usurper. But I'll be ready for him when he answers."

CHAPTER V.

NO answer to that telegram; no arriving daughter. Yet nobody showed any uneasiness or seemed surprised; that is, nobody but Washington. After three days of waiting he asked Lady Rossmore what she supposed the trouble was. She answered tranquilly:

"Oh, it's some notion of hers; you never can tell. She's a Sellers all through — at least, in some of her ways; and a Sellers can't tell you beforehand what he's going to do, because he don't know himself till he's done it. *She's* all right; no occasion to worry about *her*. When she's ready she'll come or she'll write, and you can't tell which till it's happened."

It turned out to be a letter. It was handed in at that moment, and was received by the mother without trembling hands or feverish eagerness, or any other of the manifestations common in the case of long-delayed answers to imperative telegrams. She polished her glasses with tranquillity and thoroughness, pleasantly gossiping along the while, then opened the letter and began to read aloud:

KENILWORTH KEEP, REDGAUNTLET HALL,
ROWENA-IVANHOE COLLEGE, THURSDAY.

DEAR PRECIOUS MAMMA ROSSMORE:

Oh, the joy of it! — you can't think. They had always turned up their noses at our pretensions, you know; and I had fought back as well as I could by turning up mine at theirs. They always said it might be some-

(43)

thing great and fine to be the rightful Shadow of an earldom, but to merely be shadow *of* a shadow, and two or three times removed at that — pooh-pooh! And I always retorted that not to be able to show four genera-tions of American-Colonial-Dutch-Peddler-and-Salt-Cod-McAllister-Nobility might be endurable, but to *have* to confess such an origin — pfew-few! Well, the telegram, it was just a cyclone! The messenger came right into the great Rob Roy Hall of Audience, as excited as he could be, singing out, "Dispatch for Lady Gwendolen Sellers!" and you ought to have seen that simpering chattering assemblage of pinchbeck aristocrats turn to stone! I was off in the corner, of course, by myself — it's where Cinderella belongs. I took the telegram and read it, and tried to faint — and I could have done it if I had had any preparation, but it was all so sudden, you know — but no matter, I did the next best thing: I put my handkerchief to my eyes and fled sobbing to my room, dropping the telegram as I started. I released one corner of my eye a moment — just enough to see the herd swarm for the telegram — and then continued my broken-hearted flight just as happy as a bird.

Then the visits of condolence began, and I had to accept the loan of Miss Augusta-Templeton-Ashmore Hamilton's quarters because the press was so great and there isn't room for three and a cat in mine. And I've been holding a Lodge of Sorrow ever since and defending myself against people's attempts to claim kin. And do you know, the very first girl to fetch her tears and sympathy to my market was that foolish Skimperton girl who has always snubbed me so shamefully and claimed lordship and prece-dence of the whole college because some ancestor of hers, some time or other, was a McAllister. Why, it was like the bottom bird in the menagerie putting on airs because its head ancestor was a pterodactyl.

But the ger-reatest triumph of all was — guess. But you'll never. This is it. That little fool and two others have always been fussing and fretting over which was entitled to precedence — by rank, you know. They've nearly starved themselves at it; for each claimed the right to take prece-dence of all the college in leaving the table, and so neither of them ever finished her dinner, but broke off in the middle and tried to get out ahead of the others. Well, after my first day's grief and seclusion — I was fixing up a mourning dress, you see — I appeared at the public table again, and then — what do you think? Those three fluffy goslings sat there contentedly, and squared up the long famine — lapped and lapped, munched and munched, ate and ate, till the gravy appeared in their eyes — humbly wait-ing for the Lady Gwendolen to take precedence and move out first, you see!

Oh, yes, I've been having a darling good time. And do you know, not one of these collegians has had the cruelty to ask me how I came by my new name. With some, this is due to charity, but with the others it isn't. They refrain, not from native kindness but from educated discretion. I educated them.

Well, as soon as I shall have settled up what's left of the old scores and snuffed up a few more of those pleasantly intoxicating clouds of incense, I shall pack and depart homeward. Tell papa I am as fond of him as I am of my new name. I couldn't put it stronger than that. What an inspiration it was! But inspirations come easy to him.

These, from your loving daughter,

GWENDOLEN.

Hawkins reached for the letter and glanced over it.

" Good hand," he said, " and full of confidence and animation, and goes racing right along. She's bright — that's plain."

" Oh, they're all bright — the Sellerses. Anyway, they would be, if there were any. Even those poor Latherses would have been bright if they had been Sellerses; I mean full blood. Of course they had a Sellers strain in them — a big strain of it, too — but being a Bland dollar don't make it a *dollar* just the same."

The seventh day after the date of the telegram Washington came dreaming down to breakfast and was set wide awake by an electrical spasm of pleasure. Here was the most beautiful young creature he had ever seen in his life. It was Sally Sellers Lady Gwendolen; she had come in the night. And it seemed to him that her clothes were the prettiest and the daintiest he had ever looked upon, and the most exquisitely contrived and fashioned and combined, as to decorative trimmings, and fixings, and melting harmonies of color. It was only a morning dress, and inexpensive, but he confessed to himself, in the English common to Cherokee Strip, that it was a " corker." And now, as he perceived, the reason why the Sellers household

4A

poverties and sterilities had been made to blossom like the rose, and charm the eye and satisfy the spirit, stood explained; here was the magician; here in the midst of her works, and furnishing in her own person the proper accent and climaxing finish of the whole.

"My daughter, Major Hawkins — come home to mourn; flown home at the call of affliction to help the authors of her being bear the burden of bereavement. She was very fond of the late earl — idolized him, sir, idolized him —"

"Why, father, I've never seen him."

"True — she's right, I was thinking of another — er — of her mother —"

"_I_ idolized that smoked haddock? — that sentimental, spiritless —"

"I was thinking of myself! Poor noble fellow, we were inseparable com —"

"Hear the man! Mulberry Sel — Mul — Rossmore! — hang the troublesome name, I can never — if I've heard you say once I've heard you say a thousand times that if that poor sheep —"

"I was thinking of — of — I don't know who I was thinking of, and it doesn't make any difference any way; _some_body idolized him, I recollect it as if it were yesterday; and —"

"Father, I am going to shake hands with Major Hawkins, and let the introduction work along and catch up at its leisure. I remember you very well, indeed, Major Hawkins, although I was a little child when I saw you last; and I am very, very glad, indeed, to see you again and have you in our house as one of us;" and beaming in his face she finished her cordial shake with the hope that he had not forgotten her.

He was prodigiously pleased by her outspoken heartiness, and wanted to repay her by assuring her that he remembered her, and not only that but better even than he remembered his own children, but the facts would not quite warrant this; still, he stumbled through a tangled sentence which answered just as well, since the purport of it was an awkward and unintentional confession that her extraordinary beauty had so stupefied him that he hadn't got back to his bearings yet, and therefore couldn't be certain as to whether he remembered her at all or not. The speech made him her friend; it couldn't well help it.

In truth, the beauty of this fair creature was of a rare type, and may well excuse a moment of our time spent in its consideration. It did not consist in the *fact* that she had eyes, nose, mouth, chin, hair, ears; it consisted in their arrangement. In true beauty, more depends upon right location and judicious distribution of feature than upon multiplicity of them. So also as regards color. The very combination of colors which in a volcanic irruption would add beauty to a landscape might detach it from a girl. Such was Gwendolen Sellers.

The family circle being completed by Gwendolen's arrival, it was decreed that the official mourning should now begin; that it should begin at six o'clock every evening (the dinner hour) and end with the dinner.

"It's a grand old line, Major, a sublime old line, and deserves to be mourned for almost royally; almost imperially, I may say. Er — Lady Gwendolen — but she's gone; never mind; I wanted my Peerage; I'll fetch it myself, presently, and show you a thing or two that will give you a realizing idea of what our house is. I've been glancing through *Burke*, and I find that of William the Conqueror's sixty-four natural ch — my dear, would you mind getting me that book? It's on the escritoire in our boudoir. Yes, as I was saying, there's only St. Albans, Buccleuch, and Grafton ahead of us on the list — all the rest of the British nobility are in procession behind us. Ah, thanks, my lady. Now then, we turn to William, and we find — letter for XYZ? Oh, splendid — when'd you get it?"

"Last night; but I was asleep before you came, you were out so late; and when I came to breakfast Miss Gwendolen — well, she knocked everything out of me, you know —"

"Wonderful girl, wonderful; her great origin is detectable in her step, her carriage, her features — but what does he *say?* Come, this is exciting."

"I haven't read it — er — Rossm — Mr. Rossm — er —"

"M'lord! Just cut it short like that. It's the English way. I'll open it. Ah, now let's see.

A. TO YOU KNOW WHO. Think I know you. Wait ten days. Coming to Washington.

The excitement died out of both men's faces. There was a brooding silence for a while; then the younger one said, with a sigh:

"Why, *we* can't wait ten days for the money."

"No — the man's unreasonable; we are down to the bed rock, financially speaking."

"If we could explain to him in some way that we are so situated that time is of the utmost importance to us —"

"Yes-yes, that's it — and so if it would be as convenient for him to come at once it would be a great accommodation to us, and one which we — which we — which we — wh — well, which we should sincerely appreciate —"

"That's it — and most gladly reciprocate —"

"Certainly — that'll fetch him. Worded right, if he's a *man* — got any of the *feelings* of a man, *sympathies* and all that, he'll be here inside of twenty-four hours. Pen and paper — come, we'll get right at it.''

Between them they framed twenty-two different advertisements, but none was satisfactory. A main fault in all of them was urgency. That feature was very troublesome: if made prominent, it was calculated to excite Pete's suspicion; if modified below the suspicion-point it was flat and meaningless. Finally the Colonel resigned, and said:

"I have noticed, in such literary experiences as I have had, that one of the most taking things to do is to conceal your meaning when you are *trying* to conceal it. Whereas, if you go at literature with a free conscience and nothing to conceal, you can turn out a book, every time, that the very elect can't understand. They all do.''

Then Hawkins resigned also, and the two agreed that they must manage to wait the ten days somehow or other. Next, they caught a ray of cheer; since they had something definite to go upon now they could probably borrow money on the reward — enough, at any rate, to tide them over till they got it; and meantime the materializing recipe would be perfected, and then good-bye to trouble for good and all.

The next day, May the 10th, a couple of things happened — among others. The remains of the noble Arkansas twins left our shores for England, consigned to Lord Rossmore, and Lord Rossmore's son, Kirkcudbright Llanover Marjoribanks Sellers Viscount Berkeley, sailed from Liverpool for America to place the reversion of the earldom in the hands of the rightful peer, Mulberry Sellers, of Rossmore Towers in the District of Columbia, U. S. A.

These two impressive shipments would meet and part in mid-Atlantic five days later, and give no sign.

4***

CHAPTER VI.

IN the course of time the twins arrived and were delivered to their great kinsman.   To try to describe
the rage of that old man would profit nothing, the
attempt would fall so far short of the purpose.   However, when he had worn himself out and got quiet
again, he looked the matter over and decided that the
twins had some moral rights, although they had no
legal ones; they were of his blood, and it could not
be decorous to treat them as common clay.   So he
laid them with their majestic kin in the Cholmondeley
church, with imposing state and ceremony, and added
the supreme touch by officiating as chief mourner
himself.   But he drew the line at hatchments.

Our friends in Washington watched the weary days
go by while they waited for Pete and covered his name
with reproaches because of his calamitous procrastina-
tions.   Meantime, Sally Sellers, who was as practical
and democratic as the Lady Gwendolen Sellers was
romantic and aristocratic, was leading a life of intense
interest and activity, and getting the most she could
out of her double personality.   All day long in the
privacy of her work-room Sally Sellers earned bread
for the Sellers family, and all the evening Lady Gwendolen Sellers supported the Rossmore dignity.   All
day she was American, practically, and proud of the
work of her head and hands and its commercial result;
all the evening she took holiday and dwelt in a rich

shadowland peopled with titled and coroneted fictions.
By day, to her, the place was a plain, unaffected, ramshackle old trap — just that, and nothing more; by
night it was Rossmore Towers. At college she had
learned a trade without knowing it. The girls had
found out that she was the designer of her own gowns.
She had no idle moments after that, and wanted none;
for the exercise of an extraordinary gift is the
supremest pleasure in life, and it was manifest that
Sally Sellers possessed a gift of that sort in the matter
of costume designing. Within three days after reaching home she had hunted up some work; before Pete
was yet due in Washington, and before the twins were
fairly asleep in English soil, she was already nearly
swamped with work, and the sacrificing of the family
chromos for debt had got an effective check.

"She's a brick," said Rossmore to the Major;
"just her father all over; prompt to labor with head
or hands, and not ashamed of it; capable, always
capable, let the enterprise be what it may; successful
by nature — don't know what defeat is; thus, intensely
and practically American by inhaled nationalism, and
at the same time intensely and aristocratically European
by inherited nobility of blood. Just me, exactly; Mulberry Sellers in matter of finance and invention; after
office hours, what do you find? The same clothes,
yes, but what's in them? Rossmore of the peerage."

The two friends had haunted the general post-office
daily. At last they had their reward. Toward evening on the 20th of May they got a letter for XYZ. It
bore the Washington postmark; the note itself was not
dated. It said:

Ash barrel back of lamp post Black horse Alley. If you are playing
square go and set on it to-morrow morning 21st 10.22 not sooner not later
wait till I come.
D***

The friends cogitated over the note profoundly. Presently the earl said:

"Don't you reckon he's afraid we are a sheriff with a requisition?"

"Why, m'lord?"

"Because that's no place for a séance. Nothing friendly, nothing sociable about it. And at the same time, a body that wanted to know who was roosting on that ash-barrel without exposing himself by going near it, or seeming to be interested in it, could just stand on the street corner and take a glance down the alley and satisfy himself, don't you see?"

"Yes, his idea is plain now. He seems to be a man that can't *be* candid and straightforward. He acts as if he thought we — shucks, I wish he had come out like a man and told us what hotel he —"

"Now you've struck it! you've struck it sure, Washington; he has told us."

"Has he?"

"Yes, he has; but he didn't mean to. That alley is a lonesome little pocket that runs along one side of the New Gadsby. That's his hotel."

"What makes you think that?"

"Why, I just know it. He's got a room that's just across from that lamp-post. He's going to sit there perfectly comfortable behind his shutters at 10.22 to-morrow, and when he sees us sitting on the ash-barrel, he'll say to himself, 'I saw *one* of those fellows on the train'— and then he'll pack his satchel in half a minute and ship for the ends of the earth."

Hawkins turned sick with disappointment.

"Oh, dear, it's all up, Colonel — it's exactly what he'll do."

"Indeed, he won't!"

"Won't he? Why?"

"Because *you* won't be holding the ash-barrel down;

it'll be me.   You'll be coming in with an officer and a
requisition in plain clothes — the officer, I mean — the
minute you see him arrive and open up a talk with
me.''

" Well, what a head you have got, Colonel Sellers!
I never should have thought of that in the world.''

" Neither would any earl of Rossmore, betwixt
William's contribution and Mulberry — *as* earl; but
it's office hours now, you see, and the earl in me
sleeps.   Come — I'll show you his very room.''

They reached the neighborhood of the New Gadsby
about nine in the evening, and passed down the alley
to the lamp-post.

" There you are,'' said the Colonel, triumphantly,
with a wave of his hand which took in the whole side
of the hotel.   " There it is — what did I tell you?''

" Well, but — why, Colonel, it's six stories high.   I
don't quite make out which window you —''

" All the windows, all of them.   Let him have his
choice — I'm indifferent now that I have located him.
You go and stand on the corner and wait; I'll prospect
the hotel.''

The earl drifted here and there through the swarming lobby, and finally took a waiting position in the
neighborhood of the elevator.   During an hour crowds
went up and crowds came down; and all complete as
to limbs; but at last the watcher got a glimpse of a
figure that was satisfactory — got a glimpse of the
back of it, though he had missed his chance at the face
through waning alertness.   The glimpse revealed a
cowboy hat and below it a plaided sack of rather loud
pattern, and an empty sleeve pinned up to the shoulder.   Then the elevator snatched the vision aloft, and
the watcher fled away in joyful excitement and rejoined
the fellow-conspirator.

" We've got him, Major — got him sure!   I've seen

him — seen him good; and I don't care where or when that man approaches me backwards, I'll recognize him every time. We're all right. Now for the requisition.''

They got it, after the delays usual in such cases. By half-past eleven they were at home and happy, and went to bed full of dreams of the morrow's great promise.

Among the elevator load which had the suspect for fellow-passengers was a young kinsman of Mulberry Sellers, but Mulberry was not aware of it and didn't see him. It was Viscount Berkeley.

CHAPTER VII.

ARRIVED in his room Lord Berkeley made preparations for that first and last and all-the-time duty
of the visiting Englishman — the jotting down in his
diary of his " impressions " to date. His preparations
consisted in ransacking his " box " for a pen. There
was a plenty of steel pens on his table with the ink
bottle, but he was English. The English people manu-
facture steel pens for nineteen-twentieths of the globe,
but they never use any themselves. They use exclu-
sively the prehistoric quill. My lord not only found a
quill pen, but the best one he had seen in several years
— and after writing diligently for some time, closed
with the following entry:

But in one thing I have made an immense mistake. I ought to have
sunk my title and changed my name before I started.

He sat admiring that pen awhile, and then went on:

All attempts to mingle with the common people and become permanently
one of them are going to fail, unless I can get rid of it, disappear from it,
and reappear with the solid protection of a new name. I am astonished
and pained to see how eager the most of these Americans are to get
acquainted with a lord, and how dilligent they are in pushing attentions
upon him. They lack English servility, it is true — but they could acquire
it, with practice. My quality travels ahead of me in the most mysterious
way. I write my family name without additions, on the register of this
hotel, and imagine that I am going to pass for an obscure and unknown
wanderer, but the clerk promptly calls out, " Front! show his lordship to
four-eighty-two!" and before I can get to the lift there is a reporter trying

to interview me, as they call it. This sort of thing shall cease at once. **I** will hunt up the American Claimant the first thing in the morning, accomplish my mission, then change my lodging and vanish from scrutiny under a fictitious name.

He left his diary on the table, where it would be handy in case any new "impressions" should wake him up in the night, then he went to bed and presently fell asleep. An hour or two passed, and then he came slowly to consciousness with a confusion of mysterious and augmenting sounds hammering at the gates of his brain for admission; the next moment he was sharply awake, and those sounds burst with the rush and roar and boom of an undammed freshet into his ears. Banging and slamming of shutters; smashing of windows and the ringing clash of falling glass; clatter of flying feet along the halls; shrieks, supplications, dumb moanings of despair within, hoarse shouts of command outside; cracklings and snappings, and the windy roar of victorious flames!

Bang, bang, bang! on the door, and a cry:

"Turn out — the house is on fire!"

The cry passed on, and the banging. Lord Berkeley sprang out of bed and moved with all possible speed toward the clothespress in the darkness and the gathering smoke, but fell over a chair and lost his bearings. He groped desperately about on his hands, and presently struck his head against the table and was deeply grateful, for it gave him his bearings again, since it stood close by the door. He seized his most precious possession, his journaled Impressions of America, and darted from the room.

He ran down the deserted hall toward the red lamp which he knew indicated the place of a fire-escape. The door of the room beside it was open. In the room the gas was burning full head; on a chair was a pile of clothing. He ran to the window, could not get it up, but smashed it with a chair, and stepped out on the landing of the fire-escape; below him was a crowd of men, with a sprinkling of women and youth, massed in a ruddy light. Must he go down in his spectral night-dress? No — this side of the house was not yet on fire except at the farther end; he would snatch on those clothes. Which he did. They fitted well enough, though a trifle loosely, and they were just a shade loud as to pattern. Also as to hat — which was of a new breed to him, Buffalo Bill not having been to England yet. One side of the coat went on, but the other side refused; one of its sleeves was turned up and stitched to the shoulder. He started down without waiting to get it loose, made the trip successfully, and was promptly hustled outside the limit-rope by the police.

The cowboy hat and the coat but half on made him too much of a center of attraction for comfort, although nothing could be more profoundly respectful, not to say deferential, than was the manner of the crowd toward him. In his mind he framed a discouraged remark for early entry in his diary: " It is of no use; they know a lord through any disguise, and show awe of him — even something very like fear, indeed."

Presently one of the gaping and adoring half-circle of boys ventured a timid question. My lord answered it. The boys glanced wonderingly at each other, and from somewhere fell the comment:

" *English* cowboy! Well, if that ain't curious."

Another mental note to be preserved for the diary: " Cowboy. Now what might a cowboy be? Perhaps —" But the viscount perceived that some more questions were about to be asked; so he worked his way out of the crowd, released the sleeve, put on the coat, and wandered away to seek a humble and obscure lodging. He found it, and went to bed and was soon asleep.

In the morning he examined his clothes. They were rather assertive, it seemed to him, but they were new and clean, at any rate. There was considerable property in the pockets. Item, five one hundred dollar bills. Item, near fifty dollars in small bills and silver. Plug of tobacco. Hymn-book, which refuses to open; found to contain whisky. Memorandum-book bearing no name. Scattering entries in it, recording in a sprawling, ignorant hand, appointments, bets, horse-trades, and so on, with people of strange, hyphenated name — Six-Fingered Jake, Young-Man-afraid-of-his-Shadow, and the like. No letters, no documents.

The young man muses — maps out his course. His letter of credit is burned; he will borrow the small bills and the silver in these pockets, apply part of it to advertising for the owner, and use the rest for sustenance while he seeks work. He sends out for the morning paper next, and proceeds to read about the fire. The biggest line in the display-head announces his own death! The body of the account furnishes all the particulars; and tells how, with the inherited heroism of his caste, he went on saving women and children until escape for himself was impossible; then with the eyes of weeping multitudes upon him, he stood with folded arms and sternly awaited the approach of the devouring fiend; " and so standing, amid a tossing sea of flame and on-rushing billows of smoke, the noble young heir of the great house of Rossmore was caught up in a whirlwind of fiery glory, and disappeared forever from the vision of men."

The thing was so fine and generous and knightly that it brought the moisture to his eyes. Presently he said to himself: " What to do is as plain as day now. My Lord Berkeley is dead — let him stay so. Died creditably, too; that will make the calamity the easier for my father. And I don't have to report to the Ameri-

can Claimant now. Yes, nothing could be better than
the way matters have turned out. I have only to
furnish myself with a new name, and take my new
start in life totally untrammeled. Now I breathe my
first breath of real freedom; and how fresh and breezy
and inspiring it is! At last I am a man! a man on
equal terms with my neighbor; and by my manhood,
and by it alone, I shall rise and be seen of the world,
or I shall sink from sight and deserve it. This *is* the
gladdest day, and the proudest, that ever poured its
sun upon my head!"

CHAPTER VIII.

"GOD bless my soul, Hawkins!"
        The morning paper dropped from the Colonel's nerveless grasp.

"What is it?"

"He's gone! — the bright, the young, the gifted, the noblest of his illustrious race — gone! gone up in flames and unimaginable glory!"

"Who?"

"My precious, precious young kinsman — Kirkcudbright Llanover Marjoribanks Sellers Viscount Berkeley, son and heir of usurping Rossmore."

"No!"

"It's true — too true."

"When?"

"Last night."

"Where?"

"Right here in Washington, where he arrived from England last night, the papers say."

"You don't say!"

"Hotel burned down."

"What hotel?"

"The New Gadsby!"

"Oh, my goodness! And have we lost *both* of them?"

"Both *who* ?"

"One-Arm Pete."

"Oh, great guns! I forgot all about him. Oh, I hope not!"

"Hope! Well, I should say! Oh, we *can't* spare *him!* We can better afford to lose a million viscounts than our only support and stay."

They searched the paper diligently, and were appalled to find that a one-armed man had been seen flying along one of the halls of the hotel in his underclothing and apparently out of his head with fright, and as he would listen to no one and persisted in making for a stairway which would carry him to certain death, his case was given over as a hopeless one.

"Poor fellow," sighed Hawkins; "and he had friends so near. I wish we hadn't come away from there — maybe we could have saved him."

The earl looked up and said, calmly:

"His being dead doesn't matter. He was uncertain before. We've got him sure, this time."

"Got him? How?"

"I will materialize him."

"Rossmore, don't — don't trifle with me. Do you mean that? Can you do it?"

"I can do it, just as sure as you are sitting there. And I will."

"Give me your hand, and let me have the comfort of shaking it. I was perishing, and you have put new life into me. Get at it, oh, get at it right away."

"It will take a little time, Hawkins, but there's no hurry, none in the world — in the circumstances. And of course certain duties have devolved upon me now which necessarily claim my first attention. This poor young nobleman —"

"Why, yes, I am sorry for my heartlessness, and you smitten with this new family affliction. Of course you must materialize him first — I quite understand that."

"I — I — well, I wasn't meaning just that, but — why, what am I thinking of! Of course I must

5A

materialize him. Oh, Hawkins, selfishness is the bottom trait in human nature; I was only thinking that now, with the usurper's heir out of the way — But you'll forgive that momentary weakness, and forget it. Don't ever remember it against me that Mulberry Sellers was once mean enough to think the thought that I was thinking. I'll materialize him — I will, on my honor — and I'd do it were he a thousand heirs jammed into one and stretching in a solid rank from here to the stolen estates of Rossmore, and barring the road forever to the rightful earl!''

'' There spoke the real Sellers — the other had a false ring, old friend.''

'' Hawkins, my boy, it just occurs to me — a thing I keep forgetting to mention — a matter that we've got to be mighty careful about.''

'' What is that?''

'' We must keep absolutely still about these materializations. Mind, not a hint of them must escape — not a hint. To say nothing of how my wife and daughter — high-strung, sensitive organizations — might feel about them, the negroes wouldn't stay on the place a minute.''

'' That's true, they wouldn't. It's well you spoke, for I'm not naturally discreet with my tongue when I'm not warned.''

Sellers reached out and touched a bell button in the wall, set his eye upon the rear door and waited; touched it again and waited; and just as Hawkins was remarking admiringly that the Colonel was the most progressive and most alert man he had ever seen, in the matter of impressing into his service every modern convenience the moment it was invented, and always keeping breast to breast with the drum-major in the great work of material civilization, he forsook the button (which hadn't any wire attached to it), rang a vast dinner-bell which stood on the table, and remarked that he had tried that new-fangled dry battery now to his entire satisfaction, and had got enough of it; and added:

" Nothing would do Graham Bell but I must try it; said the mere *fact* of my trying it would secure public confidence, and get it a chance to show what it could do. I *told* him that in theory a dry battery was just a curled darling and no mistake, but when it come to *practice*, sho! — and here's the result. Was I right? What should *you* say, Washington Hawkins? You've seen me try that button twice. Was I right? — that's the idea. Did I know what I was talking about, or didn't I?"

" Well, you know how I feel about you, Colonel Sellers, and always have felt. It seems to me that you always know everything about *every*thing. If that man had known you as I know you he would have taken your judgment at the start, and dropped his dry battery where it was."

" Did you ring, Marse Sellers?"

" No, Marse Sellers didn't."

" Den it was you, Marse Washington. I's heah, suh."

" No, it wasn't Marse Washington, either."

" De good lan'! who did ring her, den?"

" Lord Rossmore rang it!"

The old negro flung up his hands and exclaimed:

" Blame my skin if I hain't gone en forgit dat name agin! Come heah, Jinny — run heah, honey."

Jinny arrived.

" You take dish-yer order de lord gwine to give you. I's gwine down suller and study dat name tell I git it."

" I take de order! Who's yo' nigger las' year? De bell rung for *you*."

" Dat don't make no diffunce. When a bell ring for anybody, en old marster tell me to —"

" Clear out, and settle it in the kitchen!"

The noise of the quarreling presently sank to a murmur in the distance, and the earl added: " That's a
trouble with old house-servants that were your slaves
once and have been your personal friends always."

" Yes, and members of the family."

" Members of the family is just what they become —
the members of the family, in fact. And sometimes
master and mistress of the household. These two are
mighty good and loving and faithful and honest, but,
hang it, they do just about as they please, they chip
into a conversation whenever they want to, and the
plain fact is they ought to be killed."

It was a random remark, but it gave him an idea —
however, nothing could happen without that result.

" What I wanted, Hawkins, was to send for the
family and break the news to them."

" Oh, never mind bothering with the servants, then.
I will go and bring them down."

While he was gone the earl worked his idea.

" Yes," he said to himself, " when I've got the
materializing down to a certainty, I will get Hawkins
to kill them, and after that they will be under better
control. Without doubt a materialized negro could
easily be hypnotized into a state resembling silence.
And this could be made permanent — yes, and also
modifiable, at will — sometimes *very* silent, sometimes
turn on more talk, more action, more emotion, according to what you want. It's a prime good idea. Make
it adjustable — with a screw or something."

The two ladies entered now with Hawkins, and the
two negroes followed, uninvited, and fell to brushing
and dusting around, for they perceived that there was
matter of interest to the fore, and were willing to find
out what it was.

Sellers broke the news with stateliness and ceremony,

first warning the ladies, with gentle art, that a pang of
peculiar sharpness was about to be inflicted upon their
hearts — hearts still sore from a like hurt, still lament-
ing a like loss — then he took the paper, and with
trembling lips and with tears in his voice he gave them
that heroic death-picture.

The result was a very genuine outbreak of sorrow
and sympathy from all the hearers. The elder lady
cried, thinking how proud that great-hearted young
hero's mother would be, if she were living, and how
unappeasable her grief; and the two old servants cried
with her, and spoke out their applauses and their pitying lamentations with the eloquent sincerity and simplicity native to their race. Gwendolen was touched,
and the romantic side of her nature was strongly
wrought upon. She said that such a nature as that
young man's was rarely and truly noble, and nearly
perfect; and that with nobility of birth added it was
entirely perfect. For such a man she could endure all
things, suffer all things, even to the sacrificing of her
life. She wished she could have seen him; the slightest, the most momentary contact with such a spirit
would have ennobled her whole character, and made
ignoble thoughts and ignoble acts thereafter impossible
to her forever.

"Have they found the body, Rossmore?" asked
the wife.

"Yes; that is, they've found several. It must be
one of them, but none of them are recognizable."

"What are you going to do?"

"I am going down there and identify one of them,
and send it home to the stricken father."

"But, papa, did you ever see the young man?"

"No, Gwendolen — why?"

"How will you identify it?"

"I — well, you know, it says none of them are
5***

recognizable. I'll send his father one of them —
there's probably no choice."

Gwendolen knew it was not worth while to argue the
matter further, since her father's mind was made up,
and there was a chance for him to appear upon that
sad scene down yonder in an authentic and official way.
So she said no more — till he asked for a basket.

" A basket, papa?   What for?"

" It might be ashes."

CHAPTER IX.

THE earl and Washington started on the sorrowful errand, talking as they walked.

" And as *usual!*"

" What, Colonel?"

" Seven of them in that hotel. Actresses. And all burnt out, of course."

" Any of them burnt *up ?*"

" Oh, no, they escaped; they always do; but there's never a one of them that knows enough to fetch out her jewelry with her."

" That's strange."

" Strange — it's the most unaccountable thing in the world. Experience teaches them nothing; they can't seem to learn anything except out of a book. In some cases there's manifestly a fatality about it. For instance, take What's-her-name, that plays those sensational thunder and lightning parts. She's got a perfectly immense reputation — draws like a dog-fight — and it all came from getting burnt out in hotels."

" Why, how could that give her a reputation as an actress?"

" It didn't — it only made her name familiar. People want to see her play because her name is familiar, but they don't know what made it familiar, because they don't remember. First, she was at the bottom of the ladder, and absolutely obscure — wages thirteen dollars a week and find her own pads."

E***

" Pads?"

" Yes — things to fat up her spindles with so as to be plump and attractive.   Well, she got burnt out in a hotel and lost $30,000 worth of diamonds —"

" She?   Where'd she get them?"

" Goodness knows — given to her, no doubt, by spoony young flats and sappy old baldheads in the front row.   All the papers were full of it.   She struck for higher pay and got it.   Well, she got burnt out again and lost all her diamonds, and it gave her such a lift that she went starring."

" Well, if hotel fires are all she's got to depend on to keep up her name, it's a pretty precarious kind of a reputation, I should think."

" Not with her.   No, anything but that.   Because she's so lucky; born lucky, I reckon.   Every time there's a hotel fire she's in it.   She's always there — and if she can't be there herself, her diamonds are. Now you can't make anything out of that but just sheer luck."

" I never heard of such a thing.   She must have lost quarts of diamonds."

" Quarts! she's lost bushels of them.   It's got so that the hotels are superstitious about her.   They won't let her in.   They think there will be a fire; and, besides, if she's there it cancels the insurance.   She's been waning a little lately, but this fire will set her up. She lost $60,000 worth last night."

" I think she's a fool.   If I had $60,000 worth of diamonds I wouldn't trust them in a hotel."

" I wouldn't either; but you can't teach an actress that.   This one's been burnt out thirty-five times. And yet if there's a hotel fire in San Francisco to-night she's got to bleed again, you mark my words. Perfect ass; they say she's got diamonds in every hotel in the country."

When they arrived at the scene of the fire the poor old earl took one glimpse at the melancholy morgue and turned away his face, overcome by the spectacle. He said:

"It is too true, Hawkins — recognition is impossible; not one of the five could be identified by its nearest friend. You make the selection; I can't bear it."

"Which one had I better —"

"Oh, take any of them. Pick out the best one."

However, the officers assured the earl — for they knew him, everybody in Washington knew him — that the position in which these bodies were found made it impossible that any one of them could be that of his noble young kinsman. They pointed out the spot where, if the newspaper account was correct, he must have sunk down to destruction; and at a wide distance from this spot they showed him where the young man must have gone down in case he was suffocated in his room; and they showed still a third place, quite remote, where he might possibly have found his death if perchance he tried to escape by the side exit toward the rear. The old Colonel brushed away a tear, and said to Hawkins:

"As it turns out, there was something prophetic in my fears. Yes, it's a matter of ashes. Will you kindly step to a grocery and fetch a couple more baskets?"

Reverently they got a basket of ashes from each of those now hallowed spots, and carried them home to consult as to the best manner of forwarding them to England, and also to give them an opportunity to "lie in state" — a mark of respect which the Colonel deemed obligatory, considering the high rank of the deceased.

They set the baskets on the table in what was formerly the library, drawing-room, and work-shop —

now the Hall of Audience — and went upstairs to the lumber-room to see if they could find a British flag to use as a part of the outfit proper to the lying in state. A moment later Lady Rossmore came in from the street and caught sight of the baskets just as old Jinny crossed her field of vision. She quite lost her patience, and said:

" Well, what will you do next? What in the world possessed you to clutter up the parlor table with these baskets of ashes?"

" Ashes?" And she came to look. She put up her hands in pathetic astonishment. " Well, I *never* see de like!"

" Didn't you do it?"

" Who? me? Clah to goodness it's de fust time I've sot eyes on 'em, Miss Polly. Dat's Dan'l. Dat ole moke is losin' his mine."

But it wasn't Dan'l, for he was called, and denied it.

" Dey ain't no way to 'splain dat. Wen hit's one er dese-yer common 'currences, a body kin reckon maybe de cat —"

" Oh!" and a shudder shook Lady Rossmore to her foundations. " I see it all. Keep away from them — they're *his*."

" *His*, m'lady?"

" Yes — your young Marse Sellers from England that's burnt up."

She was alone with the ashes — alone before she could take half a breath. Then she went after Mulberry Sellers, purposing to make short work of his programme, whatever it might be; " for," said she, " when his sentimentals are up he's a numskull, and there's no knowing what extravagance he'll contrive if you let him alone." She found him. He had found the flag and was bringing it. When she heard that his idea was to have the remains " lie in state, and invite the government and the public," she broke it up. She said:

"Your intentions are all right — they always are — you want to do honor to the remains, and surely nobody can find any fault with that, for he was your kin; but you are going the wrong way about it, and you will see it yourself if you stop and think. You can't file around a basket of ashes trying to look sorry for it and make a sight that is really solemn, because the solemner it is, the more it isn't — anybody can see that. It would be so with one basket; it would be three times so with three. Well, it stands to reason that if it wouldn't be solemn with one mourner, it wouldn't be with a procession — and there would be five thousand people here. I don't know but it would be pretty near ridiculous; I think it would. No, Mulberry, they can't lie in state — it would be a mistake. Give that up and think of something else."

So he gave it up; and not reluctantly, when he had thought it over and realized how right her instinct was. He concluded to merely sit up with the remains — just himself and Hawkins. Even this seemed a doubtful attention, to his wife, but she offered no objection, for it was plain that he had a quite honest and simple-hearted desire to do the friendly and honorable thing by these forlorn poor relics which could command no hospitality in this far-off land of strangers but his. He draped the flag about the baskets, put some crape on the door-knob, and said, with satisfaction:

"There — he is as comfortable now as we can make him in the circumstances. Except — yes, we must strain a point there — one must do as one would wish to be done by — he must have it."

"Have what, dear?"

"Hatchment."

The wife felt that the house-front was standing about

all it could well stand in that way; the prospect of
another stunning decoration of that nature distressed
her, and she wished the thing had not occurred to him.
She said, hesitatingly:

"But I thought such an honor as that wasn't allowed
to any but very *very* near relations, who —"

"Right, you are quite right, my lady, perfectly
right; but there aren't any nearer relatives than relatives
by usurpation. We cannot avoid it; we are slaves of
aristocratic custom, and must submit."

The hatchments were unnecessarily generous, each
being as large as a blanket, and they were unnecessarily
volcanic, too, as to variety and violence of color, but
they pleased the earl's barbaric eye, and they satisfied
his taste for symmetry and completeness, too, for they
left no waste room to speak of on the house-front.

Lady Rossmore and her daughter assisted at the
sitting-up till near midnight, and helped the gentlemen
to consider what ought to be done next with the remains. Rossmore thought they ought to be sent
home — with a committee and resolutions — at once.
But the wife was doubtful.   She said:

"Would you send all of the baskets?"

"Oh, yes, all."

"All at once?"

"To his father? Oh, no — by no means. Think
of the shock. No — one at a time; break it to him
by degrees."

"Would *that* have that effect, father?"

"Yes, my daughter. Remember, you are young
and elastic, but he is old. To send him the whole at
once might well be more than he could bear. But
mitigated — one basket at a time, with restful intervals
between, he would be used to it by the time he got all
of him. And sending him in three ships is safer anyway. On account of wrecks and storms."

" I don't like the idea, father. If I were his father
it would be dreadful to have him coming in that — in
that —"

" On the installment plan," suggested Hawkins;
gravely, and proud of being able to help.

" Yes — dreadful to have him coming in that inco-
herent way. There would be the strain of suspense
upon me all the time. To have so depressing a thing
as a funeral impending, delayed, waiting, unaccom-
plished —"

" Oh, no, my child," said the earl, reassuringly,
" there would be nothing of that kind; so old a gentleman could not endure a long-drawn suspense like that.
There will be three funerals."

Lady Rossmore looked up surprised, and said:

" How is *that* going to make it easier for him? It's
a total mistake, to my mind. He ought to be buried
all at once; I'm sure of it."

" I should think so, too," said Hawkins.

" And certainly *I* should," said the daughter.

" You are all wrong," said the earl. " You will see
it yourselves if you think. Only one of these baskets
has got him in it."

" Very well, then," said Lady Rossmore, " the
thing is perfectly simple —- bury *that* one."

" Certainly," said Lady Gwendolen.

" But it is *not* simple," said the earl, " because we
do not know which basket he is in. We know he is in
one of them, but that is all we *do* know. You see now,
I reckon, that I was right; it takes three funerals, there
is no other way."

" And three graves and three monuments and three
inscriptions?" asked the daughter.

" Well — yes — to do it right. That is what I
should do."

" It could not be done so, father. Each of the inscriptions would give the same name and the same facts and say he was under each and all of these monuments, and that would not answer at all."

The earl nestled uncomfortably in his chair.

"No," he said, "that *is* an objection. That is a serious objection. I see no way out."

There was a general silence for a while. Then Hawkins said:

"It seems to me that if we mixed the three ramifications together —"

The earl grasped him by the hand and shook it gratefully.

"It solves the whole problem," he said. "One ship, one funeral, one grave, one monument — it is admirably conceived. It does you honor, Major Hawkins, it has relieved me of a most painful embarrassment and distress, and it will save that poor stricken old father much suffering. Yes, he shall go over in one basket."

"When?" asked the wife.

"To-morrow — immediately, of course."

"I would wait, Mulberry."

"Wait? Why?"

"*You* don't want to break that childless old man's heart."

"God knows I don't."

"Then wait till he sends for his son's remains. If you do that you will never have to give him the last and sharpest pain a parent can know — I mean, the *certainty* that his son is dead. For he will never send."

"Why won't he?"

"Because to send — and find out the truth — would rob him of the one precious thing left him: the *uncertainty*, the dim hope that maybe, after all, his boy escaped, and he will see him again some day."

" Why, Polly, he'll know by the *papers* that he was burnt up.''

" He won't let himself *believe* the papers; he'll argue against anything and everything that proves his son is dead; and he will keep that up and live on it, and on nothing else till he dies. But if the *remains* should actually come, and be put before that poor old dim-hoping soul —''

" Oh, my God, they never shall! Polly, you've saved me from a crime, and I'll bless you for it always. *Now* we know what to do. We'll place them reverently away, and he shall never know.''

CHAPTER X.

THE young Lord Berkeley, with the fresh air of freedom in his nostrils, was feeling invincibly strong for his new career; and yet — and yet — if the fight should prove a very hard one at first, very discouraging, very taxing on untoughened moral sinews, he might in some weak moment want to retreat. Not likely, of course, but possibly that might happen. And so, on the whole, it might be pardonable caution to burn his bridges behind him. Oh, without doubt. He must not stop with advertising for the owner of that money, but must put it where he could not borrow from it himself, meantime, under stress of circumstances. So he went down town and put in his advertisement, then went to a bank and handed in $500 for deposit.

" What name?"

He hesitated and colored a little; he had forgotten to make a selection. He now brought out the first one that suggested itself:

" Howard Tracy."

When he was gone, the clerks, marveling, said:

" The cowboy blushed."

The first step was accomplished. The money was still under his command and at his disposal, but the next step would dispose of that difficulty. He went to another bank and drew upon the first bank for the $500 by check. The money was collected and de-

posited a second time to the credit of Howard Tracy.
He was asked to leave a few samples of his signature,
which he did.   Then he went away, once more proud
and of perfect courage, saying:

"No help for me now, for henceforth I couldn't
draw that money without identification, and that is become legally impossible.   No resources to fall back
on.   It is work or starve from now to the end.   I am
ready — and not afraid!"

Then he sent this cablegram to his father:

Escaped unhurt from burning hotel.   Have taken fictitious name.
Good-bye.

During the evening, while he was wandering about in
one of the outlying districts of the city, he came across
a small brick church, with a bill posted there with these
words printed on it: "MECHANICS' CLUB DEBATE.
ALL INVITED."   He saw people, apparently mainly
of the working class, entering the place, and he followed and took his seat.   It was a humble little church,
quite bare as to ornamentation.   It had painted pews
without cushions, and no pulpit, properly speaking,
but it had a platform.   On the platform sat the chairman, and by his side sat a man who held a manuscript
in his hand and had the waiting look of one who is
going to perform the principal part.   The church was
soon filled with a quiet and orderly congregation of
decently dressed and modest people.   This is what the
chairman said:

"The essayist for this evening is an old member of
our club whom you all know, Mr. Parker, assistant
editor of the *Daily Democrat*.   The subject of his essay
is the American Press, and he will use as his text a
couple of paragraphs taken from Mr. Matthew Arnold's
new book.   He asks me to read these texts for him.
The first is as follows:

6A

" ' Goethe says somewhere that ' the thrill of awe,' that is to say, REVERENCE, is the best thing humanity has.'

" Mr. Arnold's other paragraph is as follows:

"I should say that if one were searching for the best means to efface and kill in a whole nation the discipline of respect, one could not do better than take the American newspapers."

Mr. Parker rose and bowed, and was received with warm applause. He then began to read in a good, round, resonant voice, with clear enunciation and careful attention to his pauses and emphases. His points were received with approval as he went on.

The essayist took the position that the most important function of a public journal in any country was the propagating of national feeling and pride in the national name — the keeping the people " in love with *their* country and *its* institutions, and shielded from the allurements of alien and inimical systems." He sketched the manner in which the reverent Turkish or Russian journalist fulfilled this function — the one assisted by the prevalent " discipline of respect " for the bastinado, the other for Siberia. Continuing, he said:

The chief function of an English journal is that of all other journals the world over: it must keep the public eye fixed admiringly upon certain things, and keep it diligently diverted from certain others. For instance, it must keep the public eye fixed admiringly upon the glories of England, a processional splendor stretching its receding line down the hazy vistas of time, with the mellowed lights of a thousand years glinting from its banners; and it must keep it diligently diverted from the fact that all these glories were for the enrichment and aggrandizement of the petted and privileged few, at cost of the blood and sweat and poverty of the unconsidered masses who achieved them, but might not enter in and partake of them. It must keep the public eye fixed in loving and awful reverence upon the throne as a sacred thing, and diligently divert it from the fact that no throne was ever set up by the unhampered vote of a majority of any nation; and that hence no throne exists that has a right to exist, and no symbol of it, flying from any flagstaff, is righteously entitled to wear any device but the skull and crossbones of that kindred industry which differs from royalty only business-wise — merely as retail differs from wholesale. It must keep the citizen's eye fixed in reverent docility upon that curious invention of machine politics, an Established Church, and upon that bald contradiction of common justice, a hereditary nobility; and diligently divert it from the fact that the one damns him if he doesn't wear its collar, and robs him under the gentle name of taxation whether he wears it or not, and the other gets all the honors while he does all the work.

The essayist thought that Mr. Arnold, with his trained eye and intelligent observation, ought to have perceived that the very quality which he so regretfully missed from our press — respectfulness, reverence — was exactly the thing which would make our press useless to us if it had it — rob it of the very thing which differentiates it from all other journalism in the world and makes it distinctively and preciously American, its frank and cheerful irreverence being by all odds the most valuable of all its qualities. "For its mission — overlooked by Mr. Arnold — is to stand guard over a nation's liberties, not its humbugs and shams." He thought that if during fifty years the institutions of the old world could be exposed to the fire of a flouting and scoffing press like ours, "monarchy and its attendant crimes would disappear from Christendom." Monarchists might doubt this; then "why not persuade the Czar to give it a trial in Russia?" Concluding, he said:

Well, the charge is, that our press has but little of that old world quality, reverence. Let us be candidly grateful that it is so. With its limited reverence it at least reveres the things which this nation reveres, as a rule, and that is sufficient: what other people revere is fairly and properly matter of light importance to us. Our press does not reverence kings, it does not reverence so-called nobilities; it does not reverence established ecclesiastical slaveries, it does not reverence laws which rob a younger son to fatten an elder one, it does not reverence any fraud or sham or infamy, howsoever old or rotten or holy, which sets one citizen above his neighbor by accident of birth; it does not reverence any law or custom, howsoever old or decayed or sacred, which shuts against the best man in the land the best place in the land and the divine right to prove property and go up and occupy it.   In the sense of the poet Goethe — that meek idolater of provincial three carat royalty and nobility — our press is certainly bankrupt in the "thrill of awe" — otherwise reverence; reverence for nickel plate and brummagem.   Let us sincerely hope that this fact will remain a fact forever; for to my mind a discriminating irreverence is the creator and protector of human liberty — even as the other thing is the creator, nurse, and steadfast protector of all forms of human slavery, bodily and mental.

Tracy said to himself, almost shouted to himself, "I'm glad I came to this country.   I was right.   I was right to seek out a land where such healthy principles and theories are in men's hearts and minds. Think of the innumerable slaveries imposed by misplaced reverence!   How well he brought that out, and how true it is.   There's manifestly prodigious force in reverence.   If you can get a man to reverence your ideals, he's your slave.   Oh, yes; in all the ages the peoples of Europe have been diligently taught to avoid reasoning about the shams of monarchy and nobility, been taught to avoid examining them, been taught to reverence them; and now, as a natural result, to reverence them is a second nature.   In order to shock them it is sufficient to inject a thought of the opposite kind into their dull minds.   For ages, any expression of so-called irreverence from their lips has been sin and crime.   The sham and swindle of all this is apparent the moment one reflects that he is himself the only legitimately qualified judge of what *is* entitled to reverence and what is not.   Come, I hadn't thought of that before, but it is true, absolutely true.   What right has Goethe, what right has Arnold, what right has any dictionary, to define the word Irreverence for me?   What their ideals are is nothing to me.   So long as I reverence my own ideals my whole duty is done, and I commit no profanation if I laugh at theirs. I may scoff at other people's ideals as much as I want to. It is my right and my privilege. No man has any right to deny it.''

Tracy was expecting to hear the essay debated, but this did not happen. The chairman said, by way of explanation:

'' I would say, for the information of the strangers present here, that in accordance with our custom the subject of this meeting will be debated at the next meeting of the club. This is in order to enable our members to prepare what they may wish to say upon the subject with pen and paper, for we are mainly mechanics and unaccustomed to speaking. We are obliged to write down what we desire to say.''

Many brief papers were now read, and several off-hand speeches made in discussion of the essay read at the last meeting of the club, which had been a laudation, by some visiting professor, of college culture, and the grand results flowing from it to the nation. One of the papers was read by a man approaching middle age, who said he hadn't had a college education, that he had got his education in a printing office, and had graduated from there into the patent office, where he had been a clerk now for a great many years. Then he continued to this effect:

The essayist contrasted the America of to-day with the America of bygone times, and certainly the result is the exhibition of a mighty progress. But I think he a little overrated the college-culture share in the production of that result. It can no doubt be easily shown that the colleges have contributed the intellectual part of this progress, and that that part is vast; but that the material progress has been immeasurably vaster, I think you will concede. Now I have been looking over a list of inventors — the creators of this amazing material development — and I find that they were not college-bred men. Of course there are exceptions — like Professor Henry of Princeton, the inventor of Mr. Morse's system of telegraphy — but these

6***

exceptions are few. It is not overstatement to say that the imagination-stunning material development of this century, the only century worth living in since time itself was invented, is the creation of men not college-bred. We think we see what these inventors have done: no, we see only the visible vast frontage of their work; behind it is their far vaster work, and it is invisible to the careless glance. They have reconstructed this nation — made it over, that is — and, metaphorically speaking, have multi-plied its numbers almost beyond the power of figures to express. I will explain what I mean. What constitutes the population of a land? Merely the numberable packages of meat and bones in it called by courtesy men and women? Shall a million ounces of brass and a million ounces of gold be held to be of the same value? Take a truer standard: the measure of a man's contributing capacity to his time and his people — the work he can do — and then number the population of this country to-day, as multiplied by what a man can now do more than his grandfather could do. By this standard of measurement, this nation, two or three generations ago, con-sisted of mere cripples, paralytics, dead men, as compared with the men of to-day. In 1840 our population was 17,000,000. By the way of rude but striking illustration, let us consider, for argument's sake, that four of these millions consisted of aged people, little children, and other incapables, and that the remaining 13,000,000 were divided and employed as follows:

2,000,000 as ginners of cotton.

6,000,000 (women) as stocking-knitters.

2,000,000 (women) as thread-spinners.

500,000 as screw-makers.

400,000 as reapers, binders, etc.

1,000,000 as corn-shellers.

40,000 as weavers.

1,000 as stitchers of shoe soles.

Now the deductions which I am going to append to these figures may sound extravagant, but they are not. I take them from Miscellaneous Documents No. 50, second session 45th Congress, and they are official and trustworthy. To-day the work of those 2,000,000 cotton-ginners is done by 2,000 men; that of the 6,000,000 stocking-knitters is done by 3,000 boys; that of the 2,000,000 thread-spinners is done by 1,000 girls; that of the 500,000 screw-makers is done by 500 girls; that of the 400,000 reapers, binders, etc., is done by 4,000 boys; that of the 1,000,000 corn-shellers is done by 7,500 men; that of the 40,000 weavers is done by 1,200 men; and that of the 1,000 stitchers of shoe soles is done by 6 men. To bunch the figures, 17,000 persons to-day do the above work, whereas fifty years ago it would have taken thirteen millions of persons to do it. Now then, how many of that ignorant race—our fathers and grandfathers—with their ignorant methods, would it take to do our work to-day? It would take forty thousand millions—a hundred times the swarming population of China—twenty times the present population of the globe. You look around you and you see a nation of sixty millions—apparently; but secreted in their hands and brains, and invisible to your eyes, is the true population of this Republic, and it numbers forty billions! It is the stupendous creation of those humble, unlettered, un-college-bred inventors—all honor to their name.

"How grand that is!" said Tracy, as he wended homeward. "What a civilization it is, and what prodigious results these are! and brought about almost wholly by common men; not by Oxford-trained aristocrats, but men who stand shoulder to shoulder in the humble ranks of life and earn the bread that they eat. Again, I'm glad I came. I have found a country at last where one may start fair, and, breast to breast with his fellow-man, rise by his own efforts, and be something in the world and be proud of that something; not be something created by an ancestor three hundred years ago."

CHAPTER XI.

DURING the first few days he kept the fact diligently before his mind that he was in a land where there was "work and bread for all." In fact, for convenience's sake he fitted it to a little tune and hummed it to himself; but as time wore on the fact itself began to take on a doubtful look, and next the tune got fatigued and presently ran down and stopped. His first effort was to get an upper clerkship in one of the departments, where his Oxford education could come into play and do him service. But he stood no chance whatever. There competency was no recommendation; political backing, without competency, was worth six of it. He was glaringly English, and that was necessarily against him in the political center of a nation where both parties prayed for the Irish cause on the house-top and blasphemed it in the cellar. By his dress he was a cowboy; that won him respect — when his back was not turned — but it couldn't get a clerkship for him. But he had said, in a rash moment, that he would wear those clothes till the owner or the owner's friends caught sight of them and asked for that money, and his conscience would not let him retire from that engagement now.

At the end of a week things were beginning to wear rather a startling look. He had hunted everywhere for work, descending gradually the scale of quality, until apparently he had sued for all the various kinds

of work a man without a special calling might hope
to be able to do, except ditching and the other
coarse manual sorts — and had got neither work nor
the promise of it.

He was mechanically turning over the leaves of his
diary meanwhile, and now his eye fell upon the first
record made after he was burnt out:

I myself did not doubt my stamina before; nobody could doubt it now,
if they could see how I am housed, and realize that I feel absolutely no
disgust with these quarters, but am as serenely content with them as any
dog would be in a similar kennel. Terms, twenty-five dollars a week. I
said I would start at the bottom. I have kept my word.

A shudder went quaking through him, and he exclaimed:

"What have I been thinking of! *This* the bottom!
Mooning along a whole week, and these terrific expenses climbing and climbing all the time! I must end
this folly straightway."

He settled up at once and went forth to find less
sumptuous lodgings. He had to wander far and seek
with diligence, but he succeeded. They made him pay
in advance — four dollars and a half; this secured
both bed and food for a week. The good-natured,
hard-worked landlady took him up three flights of
narrow, uncarpeted stairs and delivered him into his
room. There were two double bedsteads in it and
one single one. He would be allowed to sleep alone
in one of the double beds until some new boarder
should come, but he wouldn't be charged extra.

So he would presently be required to sleep with some
stranger! The thought of it made him sick. Mrs.
Marsh, the landlady, was very friendly, and hoped he
would like her house — they all liked it, she said.

"And they're a very nice set of boys. They carry
on a good deal, but that's their fun. You see, this

room opens right into this back one, and sometimes they're all in one and sometimes in the other; and hot nights they all sleep on the roof when it don't rain. They get out there the minute it's hot enough. The season's so early that they've already had a night or two up there. If you'd like to go up and pick out a place, you can. You'll find chalk in the side of the chimney where there's a brick wanting. You just take the chalk and — but, of course, you've done it before."

"Oh, no, I haven't."

"Why, of course, you haven't — what am I thinking of? Plenty of room on the Plains without chalking, I'll be bound. Well, you just chalk out a place the size of a blanket anywhere on the tin that ain't already marked off, you know, and that's your property. You and your bed-mate take turn-about carrying up the blanket and pillows and fetching them down again; or one carries them up and the other fetches them down; you fix it the way you like, you know. You'll like the boys; they're everlasting sociable — except the printer. He's the one that sleeps in that single bed — the strangest creature; why, I don't believe you could get that man to sleep with another man, not if the house was afire. Mind you, I'm not just talking, I *know*. The boys tried him to see. They took his bed out one night, and so when he got home about three in the morning — he was on a morning paper then, but he's on an evening one now — there wasn't any place for him but with the iron moulder; and if you'll believe me, he just set up the rest of the night — he did, honest. They say he's cracked, but it ain't so, he's English — they're awful particular. You won't mind my saying that. You — you're English?"

"Yes."

"I thought so. I could tell it by the way you mis-

pronounce the words that's got *a*'s in them, you know; such as saying loff when you mean laff — but you'll get over that. He's a right down good fellow, and a little sociable with the photographer's boy and the caulker and the blacksmith that work in the navy yard, but not so much with the others. The fact is, though it's private, and the others don't know it, he's a kind of an aristocrat, his father being a doctor, and *you* know what style *that* is — in England, I mean, because in this country a doctor ain't so *very* much, even if he's *that*. But over there, of course, it's different. So this chap had a falling out with his father, and was pretty high strung, and just cut for this country, and the first he knew he had to get to work or starve. Well, he'd been to college, you see, and so he judged *he* was all right — did you say anything?"

"No — I only sighed."

"And there's where he was mistaken. Why, he mighty near starved. And I reckon he would have starved sure enough if some jour' printer or other hadn't took pity on him and got him a place as apprentice. So he learned the trade, and then he was all right — but it was a close call. Once he thought he had *got* to haul in his pride and holler for his father, and — why, you're sighing again. Is anything the matter with you? — does my clatter —"

"Oh, *dear*-no. Pray go on — I like it."

"Yes, you see, he's been over here ten years; he's twenty-eight now, and he ain't pretty well satisfied in his mind, because he can't get reconciled to being a mechanic and associating with mechanics, he being, as he says to me, a *gentleman*, which is a pretty plain letting-on that the boys ain't, but of course I know enough not to let *that* cat out of the bag."

"Why — would there be any harm in it?"

"Harm in it? They'd lick him, wouldn't they?

Wouldn't *you* ? Of course you would. Don't you ever
let a man say you ain't a gentleman in *this* country.
But laws, what am I thinking about?   I reckon a body
would think twice before he said a cowboy wasn't a
gentleman.''

A trim, active, slender, and very pretty girl of
about eighteen walked into the room now, in the most
satisfied and unembarrassed way. She was cheaply
but smartly and gracefully dressed, and the mother's
quick glance at the stranger's face as he rose was of
the kind which inquires what effect has been produced,
and expects to find indications of surprise and admiration.

'' This is my daughter Hattie — we call her Puss.
It's the new boarder, Puss.''   This without rising.

The young Englishman made the awkward bow
common to his nationality and time of life in circumstances of delicacy and difficulty, and these were of
that sort; for, being taken by surprise, his natural,
lifelong self sprang to the front, and that self, of
course, would not know just how to act when introduced to a chambermaid, or to the heiress of a
mechanics' boarding house. His other self — the self
which recognized the equality of all men — would have
managed the thing better if it hadn't been caught off
guard and robbed of its chance. The young girl paid
no attention to the bow, but put out her hand frankly
and gave the stranger a friendly shake, and said:

'' How do you do?''

Then she marched to the one washstand in the
room, tilted her head this way and that before the
wreck of a cheap mirror that hung above it, dampened
her fingers with her tongue, perfected the circle of a
little lock of hair that was pasted against her forehead,
then began to busy herself with the slops.

'' Well, I must be going — it's getting toward supper

time. Make yourself at home, Mr. Tracy; you'll hear the bell when it's ready.''

The landlady took her tranquil departure without commanding either of the young people to vacate the room. The young man wondered a little that a mother who seemed so honest and respectable should be so thoughtless, and was reaching for his hat, intending to disembarrass the girl of his presence; but she said:

'' Where are you going?''

'' Well — nowhere in particular, but as I am only in the way here —''

'' Why, who said you were in the way? Sit down — I'll move you when you are in the way.''

She was making the beds now. He sat down and watched her deft and diligent performance.

'' What gave you that notion? Do you reckon I need a whole room just to make up a bed or two in?''

'' Well, no, it wasn't that, exactly. We are away up here in an empty house, and your mother being gone —''

The girl interrupted him with an amused laugh, and said:

'' Nobody to protect me? Bless you, I don't need it. I'm not afraid. I might be if I was alone, because I do hate ghosts, and I don't deny it. Not that I believe in them, for I don't. I'm only just afraid of them.''

'' How can you be afraid of them if you don't believe in them?''

'' Oh, *I* don't know the *how* of it — that's too many for *me* ; I only know it's *so*. It's the same with Maggie Lee.''

'' Who is that?''

'' One of the boarders; young lady that works in the factry.''

'' She works in a factory?''

" Yes.   Shoe factry."

" In a shoe factory; and you call her a young lady?"

" Why, she's only twenty-two; what should you call her?"

" I wasn't thinking of her age; I was thinking of the title.   The fact is, I came away from England to get away from artificial forms — for artificial forms suit artificial people only — and here you've got them, too. I'm sorry.   I hoped you had only men and women; everybody equal; no differences in rank."

The girl stopped with a pillow in her teeth and the case spread open below it, contemplating him from under her brows with a slightly puzzled expression. She released the pillow, and said:

" Why, they *are* all equal.   Where's any difference in rank?"

" If you call a factory girl a young *lady*, what do you call the President's wife?"

" Call her an *old* one."

" Oh, you make age the only distinction?"

" There ain't any other to make as far as I can see."

" Then *all* women are ladies?"

" Certainly they are.   All the respectable ones."

" Well, that puts a better face on it.   Certainly there is no harm in a title when it is given to everybody.   It is only an offense and a wrong when it is restricted to a favored few.   But Miss — er —"

" Hattie."

" Miss Hattie, be frank; confess that that title *isn't* accorded by everybody to everybody.   The rich American doesn't call her cook a lady — isn't that so?"

" Yes, it's so.   What of it?"

He was surprised and a little disappointed to see that his admirable shot had produced no perceptible effect.

" What *of* it?" he said. " Why, this: equality is *not* conceded here, after all, and the Americans are no better off then the English. In fact, there's no difference."

" Now *what* an idea. There's nothing in a title except what is *put* into it — you've said that yourself. Suppose the title is *clean*, instead of lady. You get that?"

" I believe so. Instead of speaking of a woman as a *lady*, you substitute clean and say she's a clean person."

" That's it. In England the swell folks don't speak of the working people as gentlemen and ladies?"

" Oh, no."

" And the working people don't call *themselves* gentlemen and ladies?"

" Certainly not."

" So if you used the other word there wouldn't be any change. The swell people wouldn't call anybody but themselves ' clean,' and those others would drop sort of meekly into their way of talking and *they* wouldn't call themselves clean. We don't do that way here. Everybody calls himself a lady or gentleman, and thinks he *is*, and don't care what anybody else thinks him, so long as he don't say it out loud. You think there's no difference. You *knuckle down* and we *don't*. Ain't that a difference?"

" It is a difference I hadn't thought of; I admit that. Still — *calling* one's self a lady doesn't — er —"

" I wouldn't go on if I were you."

Howard Tracy turned his head to see who it might be that had introduced this remark. It was a short man about forty years old, with sandy hair, no beard, and a pleasant face badly freckled but alive and intelligent, and he wore slop-shop clothing which was neat but showed wear. He had come from the front room beyond the hall, where he had left his hat, and he had

a chipped and cracked white wash-bowl in his hand.
The girl came and took the bowl.

"I'll get it for you. You go right ahead and *give*
it to him, Mr. Barrow. He's the new boarder — Mr.
Tracy — and I'd just got to where it was getting too
deep for me."

"Much obliged if you will, Hattie. I was coming
to borrow of the boys." He sat down at his ease on
an old trunk, and said, "I've been listening and got
interested; and as I was saying, I wouldn't go on if I
were you. You see where you are coming to, don't
you? *Calling* yourself a lady doesn't elect you; that
is what you were going to say; and you saw that if
you said it you were going to run right up against
another difference that you hadn't thought of: to wit,
Whose *right* is it to do the electing? Over there,
twenty thousand people in a million elect themselves
gentleman and ladies, and the nine hundred and eighty
thousand *accept* that decree and swallow the affront
which it puts upon them. Why, if they didn't accept
it it wouldn't *be* an election; it would be a dead letter,
and have no force at all. Over here the twenty thousand would-be exclusives come up to the polls and
vote themselves to be ladies and gentlemen. But the
thing doesn't stop there. The nine hundred and eighty
thousand come and vote themselves to be ladies and
gentlemen *too*, and that elects the whole nation. Since
the whole million vote themselves ladies and gentlemen,
there is no question about that election. It *does* make
absolute equality, and there is no fiction about it;
while over yonder the *inequality* (by decree of the
infinitely feeble, and consent of the infinitely strong)
is also absolute — as real and absolute as our equality."

Tracy had shrunk promptly into his English shell
when this speech began, notwithstanding he had now
been in severe training several weeks for contact and

intercourse with the common herd on the common herd's terms; but he lost no time in pulling himself out again, and so by the time the speech was finished his valves were open once more, and he was forcing himself to accept without resentment the common herd's frank fashion of dropping sociably into other people's conversations unembarrassed and uninvited. The process was not very difficult this time, for the man's smile and voice and manner were persuasive and winning. Tracy would even have liked him on the spot but for the fact — fact which he was not really aware of — that the equality of men was not yet a reality to him; it was only a theory; the *mind* perceived, but the *man* failed to feel it. It was Hattie's ghost over again, merely turned around. Theoretically Barrow was his equal, but it was distinctly distasteful to see him exhibit it. He presently said:

"I hope in all sincerity that what you have said is true as regards the Americans, for doubts have crept into my mind several times. It seemed that the equality must be ungenuine where the sign-names of castes were still in vogue; but those sign-names have certainly lost their offense and are wholly neutralized, nullified, and harmless if they are the undisputed property of every individual in the nation. I think I realize that caste does not exist and cannot exist except by common consent of the masses outside of its limits. I thought caste created itself and perpetuated itself; but it seems quite true that it only creates itself, and is perpetuated by the people whom it despises, and who can dissolve it at any time by assuming its mere sign-names themselves."

"It's what I think. There isn't any power on earth that can prevent England's thirty millions from electing themselves dukes and duchesses to-morrow and calling themselves so. And within six months all the

7A

former dukes and duchesses would have retired from
the business. I wish they'd try that. Royalty itself
couldn't survive such a process. A handful of frowners
against thirty million laughers in a state of erruption:
Why, it's Herculaneum against Vesuvius; it would
take another eighteen centuries to find that Herculaneum after the cataclysm. What's a Colonel in our
South? He's a nobody; because they're all colonels
down there. No, Tracy" (shudder from Tracy),
" nobody in England would call you a gentleman, and
you wouldn't call yourself one; and I tell you it's a
state of things that makes a man put himself into most
unbecoming attitudes sometimes — the broad and general recognition and acceptance of caste *as* caste does, I
mean. Makes him do it unconsciously — being bred
in him, you see, and never thought over and reasoned
out. You couldn't conceive of the Matterhorn being
flattered by the notice of one of your comely little
English hills, could you?"

" Why, no."

" Well, then, let a man in his right mind try to conceive of Darwin feeling flattered by the notice of a
princess. It's so grotesque that it — well, it paralyzes
the imagination. Yet that Memnon *was* flattered by
the notice of that statuette; he *says* so — says so himself. The system that can make a god disown his
godship and profane it — oh, well, it's all wrong, it's
all wrong and ought to be abolished, I should say."

The mention of Darwin brought on a literary discussion, and this topic roused such enthusiasm in
Barrow that he took off his coat and made himself the
more free and comfortable for it, and detained him so
long that he was still at it when the noisy proprietors
of the room came shouting and skylarking in, and
began to romp, scuffle, wash, and otherwise entertain
themselves. He lingered yet a little longer to offer

the hospitalities of his room and his bookshelf to Tracy, and ask him a personal question or two:

"What is your trade?"

"They — well, they call me a cowboy, but that is a fancy; I'm not that. I haven't any trade."

"What do you work at for your living?"

"Oh, anything — I mean I *would* work at anything I could get to do, but thus far I haven't been able to find an occupation."

"Maybe I can help you; I'd like to try."

"I shall be very glad. I've tried, myself, to weariness."

"Well, of course, where a man hasn't a regular trade he's pretty bad off in this world. What you needed, I reckon, was less book-learning and more bread-and-butter-learning. I don't know what your father could have been thinking of. You ought to have had a trade, you ought to have had a trade, by *all* means. But never mind about that; we'll stir up *something* to do, I guess. And don't you get homesick; that's a bad business. We'll talk the thing over and look around a little. You'll come out all right. Wait for me — I'll go down to supper with you."

By this time Tracy had achieved a very friendly feeling for Barrow, and would have *called* him a friend, maybe, if not taken too suddenly on a straight-out requirement to realize on his theories. He was glad of his society, anyway, and was feeling lighter hearted than before. Also he was pretty curious to know what vocation it might be which had furnished Barrow such a large acquaintanceship with books and allowed him so much time to read.

CHAPTER XII.

PRESENTLY the supper-bell began to ring in the depths of the house, and the sound proceeded steadily upward, growing in intensity all the way up toward the upper floors. The higher it came the more maddening was the noise, until at last what it lacked of being absolutely deafening was made up of the sudden crash and clatter of an avalanche of boarders down the uncarpeted stairway. The peerage did not go to meals in this fashion; Tracy's training had not fitted him to enjoy this hilarious zoölogical clamor and enthusiasm. He had to confess that there was something about this extraordinary outpouring of animal spirits which he would have to get inured to before he could accept it. No doubt in time he would prefer it; but he wished the process might be modified and made just a little more gradual, and not quite so pronounced and violent. Barrow and Tracy followed the avalanche down through an ever increasing and ever more and more aggressive stench of bygone cabbage and kindred smells; smells which are to be found nowhere but in a cheap private boarding house; smells which once encountered can never be forgotten; smells which encountered generations later are instantly recognizable, but never recognizable with pleasure. To Tracy these odors were suffocating, horrible, almost unendurable; but he held his peace and said nothing. Arrived in the basement, they entered a large dining-room where thirty-five or forty people sat at a long table. They took their places. The feast had already begun, and the conversation was going on in the liveliest way from one end of the table to the other. The tablecloth was of very coarse material, and was liberally spotted with coffee-stains and grease. The knives and forks were iron, with bone handles. The spoons appeared to be iron or sheet iron, or something of the sort. The tea and coffee cups were of the commonest and heaviest and most durable stoneware. All the furniture of the table was of the commonest and cheapest sort. There was a single large, thick slice of bread by each boarder's plate, and it was observable that he economized it as if he were not expecting it to be duplicated. Dishes of butter were distributed along the table within reach of people's arms, if they had long ones, but there were no private butter-plates. The butter was perhaps good enough, and was quiet and well behaved; but it had more bouquet than was necessary, though nobody commented upon that fact or seemed in any way disturbed by it. The main feature of the feast was a piping hot Irish stew made of the potatoes and meat left over from a procession of previous meals. Everybody was liberally supplied with this dish. On the table were a couple of great dishes of sliced ham, and there were some other eatables of minor importance — preserves and New Orleans molasses and such things. There was also plenty of tea and coffee of an infernal sort, with brown sugar and condensed milk, but the milk and sugar supply was not left at the discretion of the boarders, but was rationed out at headquarters — one spoonful of sugar and one of condensed milk to each cup, and no more. The table was waited upon by two stalwart negro women who raced back and forth from the bases of supplies with splendid dash and clatter and energy. Their labors were supplemented

7***

after a fashion by the young girl Puss. She carried
coffee and tea back and forth among the boarders, but
she made pleasure excursions rather than business ones
in this way, to speak strictly. She made jokes with
various people. She chaffed the young men pleasantly
— and wittily, as she supposed, and as the rest also
supposed, apparently, judging by the applause and
laughter which she got by her efforts. Manifestly she
was a favorite with most of the young fellows and
sweetheart of the rest of them. Where she conferred
notice she conferred happiness, as was seen by the
face of the recipient; and at the same time she conferred unhappiness — one could see it fall and dim the
faces of the other young fellows like a shadow. She
never " Mistered " these friends of hers, but called
them " Billy," " Tom," " John," and they called her
" Puss " or " Hattie."

Mr. Marsh sat at the head of the table, his wife sat
at the foot. Marsh was a man of sixty, and was an
American; but if he had been born a month earlier he
would have been a Spaniard. He was plenty good
enough Spaniard as it was; his face was very dark, his
hair very black, and his eyes were not only exceedingly black but were very intense, and there was something about them that indicated that they could burn
with passion upon occasion. He was stoop-shouldered
and lean-faced, and the general aspect of him was disagreeable; he was evidently not a very companionable
person. If looks went for anything, he was the very
opposite of his wife, who was all motherliness and
charity, good-will and good-nature. All the young
men and the women called her Aunt Rachel, which
was another sign. Tracy's wandering and interested
eye presently fell upon one boarder who had been
overlooked in the distribution of the stew. He was
very pale, and looked as if he had but lately come out

of a sick-bed, and also as if he ought to get back into
it again as soon as possible.   His face was very melancholy.   The waves of laughter and conversation broke
upon it without affecting it any more than if it had
been a rock in the sea, and the words and the laughter
veritable waters.   He held his head down and looked
ashamed.   Some of the women cast glances of pity
toward him from time to time in a furtive and half-
afraid way, and some of the youngest of the men
plainly had compassion on the young fellow — a compassion exhibited in their faces, but not in any more
active or compromising way.   But the great majority
of the people present showed entire indifference to the
youth and his sorrows.   Marsh sat with his head down,
but one could catch the malicious gleam of his eyes
through his shaggy brows.   He was watching that
young fellow with evident relish.   He had not neglected him through carelessness, and apparently the
table understood that fact.   The spectacle was making
Mrs. Marsh very uncomfortable.   She had the look of
one who hopes against hope that the impossible may
happen; but as the impossible did not happen, she
finally ventured to speak up and remind her husband
that Nat Brady hadn't been helped to the Irish stew.

Marsh lifted his head and gasped out, with mock
courtliness, " Oh, he hasn't, hasn't he?   What a pity
that is.   I don't know how I came to overlook him.
Ah, he must pardon me.   You must, indeed, Mr.—
er — Baxter — Barker, you must pardon me.   I — er
— my attention was directed to some other matter, I
don't know what.   The thing that grieves me mainly is
that it happens every meal now.   But you must try to
overlook these little things, Mr. Bunker, these little
neglects on my part.   They're always likely to happen
with me in any case, and they are especially likely to
happen where a person has — er — well, where a per-

G***

son is, say, about three weeks in arrears for his board.
You get my meaning? — you get my idea?   Here is
your Irish stew, and — er — it gives me the greatest
pleasure to send it to you, and I hope that you will
enjoy the charity as much as I enjoy conferring it.''

A blush rose in Brady's white cheeks and flowed
slowly backward to his ears and upward toward his
forehead, but he said nothing and began to eat his food
under the embarrassment of a general silence and the
sense that all eyes were fastened upon him.   Barrow
whispered to Tracy:

'' The old man's been waiting for that.   He wouldn't
have missed that chance for anything.''

'' It's a brutal business,'' said Tracy.   Then he said
to himself, purposing to set the thought down in his
diary later:

'' Well, here in this very house is a republic where
all are free and equal, if men are free and equal anywhere in the earth; therefore I have arrived at the
place I started to find, and I am a man among men,
and on the strictest equality possible to men, no doubt.
Yet here on the threshold I find an inequality.   There
are people at this table who are looked up to for some
reason or another, and here is a poor devil of a boy
who is looked down upon, treated with indifference and
shamed by humiliations, when he has committed no
crime but that common one of being poor.   Equality
ought to make men noble-minded.   In fact, I had supposed it did do that.''

After supper Barrow proposed a walk, and they
started.   Barrow had a purpose.   He wanted Tracy to
get rid of that cowboy hat.   He didn't see his way to
finding mechanical or manual employment for a person
rigged in that fashion.   Barrow presently said:

'' As I understand it, you're not a cowboy.''

'' No, I'm not.''

"Well, now if you will not think me too curious, how did you come to mount that hat? Where'd you get it?"

Tracy didn't know quite how to reply to this, but presently said:

"Well, without going into particulars, I exchanged clothes with a stranger under stress of weather, and I would like to find him and re-exchange."

"Well, why don't you find him? Where is he?"

"I don't know. I supposed the best way to find him would be to continue to wear his clothes, which are conspicuous enough to attract his attention if I should meet him on the street."

"Oh, very well," said Barrow; "the rest of the outfit is well enough, and while it's not too conspicuous, it isn't quite like the clothes that anybody else wears. Suppress the hat. When you meet your man he'll recognize the rest of his suit. That's a mighty embarrassing hat, you know, in a center of civilization like this. I don't believe an angel could get employment in Washington in a halo like that."

Tracy agreed to replace the hat with something of a modester form, and they stepped aboard a crowded car and stood with others on the rear platform. Presently, as the car moved swiftly along the rails, two men crossing the street caught sight of the backs of Barrow and Tracy, and both exclaimed at once, "There he is!" It was Sellers and Hawkins. Both were so paralyzed with joy that before they could pull themselves together and make an effort to stop the car it was gone too far, and they decided to wait for the next one. They waited a while; then it occurred to Washington that there could be no use in chasing one horse-car with another, and he wanted to hunt up a hack. But the Colonel said:

"When you come to think of it, there's no occasion

for that at all. Now that I've got him materialized, I can command his motions. I'll have him at the house by the time we get there."

Then they hurried off home in a state of great and joyful excitement.

The hat exchange accomplished, the two new friends started to walk back leisurely to the boarding house. Barrow's mind was full of curiosity about this young fellow. He said:

"You've never been to the Rocky Mountains?"

"No."

"You've never been out on the plains?"

"No."

"How long have you been in this country?"

"Only a few days."

"You've never been in America before?"

"No."

Then Barrow communed with himself. "Now what odd shapes the notions of romantic people take. Here's a fellow who's read in England about cowboys and adventures on the plains. He comes here and buys a cowboy's suit. Thinks he can play himself on folks for a cowboy, all inexperienced as he is. Now the minute he's caught in this poor little game, he's ashamed of it and ready to retire from it. It is that exchange that he has put up as an explanation. It's rather thin, too thin altogether. Well, he's young, never been anywhere, knows nothing about the world, sentimental, no doubt. Perhaps it was the natural thing for him to do, but it was a most singular choice, curious freak, altogether."

Both men were busy with their thoughts for a time; then Tracy heaved a sigh and said:

"Mr. Barrow, the case of that young fellow troubles me."

"You mean Nat Brady?"

" Yes, Brady, or Baxter, or whatever it was. The old landlord called him by several different names."

" Oh, yes, he has been very liberal with names for Brady, since Brady fell into arrears for his board. Well, that's one of his sarcasms — the old man thinks he's great on sarcasm."

" Well, what is Brady's difficulty? What is Brady — who is he?"

" Brady is a tinner. He's a young journeyman tinner who was getting along all right till he fell sick and lost his job. He was very popular before he lost his job; everybody in the house liked Brady. The old man was rather especially fond of him, but you know that when a man loses his job and loses his ability to support himself and to pay his way as he goes, it makes a great difference in the way people look at him and feel about him."

" Is that so ! *Is* it so?"

Barrow looked at Tracy in a puzzled way. " Why, of course it's so. Wouldn't you know that, naturally? Don't you know that the wounded deer is always attacked and killed by its companions and friends?"

Tracy said to himself, while a chilly and boding discomfort spread itself through his system, " In a republic of deer and men, where all are free and equal, misfortune is a crime, and the prosperous gore the unfortunate to death." Then he said aloud, " Here in the boarding house, if one would have friends and be popular, instead of having the cold shoulder turned upon him, he must be prosperous."

" Yes," Barrow said, " that is so. It's their human nature. They do turn against Brady, now that he's unfortunate, and they don't like him as well as they did before; but it isn't because of any lack in Brady — he's just as he was before, has the same nature and the same impulses, but they — well, Brady is a thorn in their conscience, you see. They know they ought to help him and they're too stingy to do it, and they're ashamed of themselves for that, and they ought also to hate themselves on that account, but instead of that they hate Brady because he makes them ashamed of themselves. I say that's human nature; that occurs everywhere; this boarding house is merely the world in little; it's the case all over — they're all alike. In prosperity we are popular; popularity comes easy in that case, but when the other thing comes our friends are pretty likely to turn against us."

Tracy's noble theories and high purposes were beginning to feel pretty damp and clammy. He wondered if by any possibility he had made a mistake in throwing his own prosperity to the winds and taking up the cross of other people's unprosperity. But he wouldn't listen to that sort of thing; he cast it out of his mind, and resolved to go ahead resolutely along the course he had mapped out for himself.

Extracts from his diary:

Have now spent several days in this singular hive. I don't know quite what to make out of these people. They have merits and virtues, but they have some other qualities, and some ways that are hard to get along with. I can't enjoy them. The moment I appeared in a hat of the period I noticed a change. The respect which had been paid me before passed suddenly away, and the people became friendly — more than that, they became familiar, and I'm not used to familiarity, and can't take to it right off; I find that out. These people's familiarity amounts to impudence, sometimes. I suppose it's all right; no doubt I can get used to it, but it's not a satisfactory process at all. I have accomplished my dearest wish; I am a man among men, on an equal footing with Tom, Dick, and Harry, and yet it isn't just exactly what I thought it was going to be. I — I miss home. Am obliged to say I am homesick. Another thing — and this is a confession — a reluctant one, but I will make it: The thing I miss most, and most severely, is the respect, the deference, with which I was treated all my life in England, and which seems to be somehow necessary to me. I get along very well without the luxury and the wealth and the sort of society I've been accustomed to, but I do miss the respect, and can't seem to get reconciled to the absence of it. There is respect, there is deference here, but it doesn't fall to my share. It is lavished on two men. One of them is a portly man of middle age who is a retired plumber. Everybody is pleased to have that man's notice. He's full of pomp and circumstance and self-complacency and bad grammar, and at table he is Sir Oracle, and when he opens his mouth not any dog in the kennel barks. The other person is a policeman at the capitol building. He represents the government. The deference paid to these two men is not so very far short of that paid to an earl in England, though the method of it differs. Not so much courtliness, but the deference is all there.

Yes, and there is obsequiousness, too.

It does rather look as if in a republic where all are free and equal prosperity and position constitute *rank*.

CHAPTER XIII.

THE days drifted by, and they grew ever more dreary. For Barrow's efforts to find work for Tracy were unavailing. Always the first question asked was, "What Union do you belong to?"

Tracy was obliged to reply that he didn't belong to any trade union.

"Very well, then, it's impossible to employ you. My men wouldn't stay with me if I should employ a 'scab,' or 'rat,'" or whatever the phrase was.

Finally, Tracy had a happy thought. He said, "Why, the thing for me to do, of course, is to *join* a trade union."

"Yes," Barrow said; "that is the thing for you to do — if you can."

"If I *can* ? Is it difficult?"

"Well, yes," Barrow said, "it's sometimes difficult — in fact, very difficult. But you can try, and of course it will be best to try."

Therefore Tracy tried; but he did not succeed. He was refused admission with a good deal of promptness, and was advised to go back home, where he belonged, not come here taking honest men's bread out of their mouths. Tracy began to realize that the situation was desperate, and the thought made him cold to the marrow. He said to himself, "So there is an aristocracy of position here, and an aristocracy of prosperity, and apparently there is also an aristocracy of

(106)

the ins as opposed to the outs, and I am with the outs.
So the ranks grow daily here. Plainly there are all
kinds of castes here, and only one that I belong to —
the outcasts." But he couldn't even smile at his small
joke, although he was obliged to confess that he had a
rather good opinion of it. He was feeling so defeated
and miserable by this time that he could no longer
look with philosophical complacency on the horse-play
of the young fellows in the upper rooms at night. At
first it had been pleasant to see them unbend and have
a good time after having so well earned it by the labors
of the day, but now it all rasped upon his feelings
and his dignity. He lost patience with the spectacle. When they were feeling good they shouted, they
scuffled, they sang songs, they romped about the place
like cattle, and they generally wound up with a pillow-
fight, in which they banged each other over the head,
and threw the pillows in all directions, and every now
and then he got a buffet himself; and they were always
inviting him to join in. They called him "Johnny
Bull," and invited him with excessive familiarity to
take a hand. At first he had endured all this with
good nature, but latterly he had shown by his manner
that it was distinctly distasteful to him, and very soon
he saw a change in the manner of these young people
toward him. They were souring on him, as they
would have expressed it in their language. He had
never been what might be called popular. That was
hardly the phrase for it; he had merely been liked,
but now dislike for him was growing. His case was
not helped by the fact that he was out of luck, couldn't
get work, didn't belong to a union, and couldn't gain
admission to one. He got a good many slights of that
small, ill-defined sort that you can't quite put your
finger on, and it was manifest that there was only one
thing which protected him from open insult, and that

was his muscle. These young people had seen him exercising mornings, after his cold sponge bath, and they had perceived by his performance and the build of his body that he was athletic, and also versed in boxing. He felt pretty naked now, recognizing that he was shorn of all respect except respect for his fists. One night when he entered his room he found about a dozen of the young fellows there carrying on a very lively conversation punctuated with horse-laughter. The talking ceased instantly, and the frank affront of a dead silence followed. He said:

" Good evening, gentlemen," and sat down.

There was no response. He flushed to the temples, but forced himself to maintain silence. He sat there in this uncomfortable stillness some time, then got up and went out.

The moment he had disappeared he heard a prodigious shout of laughter break forth. He saw that their plain purpose had been to insult him. He ascended to the flat roof, hoping to be able to cool down his spirit there and get back his tranquillity. He found the young tinner up there, alone and brooding, and entered into conversation with him. They were pretty fairly matched now in unpopularity and general ill-luck and misery, and they had no trouble in meeting upon this common ground with advantage and something of comfort to both. But Tracy's movements had been watched, and in a few minutes the tormentors came straggling one after another to the roof, where they began to stroll up and down in an apparently purposeless way. But presently they fell to dropping remarks that were evidently aimed at Tracy, and some of them at the tinner. The ringleader of this little mob was a short-haired bully and amateur prize-fighter named Allen, who was accustomed to lording it over the upper floor, and had more than once shown a dis-

position to make trouble with Tracy. Now there was
an occasional cat-call, and hootings, and whistlings,
and finally the diversion of an exchange of connected
remarks was introduced:

" How many does it take to make a pair?"

" Well, two generally makes a pair, but sometimes
there ain't stuff enough in them to make a whole pair."
General laugh.

" What were you saying about the English a while
ago?"

" Oh, nothing; the English are all right, only —
I —"

" What was it you *said* about them?"

" Oh, I only said they swallow well."

" Swallow better than other people?"

" Oh, yes; the English swallow a good deal better
than other people."

" What is it they swallow best?"

" Oh, insults."   Another general laugh.

" Pretty hard to make 'em fight, ain't it?"

" No, 'tain't hard to make 'em fight."

" Ain't it, really?"

" No, 'tain't hard. It's impossible."   Another
laugh.

" This one's kind of spiritless, that's certain."

" *Couldn't* be the other way — in his case."

" Why?"

" Don't you know the secret of his birth?"

" No!   Has *he* got a secret of his birth?"

" You bet he has."

" What is it?"

" His father was a wax-figger."

Allen came strolling by where the pair were sitting;
stopped, and said to the tinner:

" How are you off for friends these days?"

" Well enough off."

8ᴀ

" Got a good many?"

" Well, as many as I need.'

" A friend is valuable, sometimes — as a protector, you know. What do you reckon would happen if I was to snatch your cap off and slap you in the face with it?"

" Please don't trouble me, Mr. Allen, I ain't doing anything to you."

" You answer me! What do you reckon would happen?"

" Well, I don't know."

Tracy spoke up with a good deal of deliberation, and said:

" Don't trouble the young fellow. I can tell you what would happen."

" Oh, you can, can you? Boys, Johnny Bull can tell us what would happen if I was to snatch this chump's cap off and slap him in the face with it. Now you'll see."

He snatched the cap and struck the youth in the face, and before he could inquire what was going to happen it had already happened, and he was warming the tin with the broad of his back. Instantly there was a rush, and shouts of " A ring! a ring! make a ring! Fair play all round! Johnny's grit; give him a chance."

The ring was quickly chalked on the tin, and Tracy found himself as eager to begin as he could have been if his antagonist had been a prince instead of a mechanic. At bottom he was a little surprised at this, because although his theories had been all in that direction for some time, he was not prepared to find himself actually eager to measure strength with quite so common a man as this ruffian. In a moment all the windows in the neighborhood were filled with people, and the roofs also. The men squared off, and the fight began. But Allen stood no chance whatever against the young Englishman. Neither in muscle nor in science was he his equal. He measured his length on the tin time and again; in fact, as fast as he could get up he went down again, and the applause was kept up in liberal fashion from all the neighborhood around. Finally, Allen had to be helped up. Then Tracy declined to punish him further and the fight was at an end. Allen was carried off by some of his friends in a very much humbled condition, his face black-and-blue and bleeding, and Tracy was at once surrounded by the young fellows, who congratulated him, and told him that he had done the whole house a service, and that from this out Mr. Allen would be a little more particular about how he handed slights and insults and maltreatment around among the boarders.

Tracy was a hero now, and exceedingly popular. Perhaps nobody had ever been quite so popular on that upper floor before. But if being discountenanced by these young fellows had been hard to bear, their lavish commendations and approval and hero-worship were harder still to endure. He felt degraded, but he did not allow himself to analyze the reasons why too closely. He was content to satisfy himself with the suggestion that he looked upon himself as degraded by the public spectacle which he had made of himself, fighting on a tin roof for the delectation of everybody a block or two around. But he wasn't entirely satisfied with that explanation of it. Once he went a little too far, and wrote in his diary that his case was worse than that of the prodigal son. He said the prodigal son merely fed swine; he didn't have to chum with them. But he struck that out, and said, "All men are equal. I will not disown my principles. These men are as good as I am."

Tracy was become popular on the lower floors also.

Everybody was grateful for Allen's reduction to the
ranks, and for his transformation from a doer of out-
rages to a mere threatener of them.   The young girls,
of whom there were half a dozen, showed many attentions to Tracy, particularly that boarding-house pet
Hattie, the landlady's daughter.   She said to him,
very sweetly:

"I think you're ever so nice."

And when he said, "I'm glad you think so, Miss
Hattie," she said, still more sweetly:

"Don't call me Miss Hattie — call me Puss."

Ah, here was promotion!   He had struck the summit.   There were no higher heights to climb in that
boarding-house.   His popularity was complete.

In the presence of people Tracy showed a tranquil
outside, but his heart was being eaten out of him by
distress and despair.

In a little while he should be out of money, and then
what should he do?   He wished now that he had borrowed a little more liberally from that stranger's store.
He found it impossible to sleep.   A single torturing,
terrifying thought went racking round and round in
his head, wearing a groove in his brain: What should
he do — what was to become of him?   And along with
it began to intrude a something presently which was
very like a wish that he had not joined the great and
noble ranks of martyrdom, but had stayed at home
and been content to be merely an earl and nothing
better, with nothing more to do in this world of a useful sort than an earl finds to do.   But he smothered
that part of his thought as well as he could; he made
every effort to drive it away, and with fair success, but
he couldn't keep it from intruding a little now and
then, and when it intruded it came suddenly and
nipped him like a bite, a sting, a burn.   He recognized
that thought by the peculiar sharpness of its pang.

The others were painful enough, but that one cut to
the quick when it came.   Night after night he lay tossing to the music of the hideous snoring of the honest
bread-winners until two and three o'clock in the morning, then got up and took refuge on the roof, where
he sometimes got a nap and sometimes failed entirely.
His appetite was leaving him, and the zest of life was
going along with it.   Finally, one day, being near the
imminent verge of total discouragement, he said to
himself — and took occasion to blush privately when
he said it, "If my father knew what my American
name is — he — well, my duty to my father rather
requires that I furnish him my name.   I have no right
to make his days and nights unhappy, I can do enough
unhappiness for the family all by myself.   Really he
ought to know what my American name is."   He
thought over it a while, and framed a cablegram in his
mind to this effect:

   "My American name is Howard Tracy."

   That wouldn't be suggesting anything.   His father
could understand that as he chose, and doubtless he
would understand it as it was meant, as a dutiful and
affectionate desire on the part of a son to make his old
father happy for a moment.   Continuing his train of
thought, Tracy said to himself, "Ah, but if he should
cable me to come home!   I — I — couldn't do that —
I *mustn't* do that.   I've started out on a mission, and
I mustn't turn my back on it in cowardice.   No, no, I
couldn't go home, at — at — least I shouldn't want to
go home."   After a reflective pause: "Well, maybe
— perhaps — it would be my *duty* to go in the circumstances; he's very old, and he does need me by him
to stay his footsteps down the long hill that inclines
westward toward the sunset of his life.   Well, I'll
think about that.   Yes, of course it wouldn't be right
to stay here.   I — if I — well, perhaps I could just

   8***

drop him a line and put it off a little while and satisfy him in that way. It would be — well, it would mar everything to have him require me to come instantly." Another reflective pause — then: "And yet if he should do that I don't know but — oh, dear me — *home !* how good it sounds ! and a body is excusable for wanting to see his home again, now and then, anyway."

He went to one of the telegraph offices in the avenue and got the first end of what Barrow called the "usual Washington courtesy," where "they treat you as a tramp until they find out you're a Congressman, and then they slobber all over you." There was a boy of seventeen on duty there, tying his shoe. He had his foot on a chair and his back turned towards the wicket. He glanced over his shoulder, took Tracy's measure, turned back, and went on tying his shoe. Tracy finished writing his telegram and waited, still waited, and still waited, for that performance to finish, but there didn't seem to be any finish to it; so finally Tracy said:

"Can't you take my telegram?"

The youth looked over his shoulder and said, by his manner, not his words:

"Don't you think you could wait a minute if you tried?"

However, he got the shoe tied at last, and came and took the telegram, glanced over it, then looked up surprised at Tracy. There was something in his look that bordered upon respect, almost reverence, it seemed to Tracy, although he had been so long without anything of this kind he was not sure that he knew the signs of it.

The boy read the address aloud with pleased expression in face and voice.

"The Earl of Rossmore ! Cracky ! Do you know him?"

" Yes."

" Is that so? Does he know you?"

" Well — yes."

" Well, I swear! Will he answer you?"

" I think he will."

" Will he, though? Where'll you have it sent?"

" Oh, nowhere. I'll call here and get it. When shall I call?"

" Oh, I don't know — I'll send it to you. Where shall I send it? Give me your address; I'll send it to you soon's it comes."

But Tracy didn't propose to do this. He had acquired the boy's admiration and deferential respect, and he wasn't willing to throw these precious things away, a result sure to follow if he should give the address of that boarding-house. So he said again that he would call and get the telegram, and went his way.

He idled along, reflecting. He said to himself, " There *is* something pleasant about being respected. I have acquired the respect of Mr. Allen and some of those others, and almost the deference of some of them on pure merit, for having thrashed Allen. While their respect and their deference — if it is deference — is pleasant, a deference based upon a sham, a shadow, does really seem pleasanter still. It's no real merit to be in correspondence with an earl, and yet, after all, that boy makes me feel as if there was."

The cablegram was actually gone home! The thought of it gave him an immense uplift. He walked with a lighter tread. His heart was full of happiness. He threw aside all hesitancies, and confessed to himself that he was glad through and through that he was going to give up this experiment and go back to his home again. His eagerness to get his father's answer began to grow now, and it grew with marvelous celerity after it began. He waited an hour, walking about,

H***

putting in his time as well as he could, but interested in nothing that came under his eye, and at last he presented himself at the office again and asked if any answer had come yet. The boy said:

"No, no answer yet;" then glanced at the clock and added, "I don't think it's likely you'll get one to-day."

"Why not?"

"Well, you see it's getting pretty late. You can't always tell where 'bouts a man is when he's on the other side, and you can't always find him just the minute you want him, and you see it's getting about six o'clock now, and over there it's pretty late at night."

"Why, yes," said Tracy, "I hadn't thought of that."

"Yes, pretty late now — half past ten or eleven. Oh, yes, you probably won't get any answer to-night."

CHAPTER XIV.

SO Tracy went home to supper. The odors in that supper-room seemed more strenuous and more horrible that ever before, and he was happy in the thought that he was so soon to be free from them again. When the supper was over he hardly knew whether he had eaten any of it or not, and he certainly hadn't heard any of the conversation. His heart had been dancing all the time, his thoughts had been far away from these things, and in the visions of his mind the sumptuous appointments of his father's castle had risen before him without rebuke. Even the plushed flunky, that walking symbol of a sham inequality, had not been unpleasant to his dreaming view. After the meal Barrow said:

"Come with me. I'll give you a jolly evening."

"Very good. Where are you going?"

"To my club."

"What club is that?"

"Mechanics' Debating Club."

Tracy shuddered slightly. He didn't say anything about having visited that place himself. Somehow he didn't quite relish the memory of that time. The sentiments which had made his former visit there so enjoyable, and filled him with such enthusiasm, had undergone a gradual change, and they had rotted away to such a degree that he couldn't contemplate another visit there with anything strongly resembling delight;

in fact, he was a little ashamed to go.   He didn't want
to go there and find out by the rude impact of the
thought of those people upon his reorganized condition
of mind, how sharp the change had been.   He would
have preferred to stay away.   He expected that now
he should hear nothing except sentiments which would
be a reproach to him in his changed mental attitude,
and he rather wished he might be excused.   And yet
he didn't quite want to say that; he didn't want to
show how he did feel, or show any disinclination to
go; and so he forced himself to go along with Barrow,
privately purposing to take an early opportunity to get
away.

After the essayist of the evening had read his paper,
the chairman announced that the debate would now be
upon the subject of the previous meeting, " The
American Press."   It saddened the backsliding dis-
ciple to hear this anouncement.   It brought up too
many reminiscences.   He wished he had happened
upon some other subject.   But the debate began, and
he sat still and listened.

In the course of the discussion one of the speakers —
a blacksmith named Tompkins — arraigned all monarchs
and all lords in the earth for their cold selfishness in
retaining their unearned dignities.   He said that no
monarch and no son of a monarch, no lord and no son
of a lord, ought to be able to look his fellow-man in
the face without shame.   Shame for consenting to
keep his unearned titles, property, and privileges at
the expense of other people; shame for consenting to
remain, on any terms, in dishonorable possession of
these things, which represented bygone robberies and
wrongs inflicted upon the general people of the nation.
He said: " If there were a lord or the son of a lord
here I would like to reason with him, and try to show
him how unfair and how selfish his position is.   I

would try to persuade him to relinquish it, take his place among men on equal terms, earn the bread he eats, and hold of slight value all deference paid him because of artificial position, all reverence not the just due of his own personal merits.''

Tracy seemed to be listening to utterances of his own made in talks with his radical friends in England. It was as if some eavesdropping phonograph had treasured up his words and brought them across the Atlantic to accuse him with them in the hour of his defection and retreat. Every word spoken by this stranger seemed to leave a blister on Tracy's conscience, and by the time the speech was finished he felt that he was all conscience and one blister. This man's deep compassion for the enslaved and oppressed millions in Europe who had to bear with the contempt of that small class above them, throned upon shining heights whose paths were shut against them, was the very thing he had often uttered himself. The pity in this man's voice and words was the very twin of the pity that used to reside in his own heart and come from his own lips when he thought of these oppressed peoples.

The homeward tramp was accomplished in brooding silence. It was a silence most grateful to Tracy's feelings. He wouldn't have broken it for anything; for he was ashamed of himself all the way through to his spine. He kept saying to himself:

'' How unanswerable it all is — how absolutely unanswerable! It *is* basely, degradingly selfish to keep those unearned honors, and — and — oh, hang it, nobody but a cur —''

'' What an idiotic damned speech that Tompkins made!''

This outburst was from Barrow. It flooded Tracy's demoralized soul with waters of refreshment. These were the darlingest words the poor vacillating young apostate had ever heard — for they whitewashed his shame for him, and that is a good service to have when you can't get the best of all verdicts: self-acquittal.

" Come up to my room and smoke a pipe, Tracy."

Tracy had been expecting this invitation, and had had his declination all ready; but he was glad enough to accept now. Was it possible that a reasonable argument could be made against that man's desolating speech? He was burning to hear Barrow try it. He knew how to start him and keep him going; it was to seem to combat his positions — a process effective with most people.

" What is it you object to in Tompkins's speech, Barrow?"

" Oh, the leaving out of the factor of human nature; requiring another man to do what you wouldn't do yourself."

" Do you mean —"

" Why, here's what I mean; it's very simple. Tompkins is a blacksmith; has a family; works for wages; and hard, too — fooling around won't furnish the bread. Suppose it should turn out that by the death of somebody in England he is suddenly an earl — income, half a million dollars a year. What would he do?"

" Well, I — I suppose he would have to decline to —"

" Man, he would grab it in a second!"

" Do you really think he would?"

" Think? — I don't think anything about it, I know it."

" Why?"

" Why? Because he's not a fool."

" So you think that if he were a fool, he —"

"No, I don't. Fool or *no* fool, he would grab it. Anybody would. Anybody that's alive. And I've seen dead people that would get up and go for it. I would myself."

This was balm, this was healing, this was rest and peace and comfort.

"But I thought you were opposed to nobilities?"

"Transmissible ones, yes. But that's nothing. I'm opposed to millionaires, but it would be dangerous to offer me the position."

"You'd take it?"

"I would leave the funeral of my dearest enemy to go and assume its burdens and responsibilities."

Tracy thought a while, then said:

"I don't know that I quite get the bearings of your position. You say you are opposed to hereditary nobilities, and yet if you had the chance you would —"

"Take one? In a minute I would. And there isn't a mechanic in that entire club that wouldn't. There isn't a lawyer, doctor, editor, author, tinker, loafer, railroad president, saint — land, there isn't a human *being* in the United States that wouldn't jump at the chance!"

"Except me," said Tracy, softly.

"Except you!" Barrow could hardly get the words out, his scorn so choked him. And he couldn't get any further than that form of words; it seemed to dam his flow utterly. He got up and came and glared upon Tracy in a kind of outraged and unappeasable way, and said again, "Except *you !*" He walked around him — inspecting him from one point of view and then another, and relieving his soul now and then by exploding that formula at him: "Except *you !*" Finally he slumped down into his chair with the air of one who gives it up, and said:

"He's straining his viscera and he's breaking his heart trying to get some low-down job that a good dog wouldn't have, and yet wants to let on that if he had a chance to scoop an earldom he wouldn't do it. Tracy, don't put this kind of a strain on me. Lately I'm not as strong as I was."

"Well, I wasn't meaning to put a strain on you, Barrow; I was only meaning to intimate that if an earldom ever does fall in my way —"

"There — I wouldn't give myself any worry about *that* if I was you. And, besides, I can settle what you would do. Are you any different from me?"

"Well — no."

"Are you any better than me?"

"Oh — er — why, certainly not."

"Are you as *good* ? Come!"

"Indeed, I — the fact is you take me so suddenly —"

"Suddenly? What is there sudden about it? It isn't a difficult question, is it? Or doubtful? Just measure us on the only fair lines — the lines of merit — and of course you'll admit that a journeyman chair-maker that earns his twenty dollars a week, and has had the good and genuine culture of contact with men, and care, and hardship, and failure, and success, and downs and ups and ups and downs, is just a trifle the superior of a young fellow like you, who doesn't know how to do anything that's valuable, can't earn his living in any secure and steady way, hasn't had any experience of life and its seriousness, hasn't any culture but the artificial culture of books, which adorns but doesn't really educate — come! if *I* wouldn't scorn an earldom, what the devil right have *you* to do it?"

Tracy dissembled his joy, though he wanted to thank the chair-maker for that last remark. Presently a thought struck him, and he spoke up briskly and said:

"But look here, I really can't quite get the hang of your notions — your principles, if they are principles. You are inconsistent. You are opposed to aristocracies, yet you'd take an earldom if you could. Am I to understand that you don't blame an earl for being and remaining an earl?"

"I certainly don't."

"And you wouldn't blame Tompkins, or yourself, or me, or anybody, for accepting an earldom if it was offered?"

"Indeed, I wouldn't."

"Well, then, whom *would* you blame?"

"The whole nation — any bulk and mass of population anywhere, in any country, that will put up with the infamy, the outrage, the insult of a hereditary aristocracy which *they* can't enter — and on absolutely free and equal terms."

"Come, aren't you beclouding yourself with distinctions that are not differences?"

"Indeed, I am not. I am entirely clear-headed about this thing. If I could extirpate an aristocratic system by declining its honors, *then* I should be a rascal to accept them. And if enough of the mass would join me to make the extirpation possible, *then* I should be a rascal to do otherwise than help in the attempt."

"I believe I understand — yes, I think I get the idea. You have no blame for the lucky few who naturally decline to vacate the pleasant nest they were born into; you only despise the all-powerful and stupid mass of the nation for allowing the nest to exist."

"That's it, that's it! You *can* get a simple thing through your head if you work at it long enough."

"Thanks."

"Don't mention it. And I'll give you some sound advice: when you go back, if you find your nation up

and ready to abolish that hoary affront, lend a hand;
but if that isn't the state of things and you get a
chance at an earldom, don't you be a fool — you take
it."

Tracy responded with earnestness and enthusiasm:

" As I live, I'll do it!"

Barrow laughed.

" I never saw such a fellow. I begin to think you've
got a good deal of imagination. With you, the idlest
fancy freezes into a reality at a breath. Why, you
looked, then, as if it wouldn't astonish you if you did
tumble into an earldom." Tracy blushed. Barrow
added: " Earldom! Oh, yes, take it if it offers; but
meantime we'll go on looking around, in a modest
way, and if you get a chance to superintend a sausage-
stuffer at six or eight dollars a week, you just trade off
the earldom for a last year's almanac and stick to the
sausage-stuffing."

CHAPTER XV.

TRACY went to bed happy once more, at rest in his mind once more. He had started out on a high emprise — that was to his credit, he argued; he had fought the best fight he could, considering the odds against him — that was to his credit; he had been defeated — certainly there was nothing discreditable in that. Being defeated, he had a right to retire with the honors of war and go back without prejudice to the position in the world's society to which he had been born. Why not? Even the rabid republican chairmaker would do that. Yes, his conscience was comfortable once more.

He woke refreshed, happy, and eager for his cablegram. He had been born an aristocrat, he had been a democrat for a time, he was now an aristocrat again. He marveled to find that this final change was not merely intellectual, it had invaded his feeling; and he also marveled to note that this feeling seemed a good deal less artificial than any he had entertained in his system for a long time. He could also have noted, if he had thought of it, that his bearing had stiffened over night, and that his chin had lifted itself a shade. Arrived in the basement, he was about to enter the breakfast-room when he saw old Marsh in the dim light of a corner of the hall, beckoning him with his finger to approach. The blood welled slowly up in Tracy's cheek, and he said, with a grade of injured dignity almost ducal:

9A

" Is that for me?"

" Yes."

" What is the purpose of it?"

" I want to speak to you — in private."

" This spot is private enough for me."

Marsh was surprised; and not particularly pleased. He approached and said:

" Oh, in public, then, if you prefer. Though it hasn't been my way."

The boarders gathered to the spot, interested.

" Speak out," said Tracy. " What is it you want?"

" Well, haven't you — er — forgot something?"

' I? I'm not aware of it."

' Oh, you're not? Now you stop and think a minute."

" I refuse to stop and think. It doesn't interest me. If it interests you, speak out."

" Well, then," said Marsh, raising his voice to a slightly angry pitch, " you forgot to pay your board yesterday — if you're *bound* to have it public."

Oh, yes; this heir to an annual million or so had been dreaming and soaring, and had forgotten that pitiful three or four dollars. For penalty he must have it coarsely flung in his face in the presence of these people — people in whose countenances was already beginning to dawn an uncharitable enjoyment of the situation.

" Is *that* all! Take your money and give your terrors a rest."

Tracy's hand went down into his pocket with angry decision. But — it didn't come out. The color began to ebb out of his face. The countenances about him showed a growing interest; and some of them a heightened satisfaction. There was an uncomfortable pause; then he forced out, with difficulty, the words:

" I've — been robbed! "

Old Marsh's eyes flamed up with Spanish fire, and he exclaimed:

"Robbed, is it? *That's* your tune? It's too old — been played in this house too often; everybody plays it that can't get work when he wants it, and won't work when he can get it. Trot out Mr. Allen, somebody, and let *him* take a toot at it. It's *his* turn next; *he* forgot, too, last night. I'm laying for him."

One of the negro women came scrambling down stairs as pale as a sorrel horse with consternation and excitement:

"Misto Marsh, Misto Allen's skipped out!"

"What!"

"Yes-sah, and cleaned out his room *clean;* tuck bofe towels en de soap!"

"You lie, you hussy!"

"It's jes' so, jes' as I tells you — en Misto Sumner's socks is gone, en Misto Naylor's yuther shirt."

Mr. Marsh was at boiling-point by this time. He turned upon Tracy.

"Answer up now — when are you going to settle?"

"To-day — since you seem to be in a hurry."

"*To-day*, is it? Sunday — and you out of work? I like that. Come — where are you going to get the money?"

Tracy's spirit was rising again. He proposed to impress these people.

"I am expecting a cablegram from home."

Old Marsh was caught out, with the surprise of it. The idea was so immense, so extravagant, that he couldn't get his breath at first. When he did get it, it came rancid with sarcasm.

"A *cablegram* — think of it, ladies and gents, he's expecting a cablegram! *He's* expecting a cablegram — this duffer, this scrub, this bilk! From his father — eh? Yes — without a doubt. A dollar or two a word

— oh, that's nothing — *they* don't mind a little thing like that — *this* kind's fathers don't. Now his father is — er — well, I reckon his father —"

" My father is an English earl!"

The crowd fell back aghast — aghast at the sublimity of the young loafer's " cheek." Then they burst into a laugh that made the windows rattle. Tracy was too angry to realize that he had done a foolish thing. He said:

"Stand aside, please.   I —"

" Wait a minute, your lordship," said Marsh, bowing low; " where is your lordship going?"

" For the cablegram.   Let me pass."

" Excuse me, your lordship, you'll stay right where you are."

" What do you mean by that?"

" I mean that I didn't begin to keep boarding house yesterday.   It means that I am not the kind that can be taken in by every hack-driver's son that comes loafing over here because he can't bum a living at home.   It means that you can't skip out on any such —"

Tracy made a step toward the old man, but Mrs. Marsh sprang between, and said:

" Don't, Mr. Tracy, please."   She turned to her husband and said, " *Do* bridle your tongue.   What has he done to be treated so?   Can't you *see* he has lost his mind with trouble and distress?   He's not responsible."

" Thank your kind heart, madam, but I've not lost my mind; and if I can have the mere privilege of stepping to the telegraph office —"

" Well, you can't!" cried Marsh.

"— or sending —"

" Sending!   That beats everything.   If there's anybody that's fool enough to go on such a chuckle-headed errand —"

"Here comes Mr. Barrow — he will go for me. Barrow —"

A brisk fire of exclamation broke out:

"Say, Barrow, he's expecting a cablegram!"

"Cablegram from his father, you know!"

"Yes — cablegram from the wax-figger!"

"And say, Barrow, this fellow's an earl — take off your hat, pull down your vest!"

"Yes, he's come off and forgot his crown that he wears Sundays. He's cabled over to his poppy to send it."

"You step out and get that cablegram, Barrow; his majesty's a little lame to-day."

"Oh, stop," cried Barrow; "give the man a chance." He turned, and said with some severity, "Tracy, what's the matter with you? What kind of foolishness is this you've been talking? You ought to have more sense."

"I've not been talking foolishness; and if you'll go to the telegraph office —"

"Oh, don't talk so. I'm your friend in trouble and out of it, before your face and behind your back, for anything in *reason :* but you've lost your head, you see, and this moonshine about a cablegram —"

"*I'll* go there and ask for it!"

"Thank you from the bottom of my heart, Brady. Here, I'll give you a written order for it. Fly now and fetch it. We'll soon see!"

Brady flew. Immediately the sort of quiet began to steal over the crowd which means dawning doubt, misgiving; and might be translated into the words "Maybe he *is* expecting a cablegram — maybe he *has* got a father somewhere — maybe we've been just a little too fresh, just a shade too ' previous!' " Loud talk ceased; then the mutterings and low murmurings and whisperings died out. The crowd began to crumble

9***

apart. By ones and twos the fragments drifted to the breakfast table. Barrow tried to bring Tracy in; but he said:

" Not yet, Barrow — presently."

Mrs. Marsh and Hattie tried, offering gentle and kindly persuasions; but he said:

" I would rather wait — till he comes."

Even old Marsh began to have suspicions that maybe he had been a trifle too " brash," as he called it in the privacy of his soul, and he pulled himself together and started toward Tracy with invitation in his eyes; but Tracy warned him off with a gesture which was quite positive and eloquent. Then followed the stillest quarter of an hour which had ever been known in that house at that time of day. It was so still, and so solemn withal, that when somebody's cup slipped from his fingers and landed in his plate the shock made people start, and the sharp sound seemed as indecorous there and as out of place as if a coffin and mourners were imminent and being waited for. And at last when Brady's feet came clattering down the stairs the sacrilege seemed unbearable. Everybody rose softly and turned toward the door, where stood Tracy; then, with a common impulse, moved a step or two in that direction, and stopped. While they gazed young Brady arrived, panting, and put into Tracy's hand — sure enough — an envelope. Tracy fastened a bland, victorious eye upon the gazers, and kept it there till one by one they dropped their eyes, vanquished and embarrassed. Then he tore open the telegram and glanced at its message. The yellow paper fell from his fingers and fluttered to the floor, and his face turned white. There was nothing there but one word:

" *Thanks.*"

The humorist of the house, the tall, raw-boned Billy Nash, caulker from the navy yard, was standing in the rear of the crowd. In the midst of the pathetic silence that was now brooding over the place and moving some few hearts there toward compassion, he began to whimper, then he put his handkerchief to his eyes and buried his face in the neck of the bashfulest young fellow in the company, a navy-yard blacksmith, shrieked "Oh, pappy, how *could* you!" and began to bawl like a teething baby, if one may imagine a baby with the energy and the devastating voice of a jackass.

So perfect was the imitation of a child's cry, and so vast the scale of it, and so ridiculous the aspect of the performer, that all gravity was swept from the place as if by a hurricane, and almost everybody there joined in the crash of laughter provoked by the exhibition. Then the small mob began to take its revenge — revenge for the discomfort and apprehension it had brought upon itself by its own too rash freshness of a little while before. It guyed its poor victim, baited him, worried him, as dogs do with a cornered cat. The victim answered back with defiances and challenges which included everybody, and which only gave the sport new spirit and variety; but when he changed his tactics and began to single out individuals and invite them by name, the fun lost its funniness and the interest of the show died out, along with the noise.

Finally Marsh was about to take an innings, but Barrow said:

"Never mind now — leave him alone. You've no account with him but a money account. I'll take care of that myself."

The distressed and worried landlady gave Barrow a fervently grateful look for his championship of the abused stranger; and the pet of the house, a very prism in her cheap but ravishing Sunday rig blew him a kiss from the tips of her fingers and said, with the darlingest smile and a sweet little toss of her head:

I***

"You're the only man here, and I'm going to set my cap for you, you dear old thing!"

"For shame, Puss! How you talk! I *never* saw such a child!"

It took a good deal of argument and persuasion — that is to say, petting, under these disguises — to get Tracy to entertain the idea of breakfast. He at first said he would never eat again in that house; and added that he had enough firmness of character, he trusted, to enable him to starve like a man when the alternative was to eat insult with his bread.

When he had finished his breakfast, Barrow took him to his room, furnished him a pipe, and said cheerily:

"*Now*, old fellow, take in your battle-flag out of the wet; you're not in the hostile camp any more. You're a little upset by your troubles, and that's natural enough, but don't let your mind run on them any more than you can help; drag your thoughts away from your troubles — by the ears, by the heels, or any other way, so you manage it; it's the healthiest thing a body can do; dwelling on troubles is deadly, just deadly — and that's the softest name there is for it. You must keep your mind amused — you must, indeed."

"Oh, miserable me!"

"*Don't!* There's just pure heart-break in that tone. It's just as I say; you've got to get right down to it and amuse your mind, as if it was salvation."

"They're easy words to say, Barrow, but how am I going to amuse, entertain, divert a mind that finds itself suddenly assaulted and overwhelmed by disaster of a sort not dreamed of and not provided for? No-no, the bare idea of amusement is repulsive to my feelings. Let us talk of deaths and funerals."

"No — not yet. That would be giving up the ship.

We'll not give up the ship yet. I'm going to amuse you; I sent Brady out for the wherewithal before you finished breakfast.''

''You did? What is it?''

''Come, this is a good sign — curiosity. Oh, there's hope for you yet.''

CHAPTER XVI.

BRADY arrived with a box, and departed, after saying:

" They're finishing one up, but they'll be along as soon as it's done."

Barrow took a frameless oil portrait a foot square from the box, set it up in a good light, without comment, and reached for another, taking a fugitive glance at Tracy meantime. The stony solemnity in Tracy's face remained as it was, and gave out no sign of interest. Barrow placed the second portrait beside the first, and stole another glance while reaching for a third. The stone image softened a shade. No. 3 forced the ghost of a smile, No. 4 swept indifference wholly away, and No. 5 started a laugh which was still in good and hearty condition when No. 14 took its place in the row.

" Oh, *you're* all right yet," said Barrow. " You see, you're not past amusement."

The pictures were fearful as to color, and atrocious as to drawing and expression; but the feature which squelched animosity and made them funny was a feature which could not achieve its full force in a single picture, but required the wonder-working assistance of repetition. One loudly dressed mechanic in stately attitude, with his hand on a cannon, ashore, and a ship riding at anchor in the offing — this is merely odd; but when one sees the same cannon and the same ship in fourteen pictures in a row, and a different mechanic standing watch in each, the thing gets to be funny.

" Explain — explain these aberrations," said Tracy.

" Well, they are not the achievement of a single intellect, a single talent — it takes two to do these miracles. They are collaborations; the one artist does the figure, the other the accessories. The figure-artist is a German shoemaker with an untaught passion for art, the other is a simple-hearted old Yankee sailor-man whose possibilities are strictly limited to his ship, his cannon, and his patch of petrified sea. They work these things up from twenty-five cent tintypes; they get six dollars apiece for them, and they can grind out a couple a day when they strike what they call a boost — that is, an inspiration."

" People actually pay money for these calumnies?"

" They actually do — and quite willingly, too. And these abortionists could double their trade and work the women in if Captain Saltmarsh could whirl a horse in, or a piano, or a guitar, in place of his cannon. The fact is, he fatigues the market with that cannon. Even the male market, I mean. These fourteen in the procession are not all satisfied. One is an old " independent " fireman, and he wants an engine in place of the cannon; another is a mate of a tug, and wants a tug in place of the ship — and so on, and so on. But the captain can't make a tug that is deceptive, and a fire engine is many flights beyond his power."

" This *is* a most extraordinary form of robbery. I never have heard of anything like it. It's interesting."

" Yes, and so are the artists. They are perfectly honest men, and sincere. And the old sailor-man is full of sound religion, and is as devoted a student of the Bible and misquoter of it as you can find anywhere.

I don't know a better man or kinder hearted old soul than Saltmarsh, although he does swear a little sometimes."

"He seems to be perfect. I want to know him, Barrow."

"You'll have the chance. I guess I hear them coming now. We'll draw them out on their art, if you like."

The artists arrived and shook hands with great heartiness. The German was forty and a little fleshy, with a shiny bald head and a kindly face and deferential manner. Captain Saltmarsh was sixty, tall, erect, powerfully built, with coal-black hair and whiskers, and he had a well-tanned complexion, and a gait and countenance that were full of command, confidence, and decision. His horny hands and wrists were covered with tattoo-marks, and when his lips parted his teeth showed up white and blemishless. His voice was the effortless deep bass of a church organ, and would disturb the tranquillity of a gas flame fifty yards away.

"They're wonderful pictures," said Barrow. "We've been examining them."

"It is very bleasant dot you like dem," said Handel, the German, greatly pleased. "Und you, Herr Tracy, you haf peen bleased mit dem too, alretty?"

"I can honestly say I have never seen anything just like them before."

"Schön!" cried the German, delighted. "You hear, Gaptain? Here is a chentleman, yes, vot abbreciate unser aart."

The Captain was charmed, and said:

"Well, sir, we're thankful for a compliment yet, though they're not as scarce now as they used to be before we made a reputation."

"Getting the reputation is the uphill time in most things, Captain."

"It's so. It ain't enough to know how to reef a gasket, you got to make the mate know you know it. That's reputation. The good word, said at the right time, that's the word that makes us; and evil be to him that evil thinks, as Isaiah says."

"It's very relevant, and hits the point exactly," said Tracy. "Where did you study art, Captain?"

"I haven't studied; it's a natural gift."

"He is born mit dose cannon in him. He tondt haf to do noding, his chenius do all de vork. Of he is asleep, und take a pencil in his hand, out come a cannon. Py crashus, of he could do a clavier, of he could do a guitar, of he could do a vashtub, it is a fortune; heiliger Yohanniss, it is yoost a fortune!"

"Well, it is an immense pity that the business is hindered and limited in this unfortunate way."

The Captain grew a trifle excited himself now.

"You've said it, Mr. Tracy! Hindered? well, I should say so. Why, look here. This fellow here, No. 11, he's a hackman — a flourishing hackman, I may say. He wants his hack in this picture. Wants it where the cannon is. I got around that difficulty by telling him the cannon's our trademark, so to speak — proves that the picture's our work, and I was afraid if we left it out people wouldn't know for certain if it *was* a Saltmarsh-Handel — now you wouldn't yourself —"

"What, Captain? You wrong yourself, indeed you do. Any one who has once seen a genuine Saltmarsh-Handel is safe from imposture forever. Strip it, flay it, skin it out of every detail but the bare color and expression, and that man will still recognize it, still stop to worship —"

"Oh, how it makes me feel to hear dose oxpressions!"

—"still say to himself again, as he had said a hun-

dred times before, the art of the Saltmarsh-Handel is
an art apart; there is nothing in the heavens above or
in the earth beneath that resembles it —"

" Py chiminy, nur hören Sie einmal! In my lifeday
haf I never heard so brecious worts."

" So I talked him out of the hack, Mr. Tracy, and
he let up on that, and said put in a hearse, then —
because he's chief mate of a hearse, but don't own
it — stands a watch for wages, you know. But I can't
do a hearse any more than I can a hack; so here we
are — becalmed, you see. And it's the same with
women and such. They come and they want a little
johnry picture —"

" It's the accessories that make it a *genre ?*"

" Yes — cannon, or cat, or any little thing like that,
that you heave in to whoop up the effect. We could
do a prodigious trade with the women if we could fore-
ground the things they like, but they don't give a
damn for artillery. Mine's the lack," continued the
Captain, with a sigh. " Andy's end of the business is
all right — I tell you, *he's* an artist from wayback !"

" Yoost hear dot old man! He always talk 'poud
me like dot," purred the pleased German.

" Look at his work yourself ! Fourteen portraits in
a row. And no two of them alike."

" Now that you speak of it, it is true; I hadn't
noticed it before. It is very remarkable. Unique, I
suppose."

" I should say so. That's the very *thing* about
Andy — he *discriminates*. Discrimination's the thief
of time — forty-ninth Psalm; but that ain't any matter;
it's the honest thing, and it pays in the end."

" Yes, he certainly is great in that feature, one is
obliged to admit it; but — now mind, I'm not really
criticising — don't you think he is just a trifle over-
strong in technique?"

The Captain's face was knocked expressionless by this remark. It remained quite vacant while he muttered to himself: "Technique — technique — polytechnique — pyrotechnique; that's it, likely — fireworks — too much color." Then he spoke up with serenity and confidence, and said:

"Well, yes, he does pile it on pretty loud; but they all like it, you know — fact is, it's the life of the business. Take that No. 9 there — Evans the butcher. He drops into the stoodio as sober-colored as anything you ever see; *now* look at him. You can't tell him from scarlet-fever. Well, it pleases that butcher to death. I'm making a study of a sausage-wreath to hang on the cannon, and I don't really reckon I can do it right; but if I can, we can break the butcher."

"Unquestionably your confederate — I mean your — your fellow-craftsman — is a great colorist —"

"Oh, danke schön! —"

—"in fact, a quite extraordinary colorist; a colorist, I make bold to say, without imitator here or abroad — and with a most bold and effective touch, a touch like a battering-ram, and a manner so peculiar and romantic and extraneous and *ad libitum* and heart-searching that — that — he — he is an impressionist, I presume?"

"No," said the Captain, simply, "he is a Presbyterian."

"It accounts for it all — all — there's something divine about his art — soulful, unsatisfactory, yearning, dim-hearkening on the void horizon, vague-murmuring to the spirit out of ultra-marine distances and far-sounding cataclysms of uncreated space — oh, if he — if he — has he ever tried distemper?"

The Captain answered up, with energy:

"Not if he knows himself! But his dog has, and —"

" Oh, no, it vas not *my* dog."

" Why, you *said* it was your dog."

" Oh, no, Gaptain, I —''

" It was a white dog, wasn't it, with his tail docked, and one ear gone, and —"

" Dot's him, dot's him! — der fery dog. Wy, py Chorge, dot dog he vould eat baint yoost de same like —''

" Well, never mind that now —'vast heaving — I never saw such a man. You start him on that dog and he'll dispute a year. Blamed if I haven't *seen* him keep it up a level two hours and a half."

" Why, Captain!'' said Barrow. " I guess that must be hearsay."

" No, sir, no hearsay about it — he disputed with me.''

" I don't see how you stood it."

" Oh, you've got to — if you run with Andy. But it's the only fault he's got."

" Ain't you afraid of acquiring it?''

" Oh, no,'' said the Captain, tranquilly; " no danger of that, I reckon."

The artists presently took their leave. Then Barrow put his hands on Tracy's shoulders and said:

" Look me in the eye, my boy. Steady, steady. There — it's just as I thought — hoped, anyway; *you're* all right, thank goodness. Nothing the matter with your mind. But don't do that again — even for fun. It isn't wise. They wouldn't have believed you if you'd *been* an earl's son. Why, they *couldn't* — don't you know that? What ever possessed you to take such a freak? But never mind about that; let's not talk of it. It was a mistake; you see that yourself."

" Yes — it *was* a mistake."

" Well, just drop it out of your mind; it's no harm;

we all make them. Pull your courage together, and don't brood, and don't give up. I'm at your back, and we'll pull through, don't you be afraid."

When he was gone, Barrow walked the floor a good while, uneasy in his mind. He said to himself, "I'm troubled about him. He never would have made a break like that if he hadn't been a little off his balance. But I know what being out of work and no prospect ahead can do for a man. First it knocks the pluck out of him and drags his pride in the dirt; worry does the rest, and his mind gets shaky. I must talk to these people. No — if there's any humanity in them — and there is, at bottom — they'll be easier on him if they think his troubles have disturbed his reason. But I've *got* to find him some work; work's the only medicine for his disease. Poor devil! away off here, and not a friend."

10A

CHAPTER XVII.

THE moment Tracy was alone his spirits vanished
away, and all the misery of his situation was
manifest to him. To be moneyless and an object of
the chair-maker's charity — this was bad enough; but
his folly in proclaiming himself an earl's son to that
scoffing and unbelieving crew, and, on top of that, the
humiliating result — the recollection of these things
was a sharper torture still. He made up his mind that
he would never play earl's son again before a doubtful
audience.

His father's answer was a blow he could not understand. At times he thought his father imagined he
could get work to do in America without any trouble,
and was minded to let him try it and cure himself of
his radicalism by hard, cold, disenchanting experience.
That seemed the most plausible theory, yet he could
not content himself with it. A theory that pleased
him better was that this cablegram would be followed
by another, of a gentler sort, requiring him to come
home. Should he write and strike his flag, and ask
for a ticket home? Oh, no; that he couldn't *ever* do
— at least, not yet. That cablegram would come, it
certainly would. So he went from one telegraph
office to another every day for nearly a week, and
asked if there was a cablegram for Howard Tracy.
No, there wasn't any. So they answered him at first.
Later, they said it before he had a chance to ask.

Later still they merely shook their heads impatiently as soon as he came in sight. After that he was ashamed to go any more.

He was down in the lowest depths of despair now, for the harder Barrow tried to find work for him the more hopeless the possibilities seemed to grow. At last he said to Barrow:

"Look here. I want to make a confession. I have got down now to where I am not only willing to acknowledge to myself that I am a shabby creature and full of false pride, but am willing to acknowledge it to you. Well, I've been allowing you to wear yourself out hunting for work for me when there's been a chance open to me all the time. Forgive my pride — what was left of it. It is all gone now, and I've come to confess that if those ghastly artists want another confederate I'm their man — for at last I am dead to shame."

"No? Really, can you paint?"

"Not as badly as *they*. No, I don't claim that, for I am not a genius; in fact, I am a very indifferent amateur, a slouchy dabster, a mere artistic sarcasm; but drunk or asleep I can beat *those* buccaneers."

"Shake! I want to shout! Oh, I tell you, I am immensely delighted and relieved. Oh, just to work — that is life! No matter what the work is — that's of no consequence. Just work itself is bliss when a man's been starving for it. I've *been* there! Come right along, we'll hunt the old boys up. Don't you feel good? I tell you *I* do."

The freebooters were not at home. But their "works" were — displayed in profusion all about the little ratty studio. Cannon to the right of them, cannon to the left of them, cannon in front — it was Balaklava come again.

"Here's the uncontented hackman, Tracy. Buckle

to — deepen the sea-green to turf, turn the ship into a hearse. Let the boys have a taste of your quality."

The artists arrived just as the last touch was put on. They stood transfixed with admiration.

"My souls but she's a stunner, that hearse! The hackman will just go all to pieces when he sees that — won't he, Andy?"

"Oh, it is sphlennid, sphlennid! Herr Tracy, why haf you not said you vas a so sublime aartist? Lob' Gott, of you had lif'd in Paris you would be a Pree de Rome, dot's vot's de matter!"

The arrangements were soon made. Tracy was taken into full and equal partnership, and he went straight to work, with dash and energy, to reconstructing gems of art whose accessories had failed to satisfy. Under his hand, on that and succeeding days, artillery disappeared and the emblems of peace and commerce took its place — cats, hacks, sausages, tugs, fire engines, pianos, guitars, rocks, gardens, flower pots, landscapes — whatever was wanted, he flung it in; and the more out of place and absurd the required object was, the more joy he got out of fabricating it. The pirates were delighted, the customers applauded, the sex began to flock in, great was the prosperity of the firm. Tracy was obliged to confess to himself that there was something about work — even such grotesque and humble work as this — which most pleasantly satisfied a something in his nature which had never been satisfied before, and also gave him a strange new dignity in his own private view of himself.

The Unqualified Member from Cherokee Strip was in a state of deep dejection. For a good while now he had been leading a sort of life which was calculated to kill; for it had consisted in regularly alternating days of brilliant hope and black disappointment. The brilliant hopes were created by the magician Sellers, and they always promised that *now* he had got the trick sure, and would effectively influence that materialized cowboy to call at the Towers before night. The black disappointments consisted in the persistent and monotonous failure of these prophecies.

At the date which this history has now reached, Sellers was appalled to find that the usual remedy was inoperative, and that Hawkins's low spirits refused absolutely to lift. Something must be done, he reflected; it was heart-breaking, this woe, this smileless misery, this dull despair that looked out from his poor friend's face. Yes, he must be cheered up. He mused a while, then he saw his way. He said, in his most conspicuously casual vein:

"Er-uh — by the way, Hawkins, we are feeling disappointed about this thing — the way the materializee is acting, I mean — we are disappointed; you concede that?"

"Concede it? Why, yes, if you like the term."

"Very well; so far, so good. Now for the *basis* of the feeling. It is not that your heart, your affections are concerned; that is to say, it is not that you *want* the materializee *Itself*. You concede that?"

"Yes, I concede that, too — cordially."

"Very well, again; we are making progress. To sum up: The feeling, it is conceded, is not engendered by the mere conduct of the materializee; it is conceded that it does not arise from any pang which the *personality* of the materializee could assuage. Now, then," said the earl, with the light of triumph in his eye, "the inexorable logic of the situation narrows us down to this: our feeling has its source in the *money*-loss involved. Come — isn't that so?"

"Goodness knows I concede that, with all my heart."

10***

"Very well. When you've found out the source of a disease, you've also found out what remedy is required — just as in this case. In this case money is required. And *only* money."

The old, old seduction was in that airy, confident tone and those significant words — usually called pregnant words in books. The old answering signs of faith and hope showed up in Hawkins's countenance, and he said:

"*Only* money? Do you mean that you know a way to —"

"Washington, have you the impression that I have no resources but those I allow the public and my intimate friends to know about?"

"Well, I — er —"

"Is it *likely*, do you think, that a man moved by nature and taught by experience to keep his affairs to himself, and a cautious and reluctant tongue in his head, wouldn't be thoughtful enough to keep a few resources in reserve for a rainy day, when he's got as many as I have to select from?"

"Oh, you make me feel so much better already, Colonel!"

"Have you ever been in my laboratory?"

"Why no."

"That's it. You see, you didn't even know that I had one. Come along. I've got a little trick there that I want to show you. I've kept it perfectly quiet, not fifty people know anything about it. But that's my way, always been my way. Wait till you're *ready*, that's the idea; and *when* you're ready, *zzip!* — let her go!"

"Well, Colonel, I've never seen a man that I've had such unbounded confidence in as you. When you say a thing right out, I always feel as if that ends it; as if that is evidence, and proof, and everything else."

The old earl was profoundly pleased and touched.

" I'm glad *you* believe in me, Washington; not everybody is so just."

" I always have believed in you; and I always shall as long as I live."

" Thank you, my boy. You sha'n't repent it. And you *can't*." Arrived in the " laboratory," the earl continued, " Now, cast your eye around this room — what do you see? *Apparently* a junk-shop; *apparently* a hospital connected with a patent office — in *reality*, the mines of Golconda in disguise! Look at that thing there. Now what would you take that thing to be?"

" I don't believe I could ever imagine."

" Of course you couldn't. It's my grand adaptation of the phonograph to the marine service. You store up profanity in it for use at sea. You know that sailors don't fly around worth a cent unless you swear at them — so the mate that can do the best job of swearing is the most valuable man. In great emergencies his talent saves the ship. But a ship is a large thing, and he can't be everywhere at once; so there have been times when one mate has lost a ship which could have been saved if they had had a hundred. Prodigious storms, you know. Well, a ship can't afford a hundred mates; but she can afford a hundred Cursing Phonographs, and distribute them all over the vessel — and there, you see, she's armed at every point. Imagine a big storm, and a hundred of my machines all cursing away at once — splendid spectacle, splendid! — you couldn't hear yourself think. Ship goes through that storm perfectly serene — she's just as safe as she'd be on shore."

" It's a wonderful idea. How do you prepare the thing?"

" Load it — simply load it."

" How?"

J***

" Why, you just stand over it and swear into it."

" That loads it, does it?"

" Yes; because every word it collars it *keeps* — keeps it forever. Never wears out. Any time you turn the crank, out it'll come. In times of great peril you can reverse it, and it'll swear backwards. *That* makes a sailor hump himself!"

" Oh, I see. Who loads them? — the mate?"

" Yes, if he chooses. Or I'll furnish them already loaded. I can hire an expert for $75 a month who will load a hundred and fifty phonographs in one hundred and fifty hours, and do it *easy*. And an expert can furnish a stronger article, of course, than the mere average uncultivated mate could. Then, you see, all the ships of the world will buy them ready loaded — for I shall have them loaded in any language a customer wants. Hawkins, it will work the grandest moral reform of the nineteenth century. Five years from now *all* the swearing will be done by machinery — you won't ever hear a profane word come from human lips on a ship. Millions of dollars have been spent by the churches in the effort to abolish profanity in the commercial marine. Think of it — my name will live forever in the affections of good men as the man who, solitary and alone, accomplished this noble and elevating reform."

" Oh, it *is* grand and beneficent and beautiful. How *did* you ever come to think of it? You have a wonderful mind. How did you say you loaded the machine?"

" Oh, it's no trouble — perfectly simple. If you want to load it up loud and strong, you stand right over it and shout. But if you leave it open and all set, it'll *eavesdrop*, so to speak — that is to say, it will load itself up with any sounds that are made within six feet of it. Now I'll show you how it works. I had an expert come and load this one up yesterday. Hello, it's been left open — it's too bad — still I reckon it hasn't had much chance to collect irrelevant stuff. All you do is to press this button in the floor — so.''

The phonograph began to sing in a plaintive voice:

> There is a boarding-house, far far away,
> Where they have ham and eggs, three times a day.

" Hang it, *that* ain't it. Somebody's been singing around here.''

The plaintive song began again, mingled with a low, gradually rising wail of cats slowly warming up towards a fight:

> O, *how* the boarders yell,
> When they hear that dinner-bell —
> They give that landlord——

(momentary outburst of terrific cat-fight which drowns out one word)

> Three times a day.

(Renewal of furious cat-fight for a moment. The plaintive voice on a high fierce key, " *Scat*, you devils!'' and a racket as of flying missiles.)

" Well, never mind — let it go. I've got some sailor profanity down in there somewhere, if I could get to it. But it isn't any matter; you see how the machine works.''

Hawkins responded, with enthusiasm:

" Oh, it works admirably! I know there's a hundred fortunes in it.''

" And mind, the Hawkins family get their share, Washington.''

" Oh, thanks, thanks; you are just as generous as ever. Ah, it's the grandest invention of the age!''

" Ah, well, we live in wonderful times. The elements are crowded *full* of beneficent forces — always *have* been — and ours is the first generation to turn them to account and make them work for us. Why, Hawkins, *everything* is useful — *nothing* ought ever to be wasted. Now look at sewer-gas, for instance. Sewer-gas has always been wasted heretofore; nobody tried to save up sewer-gas — you can't name me a man. Ain't that so? *You* know perfectly well it's so."

" Yes, it is so — but I never — er — I don't quite see why a body —"

" Should *want* to save it up? Well, I'll tell you. Do you see this little invention here? — it's a decomposer — I call it a decomposer. I give you my word of honor that if you show me a house that produces a given quantity of sewer-gas in a day, I'll engage to set up my decomposer there and make that house produce a hundred times that quantity of sewer-gas in less than half an hour."

" Dear me, but why should you want to?"

" *Want* to? Listen, and you'll see. My boy, for illuminating purposes and economy combined, there's nothing in the world that begins with sewer-gas. And really it don't cost a cent. You put in a good inferior article of plumbing — such as you find everywhere — and add my decomposer, and there you are. Just use the ordinary gas-pipes — and there your expense ends. Think of it. Why, Major, in five years from now you won't see a house lighted with anything but sewer-gas. Every physician I talk to recommends it, and every plumber."

" But isn't it dangerous?"

" Oh, yes, more or less, but everything is — coal-gas, candles, electricity — there isn't anything that ain't."

" It lights up well, does it?"

" Oh, magnificently."

" Have you given it a good trial?"

" Well, no, not a first-rate one. Polly's prejudiced, and she won't let me put it in here; but I'm playing my cards to get it adopted in the President's house, and *then* it'll go — don't you doubt it. I shall not need this one for the present, Washington; you may take it down to some boarding-house and give it a trial if you like."

CHAPTER XVIII.

WASHINGTON shuddered slightly at the suggestion; then his face took on a dreamy look and he dropped into a trance of thought. After a little Sellers asked him what he was grinding in his mental mill.

" Well, this. Have you got some secret project in your head which requires a Bank of England back of it to make it succeed?"

The Colonel showed lively astonishment, and said:

" Why, Hawkins, are you a mind-reader?"

" I? I never thought of such a thing."

" Well, then, how did you happen to drop on to that idea in this curious fashion? It's just mind-reading — that's what it is, though you may not know it. Because I *have* got a private project that requires a Bank of England at its back. How could you divine that? What was the process? This is interesting."

" There wasn't any process. A thought like this happened to slip through my head by accident: How much would make you or me comfortable? A hundred thousand. Yet you are expecting two or three of these inventions of yours to turn out some billions of money — and you are *wanting* them to do that. If you wanted ten millions, I could understand that — it's inside the human limits. But billions! That's clear outside the limits. There must be a definite project back of that somewhere."

The earl's interest and surprise augmented with every word, and when Hawkins finished he said, with strong admiration:

"It's wonderfully reasoned out, Washington, it certainly is. It shows what I think is quite extraordinary penetration. For you've hit it; you've driven the center, you've plugged the bull's-eye of my dream. Now I'll tell you the whole thing, and you'll understand it. I don't need to ask you to keep it to yourself, because you'll see that the project will prosper all the better for being kept in the background till the right time. Have you noticed how many pamphlets and books I've got lying around relating to Russia?"

"Yes, I think most anybody would notice that — anybody who wasn't dead."

"Well, I've been posting myself a good while. That's a great and splendid nation, and deserves to be set free." He paused; then added, in a quite matter-of-fact way, "When I get this money I'm going to set it free."

"Great guns!"

"Why, what makes you jump like that?"

"Dear me, when you are going to drop a remark under a man's chair that is likely to blow him out through the roof, why don't you put some expression, some force, some noise into it that will prepare him? You shouldn't flip out such a gigantic thing as this in that colorless kind of a way. You do jolt a person up so. Go on now, I'm all right again. Tell me all about it. I'm all interest — yes, and sympathy, too."

"Well, I've looked the ground over, and concluded that the methods of the Russian patriots, while good enough considering the way the boys are hampered, are not the best — at least, not the quickest. They are trying to revolutionize Russia from *within ;* that's pretty slow, you know, and liable to interruption all the time, and is full of perils for the workers. Do you know how Peter the Great started his army? He didn't start it on the family premises under the noses of the Strelitzes; no, he started it away off yonder, privately — only just one regiment, you know, and he built to *that*. The first thing the Strelitzes knew, the regiment was an *army*, their position was turned, and they had to take a walk. Just that little idea *made* the biggest and worst of all the despotisms the world has seen. The same idea can *un*make it. I'm going to prove it. I'm going to get out to one side and work my scheme the way Peter did."

" This is mighty interesting, Rossmore. What is it you are going to do?"

" I am going to buy Siberia and start a republic."

" There — bang you go again without giving any notice! Going to *buy* it?"

" Yes, as soon as I get the money. I don't care what the price is, I shall take it. I can afford it, and I will. Now, then, consider this — and you've never thought of it, I'll warrant. Where is the place where there is twenty-five times more manhood, pluck, true heroism, unselfishness, devotion to high and noble ideals, adoration of liberty, wide education, and *brains*, per thousand of population, than any other domain in the whole world can show?"

" Siberia!"

" Right."

" It is true; it certainly is true, but I never thought of it before."

" Nobody ever thinks of it. But it's so, just the same. In those mines and prisons are gathered together the very finest and noblest and capablest multitude of human beings that God is able to create. Now if you had that kind of a population to sell, would you offer it to a despotism? No, the despotism has no use for it; you would lose money. A despotism has no use for anything but human cattle. But suppose you want to start a republic?"

" Yes, I see. It's just the material for it."

" Well, I should say so! There's Siberia, with just the very finest and choicest material on the globe for a republic, and more coming — more coming all the time, don't you see! It is being daily, weekly, monthly recruited by the most perfectly devised system that has ever been invented perhaps. By this system the whole of the hundred millions of Russia are being constantly and patiently sifted, sifted, sifted by myriads of trained experts, spies appointed by the emperor personally; and whenever they catch a man, woman, or child that has got any brains or education or character they ship that person straight to Siberia. It is admirable, it is wonderful. It is so searching and so effective that it keeps the general level of Russian intellect and education down to that of the Czar."

" Come, that sounds like exaggeration."

" Well, it's what they say anyway. But I think, myself, it's a lie. And it doesn't seem right to slander a whole nation that way, anyhow. Now, then, you see what the material is, there in Siberia, for a republic." He paused, and his breast began to heave and his eye to burn under the impulse of strong emotion. Then his words began to stream forth with constantly increasing energy and fire, and he rose to his feet as if to give himself larger freedom. " The minute I organize that republic, the light of liberty, intelligence, justice, humanity, bursting from it, flooding from it, flaming from it, will concentrate the gaze of the whole astonished world as upon the miracle of a new sun; Russia's countless multitudes of slaves will rise up and march, march! — eastward, with that great light transfiguring their faces as they come, and far back of them you will see — what will you see? — a vacant throne in an empty land!   It can be done, and by God I will do it!''

He stood a moment bereft of earthly consciousness by his exaltation; then consciousness returned, bringing him a slight shock, and he said, with grave earnestness:

"I must ask you to pardon me, Major Hawkins.   I have never used that expression before, and I beg you will forgive it this time."

Hawkins was quite willing.

"You see, Washington, it is an error which I am by nature not liable to.   Only excitable people, impulsive people, are exposed to it.   But the circumstances of the present case — I being a democrat by birth and preference, and an aristocrat by inheritance and relish —"

The earl stopped suddenly, his frame stiffened, and he began to stare speechless through the curtainless window.   Then he pointed, and gasped out a single rapturous word:

"Look!"

"What *is* it, Colonel?"

"*It!*"

"No!"

"Sure as you're born.   Keep perfectly still.   I'll apply the influence — I'll turn on all my force.   I've brought It thus far — I'll fetch It right into the house. You'll see."

He was making all sorts of passes in the air with his hands.

"There!   Look at that.   I've made It smile! See?"

Quite true.   Tracy, out for an afternoon stroll, had come unexpectantly upon his family arms displayed upon this shabby house-front.   The hatchments made him smile; which was nothing, they had made the neighborhood cats do that.

" Look, Hawkins, look! I'm drawing It over!"

" You're drawing It sure, Rossmore. If I ever had any doubts about materialization, they're gone now, and gone for good. Oh, this is a joyful day!"

Tracy was sauntering over to read the doorplate. Before he was half-way over he was saying to himself, " Why, manifestly these are the American Claimant's quarters."

" It's coming — coming right along. I'll slide down and pull It in. You follow after me."

Sellers, pale and a good deal agitated, opened the door and confronted Tracy. The old man could not at once get his voice; then he pumped out a scattering and hardly coherent salutation, and followed it with:

" Walk in, walk right in, Mr.— er —"

" Tracy — Howard Tracy."

—" Tracy — thanks — walk right in, you're expected."

Tracy entered, considerably puzzled, and said:

" Expected? I think there must be some mistake."

" Oh, I judge not," said Sellers, who noticing that Hawkins had arrived, gave him a sidewise glance intended to call his close attention to a dramatic effect which he was proposing to produce by his next remark. Then he said, slowly and impressively: " I am — *You Know Who.*"

To the astonishment of both conspirators the remark produced no dramatic effect at all; for the new-comer responded, with a quite innocent and unembarrassed air:

" No, pardon me. I don't *know* who you are. I only suppose — but no doubt correctly — that you are the gentleman whose title is on the doorplate."

" Right, quite right — sit down, pray sit down."

11A

The earl was rattled, thrown off his bearings, his head was in a whirl. Then he noticed Hawkins standing apart and staring idiotically at what to him was the apparition of a defunct man, and a new idea was born to him. He said to Tracy, briskly:

"But a thousand pardons, dear sir, I am forgetting courtesies due to a guest and stranger. Let me introduce my friend General Hawkins — General Hawkins, our new Senator — Senator from the latest and grandest addition to the radiant galaxy of sovereign States, Cherokee Strip"— (to himself, "that name will shrivel him up!"— but it didn't in the least, and the Colonel resumed the introduction piteously disheartened and amazed)—"Senator Hawkins, Mr. Howard Tracy, of — er —"

"England."

"England! — Why, that's im — "

"England, yes, native of England."

"Recently from there?"

"Yes, quite recently."

Said the Colonel to himself, "This phantom lies like an expert. Purifying this kind by fire don't work. I'll sound him a little further, give him another chance or two to work his gift." Then aloud, with deep irony:

"Visiting our great country for recreation and amusement, no doubt. I suppose you find that traveling in the majestic expanses of our Far West is —"

"I haven't been West, and haven't been devoting myself to amusement with any sort of exclusiveness, I assure you. In fact, to merely live, an artist has got to work, not play."

"Artist!" said Hawkins to himself, thinking of the rifled bank; "that *is* a name for it!"

"Are *you* an artist?" asked the Colonel. And added to himself, "*Now* I'm going to catch him."

"In a humble way, yes."

"What line?" pursued the sly veteran.

"Oils."

"I've got him!" said Sellers to himself. Then aloud, "This is fortunate. Could I engage you to restore some of my paintings that need that attention?"

"I shall be very glad. Pray let me see them."

No shuffling, no evasion, no embarrassment, even under this crucial test. The Colonel was nonplussed. He led Tracy to a chromo which had suffered damage in a former owner's hands through being used as a lamp-mat, and said, with a flourish of his hand toward the picture:

"This del Sarto —"

"Is *that* a del Sarto?"

The Colonel bent a look of reproach upon Tracy, allowed it to sink home, then resumed as if there had been no interruption:

"This del Sarto is perhaps the only original of that sublime master in our country. You see, yourself, that the work is of such exceeding delicacy that the risk — could — er — would you mind giving me a little example of what you can do before we —"

"Cheerfully, cheerfully. I will copy one of these marvels."

Water-color materials — relics of Miss Sally's college life — were brought. Tracy said he was better in oils, but would take a chance with these. So he was left alone. He began his work, but the attractions of the place were too strong for him, and he got up and went drifting about, fascinated; also amazed.

CHAPTER XIX.

MEANTIME the earl and Hawkins were holding a troubled and anxious private consultation. The earl said:

"The mystery that bothers me is, Where did It get its other arm?"

"Yes; it worries me, too. And another thing troubles me — the apparition is English. How do you account for that, Colonel?"

"Honestly, I don't know, Hawkins, I don't really know. It is very confusing and awful."

"Don't you think maybe we've waked up the wrong one?"

"The wrong one? How do you account for the clothes?"

"The clothes *are* right, there's no getting around it. What are we going to do? We can't collect, as I see. The reward is for a one-armed American. This is a two-armed Englishman."

"Well, it may be that that is not objectionable. You see, it isn't *less* than is called for; it is *more*, and so —"

But he saw that this argument was weak, and dropped it. The friends sat brooding over their perplexities some time in silence. Finally the earl's face began to glow with an inspiration, and he said, impressively:

"Hawkins, this materialization is a grander and

nobler science than we have dreamed of. We have little imagined what a solemn and stupendous thing we have done. The whole secret is perfectly clear to me now, clear as day. *Every man is made up of heredities*, long-descended atoms and particles of his ancestors. This present materialization is incomplete. We have only brought it down to perhaps the beginning of this century."

"What do you mean, Colonel?" cried Hawkins, filled with vague alarms by the old man's awe-compelling words and manner.

"This: We've materialized this burglar's ancestor!"

"Oh, don't — don't say that. It's hideous."

"But it's true, Hawkins; I *know* it. Look at the facts. This apparition is distinctly English — note that. It uses good grammar — note that. It is an artist — note that. It has the manners and carriage of a gentleman — note that. Where's your cowboy? Answer me that."

"Rossmore, this is dreadful — it's too dreadful to think of!"

"Never resurrected a rag of that burglar but the clothes, not a solitary rag of him but the clothes."

"Colonel, do you really mean —"

The Colonel brought his fist down with emphasis, and said:

"I mean exactly this: This materialization was immature, the burglar has evaded us; this is nothing but a damned ancestor!"

He rose and walked the floor in great excitement. Hawkins said, plaintively:

"It's a bitter disappointment — bitter."

"I know it. I know it, Senator; I feel it as deeply as anybody could. But we've got to submit — on moral grounds. I need money, but God knows I am not poor enough or shabby enough to be an accessory

11***

to the punishing of a man's ancestor for crimes committed by that ancestor's posterity."

" But, Colonel!" implored Hawkins, " stop and think; don't be rash; you know it's the *only* chance we've got to get the money; and, besides, the Bible itself says posterity to the fourth generation shall be punished for the sins and crimes committed by ancestors four generations back that hadn't anything to do with them; and so it's only fair to turn the rule around and make it work both ways."

The Colonel was struck with the strong logic of this position. He strode up and down, and thought it painfully over. Finally he said:

" There's reason in it; yes, there's reason in it. And so, although it seems a piteous thing to sweat this poor ancient devil for a burglary he hadn't the least hand in, still if duty commands I suppose we must give him up to the authorities."

" *I* would," said Hawkins, cheered and relieved; " I'd give him up if he was a thousand ancestors compacted into one."

" Lord bless me, that's just what he is!" said Sellers, with something like a groan; " it's exactly what he is; there's a contribution in him from every ancestor he ever had. In him there's atoms of priests, soldiers, crusaders, poets, and sweet and gracious women — all kinds and conditions of folk who trod this earth in old, old centuries, and vanished out of it ages ago, and now by act of ours they are summoned from their holy peace to answer for gutting a one-horse bank away out on the borders of Cherokee Strip, and it's just a howling outrage!"

" Oh, don't talk like that, Colonel; it takes the heart all out of me, and makes me ashamed of the part I am proposing to —"

" Wait — I've got it!"

"A saving hope? Shout it out, I am perishing."

"It's perfectly simple; a child would have thought of it. He is all right, not a flaw in him, as far as I have carried the work. If I've been able to bring him as far as the beginning of this century, what's to stop me now? I'll go on and materialize him down to date."

"Land, I never thought of that!" said Hawkins, all ablaze with joy again. "It's the very thing. What a brain you have got! And will he shed the superfluous arm?"

"He will."

"And lose his English accent?"

"It will wholly disappear. He will speak Cherokee Strip — and other forms of profanity."

"Colonel, maybe he'll confess!"

"Confess? Merely that bank robbery?"

"Merely? Yes, but why ' merely '?"

The Colonel said, in his most impressive manner:

"Hawkins, he will be wholly under my command. I will make him confess every crime he ever committed. There must be a thousand. Do you get the idea?"

"Well — not quite."

"The rewards will come to us."

"Prodigious conception! I *never* saw such a head for seeing with a lightning glance all the outlying ramifications and possibilities of a central idea."

"It is nothing; it comes natural to me. When his time is out in one jail he goes to the next and the next, and we shall have nothing to do but collect the rewards as he goes along. It is a perfectly steady income as long as we live, Hawkins. And much better than other kinds of investments, because he is indestructible."

"It looks — it really does look the way you say; it does, indeed."

K***

" Look? — why, it *is*. It will not be denied that I have had a pretty wide and comprehensive financial experience, and I do not hesitate to say that I consider this one of the most valuable properties I have ever controlled.''

" Do you really think so?''

" I do, indeed.''

" Oh, Colonel, the wasting grind and grief of poverty! If we could realize immediately. I don't mean sell it all, but sell part — enough, you know, to —''

" See how you tremble with excitement. That comes of lack of experience. My boy, when you have been familiar with vast operations as long as I have you'll be different. Look at me. Is my eye dilated? Do you notice a quiver anywhere? Feel my pulse: plunk — plunk — plunk — same as if I were asleep. And yet, what is passing through my calm, cold mind? A procession of figures which would make a financial novice drunk — just the sight of them. Now it is by keeping cool, and looking at a thing all around, that a man sees what's really in it, and saves himself from the novice's unfailing mistake — the one you've just suggested — eagerness to *realize*. Listen to me. Your idea is to sell a part of him for ready cash. Now mine is — guess.''

" I haven't an idea. What is it?''

" Stock him — of course.''

" Well, I should never have thought of that.''

" Because you are not a financier. Say he has committed a thousand crimes. Certainly that's a low estimate. By the look of him, even in his unfinished condition, he has committed all of a million. But call it only a thousand to be perfectly safe; five thousand reward, multiplied by a thousand, gives us a dead sure cash basis of — what? Five million dollars!''

" Wait — let me get my breath.''

" And the property indestructible. Perpetually fruit-ful — perpetually; for a property with his disposition will go on committing crimes and winning rewards.''

" You daze me, you make my head whirl!''

" Let it whirl, it won't do it any harm. Now that matter is all fixed — leave it alone. I'll get up the company and issue the stock, all in good time. Just leave it in my hands. I judge you don't doubt my ability to work it up for all it is worth.''

" Indeed, I don't. I can say that with truth.''

" All right, then. That's disposed of. Everything in its turn. We old operators go by order and system — no helter-skelter business with us. What's the next thing on the docket? The carrying on of the materiali-zation — the bringing it down to date. I will begin on that at once. I think —''

" Look here, Rossmore. You didn't lock It in. A hundred to one it has escaped!''

" Calm yourself as to that; don't give yourself any uneasiness.''

" But why shouldn't it escape?''

" Let it, if it wants to? What of it?''

" Well, *I* should consider it a pretty serious calamity.''

" Why, my dear boy, once in my power, always in my power. It may go and come freely. I can pro-duce it here whenever I want it, just by the exercise of my will.''

" Well, I am truly glad to hear that, I do assure you.''

" Yes, I shall give it all the painting it wants to do, and we and the family will make it as comfortable and contented as we can. No occasion to restrain its movements. I hope to persuade it to remain pretty quiet, though, because a materialization which is in a

state of arrested development must of necessity be
pretty soft and flabby and substanceless, and — er —
by the way, I wonder where It comes from?"

" How? What do you mean?"

The earl pointed significantly — and interrogatively
— toward the sky. Hawkins started; then settled into
deep reflection; finally shook his head sorrowfully and
pointed downward.

" What makes you think so, Washington?"

" Well, I hardly know, but really you can see yourself that he doesn't seem to be pining for his last
place."

" It's well thought! Soundly deduced. We've
done that Thing a favor. But I believe I will pump
it a little, in a quiet way, and find out if we are right."

" How long is it going to take to finish him off and
fetch him down to date, Colonel?"

" I wish I knew, but I don't. I am clear knocked
out by this new detail — this unforeseen necessity of
working a subject down gradually from his condition
of ancestor to his ultimate result as posterity. But
I'll make him hump himself, anyway."

" Rossmore!"

" Yes, dear. We're in the laboratory. Come —
Hawkins is here. Mind now, Hawkins — he's a sound,
living *human being* to all the family — *don't* forget
that. Here she comes."

" Keep your seats, I'm not coming in. I just
wanted to ask, who is it that's painting down there?"

" That? Oh, that's a young artist; young Englishman named Tracy; very promising — favorite pupil of
Hans Christian Andersen or one of the other old
masters — Andersen I'm pretty sure it is; he's going
to half-sole some of our old Italian masterpieces.
Been talking to him?"

" Well, only a word. I stumbled right in on him

without expecting anybody was there. I tried to be polite to him; offered him a snack " (Sellers delivered a large wink to Hawkins from behind his hand), " but he declined, and said he wasn't hungry " (another sarcastic wink); " so I brought some apples " (double wink), " and he ate a couple of —"

" What!" And the Colonel sprang some yards toward the ceiling, and came down quaking with astonishment.

Lady Rossmore was smitten dumb with amazement. She gazed at the sheepish relic of Cherokee Strip, then at her husband, and then at the guest again. Finally she said:

" What is the matter with you, Mulberry?"

He did not answer immediately. His back was turned; he was bending over his chair, feeling the seat of it. But he answered next moment, and said:

" Ah, there it is; it was a tack."

The lady contemplated him doubtfully a moment, then said, pretty snappishly:

" All that for a tack! Praise goodness it wasn't a shingle nail, it would have landed you in the Milky Way. I do hate to have my nerves shook up so." And she turned on her heel and went her way.

As soon as she was safely out, the Colonel said in a suppressed voice:

" Come — we must see for ourselves. It *must* be a mistake."

They hurried softly down and peeped in. Sellers whispered, in a sort of despair:

" It *is* eating! What a grisly spectacle! Hawkins, it's horrible! Take me away — I can't stand it "

They tottered back to the laboratory.

CHAPTER XX.

TRACY made slow progress with his work, for his mind wandered a good deal. Many things were puzzling him. Finally a light burst upon him all of a sudden — seemed to, at any rate — and he said to himself, " I've got the clew at last — this man's mind is off its balance; I don't know how much, but it's off a point or two, sure; off enough to explain this mess of perplexities, anyway. These dreadful chromos — which he takes for old masters; these villainous portraits — which to his frantic mind represent Rossmores; the hatchments; the pompous name of this ramshackle old crib — Rossmore Towers; and that odd assertion of his, that I was expected. How could I be expected? that is, Lord Berkeley. He knows by the papers that that person was burned up in the New Gadsby. Why, hang it, he really doesn't know *whom* he was expecting; for his talk showed that he was not expecting an Englishman, or yet an artist, yet I answer his requirements notwithstanding. He seems sufficiently satisfied with me. Yes, he is a little off; in fact, I am afraid he is a good deal off, poor old gentleman. But he's interesting — all people in about his condition are, I suppose. I hope he'll like my work; I would like to come every day and study him. And when I write my father — ah, that hurts! I mustn't get on that subject; it isn't good for my spirits. Somebody coming — I must get to work. It's the old

(168)

gentleman again. He looks bothered. Maybe my clothes are suspicious; and they are — for an artist. If my conscience would allow me to make a change — but that is out of the question. I wonder what he's making those passes in the air for with his hands. I seem to be the object of them. Can he be trying to mesmerize me? I don't quite like it. There's something uncanny about it."

The Colonel muttered to himself, "It has an effect on him, I can see it myself. That's enough for one time, I reckon. He's not very solid yet I suppose, and I might disintegrate him. I'll just put a sly question or two at him now, and see if I can find out what his condition is and where he's from."

He approached and said, affably:

"Don't let me disturb you, Mr. Tracy; I only want to take a little glimpse of your work. Ah, that's fine — that's very fine, indeed. You are doing it elegantly. My daughter will be charmed with this. May I sit down by you?"

"Oh, do; I shall be glad."

"It won't disturb you? I mean, won't dissipate your inspirations?"

Tracy laughed and said they were not ethereal enough to be very easily discommoded.

The Colonel asked a number of cautious and well-considered questions — questions which seemed pretty odd and flighty to Tracy — but the answers conveyed the information desired apparently, for the Colonel said to himself, with mixed pride and gratification:

"It's a good job as far as I've got with it. He's solid. Solid, and going to last; solid as the real thing. It's wonderful — wonderful. I believe I could petrify him."

After a little he asked, warily:

"Do you prefer being here, or — or there?"

" There ? Where ? "

" Why — er — where you've been ? "

Tracy's thought flew to his boarding-house, and he answered with decision :

" Oh, *here*, much ! "

The Colonel was startled, and said to himself, " There's no uncertain ring about that. It indicates where *he's* been to, poor fellow. Well, I am satisfied now. I'm glad I got him out."

He sat thinking and thinking, and watching the brush go. At length he said to himself, " Yes, it certainly seems to account for the failure of my endeavors in poor Berkeley's case. *He* went in the other direction. Well, it's all right. He's better off."

Sally Sellers entered from the street now, looking her divinest, and the artist was introduced to her. It was a violent case of mutual love at first sight, though neither party was entirely aware of the fact, perhaps. The Englishman made this irrelevant remark to himself : " Perhaps he is not insane, after all." Sally sat down and showed an interest in Tracy's work which greatly pleased him, and a benevolent forgiveness of it which convinced him that the girl's nature was cast in a large mould. Sellers was anxious to report his discoveries to Hawkins ; so he took his leave, saying that if the two " young devotees of the colored Muse " thought they could manage without him, he would go and look after his affairs. The artist said to himself, " I think he *is* a little eccentric, perhaps, but that is all." He reproached himself for having injuriously judged a man without giving him any fair chance to show what he really was.

Of course the stranger was very soon at his ease and chatting along comfortably. The average American girl possesses the valuable qualities of naturalness, honesty, and inoffensive straightforwardness ; she is

nearly barren of troublesome conventions and artificial-
ities; consequently, her presence and her ways are
unembarrassing, and one is acquainted with her and on
the pleasantest terms with her before he knows how it
came about.   This new acquaintanceship — friendship,
indeed — progressed swiftly; and the unusual swiftness
of it and the thoroughness of it are sufficiently evi-
denced and established by one noteworthy fact — that
within the first half hour both parties had ceased to be
conscious of Tracy's clothes.   Later this consciousness
was reawakened; it was then apparent to Gwendolen
that she was almost reconciled to them, and it was apparent to Tracy that he wasn't.   The reawakening was
brought about by Gwendolen's inviting the artist to
stay to dinner.   He had to decline because he wanted
to live now — that is, now that there was something to
live for — and he could not survive in those clothes at
a gentleman's table.   He thought he knew that.   But
he went away happy, for he saw that Gwendolen was
disappointed.

And whither did he go?   He went straight to a
slop-shop and bought as neat and reasonably well-fitting
a suit of clothes as an Englishman could be persuaded
to wear.   He said — *to* himself, but *at* his conscience —
"I know it's wrong; but it would be wrong *not* to do
it; and two wrongs do not make a right."

This satisfied him, and made his heart light.   Perhaps it will also satisfy the reader — if he can make
out what it means.

The old people were troubled about Gwendolen at
dinner, because she was so distraught and silent.   If
they had noticed, they would have found that she was
sufficiently alert and interested whenever the talk
stumbled upon the artist and his work; but they
didn't notice, and so the chat would swap around to
some other subject, and then somebody would pres-

ently be privately worrying about Gwendolen again,
and wondering if she were not well, or if something
had gone wrong in the millinery line.   Her mother
offered her various reputable patent medicines and tonics
with iron and other hardware in them, and her father
even proposed to send out for wine, relentless prohibi-
tionist and head of the order in the District of Columbia
as he was, but these kindnesses were all declined —
thankfully, but with decision.   At bedtime, when the
family were breaking up for the night, she privately
looted one of the brushes, saying to herself, " It's the
one he has used the most."

The next morning Tracy went forth wearing his new
suit, and equipped with a pink in his button-hole — a
daily attention from Puss.   His whole soul was full of
Gwendolen Sellers, and this condition was an inspiration, art-wise.   All the morning his brush pawed nimbly
away at the canvases, almost without his awarity —
awarity, in this sense, being the sense of being aware,
though disputed by some authorities — turning out
marvel upon marvel, in the way of decorative accessories to the portraits, with a felicity and celerity which
amazed the veterans of the firm and fetched out of
them continuous explosions of applause.

Meantime Gwendolen was losing her morning and
many dollars.   She supposed Tracy was coming in the
forenoon — a conclusion which she had jumped to
without outside help.   So she tripped down stairs
every little while from her work-parlor to arrange the
brushes and things over again and see if he had arrived.
And when she was in her work-parlor it was not profitable, but just the other way — as she found out to her
sorrow.   She had put in her idle moments during the
last little while back in designing a particularly rare
and capable gown for herself, and this morning she set
about making it up; but she was absentminded, and

made an irremediable botch of it. When she saw what she had done she knew the reason of it and the meaning of it, and she put her work away from her and said she would accept the sign. And from that time forth she came no more away from the Audience Chamber, but remained there and waited. After luncheon she waited again. A whole hour. Then a great joy welled up in her heart, for she saw him coming. So she flew back up stairs thankful, and could hardly wait for him to miss the principal brush, which she had mislaid down there, but knew where she had mislaid it. However, all in good time the others were called in and couldn't find the brush, and then she was sent for, and she couldn't find it herself for some little time; but then she found it when the others had gone away to hunt in the kitchen and down cellar and in the woodshed, and all those other places where people look for things whose ways they are not familiar with. So she gave him the brush, and remarked that she ought to have seen that everything was ready for him, but it hadn't seemed necessary, because it was so early that she wasn't expecting — but she stopped there, surprised at herself for what she was saying; and he felt caught and ashamed, and said to himself, " I knew my impatience would drag me here before I was expected and betray me, and that is just what it has done; she sees straight through me — and is laughing at me inside, of course.''

Gwendolen was very much pleased on one account, and a little the other way in another; pleased with the new clothes and the improvement which they had achieved; less pleased by the pink in the buttonhole. Yesterday's pink had hardly interested her; this one was just like it, but somehow it had got her immediate attention, and kept it. She wished she could think of some way of getting at its history in a properly color-

less and indifferent way. Presently she made a venture. She said:

"Whatever a man's age may be, he can reduce it
several years by putting a bright-colored flower in his
buttonhole. I have often noticed that. Is that your
sex's reason for wearing a boutonnière?"

"I fancy not, but certainly that reason would be a
sufficient one. I've never heard of the idea before."

"You seem to prefer pinks. Is it on account of the
color, or the form?"

"Oh, no," he said, simply, "they are given to me.
I don't think I have any preference."

"They are given to him," she said to herself, and
she felt a coldness towards that pink. "I wonder who
it is, and what she is like." The flower began to take
up a good deal of room; it obtruded itself everywhere;
it intercepted all views, and marred them; it was becoming exceedingly annoying and conspicuous for a
little thing. "I wonder if he cares for her." That
thought gave her a quite definite pain.

CHAPTER XXI.

SHE had made everything comfortable for the artist; there was no further pretext for staying. So she said she would go now, and asked him to summon the servants in case he should need anything. She went away unhappy, and she left unhappiness behind her; for she carried away all the sunshine. The time dragged heavily for both now. He couldn't paint for thinking of her; she couldn't design or millinerize with any heart for thinking of him. Never before had painting seemed so empty to him, never before had millinerizing seemed so void of interest to her. She had gone without repeating that dinner-invitation — an almost unendurable disappointment to him. On her part — well, she was suffering, too; for she had found she *couldn't* invite him. It was not hard yesterday, but it was impossible to-day. A thousand innocent privileges seemed to have been filched from her unawares in the past twenty-four hours. To-day she felt strangely hampered, restrained of her liberty. To-day she couldn't propose to herself to do anything or say anything concerning this young man without being instantly paralyzed into non-action by the fear that he might " suspect." Invite him to dinner *to-day ?* It made her shiver to think of it.

And so her afternoon was one long fret — broken at intervals. Three times she had to go downstairs on errands — that is, she thought she had to go downstairs on errands. Thus, going and coming, she had six glimpses of him in the aggregate, without seeming to look in his direction; and she tried to endure these electric ecstasies without showing any sign, but they fluttered her up a good deal, and she felt that the naturalness she was putting on was overdone and quite too frantically sober and hysterically calm to deceive.

The painter had his share of the rapture; he had his six glimpses, and they smote him with waves of pleasure that assaulted him, beat upon him, washed over him deliciously, and drowned out all consciousness of what he was doing with his brush. So there were six places in his canvas which had to be done over again.

At last Gwendolen got some peace of mind by sending word to the Thompsons, in the neighborhood, that she was coming there to dinner. She wouldn't be reminded, at *that* table, that there was an absentee who ought to be a presentee — a word which she meant to look out in the dictionary at a calmer time.

About this time the old earl dropped in for a chat with the artist, and invited him to stay to dinner. Tracy cramped down his joy and gratitude by a sudden and powerful exercise of all his forces; and he felt that now that he was going to be close to Gwendolen, and hear her voice and watch her face during several precious hours, earth had nothing valuable to add to his life for the present.

The earl said to himself, " This specter can eat apples, apparently. We shall find out now if that is a specialty. I think, myself, it's a specialty. Apples, without doubt, constitute the spectral limit. It was the case with our first parents. No, I am wrong — at least, only partly right. The line *was* drawn at apples, just as in the present case, but it was from the other direction.'' The new clothes gave him a thrill of pleasure and pride. He said to himself, "I've got part of him down to date, anyway."

Sellers said he was pleased with Tracy's work; and he went on and engaged him to restore his old masters, and said he should also want him to paint his portrait and his wife's and possibly his daughter's. The tide of the artist's happiness was at flood now. The chat flowed pleasantly along while Tracy painted and Sellers carefully unpacked a picture which he had brought with him. It was a chromo; a new one, just out. It was the smirking, self-satisfied portrait of a man who was inundating the Union with advertisements inviting everybody to buy his specialty, which was a three-dollar shoe or a dress-suit or something of that kind. The old gentleman rested the chromo flat upon his lap and gazed down tenderly upon it, and became silent and meditative. Presently Tracy noticed that he was dripping tears on it. This touched the young fellow's sympathetic nature, and at the same time gave him the painful sense of being an intruder upon a sacred privacy, an observer of emotions which a stranger ought not to witness. But his pity rose superior to other considerations, and compelled him to try to comfort the old mourner with kindly words and a show of friendly interest. He said:

"I am very sorry — is it a friend whom —"

"Ah, more than that, far more than that — a relative, the dearest I had on earth, although I was never permitted to see him. Yes, it is young Lord Berkeley, who perished so heroically in the awful confla — Why, what is the matter?"

"Oh, nothing, nothing. It was a little startling to be so suddenly brought face to face, so to speak, with a person one has heard so much talk about. Is it a good likeness?"

"Without doubt, yes. I never saw him, but you

12***

can easily see the resemblance to his father," said
Sellers, holding up the chromo, and glancing from it
to the chromo misrepresenting the Usurping Earl, and
back again with an approving eye.

"Well, no — I am not sure that I make out the likeness. It is plain that the Usurping Earl there has a
great deal of character and a long face like a horse's,
whereas his heir here is smirky, moon-faced, and
characterless."

"We are all that way in the beginning — all the
line," said Sellers, undisturbed. "We all start as
moon-faced fools, then later we tadpole along into
horse-faced marvels of intellect and character. It is
by that sign and by that fact that I detect the resemblance here, and know this portrait to be genuine and
perfect. Yes, all our family are fools at first."

"This young man seems to meet the hereditary requirement, certainly."

"Yes, yes, he was a fool, without any doubt.
Examine the face, the shape of the head, the expression. It's all fool, fool, fool, straight through."

"Thanks," said Tracy, involuntarily.

"Thanks?"

"I mean for explaining it to me. Go on, please."

"As I was saying, fool is printed all over the face.
A body can even read the *de*tails."

"What do they say?"

"Well, added up, he is a wobbler."

"A which?"

"Wobbler. A person that's always taking a firm
stand about something or other — kind of a Gibraltar
stand, *he* thinks, for unshakable fidelity and everlasting-
ness — and then, inside of a little while, he begins to
wobble; no more Gibraltar there; no, sir, a mighty
ordinary commonplace weakling wobbling around on
stilts. That's Lord Berkeley to a dot, you can *see* it —

look at that sheep! But — why are you blushing like sunset? Dear sir, have I unwittingly offended in some way?"

"Oh, no indeed, no indeed. Far from it. But it always makes me blush to hear a man revile his own blood." He said to himself, "How strangely his vagrant and unguided fancies have hit upon the truth. By accident he has described me. I am that contemptible thing. When I left England I thought I knew myself; I thought I was a very Frederick the Great for resolution and staying capacity; whereas in truth I am just a Wobbler, simply a Wobbler. Well — after all, it is at least creditable to *have* high ideals and give birth to lofty resolutions; I will allow myself that comfort." Then he said aloud, "Could this sheep, as you call him, breed a great and self-sacrificing idea in his head, do you think? Could he meditate such a thing, for instance, as the renunciation of the earldom and its wealth and its glories, and voluntary retirement to the ranks of the commonalty, there to rise by his own merit or remain forever poor and obscure?"

"*Could* he? Why, look at him — look at this simpering, self-righteous mug! There is your answer. It's the very thing he would think of. And he would start in to do it, too."

"And then?"

"He'd wobble."

"And back down?"

"Every time."

"Is that to happen with *all* my — I mean would that happen to *all* his high resolutions?"

"Oh, certainly — certainly. It's the Rossmore of it."

"Then this creature was fortunate to die! Suppose, for argument's sake, that I was a Rossmore, and —"

"It can't be done."

L***

" Why?"

" Because it's not a supposable case. To be a Ross-more at your age you'd have to be a fool, and you're not a fool. And you'd have to be a Wobbler, whereas anybody that is an expert in reading character can see at a glance that when you set your foot down once, it's there to stay; an earthquake can't wobble it." He added to himself, " That's enough to say to him, but it isn't half strong enough for the facts. The more I observe him now the more remarkable I find him. It is the strongest face I have ever examined. There is almost superhuman firmness here, immovable purpose, iron steadfastness of will. A most extraordinary young man."

He presently said, aloud:

" Some time I want to ask your advice about a little matter, Mr. Tracy. You see, I've got that young lord's remains — my goodness, how you jump!"

" Oh, it's nothing, pray go on. You've got his remains?"

" Yes."

" Are you sure they are his, and not somebody else's?"

" Oh, perfectly sure. Samples, I mean. Not all of him."

" Samples?"

" Yes — in baskets. Some time you will be going home; and if you wouldn't mind taking them along—"

" Who? I?"

" Yes — certainly. I don't mean *now;* but after a while; after — but look here, would you like to see them?"

" No! Most certainly not. I don't want to see them."

" Oh, very well. I only thought. Heyo, where are you going, dear?"

" Out to dinner, papa."

Tracy was aghast. The Colonel said, in a disappointed voice :

" Well, I'm sorry. Sho, I didn't know she was going out, Mr. Tracy." Gwendolen's face began to take on a sort of apprehensive What-have-I-done expression. " Three old people to one young one — well, it *isn't* a good team, that's a fact." Gwendolen's face betrayed a dawning hopefulness, and she said, with a tone of reluctance which hadn't the hall-mark on it :

" If you prefer, I will send word to the Thompsons that I —"

" Oh, is it the Thompsons? That simplifies it — sets everything right. We can fix it without spoiling your arrangements, my child. You've got your heart set on —"

" But, papa, I'd *just* as soon go there some other—"

" No, I won't have it. You are a good, hardworking, darling child, and your father is not the man to disappoint you when you —"

" But, papa, I —"

" Go along, I won't hear a word. We'll get along, dear."

Gwendolen was ready to cry with vexation. But there was nothing to do but start ; which she was about to do when her father hit upon an idea which filled him with delight because it so deftly covered all the difficulties of the sitation, and made things smooth and satisfactory :

" I've got it, my love, so that you won't be robbed of your holiday, and at the same time we'll be pretty satisfactorily fixed for a good time here. You send Belle Thompson here — perfectly beautiful creature, Tracy, per-fectly beautiful. I want you to see that girl ; why, you'll just go mad — you'll go mad inside

of a minute. Yes, you send her right along, Gwendolen, and tell her — Why, she's gone!'' He turned
— she was already passing out at the gate. He muttered, '' I wonder what's the matter; I don't know
what her mouth's doing, but I think her shoulders are
swearing. Well,'' said Sellers, blithely, to Tracy, '' I
shall miss her — parents always miss the children as
soon as they're out of sight; it's only a natural and
wisely ordained partiality; but you'll be all right, because Miss Belle will supply the youthful element for
you and to your entire content; and we old people
will do our best, too. We shall have a good enough
time. And you'll have a chance to get better acquainted with Admiral Hawkins. That's a rare character, Mr. Tracy — one of the rarest and most engaging
characters the world has produced. You'll find him
worth studying. I've studied him ever since he was a
child, and have always found him developing. I really
consider that one of the main things that has enabled
me to master the difficult science of character-reading
was the vivid interest I always felt in that boy, and the
baffling inscrutabilities of his ways and inspirations.''

Tracy was not hearing a word. His spirits were
gone, he was desolate.

'' Yes, a most wonderful character. Concealment —
that's the basis of it. Always the first thing you want
to do is to find the keystone a man's character is
built on — then you've got it. No misleading and apparently inconsistent peculiarities can fool you then.
What do you read on the Senator's surface? Simplicity
— a kind of rank and protuberant simplicity; whereas,
in fact, that's one of the deepest minds in the world.
A perfectly honest man — an absolutely honest and
honorable man — and yet, without doubt, the profoundest master of dissimulation the world has ever
seen.''

"Oh, it's devilish!" This was wrung from the un-listening Tracy by the anguished thought of what might have been if only the dinner arrangements hadn't got mixed.

"No, I shouldn't call it that," said Sellers, who was now placidly walking up and down the room with his hands under his coat-tails and listening to himself talk. "One could quite properly call it devilish in another man, but not in the Senator. Your *term* is right, perfectly right — I grant that; but the applica-tion is wrong. It makes a great difference. Yes, he is a marvelous character. I do not suppose that any other statesman ever had such a colossal sense of humor, combined with the ability to totally conceal it. I may except George Washington and Cromwell, and perhaps Robespierre, but I draw the line there. A person not an expert might be in Judge Hawkins's company a lifetime and never find out he had any more sense of humor than a cemetery."

A deep-drawn, yard-long sigh from the distraught and dreaming artist, followed by a murmured "Miser-able, oh, miserable!"

"Well, no, I shouldn't say *that* about it, quite. On the contrary, I admire his ability to conceal his humor even more if possible than I admire the gift itself, stupendous as it is. Another thing — General Hawkins is a thinker; a keen, logical, exhaustive, analytical thinker — perhaps the ablest of modern times. That is, of course, upon themes suited to his size, like the glacial period, and the correlation of forces, and the evolution of the Christian from the caterpillar — any of those things; give him a subject according to his size, and just stand back and watch him think! Why, you can see the place rock! Ah, yes, you must know him; you must get on the inside of him. Perhaps the most extraordinary mind since Aristotle."

Dinner was kept waiting for a while for Miss Thompson, but as Gwendolen had not delivered the invitation to her the waiting did no good, and the household presently went to the meal without her. Poor old Sellers tried everything his hospitable soul could devise to make the occasion an enjoyable one for the guest, and the guest tried his honest best to be cheery and chatty and happy for the old gentleman's sake; in fact, all hands worked hard in the interest of a mutual good time, but the thing was a failure from the start; Tracy's heart was lead in his bosom; there seemed to be only one prominent feature in the landscape, and that was a vacant chair; he couldn't drag his mind away from Gwendolen and his hard luck; consequently, his distractions allowed deadly pauses to slip in every now and then when it was his turn to say something, and of course this disease spread to the rest of the conversation — wherefore, instead of having a breezy sail in sunny waters, as anticipated, everybody was bailing out and praying for land. What *could* the matter be? Tracy alone could have told, the others couldn't even invent a theory.

Meanwhile they were having a similarly dismal time at the Thompson house; in fact, a twin experience. Gwendolen was ashamed of herself for allowing her disappointment to so depress her spirits, and make her so strangely and profoundly miserable; but feeling ashamed of herself didn't improve the matter any; it only seemed to aggravate the suffering. She explained that she was not feeling very well, and everybody could see that this was true; so she got sincere sympathy and commiseration; but that didn't help the case. Nothing helps that kind of a case. It is best to just stand off and let it fester. The moment the dinner was over the girl excused herself, and she hurried home, feeling unspeakably grateful to get away from that house and that intolerable captivity and suffering.

Will he be gone? The thought arose in her brain but took effect in her heels. She slipped into the house, threw off her things, and made straight for the dining-room. She stopped and listened. Her father's voice — with no life in it; presently her mother's — no life in that; a considerable vacancy, then a sterile remark from Washington Hawkins. Another silence; then, not Tracy's but her father's voice again.

"He's gone," she said to herself, despairingly, and listlessly opened the door and stepped within.

"Why, my child," cried the mother, "how white you are! Are you — has anything —"

"White?" exclaimed Sellers. "It's gone like a flash; 'twasn't serious. Already she's as red as the soul of a watermelon! Sit down, dear, sit down — goodness knows you're welcome. Did you have a good time? We've had great times here — immense. Why didn't Miss Belle come? Mr. Tracy is not feeling well, and she'd have made him forget it."

She was content now; and out from her happy eyes there went a light that told a secret to another pair of eyes there and got a secret in return. In just that infinitely small fraction of a second those two great confessions were made, received and perfectly understood. All anxiety, apprehension, uncertainty, vanished out of these young people's hearts and left them filled with a great peace.

Sellers had had the most confident faith that with the new reinforcement victory would be at this last moment snatched from the jaws of defeat, but it was an error. The talk was as stubbornly disjointed as ever. He was proud of Gwendolen, and liked to show her off, even against Miss Belle Thompson, and here had been a great opportunity, and what had she made of it? He

felt a good deal put out.   It vexed him to think that
this Englishman, with the traveling Briton's everlasting
disposition to generalize whole mountain ranges from
single sample-grains of sand, would jump to the conclusion that American girls were as dumb as himself —
generalizing the whole tribe from this single sample,
and she at her poorest, there being nothing at that
table to inspire her, give her a start, keep her from
going to sleep.   He made up his mind that for the
honor of the country he would bring these two together
again over the social board before long.   There would
be a different result another time, he judged.   He said
to himself, with a deep sense of injury, " He'll put in
his diary — they all keep diaries — he'll put in his
diary that she was miraculously uninteresting — dear,
dear, but *wasn't* she! — I never saw the like — and
yet looking as beautiful as Satan, too — and couldn't
seem to do anything but paw bread crumbs, and pick
flowers to pieces, and look fidgety.   And it isn't any
better here in the Hall of Audience.   I've had enough;
I'll haul down my flag; the others may fight it out if
they want to."

He shook hands all around and went off to do some
work which he said was pressing.   The idolaters were
the width of the room apart, and apparently unconscious of each other's presence.   The distance got
shortened a little now.   Very soon the mother withdrew.   The distance narrowed again.   Tracy stood before a chromo of some Ohio politician which had been
retouched and chain-mailed for a crusading Rossmore,
and Gwendolen was sitting on the sofa not far from his
elbow, artificially absorbed in examining a photograph
album that hadn't any photographs in it.

The " Senator " still lingered.   He was sorry for
the young people; it had been a dull evening for them.
In the goodness of his heart he tried to make it pleasant

for them now; tried to remove the ill-impression necessarily left by the general defeat; tried to be chatty,
even tried to be gay. But the responses were sickly,
there was no starting any enthusiasm; he would give it
up and quit — it was a day specially picked out and
consecrated to failures.

But when Gwendolen rose up promptly and smiled a
glad smile, and said, with thankfulness and blessing,
" *Must* you go?" it seemed cruel to desert, and he sat
down again.

He was about to begin a remark when — when he
didn't. We have all been there. He didn't know how
he knew his concluding to stay longer had been a mistake, he merely knew it; and knew it for dead certain,
too. And so he bade good night and went mooning
out, wondering what he could have done that changed
the atmosphere that way. As the door closed behind
him those two were standing side by side, looking at
that door — looking at it in a waiting, second-counting,
but deeply grateful kind of way. And the instant it
closed they flung their arms about each other's necks,
and there, heart to heart and lip to lip —

" Oh, my God, she's kissing it!"

Nobody heard this remark, because Hawkins, who
bred it, only thought it; he didn't utter it. He had
turned the moment he had closed the door, and had
pushed it open a little, intending to re-enter and ask
what ill-advised thing he had done or said, and apologize for it. But he didn't re-enter; he staggered off
stunned, terrified, distressed.

CHAPTER XXII.

FIVE minutes later he was sitting in his room, with his head bowed within the circle of his arms, on the table — final atttiude of grief and despair. His tears were flowing fast, and now and then a sob broke upon the stillness. Presently he said:

"I knew her when she was a little child and used to climb about my knees; I love her as I love my own, and now — oh, poor thing, poor thing, I cannot bear it! — she's gone and lost her heart to this mangy materializee! Why *didn't* we see that that might happen? But how could we? Nobody could; nobody could ever have dreamed of such a thing. You couldn't expect a person would fall in love with a wax-work. And this one doesn't even amount to that."

He went on grieving to himself, and now and then giving voice to his lamentations.

"It's done, oh, it's done, and there's no help for it, no undoing the miserable business. If I had the nerve, I would kill it. But that wouldn't do any good. *She* loves it; she thinks it's genuine and authentic. If she lost it she would grieve for it just as she would for a real person. And who's to break it to the family? Not I — I'll die first. Sellers is the best human being I ever knew, and I wouldn't any more think of — oh, dear, why it'll break his heart when he finds it out. And Polly's, too. *This* comes of meddling with such infernal matters! But for this the creature would still be roasting in Sheol, where it belongs. How is it that

(188)

these people don't smell the brimstone? Sometimes I can't come into the same room with him without nearly suffocating."

After a while he broke out again:

"Well, there's *one* thing sure. The materializing has got to stop right where it is. If she's got to marry a specter, let her marry a decent one out of the Middle Ages, like this one — not a cowboy and a thief such as this protoplasmic tadpole's going to turn into if Sellers keeps on fussing at it. It costs five thousand dollars cash and shuts down on the incorporated company to stop the works at this point, but Sally Sellers's happiness is worth more than that."

He heard Sellers coming, and got himself to rights. Sellers took a seat, and said:

"Well, I've got to confess I'm a good deal puzzled. It did certainly eat, there's no getting around it. Not eat, exactly, either, but it nibbled; nibbled in an appetiteless way, but still it nibbled; and that's just a marvel. Now the question is, What does it do with those nibblings? That's it — what does it do with them? My idea is that we don't begin to know all there is to this stupendous discovery yet. But time will show — time and science — give us a chance, and don't get impatient."

But he couldn't get Hawkins interested; couldn't make him talk to amount to anything; couldn't drag him out of his depression. But at last he took a turn that arrested Hawkins's attention.

"I'm coming to like him, Hawkins. He is a person of stupendous character — absolutely gigantic. Under that placid exterior is concealed the most dare-devil spirit that was ever put into a man; he's just a Clive over again. Yes, I'm all admiration for him on account of his character, and liking naturally follows admiration, you know. I'm coming to like him im-

13A

mensely. Do you know, I haven't the heart to degrade
such a character as that down to the burglar estate for
money or for anything else; and I've come to ask if
you are willing to let the reward go and leave this poor
fellow —"

"Where he is?"

"Yes — not bring him down to date."

"Oh, there's my hand; and my heart's in it, too!"

"I'll never forget you for this, Hawkins," said the
old gentleman, in a voice which he found it hard to
control. "You are making a great sacrifice for me,
and one which you can ill afford, but I'll never forget
your generosity, and if I live you shall not suffer for it,
be sure of that."

Sally Sellers immediately and vividly realized that
she was become a new being; a being of a far higher
and worthier sort than she had been such a little while
before; an earnest being, in place of a dreamer; and
supplied with a reason for her presence in the world,
where merely a wistful and troubled curiosity about it
had existed before. So great and so comprehensive
was the change which had been wrought that she
seemed to herself to be a real person who had lately
been a shadow; a something, which had lately been a
nothing; a purpose, which had lately been a fancy; a
finished temple, with the altar-fires lit and the voice of
worship ascending, where before had been but an
architect's confusion of ·arid working plans, unintelli-
gible to the passing eye and prohesying nothing.

"Lady" Gwendolen! The pleasantness of that
sound was all gone; it was an offense to her ear now.
She said:

"There — that sham belongs to the past; I will not
be called by it any more."

"I may call you simply Gwendolen? You will allow

me to drop the formalities straightway and name you by your dear first name without additions?"

She was dethroning the pink and replacing it with a rosebud.

"There — that is better. I hate pinks — some pinks. Indeed, yes, you are to call me by my first name without additions — that is — well, I don't mean without additions *entirely*, but —"

It was as far as she could get. There was a pause; his intellect was struggling to comprehend; presently it did manage to catch the idea in time to save embarrassment all around, and he said, gratefully:

"*Dear* Gwendolen! I may say that?"

"Yes — part of it. But — don't kiss me when I am talking; it makes me forget what I was going to say. You can call me by part of that form, but not the last part. Gwendolen is not my name."

"Not your name?" This in a tone of wonder and surprise.

The girl's soul was suddenly invaded by a creepy apprehension, a quite definite sense of suspicion and alarm. She put his arms away from her, looked searchingly in the eye, and said:

"Answer me truly, on your honor. You are not seeking to marry me on account of my *rank ?*"

The shot almost knocked him through the wall, he was so little prepared for it. There was something so finely grotesque about the question and its parent suspicion that he stopped to wonder and admire, and thus was he saved from laughing. Then, without wasting precious time, he set about the task of convincing her that he had been lured by herself alone, and had fallen in love with her only, not her title and position; that he loved her with all his heart, and could not love her more if she were a duchess, or less if she were without home, name, or family. She watched his face wistfully, eagerly, hopefully, translating his words by its expression; and when he had finished there was gladness in her heart — a tumultuous gladness, indeed, though outwardly she was calm, tranquil, even judicially austere. She prepared a surprise for him now, calculated to put a heavy strain upon those disinterested protestations of his; and thus she delivered it, burning it away word by word as the fuse burns down to a bombshell, and watching to see how far the explosion would lift him.

"Listen — and do not doubt me — for I shall speak the exact truth. Howard Tracy, I am no more an earl's child than you are!"

To her joy — and secret surprise also — it never phased him. He was ready this time, and saw his chance. He cried out, with enthusiasm, "Thank Heaven for that!" and gathered her to his arms.

To express her happiness was almost beyond her gift of speech.

"You make me the proudest girl in all the earth," she said, with her head pillowed on his shoulder. "I thought it only natural that you should be dazzled by the title — maybe even unconsciously, you being English — and that you might be deceiving yourself in thinking you loved only me, and find you didn't love me when the deception was swept away; so it makes me proud that the revelation stands for nothing and that you *do* love just me, only me — oh, prouder than any words can tell!"

"It is only you, sweetheart; I never gave one envying glance towards your father's earldom. That is utterly true, dear Gwendolen."

"There — you mustn't call me that. I hate that false name. I told you it wasn't mine. My name is Sally Sellers — or Sarah, if you like. From this time I banish dreams, visions, imaginings, and will no more

of them. I am going to be myself — my genuine
self, my honest self, my natural self, clear and clean of
sham and folly and fraud, and worthy of you.   There
is no grain of social inequality between us; I, like you,
am poor; I, like you, am without position or distinction; you are a struggling artist; I am that, too, in my
humbler way.   Our bread is honest bread; we work
for our living.   Hand in hand we will walk hence to
the grave, helping each other in all ways, living for
each other, being and remaining one in heart and purpose, one in hope and aspiration, inseparable to the
end.   And though our place is low, judged by the
world's eye, we will make it as high as the highest in
the great essentials of honest work for what we eat and
wear, and conduct above reproach.   We live in a land,
let us be thankful, where this is all-sufficient, and no
man is better than his neighbor by the grace of God,
but only by his own merit."

Tracy tried to break in, but she stopped him, and
kept the floor herself.

"I am not through yet.   I am going to purge
myself of the last vestiges of artificiality and pretense,
and then start fair on your own honest level, and be
worthy mate to you thenceforth.   My father honestly
thinks he is an earl.   Well, leave him his dream; it
pleases him, and does no one any harm.   It was the
dream of his ancestors before him.   It has made fools
of the house of Sellers for generations, and it made
something of a fool of me, but took no deep root.   I
am done with it now, and for good.   Forty-eight hours
ago I was privately proud of being the daughter of a
pinchbeck earl, and thought the proper mate for me
must be a man of like degree; but to-day — oh, how
grateful I am for your love, which has healed my sick
brain and restored my sanity! — I could make oath
that no earl's son in all the world —"

13***

" Oh — well, but — but —"

" Why, you look like a person in a panic. What is it? What is the matter?"

" Matter? Oh, nothing — nothing. I was only going to say "— but in his flurry nothing occurred to him to say for a moment; then by a lucky inspiration he thought of something entirely sufficient for the occasion, and brought it out with eloquent force: " Oh, how beautiful you are! You take my breath away when you look like that."

It was well conceived, well timed, and cordially delivered — and it got its reward.

" Let me see. Where was I? Yes, my father's earldom is pure moonshine. Look at those dreadful things on the wall. You have of course supposed them to be portraits of his ancestors, earls of Rossmore. Well, they are not. They are chromos of distinguished Americans — all moderns; but he has carried them back a thousand years by relabeling them. Andrew Jackson there is doing what he can to be the late American earl; and the newest treasure in the collection is supposed to be the young English heir — I mean the idiot with the crape; but in truth it's a shoemaker, and not Lord Berkeley at all."

" Are you sure?"

" Why, of course I am. He wouldn't look like that."

" Why?"

" Because his conduct in his last moments, when the fire was sweeping around him, shows that he was a man. It shows that he was a fine, high-souled young creature."

Tracy was strongly moved by these compliments, and it seemed to him that the girl's lovely lips took on a new loveliness when they were delivering them. He said, softly:

" It is a pity he could not know what a gracious

impression his behavior was going to leave with the dearest and sweetest stranger in the land of —''

" Oh, I almost loved him! Why, I think of him every day. He is always floating about in my mind.''

Tracy felt that this was a little more than was necessary. He was conscious of the sting of jealousy. He said:

" It is quite right to think of him — at least, now and then — that is, at intervals — in perhaps an admiring way — but it seems to me that —''

" Howard Tracy, are you jealous of that dead man?''

He was ashamed — and at the same time not ashamed. He was jealous — and at the same time he was not jealous. In a sense the dead man was himself; in that case compliments and affection lavished upon that corpse went into his own till and were clear profit. But in another sense the dead man was not himself; and in that case all compliments and affection lavished there were wasted, and a sufficient basis for jealousy. A tiff was the result of the dispute between the two. Then they made it up, and were more loving than ever. As an affectionate clincher of the reconciliation, Sally declared that she had now banished Lord Berkeley from her mind; and added, " And in order to make sure that he shall never make trouble between us again, I will teach myself to detest that name and all that have ever borne it or ever shall bear it.''

This inflicted another pang, and Tracy was minded to ask her to modify that a little — just on general principles, and as practice in not overdoing a good thing — perhaps he might better leave things as they were and not risk bringing on another tiff. He got away from that particular, and sought less tender ground for conversation.

" I suppose you disapprove wholly of aristocracies

M ***

and nobilities, now that you have renounced your title and your father's earldom?''

"*Real* ones? Oh, dear no; but I've thrown aside our sham one for good."

This answer fell just at the right time and just in the right place to save the poor, unstable young man from changing his political complexion once more. He had been on the point of beginning to totter again, but this prop shored him up and kept him from floundering back into democracy and re-renouncing aristocracy. So he went home glad that he had asked the fortunate question. The girl would accept a little thing like a genuine earldom; she was merely prejudiced against the brummagem article. Yes, he could have his girl and have his earldom, too; that question was a fortunate stroke.

Sally went to bed happy, too; and remained happy, deliriously happy, for nearly two hours; but at last, just as she was sinking into a contented and luxurious unconsciousness, the shady devil who lives and lurks and hides and watches inside of human beings and is always waiting for a chance to do the proprietor a malicious damage, whispered to her soul and said, "That question had a harmless look, but what was *back* of it? — what was the secret motive of it? — what suggested it?"

The shady devil had knifed her, and could retire now and take a rest; the wound would attend to business for him. And it did.

Why should Howard Tracy ask that question? If he was not trying to marry her for the sake of her rank, what should suggest that question to him? Didn't he plainly look gratified when she said her objections to aristocracy had their limitations? Ah, he is after that earldom, that gilded sham — it isn't poor me he wants.

So she argued, in anguish and tears. Then she argued the opposite theory, but made a weak, poor business of it, and lost the case. She kept the arguing up, one side and then the other, the rest of the night, and at last fell asleep at dawn; fell in the fire at dawn, one may say; for that kind of sleep resembles fire, and one comes out of it with his brain baked and his physical forces fried out of him.

CHAPTER XXIII.

TRACY wrote his father before he sought his bed. He wrote a letter which he believed would get better treatment than his cablegram received, for it contained what ought to be welcome news: namely, that he had tried equality and working for a living; had made a fight which he could find no reason to be ashamed of, and in the matter of earning a living had proved that he was able to do it; but that on the whole he had arrived at the conclusion that he could not reform the world single-handed, and was willing to retire from the conflict with the fair degree of honor which he had gained, and was also willing to return home and resume his position and be content with it and thankful for it for the future, leaving further experiment of a missionary sort to other young people needing the chastening and quelling persuasions of experience, the only logic sure to convince a diseased imagination and restore it to rugged health. Then he approached the subject of marriage with the daughter of the American Claimant with a good deal of caution and much painstaking art. He said praiseful and appreciative things about the girl, but didn't dwell upon that detail or make it prominent. The thing which he made prominent was the opportunity now so happily afforded to reconcile York and Lancaster, graft the warring roses upon one stem, and end forever a crying injustice which had already lasted far too long. One could

infer that he had thought this thing all out and chosen
this way of making all things fair and right because it
was sufficiently fair and considerably wiser than the
renunciation scheme which he had brought with him
from England. One could infer that, but he didn't
say it. In fact, the more he read his letter over, the
more he got to inferring it himself.

When the old earl received that letter the first part
of it filled him with a grim and snarly satisfaction; but
the rest of it brought a snort or two out of him that
could be translated differently. He wasted no ink in
this emergency, either in cablegrams or letters; he
promptly took ship for America to look into the matter
himself. He had stanchly held his grip all this long
time, and given no sign of the hunger at his heart to
see his son; hoping for the cure of his insane dream,
and resolute that the process should go through all the
necessary stages without assuaging telegrams or other
nonsense from home, and here was victory at last —
victory, but stupidly marred by this idiotic marriage
project. Yes, he would step over and take a hand in
this matter himself.

During the first ten days following the mailing of the
letter Tracy's spirits had no idle time; they were
always climbing up into the clouds or sliding down
into the earth as deep as the law of gravitation reached.
He was intensely happy or intensely miserable by
turns, according to Miss Sally's moods. He never
could tell when the mood was going to change, and
when it changed he couldn't tell what it was that had
changed it. Sometimes she was so in love with him
that her love was tropical, torrid, and she could find
no language fervent enough for its expression; then
suddenly, and without warning or any apparent reason,
the weather would change, and the victim would find
himself adrift among the icebergs and feeling as lone·

some and friendless as the north pole. It sometimes seemed to him that a man might better be dead than exposed to these devastating varieties of climate.

The case was simple. Sally *wanted* to believe that Tracy's preference was disinterested; so she was always applying little tests of one sort or another, hoping and expecting that they would bring out evidence which would confirm or fortify her belief. Poor Tracy did not know that these experiments were being made upon him, consequently he walked promptly into all the traps the girl set for him. These traps consisted in apparently casual references to social distinction, aristocratic title and privilege, and such things. Often Tracy responded to these references heedlessly and not much caring what he said, provided it kept the talk going and prolonged the séance. He didn't suspect that the girl was watching his face and listening for his words as one who watches the judge's face and listens for the words which will restore him to home and friends and freedom, or shut him away from the sun and human companionship forever. He didn't suspect that his careless words were being weighed, and so he often delivered sentence of death when it would have been just as handy and all the same to him to pronounce acquittal. Daily he broke the girl's heart, nightly he sent her to the rack for sleep. He couldn't understand it.

Some people would have put this and that together and perceived that the weather never changed until one particular subject was introduced, and that then it *always* changed. And they would have looked further, and perceived that that subject was always introduced by the one party, never the other. They would have argued then that this was done for a purpose. If they could not find out what that purpose was in any simpler or easier way they would *ask*.

But Tracy was not deep enough or suspicious enough to think of these things.   He noticed only one particular: that the weather was always sunny when a visit *began*.   No matter how much it might cloud up later, it always began with a clear sky.   He couldn't explain this curious fact to himself; he merely knew it to be a fact.   The truth of the matter was that by the time Tracy had been out of Sally's sight six hours she was so famishing for a sight of him that her doubts and suspicions were all consumed away in the fire of that longing, and so always she came into his presence as surprisingly radiant and joyous as she wasn't when she went out of it.

In circumstances like these a growing portrait runs a good many risks.   The portrait of Sellers, by Tracy, was fighting along day by day through this mixed weather, and daily adding to itself ineradicable signs of the checkered life it was leading.   It was the happiest portrait, in spots, that was ever seen; but in other spots a damned soul looked out from it; a soul that was suffering all the different kinds of distress there are, from stomach-ache to rabies.   But Sellers liked it. He said it was just himself all over — a portrait that sweated moods from every pore, and no two moods alike.   He said he had as many different kinds of emotions in him as a jug.

It was a kind of a deadly work of art, maybe, but it was a starchy picture for show; for it was life-size, full length, and represented the American earl in a peer's scarlet robe, with the three ermine bars indicative of an earl's rank, and on the gray head an earl's coronet tilted just a wee bit to one side in a most gallus and winsome way.   When Sally's weather was sunny the portrait made Tracy chuckle, but when her weather was overcast it disordered his mind and stopped the circulation of his blood.

Late one night when the sweethearts had been having a flawless visit together, Sally's interior devil began to work his specialty, and soon the conversation was drifting towards the customary rock. Presently, in the midst of Tracy's serene flow of talk, he felt a shudder which he knew was not his shudder, but exterior to his breast although immediately against it. After the shudder came sobs: Sally was crying.

" Oh, my darling, what have I done — what have I said? It has happened again! What *have* I done to wound you?"

She disengaged herself from his arms and gave him a look of deep reproach.

" What have you done? I will tell you what you have done. You have unwittingly revealed — oh, for the twentieth time, though I *could* not believe it, *would* not believe it! — that it is not me you love, but that foolish sham, my father's imitation earldom; and you have broken my heart!"

" Oh, my child, what are you saying? I never dreamed of such a thing!"

" Oh, Howard! Howard! the things you have uttered when you were forgetting to guard your tongue have betrayed you!"

" Things I have uttered when I was *forgetting* to guard my tongue? These are hard words. When have I *remembered* to guard it? Never in one instance. It has no office but to speak the truth. It needs no guarding for that."

" Howard, I have noted your words and weighed them when you were not thinking of their significance — and they have told me more than you meant they should."

" Do you mean to say you have answered the trust I had in you by using it as an ambuscade from which you could set snares for my unsuspecting tongue and

be safe from detection while you did it? You have
not done this — surely you have not done this thing.
Oh, one's enemy could not do it!"

This was an aspect of the girl's conduct which she
had not clearly perceived before. Was it treachery?
Had she abused a trust? The thought crimsoned her
cheeks with shame and remorse.

"Oh, forgive me," she said; "I did not know
what I was doing. I have been so tortured — you *will*
forgive me, you *must;* I have suffered so much, and I
am so sorry and so humble; you *do* forgive me, *don't*
you? Don't turn away, don't refuse me; it is only
my love that is at fault, and you *know* I love you —
love you with all my heart; I couldn't bear to — oh,
dear, dear, I am so miserable, and I *never* meant any
harm, and I didn't see where this insanity was carrying
me, and how it was wronging and abusing the dearest
heart in all the world to me — and — and — oh, take
me in your arms again; I have no other refuge, no
other home and hope!"

There was reconciliation again — immediate, perfect,
all-embracing — and with it utter happiness. This
would have been a good time to adjourn. But no,
now that the cloud-breeder was revealed at last; now
that it was manifest that all the sour weather had come
from this girl's dread that Tracy was lured by her rank
and not herself, he resolved to lay that ghost immediately and permanently by furnishing the best possible
proof that he *couldn't* have had back of him at any
time the suspected motive. So he said:

"Let me whisper a little secret in your ear — a
secret which I have kept shut up in my breast all this
time. Your rank *couldn't* ever have been an entice-
ment. I am son and heir to an English earl!"

The girl stared at him — one, two, three moments,
maybe a dozen — then her lips parted.

" You?" she said, and moved away from him, still gazing at him in a kind of blank amazement.

" Why — why, certainly I am. Why do you act like this? What have I done *now* ?"

" What have you done? You have certainly made a most strange statement. You must see that yourself."

" Well," with a timid little laugh, " it may be a strange enough statement; but of what consequence is that if it is true?"

" *If* it is true. You are already retiring from it."

" Oh, not for a moment! You should not say that. I have not deserved it. I have spoken the truth; why do you doubt it?"

Her reply was prompt.

" Simply because you didn't speak it earlier."

" Oh!" It wasn't a groan exactly, but it was an intelligible enough expression of the fact that he saw the point and recognized that there was reason in it.

" You have seemed to conceal nothing from me that I ought to know concerning yourself, and you were not privileged to keep back such a thing as this from me a moment after — after — well, after you had determined to pay your court to me."

" It's true, it's true, I know it! But there were circumstances — in — in the way — circumstances which —"

She waved the circumstances aside.

" Well, you see," he said, pleadingly, " you seemed so bent on our traveling the proud path of honest labor and honorable poverty that I was terrified — that is, I was afraid — of — of — well, *you* know how you talked."

" Yes, I know how I talked. And I also know that before the talk was finished you inquired how I stood as regards aristocracies, and my answer was calculated to relieve your fears."

He was silent a while. Then he said, in a discouraged way:

"I don't see any way out of it. It was a mistake. That is in truth all it was, just a mistake. No harm was meant, no harm in the world. I didn't see how it might some time look. It is my way. I don't seem to see far."

The girl was almost disarmed for a moment. Then she flared up again.

"An earl's son! Do earls' sons go about working in lowly callings for their bread and butter?"

"God knows they don't! I have wished they did."

"Do earls' sons sink their degree in a country like this, and come sober and decent to sue for the hand of a born child of poverty when they can go drunk, profane, and steeped in dishonorable debt and buy the pick and choice of the millionaires' daughters of America? *You* an earl's son! Show me the signs."

"I thank God I am not able —if those are the signs. But yet I am an earl's son and heir. It is all I can say. I wish you would believe me, but you will not. I know no way to persuade you."

She was about to soften again, but his closing remark made her bring her foot down with smart vexation, and she cried out:

"Oh, you drive all patience out of me! Would you have one believe that you haven't your proofs at hand, and yet are what you say you are? You do not put your hand in your pocket *now* — for you have nothing there. You make a claim like this, and then venture to travel without credentials. These are simply incredibilities. Don't you see that yourself?"

He cast about in his mind for a defense of some kind or other — hesitated a little, and then said, with difficulty and diffidence:

"I will tell you just the truth, foolish as it will seem

14A

to you — to anybody, I suppose — but it *is* the truth.
I had an ideal — call it a dream, a folly, if you will —
but I wanted to renounce the privileges and unfair advantages enjoyed by the nobility and wrung from the
nation by force and fraud, and purge myself of my
share of those crimes against right and reason by
thenceforth comrading with the poor and humble on
equal terms, earning with my own hands the bread I
ate, and rising by my own merit if I rose at all.''

The young girl scanned his face narrowly while he
spoke; and there was something about his simplicity
of manner and statement which touched her — touched
her almost to the danger point; but she set her grip
on the yielding spirit and choked it to quiescence; it
could not be wise to surrender to compassion or any
kind of sentiment yet; she must ask one or two more
questions. Tracy was reading her face; and what he
read there lifted his drooping hopes a little.

'' An earl's son to do that! Why, he were a man!
A man to love! — oh, more, a man to worship!''

'' Why, I —''

'' But he never lived! He is not born, he will not
be born. The self-abnegation that could do that —
even in utter folly, and hopeless of conveying benefit
to any, beyond the mere example — could be mistaken
for greatness; why, it would *be* greatness in this cold
age of sordid ideals! A moment — wait — let me
finish; I have one question more. Your father is earl
of what?''

'' Rossmore — and I am Viscount Berkeley.''

The fat was in the fire again. The girl felt so outraged that it was difficult for her to speak.

'' How *can* you venture such a brazen thing! You
know that he is dead, and you know that I know it.
Oh, to rob the living of name and honors for a selfish
and temporary advantage is crime enough, but to rob

the defenseless dead — why, it is more than crime: it *degrades* crime!''

'' Oh, listen to me — just a word — don't turn away like that. Don't go — don't leave me so — stay one moment. On my honor —''

'' Oh, on your honor!''

'' On my honor I am what I say! And I will prove it, and you will believe, I know you will. I will bring you a message — a cablegram —''

'' When?''

'' To-morrow — next day —''

'' Signed ' Rossmore '?''

'' Yes — signed Rossmore.''

'' What will that prove?''

'' What will it prove? What *should* it prove?''

'' If you force me to say it — possibly the presence of a confederate somewhere.''

This was a hard blow, and staggered him. He said, dejectedly:

'' It is true. I did not think of it. Oh, my God, I do not know any way to do; I do everything wrong. You are going? — and you won't say even good night — or good-bye? Ah, we have not parted like this before.''

'' Oh, I *want* to run and — no, go now.'' A pause — then she said, '' You may bring the message when it comes.''

'' Oh, may I? God bless you.''

He was gone; and none too soon; her lips were already quivering, and now she broke down. Through her sobbings her words broke from time to time.

'' Oh, he is gone. I have lost him, I shall never see him any more. And he didn't kiss me good-bye; never even offered to force a kiss from me, and he *knowing* it was the very, very last, and I expecting he would, and never *dreaming* he would treat me so after all we have been to each other. Oh, oh, oh, oh, what shall I do, what *shall* I do? He is a dear, poor, miserable, good-hearted, transparent liar and humbug, but oh, I *do* love him so!" After a little she broke into speech again. "How dear he is! and I shall miss him so, I shall miss him so! Why *won't* he ever think to *forge* a message and fetch it? — but no, he never will, he never thinks of anything; he's so honest and simple it wouldn't ever occur to him. Oh, what *did* possess him to think he could succeed as a fraud — and he hasn't the first requisite except duplicity that I can see. Oh, dear, I'll go to bed and give it all up. Oh, I *wish* I had told him to come and tell me whenever he didn't get any telegram — and now it's all my own fault if I never see him again. How my eyes must look!"

CHAPTER XXIV.

NEXT day, sure enough, the cablegram didn't come. This was an immense disaster; for Tracy couldn't go into the presence without that ticket, although it wasn't going to possess any value as evidence. But if the failure of the cablegram on that first day may be called an immense disaster, where is the dictionary that can turn out a phrase sizable enough to describe the tenth day's failure? Of course every day that the cablegram didn't come made Tracy all of twenty-four hours more ashamed of himself than he was the day before, and made Sally fully twenty-four hours more certain than ever that he not only hadn't any father anywhere, but hadn't even a confederate — and so it followed that he was a double-dyed humbug, and couldn't be otherwise.

These were hard days for Barrow and the art firm. All these had their hands full trying to comfort Tracy. Barrow's task was particularly hard, because he was made a confidant in full, and therefore had to humor Tracy's delusion that he had a father, and that the father was an earl, and that he was going to send a cablegram. Barrow early gave up the idea of trying to convince Tracy that he hadn't any father, because this had such a bad effect on the patient, and worked up his temper to such an alarming degree. He had tried, as an experiment, letting Tracy think he had a father; the result was so good that he went further,

14***

14***   (209)

with proper caution, and tried letting him think his father was an earl; this wrought so well that he grew bold, and tried letting him think he had two fathers, if he wanted to, but he didn't want to, so Barrow withdrew one of them and substituted letting him think he was going to get a cablegram — which Barrow judged he wouldn't, and was right; but Barrow worked the cablegram daily for all it was worth, and it was the one thing that kept Tracy alive; that was Barrow's opinion.

And these were bitter, hard days for poor Sally, and mainly delivered up to private crying. She kept her furniture pretty damp, and so caught cold, and the dampness and the cold and the sorrow together undermined her appetite, and she was a pitiful enough object, poor thing! Her state was bad enough, as per statement of it above quoted; but all the forces of nature and circumstance seemed conspiring to make it worse — and succeeding. For instance, the morning after her dismissal of Tracy, Hawkins and Sellers read in the Associated Press dispatches that a toy puzzle called Pigs in the Clover had come into sudden favor within the past few weeks, and that from the Atlantic to the Pacific all the populations of all the States had knocked off work to play with it, and that the business of the country had now come to a standstill by consequence; that judges, lawyers, burglars, parsons, thieves, merchants, mechanics, murderers, women, children, babies — everybody, indeed, could be seen from morning till midnight absorbed in one deep project and purpose, and only one: to pen those pigs, work out that puzzle successfully; that all gayety, all cheerfulness, had departed from the nation, and in its place care, preoccupation, and anxiety sat upon every countenance, and all faces were drawn, distressed, and furrowed with the signs of age and trouble, and marked with the still sadder signs of mental decay and incipient madness; that factories were at work night and day in eight cities, and yet to supply the demand for the puzzle was thus far impossible. Hawkins was wild with joy, but Sellers was calm. Small matters could not disturb his serenity. He said:

"That's just the way things go. A man invents a thing which could revolutionize the arts, produce mountains of money, and bless the earth, and who will bother with it or show any interest in it? — and so you are just as poor as you were before. But you invent some worthless thing to amuse yourself with, and would throw it away if let alone, and all of a sudden the whole world makes a snatch for it and out crops a fortune. Hunt up that Yankee and collect, Hawkins — half is yours, you know. Leave me to potter at my lecture."

This was a temperance lecture. Sellers was head chief in the Temperance camp, and had lectured, now and then, in that interest, but had been dissatisfied with his efforts; wherefore he was now about to try a new plan. After much thought he had concluded that a main reason why his lectures lacked fire or something was that they were too transparently amateurish; that is to say, it was probably too plainly perceptible that the lecturer was trying to tell people about the horrid effects of liquor when he didn't really know anything about those effects except from hearsay, since he had hardly ever tasted an intoxicant in his life. His scheme now was to prepare himself to speak from bitter experience. Hawkins was to stand by with the bottle, calculate the doses, watch the effects, make notes of results, and otherwise assist in the preparation. Time was short, for the ladies would be along about noon — that is to say, the temperance organization called the Daughters of Siloam — and Sellers must be ready to head the procession.

N ***

The time kept slipping along — Hawkins did not return — Sellers could not venture to wait longer; so he attacked the bottle himself, and proceeded to note the effects. Hawkins got back at last; took one comprehensive glance at the lecturer, and went down and headed off the procession. The ladies were grieved to hear that the champion had been taken suddenly ill and violently so, but glad to hear that it was hoped he would be out again in a few days.

As it turned out, the old gentleman didn't turn over or show any signs of life worth speaking of for twenty-four hours. Then he asked after the procession, and learned what had happened about it. He was sorry; said he had been " fixed " for it. He remained abed several days, and his wife and daughter took turns in sitting with him and ministering to his wants. Often he patted Sally's head and tried to comfort her.

" Don't cry, my child, don't cry so; *you* know your old father did it by mistake, and didn't mean a bit of harm; you know he wouldn't intentionally do anything to make you ashamed for the world; you know he was trying to do good, and only made the mistake through ignorance, not knowing the right doses and Washington not there to help. Don't cry so, dear, it breaks my old heart to see you, and think I've brought this humiliation on you, and you so dear to me and so good. I won't ever do it again, indeed I won't; now be comforted, honey, that's a good child."

But when she wasn't on duty at the bedside the crying went on just the same; then the mother would try to comfort her, and say:

" Don't cry, dear, *he* never meant any harm; it was all one of those happens that you can't guard against when you are trying experiments that way. You see, *I* don't cry. It's because I know him so well. I could never look anybody in the face again if he had

got into such an amazing condition as that a-purpose;
but, bless you, his intention was pure and high, and
that makes the *act* pure, though it was higher than was
necessary. We're not humiliated, dear; he did it
under a noble impulse, and we don't need to be
ashamed. There, don't cry any more, honey."

Thus the old gentleman was useful to Sally during
several days as an explanation of her tearfulness. She
felt thankful to him for the shelter he was affording
her, but often said to herself, "It's a shame to let him
see in my crying a reproach — as if he could ever do
anything that could make me reproach him! But I
can't confess; I've got to go on using him for a pretext; he's the only one I've got in the world, and I do
need one so much."

As soon as Sellers was out again, and found that
stacks of money had been placed in bank for him and
Hawkins by the Yankee, he said, "*Now* we'll soon
see who's the Claimant and who's the Authentic. I'll
just go over there and warm up that House of Lords."
During the next few days he and his wife were so
busy with preparations for the voyage that Sally had
all the privacy she needed, and all the chance to cry
that was good for her. Then the old pair left for New
York — and England.

Sally had also had a chance to do another thing.
That was, to make up her mind that life was not worth
living upon the present terms. If she *must* give up
her impostor and die, doubtless she must submit; but
might she not lay her whole case before some disinterested person first, and see if there wasn't perhaps some
saving way out of the matter? She turned this idea
over in her mind a good deal. In her first visit with
Hawkins after her parents were gone, the talk fell
upon Tracy, and she was impelled to set her case
before the statesman and take his counsel. So she

poured out her heart, and he listened with painful
solicitude. She concluded, pleadingly, with:

"*Don't* tell me he is an impostor. I suppose he is,
but doesn't it look to you as if he isn't? You are
cool, you know, and outside; and so, maybe it can
look to you as if he isn't one, when it can't to me.
Doesn't it look to you as if he isn't? Couldn't you —
can't it look to you that way — for — for my sake?"

The poor man was troubled, but he felt obliged to
keep in the neighborhood of the truth. He fought
around the present detail a little while, then gave it up,
and said he couldn't see his way to clearing Tracy.

"No," he said; "the truth is, he's an impostor."

"That is, you — you feel a little certain, but not
entirely — oh, not *entirely*, Mr. Hawkins!"

"It's a pity to have to say it — I do hate to say
it — but I don't think anything about it, I *know* he's
an impostor."

"Oh, now, Mr. Hawkins, you *can't* go that far. A
body *can't* really know it, you know. It isn't *proved*
that he's not what he says he is."

Should he come out and make a clean breast of the
whole wretched business? Yes — at least, the most of
it — it ought to be done. So he set his teeth and
went at the matter with determination, but purposing
to spare the girl one pain — that of knowing that
Tracy was a criminal.

"Now I am going to tell you a plain tale; one not
pleasant for me to tell or for you to hear, but we've
got to stand it. I know all about that fellow, and I
know he is no earl's son."

The girl's eyes flashed, and she said:

"I don't care a snap for that — go on!"

This was so wholly unexpected that it at once ob-
structed the narrative; Hawkins was not even sure that
he had heard aright. He said:

" I don't know that I quite understand. Do you mean to say that if he was all right and proper otherwise, you'd be indifferent about the earl part of the business?"

" Absolutely."

" You'd be entirely satisfied with him, and wouldn't *care* for his not being an earl's son — that *being* an earl's son wouldn't add any value to him?"

" Not the least value that I would care for. Why, Mr. Hawkins, I've gotten over all that day-dreaming about earldoms and aristocracies and all such nonsense, and am become just a plain ordinary nobody and content with it; and it is to *him* I owe my cure. And as to anything being able to add a value to him, nothing can do that. He is the whole world to me, just as he is; he comprehends *all* the values there are — then how can you *add* one?"

" She's pretty far gone." He said that to himself. He continued, still to himself, " I must change my plan again; I can't seem to strike one that will stand the requirements of this most variegated emergency five minutes on a stretch. Without making this fellow a criminal, I believe I will invent a name and a character for him calculated to disenchant her. If it fails to do it, then I'll know that the next rightest thing to do will be to help her to her fate, poor thing, not hinder her."

Then he said aloud:

" Well, Gwendolen —"

" I want to be called Sally."

" I'm glad of it; I like it better myself. Well, then, I'll tell you about this man Snodgrass."

" Snodgrass! Is *that* his name?"

" Yes — Snodgrass. The other's his *nom de plume*."

" It's hideous?"

" I know it is, but we can't help our names."

" And that is truly his real name — and not Howard Tracy?"

Hawkins answered, regretfully:

" Yes; it seems a pity."

The girl sampled the name musingly once or twice:

" Snodgrass! Snodgrass! No, I could not endure that. I could not get used to it. No, I should call him by his first name. What is his first name?"

" His — er — his initials are S. M."

" His initials? I don't care anything about his initials. I can't call him by his initials. What do they *stand* for?"

" Well, you see, his father was a physician, and he — he — well, he was an idolater of his profession, and he — well, he was a very eccentric man, and —"

" What do they *stand* for? What are you shuffling about?"

" They — well, they stand for Spinal Meningitis. His father being a phy —"

" I never heard such an infamous name! Nobody can ever call a person *that* — a person they love. I wouldn't call an enemy by such a name. It sounds like an epithet." After a moment she added, with a kind of consternation, " Why, it would be *my* name! Letters would come with it on."

" Yes — Mrs. Spinal Meningitis Snodgrass."

" Don't repeat it — don't; I can't bear it. Was the father a lunatic?"

" No, that is not charged."

" I am glad of that, because that is transmissible. What do you think *was* the matter with him, then?"

" Well, I don't really know. The family used to run a good deal to idiots, and so, maybe —"

" Oh, there isn't any maybe about it. This one was an idiot."

"Well, yes — he could have been. He was suspected."

"Suspected!" said Sally, with irritation. "Would
one *suspect* there was going to be a dark time if he saw
the constellations fall out of the sky? But that is
enough about the idiot, I don't take any interest in
idiots; tell me about the son."

'Very well then; this one was the eldest, but not
the favorite. His brother, Zylobalsamum —"

"Wait — give me a chance to realize that. It is
perfectly stupefying. Zylo — what did you call it?"

"Zylobalsamum."

"I never heard such a name. It sounds like a disease. Is it a disease?"

"No, I don't think it's a disease. It's either Scriptural or —"

"Well, it's not Scriptural."

"Then it's anatomical. I knew it was one or the
other. Yes, I remember now, it *is* anatomical. It's a
ganglion — a nerve center — it is what is called the
zylobalsamum process."

"Well, go on; and if you come to any more of
them, omit the names; they make one feel so uncomfortable."

"Very well, then. As I said, this one was not a
favorite in the family, and so he was neglected in every
way — never sent to school, always allowed to associate with the worst and coarsest characters, and so of
course he has grown up a rude, vulgar, ignorant, dissipated ruffian, and —"

"He? It's no such thing! You ought to be more
generous than to make such a statement as that about
a poor young stranger who — who — why, he is the
very opposite of that! He is considerate, courteous,
obliging, modest, gentle, refined, cultivated — *oh*, for
shame! how can you say such things about him?"

" I don't blame you, Sally — indeed, I haven't a word of blame for you for being blinded by your affection — blinded to these minor defects which are so manifest to others who —"

" Minor defects?   Do you call these minor defects? What are murder and arson, pray?"

" It is a difficult question to answer straight off — and of course estimates of such things vary with environment.   With us, out our way, they would not necessarily attract as much attention as with you, yet they are often regarded with disapproval —"

" Murder and arson are regarded with disapproval?"

" Oh, frequently."

" With disapproval!   Who *are* those Puritans you are talking about?   But wait — how did you come to know so much about this family?   Where did you get all this hearsay evidence?"

" Sally, it isn't hearsay evidence.   That is the serious part of it.   I *knew* that family — personally."

This was a surprise.

" You?   You actually knew them?"

" Knew Zylo, as we used to call him, and knew his father, Dr. Snodgrass.   I didn't know your own Snodgrass, but have had glimpses of him from time to time, and I heard about him all the time.   He was the common talk, you see, on account of his —"

" On account of his not being a house-burner or an assassin, I suppose.   That would have made him commonplace.   Where did you know these people?"

" In Cherokee Strip."

" Oh, how preposterous!   There are not enough people in Cherokee Strip to *give* anybody a reputation, good or bad.   There isn't a quorum.   Why, the whole population consists of a couple of wagon loads of horse thieves."

Hawkins answered, placidly:

" Our friend was one of those wagon loads."

Sally's eyes burned, and her breath came quick and fast, but she kept a fairly good grip on her anger, and did not let it get the advantage of her tongue. The statesman sat still and waited for developments. He was content with his work. It was as handsome a piece of diplomatic art as he had ever turned out, he thought; and now let the girl make her own choice. He judged she would let her specter go; he hadn't a doubt of it, in fact; but anyway let the choice be made, and he was ready to ratify it and offer no further hindrance.

Meantime Sally had thought her case out and made up her mind. To the Major's disappointment the verdict was against him. Sally said:

" He has no friend but me, and I will not desert him now. I will not marry him if his moral character is bad; but if he can prove that it isn't, I will — and he shall have the chance. To me he seems utterly good and dear; I've never seen anything about him that looked otherwise — except, of course, his calling himself an earl's son. Maybe that is only vanity, and no real harm when you get to the bottom of it. I do *not* believe he is any such person as you have painted him. I want to see him. I want you to find him and send him to me. I will implore him to be honest with me, and tell me the whole truth, and not be afraid."

" Very well; if that is your decision, I will do it. But, Sally, you know he's poor, and —"

" Oh, *I* don't care anything about that. That's neither here nor there. Will you bring him to me?"

" I'll do it. When?"

" Oh, dear, it's getting towards dark now, and so you'll have to put it off till morning. But you *will* find him in the morning, *won't* you? Promise."

" I'll have him here by daylight."

" Oh, *now* you're your own old self again — and lovelier than ever!"

" I couldn't ask fairer than that. Good-bye, dear."

Sally mused a moment alone; then said, earnestly, " I love him in *spite* of his name!" and went about her affairs with a light heart.

CHAPTER XXV.

HAWKINS went straight to the telegraph office and disburdened his conscience. He said to himself, "She's not going to give this galvanized cadaver up, that's plain. Wild horses can't pull her away from him. I've done my share; it's for Sellers to take an innings now." So he sent this message to New York:

Come back. Hire special train. She's going to marry the materializee.

Meantime a note came to Rossmore Towers to say that the Earl of Rossmore had just arrived from England, and would do himself the pleasure of calling in the evening. Sally said to herself, "It is a pity he didn't stop in New York; but it's no matter; he can go up to-morrow and see my father. He has come over here to tomahawk papa very likely, or buy out his claim. This thing would have excited me a while back, but it has only one interest for me now, and only one value. I can say to — to — Spine, Spiny, Spinal — I don't like any *form* of that name! — I can say to him to-morrow, '*Don't* try to keep it up any more, or I shall have to tell you whom I have been talking with last night, and then you will be embarrassed."

Tracy couldn't know he was to be invited for the morrow, or he might have waited. As it was, he was too miserable to wait any longer; for his last hope — a letter — had failed him. It was fully due to-day; it had not come. Had his father really flung him away? It looked so. It was not like his father, but it surely looked so. His father was a rather tough nut, in truth, but had never been so with his son — still, this implacable silence had a calamitous look. Anyway, Tracy would go to the Towers and — then what? He didn't know; his head was tired out with thinking — he wouldn't think about what he must do or say — let it all take care of itself. So that he saw Sally once more he would be satisfied, happen what might; he wouldn't care.

He hardly knew how he got to the Towers, or when. He knew and cared for only one thing — he was alone with Sally. She was kind, she was gentle, there was moisture in her eyes, and a yearning something in her face and manner which she could not wholly hide — but she kept her distance. They talked. By and by she said, watching his downcast countenance out of the corner of her eye:

" It's so lonesome — with papa and mamma gone. I try to read, but I can't seem to get interested in any book. I try the newspapers, but they do put such rubbish in them! You take up a paper and start to read something you think's interesting, and it goes on and on and on about how somebody — well, Dr. Snodgrass, for instance —"

Not a movement from Tracy, not the quiver of a muscle. Sally was amazed — what command of himself he must have! Being disconcerted, she paused so long that Tracy presently looked up wearily and said:

" Well?"

" Oh, I thought you were not listening. Yes, it goes on and on about this Dr. Snodgrass till you are *so* tired, and then about his younger son — *the favorite son* — Zylobalsamum Snodgrass —"

Not a sign from Tracy, whose head was drooping again. What supernatural self-possession! Sally fixed her eye on him and began again, resolved to blast him out of his serenity this time if she knew how to apply the dynamite that is concealed in certain forms of words when those words are properly loaded with unexpected meanings.

"And next it goes on and on and on about the eldest son — *not* the favorite, this one — and how he is neglected in his poor barren boyhood, and allowed to grow up unschooled, ignorant, coarse, vulgar, the comrade of the community's scum, and become in his completed manhood a rude, profane, dissipated ruffian —"

That head still dropped! Sally rose, moved softly and solemnly a step or two, and stood before Tracy — his head came slowly up, his meek eyes met her intense ones — then she finished, with deep impressiveness:

"— named Spinal Meningitis Snodgrass!"

Tracy merely exhibited signs of increased fatigue. The girl was outraged by this iron indifference and callousness, and cried out:

"What *are* you made of?"

"I? Why?"

"Haven't you *any* sensitiveness? Don't these things touch any poor *remnant* of delicate feeling in you?"

"N-no," he said, wonderingly, "they don't seem to. Why should they?"

"Oh, dear me, *how* can you look so innocent, and foolish, and good, and empty, and gentle, and all that, right in the hearing of such things as those! Look me in the eye — straight in the eye. There, now then, answer me without a flinch. Isn't Dr. Snodgrass your father, and isn't Zylobalsamum your brother" [here Hawkins was about to enter the room, but changed his mind upon hearing these words, and elected for a walk down town, and so glided swiftly away], "and isn't your name Spinal Meningitis, and isn't your father a doctor and an idiot, like all the family for generations, and doesn't he name all his children after poisons and pestilences and abnormal anatomical eccentricities of the human body? Answer me, some way or somehow — and quick. *Why* do you sit there looking like an envelope without any address on it and see me going mad before your face with suspense?"

"Oh, I wish I could do — do — I wish I could do something, *anything* that would give you peace again and make you happy; but I know of nothing — I know of no way. I have never heard of these awful people before."

"What? Say it again!"

"I have never — never in my life till now."

"Oh, you *do* look so honest when you say that! It *must* be true — surely you *couldn't* look that way, you *wouldn't* look that way if it were not true — *would* you?"

"I couldn't and wouldn't. It *is* true. Oh, let us end this suffering — take me back into your heart and confidence —"

"Wait — one more thing. Tell me you told that falsehood out of mere vanity and are sorry for it; that you're *not* expecting to ever wear the coronet of an earl —"

"Truly I am cured — cured this very day — I am *not* expecting it!"

"Oh, now you *are* mine! I've got you back in the beauty and glory of your unsmirched poverty and your honorable obscurity, and nobody shall ever take you from me again but the grave! And if —"

"De Earl of Rossmore, fum Englan'!"

"My father!" The young man released the girl and hung his head.

The old gentleman stood surveying the couple — the one with a strongly complimentary right eye, the other with a mixed expression done with the left. This is difficult, and not often resorted to. Presently his face relaxed into a kind of constructive gentleness, and he said to his son:

"Don't you think you could embrace me, too?"

The young man did it with alacrity.

"Then you *are* the son of an earl after all," said Sally, reproachfully.

"Yes, I—"

"Then I won't have you!"

"Oh, but you know—"

"No, I will not. You've told me another fib."

"She's right. Go away and leave us. I want to talk with her."

Berkeley was obliged to go. But he did not go far. He remained on the premises. At midnight the conference between the old gentleman and the young girl was still going blithely on, but it presently drew to a close, and the former said:

"I came all the way over here to inspect you, my dear, with the general idea of breaking off this match if there were *two* fools of you, but as there's only one, you can have him if you'll take him."

"Indeed, I will, then! May I kiss you?"

"You may. Thank you. Now you shall have that privilege whenever you are good."

Meantime Hawkins had long ago returned and slipped up into the laboratory. He was rather disconcerted to find his late invention, Snodgrass, there. The news was told him: that the English Rossmore was come, "and I'm his son, Viscount Berkeley, not Howard Tracy any more."

Hawkins was aghast. He said:

"Good gracious, then you're dead!"

"Dead?"

"Yes, you are — we've got your ashes."

15***

"Hang those ashes, I'm tired of them; I'll give them to my father."

Slowly and painfully the statesman worked the truth into his head that this was really a flesh and blood young man, and not the insubstantial resurrection he and Sellers had so long supposed him to be. Then he said, with feeling:

"I'm so glad; so glad on Sally's account, poor thing. We took you for a departed materialized bank thief from Tahlequah. This will be a heavy blow to Sellers." Then he explained the whole matter to Berkeley, who said:

"Well, the Claimant must manage to stand the blow, severe as it is. But he'll get over the disappointment."

"Who — the Colonel? He'll get over it the minute he invents a new miracle to take its place. And he's already at it by this time. But look here — what do you suppose became of the man you've been *representing* all this time?"

"I don't know. I saved his clothes — it was all I could do. I am afraid he lost his life."

"Well, you must have found twenty or thirty thousand dollars in those clothes in money or certificates of deposit."

"No, I found only five hundred and a trifle. I borrowed the trifle and banked the five hundred."

"What'll we do about it?"

"Return it to the owner."

"It's easy said, but not easy to manage. Let's leave it alone till we get Sellers's advice. And that reminds me. I've got to run and meet Sellers and explain who you are *not* and who you *are*, or he'll come thundering in here to stop his daughter from marrying a phantom. But — suppose your father came over here to break off the match?"

"Well, isn't he downstairs getting acquainted with Sally? That's all safe."

So Hawkins departed to meet and prepare the Sellerses.

Rossmore Towers saw great times and late hours during the succeeding week. The two earls were such opposites in nature that they fraternized at once. Sellers said privately that Rossmore was the most extraordinary character he had ever met — a man just made out of the condensed milk of human kindness, yet with the ability to totally hide the fact from any but the most practiced character-reader; a man whose whole being was sweetness, patience, and charity, yet with a cunning so profound, an ability so marvelous in the acting of a double part, that many a person of considerable intelligence might live with him for centuries and never suspect the presence in him of these characteristics.

Finally there was a quiet wedding at the Towers, instead of a big one at the British embassy, with the militia and the fire brigades and the temperance organizations on hand in torchlight procession, as at first proposed by one of the earls. The art firm and Barrow were present at the wedding, and the tinner and Puss had been invited, but the tinner was ill and Puss was nursing him — for they were engaged.

The Sellerses were to go to England with their new allies for a brief visit, but when it was time to take the train from Washington the Colonel was missing. Hawkins was going as far as New York with the party, and said he would explain the matter on the road. The explanation was in a letter left by the Colonel in Hawkins's hands. In it he promised to join Mrs. Sellers later in England, and then went on to say:

The truth is, my dear Hawkins, a mighty idea has been born to me within the hour, and I must not even stop to say good-bye to my dear ones.

o***

A man's highest duty takes precedence of all minor ones, and must be attended to with his best promptness and energy, at whatsoever cost to his affections or his convenience. And first of all a man's duties is his duty to his own honor — he must keep that spotless. Mine is threatened. When I was feeling sure of my imminent future solidity, I forwarded to the Czar of Russia — perhaps prematurely — an offer for the purchase of Siberia, naming a vast sum. Since then an episode has warned me that the method by which I was expecting to acquire this money — materialization upon a scale of limitless magnitude — is marred by a taint of temporary uncertainty. His imperial majesty may accept my offer at any moment. If this should occur now, I should find myself painfully embarrassed — in fact, financially inadequate. I could not take Siberia. This would become known, and my credit would suffer.

Recently my private hours have been dark indeed, but the sun shines again now; I see my way; I shall be able to meet my obligation, and without having to ask an extension of the stipulated time, I think. This grand new idea of mine — the sublimest I have ever conceived — will save me whole, I am sure. I am leaving for San Francisco this moment to test it by the help of the great Lick telescope. Like all of my more notable discoveries and inventions, it is based upon hard, practical scientific laws; all other bases are unsound, and hence untrustworthy.

In brief, then, I have conceived the stupendous idea of reorganizing the climates of the earth according to the desire of the populations interested. That is to say, I will furnish climates to order, for cash or negotiable paper, taking the old climates in part payment, of course, at a fair discount, where they are in condition to be repaired at small cost and let out for hire to poor and remote communities not able to afford a good climate and not caring for an expensive one for mere display. My studies have convinced me that the regulation of climates and the breeding of new varieties at will from the old stock is a feasible thing; indeed, I am convinced that it has been done before, done in prehistoric times by now forgotten and unrecorded civilizations. Everywhere I find hoary evidences of artificial manipulation of climates in bygone times. Take the glacial period. Was that produced by accident? Not at all; it was done for money. I have a thousand proofs of it, and will some day reveal them.

I will confide to you an outline of my idea. It is to utilize the spots on the sun — get control of them, you understand, and apply the stupendous energies which they wield to beneficent purposes in the reorganization of our climates. At present they merely make trouble and do harm in the evoking of cyclones and other kinds of electric storms; but once under humane and intelligent control this will cease, and they will become a boon to man.

I have my plan all mapped out, whereby I hope and expect to acquire complete and perfect control of the sun-spots, also details of the method whereby I shall employ the same commercially; but I will not venture to go into particulars before the patents shall have been issued. I shall hope and expect to sell shop-rights to the minor countries at a reasonable figure, and supply a good business article of climate to the great empires at special rate, together with fancy brands for coronations, battles, and other great and particular occasions. There are billions of money in this enterprise, no expensive plant is required, and I shall begin to realize in a few days — in a few weeks at furthest. I shall stand ready to pay cash for Siberia the moment it is delivered, and thus save my honor and my credit. I am confident of this.

I would like you to provide a proper outfit and start north as soon as I telegraph you, be it night or be it day. I wish you to take up all the country stretching away from the north pole on all sides for many degrees south, and buy Greenland and Iceland at the best figure you can get now while they are cheap. It is my intention to move one of the tropics up there and transfer the frigid zone to the equator. I will have the entire Arctic Circle in the market as a summer resort next year, and will use the surplusage of the old climate, over and above what can be utilized on the equator, to reduce the temperature of opposition resorts. But I have said enough to give you an idea of the prodigious nature of my scheme and the feasible and enormously profitable character of it. I shall join all you happy people in England as soon as I shall have sold out some of my principal climates and arranged with the Czar about Siberia.

Meantime, watch for a sign from me. Eight days from now we shall be wide asunder; for I shall be on the border of the Pacific, and you far out on the Atlantic, approaching England. That day, if I am alive and my sublime discovery is proved and established, I will send you greeting, and my messenger shall deliver it where you are, in the solitudes of the sea; for I will waft a vast sun-spot across the disk like drifting smoke, and you will know it for my love-sign, and will say, " Mulberry Sellers throws us a kiss across the universe."

APPENDIX

WEATHER FOR USE IN THIS BOOK

Selected from the best authorities

A brief though violent thunder-storm which had raged over the city was passing away; but still, though the rain had ceased more than an hour before, wild piles of dark and coppery clouds, in which a fierce and rayless glow was laboring, gigantically overhung the grotesque and huddled vista of dwarf houses, while in the distance, sheeting high over the low, misty confusion of gables and chimneys, spread a pall of dead, leprous blue, suffused with blotches of dull, glistening yellow, and with black plague-spots of vapor floating and faint lightnings crinkling on its surface. Thunder, still muttering in the close and sultry air, kept the scared dwellers in the street within, behind their closed shutters; and all deserted, cowed, dejected, squalid, like poor, stupid, top-heavy things that had felt the wrath of the summer tempest, stood the drenched structures on either side of the narrow and crooked way, ghastly and picturesque under the giant canopy. Rain dripped wretchedly in slow drops of melancholy sound from their projecting eaves upon the broken flagging, lay there in pools or trickled into the swollen drains, where the fallen torrent sullenly gurgled on its way to the river.—" *The Brazen Android:* " *W. D. O' Connor.*

> The fiery mid-March sun a moment hung
> Above the bleak Judean wilderness;
> Then darkness swept upon us, and 'twas night.
> —" *Easter-Eve at Kerak-Moab :* " *Clinton Scollard.*

The quick-coming winter twilight was already at hand. Snow was again falling, sifting delicately down, incidentally as it were.—" *Felicia :* " *Fanny N. D. Murfree.*

(230)

Merciful heavens! The whole west, from right to left, blazes up with a fierce light, and next instant the earth reels and quivers with the awful shock of ten thousand batteries of artillery. It is the signal for the Fury to spring — for a thousand demons to scream and shriek — for innumerable serpents of fire to writhe and light up the blackness.

Now the rain falls — now the wind is let loose with a terrible shriek — now the lightning is so constant that the eyes burn, and the thunderclaps merge into an awful roar, as did the 800 cannon at Gettysburg. Crash! Crash! Crash! It is the cottonwood trees falling to earth. Shriek! Shriek! Shriek! It is the Demon racing along the plain and uprooting even the blades of grass. Shock! Shock! Shock! It is the Fury flinging his fiery bolts into the bosom of the earth.—" *The Demon and the Fury:*" *M. Quad.*

Away up the gorge all diurnal fancies trooped into the wide liberties of endless luminous vistas of azure sunlit mountains beneath the shining azure heavens. The sky, looking down in deep blue placidities, only here and there smote the water to azure emulations of its tint.—" *In the 'Stranger People's' Country:*" *Charles Egbert Craddock.*

There was every indication of a dust-storm, though the sun still shone brilliantly. The hot wind had become wild and rampant. It was whipping up the sandy coating of the plain in every direction. High in the air were seen whirling spires and cones of sand — a curious effect against the deep-blue sky. Below, puffs of sand were breaking out of the plain in every direction, as though the plain were alive with invisible horsemen. These sandy cloudlets were instantly dissipated by the wind; it was the larger clouds that were lifted whole into the air, and the larger clouds of sand were becoming more and more the rule.

Alfred's eye, quickly scanning the horizon, descried the roof of the boundary-rider's hut still gleaming in the sunlight. He remembered the hut well. It could not be further than four miles, if as much as that, from this point of the track. He also knew these dust-storms of old; Bindarra was notorious for them. Without thinking twice, Alfred put spurs to his horse and headed for the hut. Before he had ridden half the distance the detached clouds of sand banded together in one dense whirlwind, and it was only owing to his horse's instinct that he did not ride wide of the hut altogether; for during the last half-mile he never saw the hut, until its outline loomed suddenly over his horse's ears; and by then the sun was invisible.—"*A Bride from the Bush.*"

It rained forty days and forty nights.— *Genesis.*

MERRY TALES

Acknowledgment should be made to the Century Company and to Messrs. Harper & Brothers for kind permission to reprint several of these stories from the "Century" and "Harper's Magazine."

THE PRIVATE HISTORY OF A CAMPAIGN THAT FAILED

YOU have heard from a great many people who did something in the war; is it not fair and right that you listen a little moment to one who started out to do something in it, but didn't? Thousands entered the war, got just a taste of it, and then stepped out again permanently. These, by their very numbers, are respectable, and are therefore entitled to a sort of voice — not a loud one, but a modest one; not a boastful one, but an apologetic one. They ought not to be allowed much space among better people — people who did something. I grant that; but they ought at least to be allowed to state why they didn't do anything, and also to explain the process by which they didn't do anything. Surely this kind of light must have a sort of value.

Out West there was a good deal of confusion in men's minds during the first months of the great trouble — a good deal of unsettledness, of leaning first this way, then that, then the other way. It was hard for us to get our bearings. I call to mind an instance of this. I was piloting on the Mississippi when the news came that South Carolina had gone out of the Union on the 20th of December, 1860. My pilot mate was a New Yorker. He was strong for the Union; so was I. But he would not listen to me with any patience; my loyalty was smirched, to his eye,

(235)

because my father had owned slaves. I said, in pallia-
tion of this dark fact, that I had heard my father say,
some years before he died, that slavery was a great
wrong, and that he would free the solitary negro he
then owned if he could think it right to give away the
property of the family when he was so straitened in
means. My mate retorted that a mere impulse was
nothing — anybody could pretend to a good impulse;
and went on decrying my Unionism and libeling my
ancestry. A month later the secession atmosphere
had considerably thickened on the Lower Mississippi,
and I became a rebel; so did he. We were together
in New Orleans the 26th of January, when Louisiana
went out of the Union. He did his full share of the
rebel shouting, but was bitterly opposed to letting me
do mine. He said that I came of bad stock — of a
father who had been willing to set slaves free. In the
following summer he was piloting a Federal gunboat
and shouting for the Union again, and I was in the
Confederate army. I held his note for some borrowed
money. He was one of the most upright men I
ever knew, but he repudiated that note without hesitation because I was a rebel and the son of a man
who owned slaves.

In that summer — of 1861 — the first wash of the
wave of war broke upon the shores of Missouri. Our
State was invaded by the Union forces. They took
possession of St. Louis, Jefferson Barracks, and some
other points. The Governor, Claib Jackson, issued
his proclamation calling out fifty thousand militia to
repel the invader.

I was visiting in the small town where my boyhood
had been spent — Hannibal, Marion County. Several
of us got together in a secret place by night and
formed ourselves into a military company. One Tom
Lyman, a young fellow of a good deal of spirit but of

no military experience, was made captain; I was made second lieutenant. We had no first lieutenant; I do not know why; it was long ago. There were fifteen of us. By the advice of an innocent connected with the organization we called ourselves the Marion Rangers. I do not remember that any one found fault with the name. I did not; I thought it sounded quite well. The young fellow who proposed this title was perhaps a fair sample of the kind of stuff we were made of. He was young, ignorant, good-natured, well-meaning, trivial, full of romance, and given to reading chivalric novels and singing forlorn love-ditties. He had some pathetic little nickel-plated aristocratic instincts, and detested his name, which was Dunlap; detested it, partly because it was nearly as common in that region as Smith, but mainly because it had a plebeian sound to his ear. So he tried to ennoble it by writing it in this way: *d' Unlap*. That contented his eye, but left his ear unsatisfied, for people gave the new name the same old pronunciation — emphasis on the front end of it. He then did the bravest thing that can be imagined — a thing to make one shiver when one remembers how the world is given to resenting shams and affectations; he began to write his name so: *d' Un Lap*. And he waited patiently through the long storm of mud that was flung at this work of art, and he had his reward at last; for he lived to see that name accepted, and the emphasis put where he wanted it by people who had known him all his life, and to whom the tribe of Dunlaps had been as familiar as the rain and the sunshine for forty years. So sure of victory at last is the courage that can wait. He said he had found, by consulting some ancient French chronicles, that the name was rightly and originally written d'Un Lap; and said that if it were translated into English it would mean Peterson: *Lap*, Latin or Greek,

16A

he said, for stone or rock, same as the French *pierre*, that is to say, Peter; *d'*, of or from; *un*, a or one; hence, d'Un Lap, of or from a stone or a Peter; that is to say, one who is the son of a stone, the son of a Peter — Peterson. Our militia company were not learned, and the explanation confused them; so they called him Peterson Dunlap. He proved useful to us in his way; he named our camps for us, and he generally struck a name that was " no slouch," as the boys said.

That is one sample of us. Another was Ed Stevens, son of the town jeweler — trim-built, handsome, graceful, neat as a cat; bright, educated, but given over entirely to fun. There was nothing serious in life to him. As far as he was concerned, this military expedition of ours was simply a holiday. I should say that about half of us looked upon it in the same way; not consciously perhaps, but unconsciously. We did not think; we were not capable of it. As for myself, I was full of unreasoning joy to be done with turning out of bed at midnight and four in the morning for a while; grateful to have a change, new scenes, new occupations, a new interest. In my thoughts that was as far as I went; I did not go into the details; as a rule, one doesn't at twenty-four.

Another sample was Smith, the blacksmith's apprentice. This vast donkey had some pluck, of a slow and sluggish nature, but a soft heart; at one time he would knock a horse down for some impropriety, and at another he would get homesick and cry. However, he had one ultimate credit to his account which some of us hadn't: he stuck to the war, and was killed in battle at last.

Jo Bowers, another sample, was a huge, good-natured, flax-headed lubber; lazy, sentimental, full of harmless brag, a grumbler by nature; an experienced, industrious, ambitious, and often quite picturesque liar, and yet not a successful one, for he had had no intelligent training, but was allowed to come up just any way. This life was serious enough to him, and seldom satisfactory. But he was a good fellow anyway, and the boys all liked him. He was made orderly sergeant; Stevens was made corporal.

These samples will answer — and they are quite fair ones. Well, this herd of cattle started for the war. What could you expect of them? They did as well as they knew how; but really what was justly to be expected of them? Nothing, I should say. That is what they did.

We waited for a dark night, for caution and secrecy were necessary; then, towards midnight, we stole in couples and from various directions to the Griffith place, beyond the town; from that point we set out together on foot. Hannibal lies at the extreme southeastern corner of Marion County, on the Mississippi River; our objective point was the hamlet of New London, ten miles away, in Ralls County.

The first hour was all fun, all idle nonsense and laughter. But that could not be kept up. The steady trudging came to be like work; the play had somehow oozed out of it; the stillness of the woods and the somberness of the night began to throw a depressing influence over the spirits of the boys, and presently the talking died out and each person shut himself up in his own thoughts. During the last half of the second hour nobody said a word.

Now we approached a log farmhouse where, according to report, there was a guard of five Union soldiers. Lyman called a halt; and there, in the deep gloom of the overhanging branches, he began to whisper a plan of assault upon that house, which made the gloom more depressing than it was before. It was a crucial moment; we realized, with a cold suddenness, that

here was no jest — we were standing face to face with
actual war. We were equal to the occasion. In our
response there was no hesitation, no indecision: we
said that if Lyman wanted to meddle with those soldiers,
he could go ahead and do it; but if he waited for us to
follow him, he would wait a long time.

Lyman urged, pleaded, tried to shame us, but it had
no effect. Our course was plain, our minds were made
up: we would flank the farmhouse — go out around.
And that was what we did.

We struck into the woods and entered upon a rough
time, stumbling over roots, getting tangled in vines,
and torn by briers. At last we reached an open place
in a safe region, and sat down, blown and hot, to cool
off and nurse our scratches and bruises. Lyman was
annoyed, but the rest of us were cheerful; we had
flanked the farmhouse, we had made our first military
movement, and it was a success; we had nothing to
fret about, were were feeling just the other way.
Horse-play and laughing began again; the expedition
was become a holiday frolic once more.

Then we had two more hours of dull trudging and
ultimate silence and depression; then, about dawn, we
straggled into New London, soiled, heel-blistered,
fagged with our little march, and all of us except
Stevens in a sour and raspy humor and privately down
on the war. We stacked our shabby old shotguns in
Colonel Ralls's barn, and then went in a body and
breakfasted with that veteran of the Mexican War.
Afterwards he took us to a distant meadow, and there
in the shade of a tree we listened to an old-fashioned
speech from him, full of gunpowder and glory, full of
that adjective-piling, mixed metaphor, and windy
declamation which were regarded as eloquence in that
ancient time and that remote region; and then he
swore us on the Bible to be faithful to the State of

Missouri and drive all invaders from her soil, no matter whence they might come or under what flag they might march. This mixed us considerably, and we could not make out just what service we were embarked in; but Colonel Ralls, the practiced politician and phrase-juggler, was not similarly in doubt; he knew quite clearly that he had invested us in the cause of the Southern Confederacy. He closed the solemnities by belting around me the sword which his neighbor, Colonel Brown, had worn at Buena Vista and Molino del Rey; and he accompanied this act with another impressive blast.

Then we formed in line of battle and marched four miles to a shady and pleasant piece of woods on the border of the far-reaching expanses of a flowery prairie. It was an enchanting region for war — our kind of war.

We pierced the forest about half a mile, and took up a strong position, with some low, rocky, and wooded hills behind us, and a purling, limpid creek in front. Straightway half the command were in swimming and the other half fishing. The ass with the French name gave this position a romantic title, but it was too long, so the boys shortened and simplified it to Camp Ralls.

We occupied an old maple sugar camp, whose half-rotted troughs were still propped against the trees. A long corn-crib served for sleeping quarters for the battalion. On our left, half a mile away, were Mason's farm and house; and he was a friend to the cause. Shortly after noon the farmers began to arrive from several directions, with mules and horses for our use, and these they lent us for as long as the war might last, which they judged would be about three months. The animals were of all sizes, all colors, and all breeds. They were mainly young and frisky, and nobody in the command could stay on them long at a time; for

16***

we were town boys, and ignorant of horsemanship. The creature that fell to my share was a very small mule, and yet so quick and active that it could throw me without difficulty; and it did this whenever I got on it. Then it would bray — stretching its neck out, laying its ears back, and spreading its jaws till you could see down to its works. It was a disagreeable animal in every way. If I took it by the bridle and tried to lead it off the grounds, it would sit down and brace back, and no one could budge it. However, I was not entirely destitute of military resources, and I did presently manage to spoil this game; for I had seen many a steamboat aground in my time, and knew a trick or two which even a grounded mule would be obliged to respect. There was a well by the corn-crib; so I substituted thirty fathom of rope for the bridle, and fetched him home with the windlass.

I will anticipate here sufficiently to say that we did learn to ride, after some days' practice, but never well. We could not learn to like our animals; they were not choice ones, and most of them had annoying peculiarities of one kind or another. Stevens's horse would carry him, when he was not noticing, under the huge excrescences which form on the trunks of oak trees, and wipe him out of the saddle; in this way Stevens got several bad hurts. Sergeant Bowers's horse was very large and tall, with slim, long legs, and looked like a railroad bridge. His size enabled him to reach all about, and as far as he wanted to, with his head; so he was always biting Bowers's legs. On the march, in the sun, Bowers slept a good deal; and as soon as the horse recognized that he was asleep he would reach around and bite him on the leg. His legs were black and blue with bites. This was the only thing that could ever make him swear, but this always did; whenever his horse bit him he always swore, and of course Stevens, who laughed at everything, laughed at this, and would even get into such convulsions over it as to lose his balance and fall off his horse; and then Bowers, already irritated by the pain of the horse-bite, would resent the laughter with hard language, and there would be a quarrel; so that horse made no end of trouble and bad blood in the command.

However I will get back to where I was — our first afternoon in the sugar-camp. The sugar-troughs came very handy as horse-troughs, and we had plenty of corn to fill them with. I ordered Sergeant Bowers to feed my mule; but he said that if I reckoned he went to war to be a dry-nurse to a mule, it wouldn't take me very long to find out my mistake. I believed that this was insubordination, but I was full of uncertainties about everything military, and so I let the thing pass, and went and ordered Smith, the blacksmith's apprentice, to feed the mule; but he merely gave me a large, cold, sarcastic grin, such as an ostensibly seven-year-old horse gives you when you lift his lip and find he is fourteen, and turned his back on me. I then went to the captain, and asked if it was not right and proper and military for me to have an orderly. He said it was, but as there was only one orderly in the corps, it was but right that he himself should have Bowers on his staff. Bowers said he wouldn't serve on anybody's staff; and if anybody thought he could make him, let him try it. So, of course, the thing had to be dropped; there was no other way.

Next, nobody would cook; it was considered a degradation; so we had no dinner. We lazied the rest of the pleasant afternoon away, some dozing under the trees, some smoking cob-pipes and talking sweethearts and war, some playing games. By late suppertime all hands were famished; and to meet the difficulty all hands turned to, on an equal footing, and gathered

Y***

wood, built fires, and cooked the meal. Afterwards everything was smooth for a while; then trouble broke out between the corporal and the sergeant, each claiming to rank the other. Nobody knew which was the higher office; so Lyman had to settle the matter by making the rank of both officers equal. The commander of an ignorant crew like that has many troubles and vexations which probably do not occur in the regular army at all. However, with the song-singing and yarn-spinning around the camp-fire, everything presently became serene again; and by and by we raked the corn down level in one end of the crib, and all went to bed on it, tying a horse to the door, so that he would neigh if any one tried to get in.*

We had some horsemanship drill every forenoon; then, afternoons, we rode off here and there in squads a few miles, and visited the farmers' girls, and had a youthful good time, and got an honest good dinner or supper, and then home again to camp, happy and content.

For a time life was idly delicious, it was perfect; there was nothing to mar it. Then came some farmers with an alarm one day. They said it was rumored that the enemy were advancing in our direction from over Hyde's prairie. The result was a sharp stir among us, and general consternation. It was a rude awakening from our pleasant trance. The rumor was but a rumor

---

* It was always my impression that that was what the horse was there for, and I know that it was also the impression of at least one other of the command, for we talked about it at the time, and admired the military ingenuity of the device; but when I was out West, three years ago, I was told by Mr. A. G. Fuqua, a member of our company, that the horse was his; that the leaving him tied at the door was a matter of mere forgetfulness, and that to attribute it to intelligent invention was to give him quite too much credit. In support of his position he called my attention to the suggestive fact that the artifice was not employed again. I had not thought of that before.

— nothing definite about it; so, in the confusion, we did not know which way to retreat. Lyman was for not retreating at all in these uncertain circumstances; but he found that if he tried to maintain that attitude he would fare badly, for the command were in no humor to put up with insubordination. So he yielded the point and called a council of war — to consist of himself and the three other officers; but the privates made such a fuss about being left out that we had to allow them to remain, for they were already present, and doing the most of the talking too. The question was, which way to retreat; but all were so flurried that nobody seemed to have even a guess to offer. Except Lyman. He explained in a few calm words that, inasmuch as the enemy were approaching from over Hyde's prairie, our course was simple: all we had to do was not to retreat *towards* him; any other direction would answer our needs perfectly. Everybody saw in a moment how true this was, and how wise; so Lyman got a great many compliments. It was now decided that we should fall back on Mason's farm.

It was after dark by this time, and as we could not know how soon the enemy might arrive, it did not seem best to try to take the horses and things with us; so we only took the guns and ammunition, and started at once. The route was very rough and hilly and rocky, and presently the night grew very black and rain began to fall; so we had a troublesome time of it, struggling and stumbling along in the dark; and soon some person slipped and fell, and then the next person behind stumbled over him and fell, and so did the rest, one after the other; and then Bowers came with the keg of powder in his arms, while the command were all mixed together, arms and legs, on the muddy slope; and so he fell, of course, with the keg, and this started the whole detachment down the hill in a body, and they landed in the brook at the bottom in a pile, and each that was undermost pulling the hair and scratching and biting those that were on top of him; and those that were being scratched and bitten scratching and biting the rest in their turn, and all saying they would die before they would ever go to war again if they ever got out of this brook this time, and the invader might rot for all they cared, and the country along with him — and all such talk as that, which was dismal to hear and take part in, in such smothered, low voices, and such a grisly dark place and so wet, and the enemy, maybe, coming any moment.

The keg of powder was lost, and the guns, too; so the growling and complaining continued straight along while the brigade pawed around the pasty hillside and slopped around in the brook hunting for these things; consequently we lost considerable time at this; and then we heard a sound, and held our breath and listened, and it seemed to be the enemy coming, though it could have been a cow, for it had a cough like a cow; but we did not wait, but left a couple of guns behind and struck out for Mason's again as briskly as we could scramble along in the dark. But we got lost presently among the rugged little ravines, and wasted a deal of time finding the way again, so it was after nine when we reached Mason's stile at last; and then before we could open our mouths to give the countersign several dogs came bounding over the fence, with great riot and noise, and each of them took a soldier by the slack of his trousers and began to back away with him. We could not shoot the dogs without endangering the persons they were attached to; so we had to look on helpless, at what was perhaps the most mortifying spectacle of the Civil War. There was light enough, and to spare, for the Masons had now run out on the porch with candles in their hands. The

old man and his son came and undid the dogs without
difficulty, all but Bowers's; but they couldn't undo his
dog, they didn't know his combination; he was of the
bull kind, and seemed to be set with a Yale time-lock;
but they got him loose at last with some scalding water,
of which Bowers got his share and returned thanks.
Peterson Dunlap afterwards made up a fine name for
this engagement, and also for the night march which
preceded it, but both have long ago faded out of my
memory.

We now went into the house, and they began to ask
us a world of questions, whereby it presently came out
that we did not know anything concerning who or what
we were running from; so the old gentleman made
himself very frank, and said we were a curious breed
of soldiers, and guessed we could be depended on to
end up the war in time, because no government could
stand the expense of the shoe-leather we should cost it
trying to follow us around. "Marion *Rangers!* good
name, b'gosh!" said he. And wanted to know why
we hadn't had a picket-guard at the place where the
road entered the prairie, and why we hadn't sent out a
scouting party to spy out the enemy and bring us an
account of his strength, and so on, before jumping up
and stampeding out of a strong position upon a mere
vague rumor — and so on, and so forth, till he made
us all feel shabbier than the dogs had done, not half so
enthusiastically welcome. So we went to bed shamed
and low-spirited; except Stevens. Soon Stevens began
to devise a garment for Bowers which could be made
to automatically display his battle-scars to the grateful,
or conceal them from the envious, according to his
occasions; but Bowers was in no humor for this, so
there was a fight, and when it was over Stevens had
some battle-scars of his own to think about.

Then we got a little sleep. But after all we had

gone through, our activities were not over for the
night; for about two o'clock in the morning we heard
a shout of warning from down the lane, accompanied
by a chorus from all the dogs, and in a moment everybody was up and flying around to find out what the
alarm was about. The alarmist was a horseman who
gave notice that a detachment of Union soldiers was
on its way from Hannibal with orders to capture and
hang any bands like ours which it could find, and said
we had no time to lose. Farmer Mason was in a flurry
this time himself. He hurried us out of the house with
all haste, and sent one of his negroes with us to show
us where to hide ourselves and our telltale guns among
the ravines half a mile away. It was raining heavily.

We struck down the lane, then across some rocky
pasture-land which offered good advantages for stumbling; consequently we were down in the mud most of
the time, and every time a man went down he blackguarded the war, and the people that started it, and
everybody connected with it, and gave himself the
master dose of all for being so foolish as to go into it.
At last we reached the wooded mouth of a ravine, and
there we huddled ourselves under the streaming trees,
and sent the negro back home. It was a dismal and
heart-breaking time. We were like to be drowned
with the rain, deafened with the howling wind and the
booming thunder, and blinded by the lightning. It
was, indeed, a wild night. The drenching we were
getting was misery enough, but a deeper misery still
was the reflection that the halter might end us before
we were a day older. A death of this shameful sort
had not occurred to us as being among the possibilities
of war. It took the romance all out of the campaign,
and turned our dreams of glory into a repulsive night-
mare. As for doubting that so barbarous an order had
been given, not one of us did that.

The long night wore itself out at last, and then the negro came to us with the news that the alarm had manifestly been a false one, and that breakfast would soon be ready. Straightway we were light-hearted again, and the world was bright, and life as full of hope and promise as ever — for we were young then. How long ago that was! Twenty-four years.

The mongrel child of philology named the night's refuge Camp Devastation, and no soul objected. The Masons gave us a Missouri country breakfast, in Missourian abundance, and we needed it: hot biscuits; hot "wheat bread," prettily criss-crossed in a lattice pattern on top; hot corn pone; fried chicken; bacon, coffee, eggs, milk, buttermilk, etc.; and the world may be confidently challenged to furnish the equal of such a breakfast, as it is cooked in the South.

We stayed several days at Mason's; and after all these years the memory of the dullness, and stillness, and lifelessness of that slumberous farmhouse still oppresses my spirit as with a sense of the presence of death and mourning. There was nothing to do, nothing to think about; there was no interest in life. The male part of the household were away in the fields all day, the women were busy and out of our sight; there was no sound but the plaintive wailing of a spinning-wheel, forever moaning out from some distant room — the most lonesome sound in nature, a sound steeped and sodden with homesickness and the emptiness of life. The family went to bed about dark every night, and as we were not invited to intrude any new customs we naturally followed theirs. Those nights were a hundred years long to youths accustomed to being up till twelve. We lay awake and miserable till that hour every time, and grew old and decrepit waiting through the still eternities for the clock-strikes. This was no place for town boys. So at last it was with something very like joy that we received news that the enemy were on our track again. With a new birth of the old warrior spirit we sprang to our places in line of battle and fell back on Camp Ralls.

Captain Lyman had take a hint from Mason's talk, and he now gave orders that our camp should be guarded against surprise by the posting of pickets. I was ordered to place a picket at the forks of the road in Hyde's prairie. Night shut down black and threatening. I told Sergeant Bowers to go out to that place and stay till midnight; and, just as I was expecting, he said he wouldn't do it. I tried to get others to go, but all refused. Some excused themselves on account of the weather; but the rest were frank enough to say they wouldn't go in any kind of weather. This kind of thing sounds odd now, and impossible, but there was no surprise in it at the time. On the contrary, it seemed a perfectly natural thing to do. There were scores of little camps scattered over Missouri where the same thing was happening. These camps were composed of young men who had been born and reared to a sturdy independence, and who did not know what it meant to be ordered around by Tom, Dick, and Harry, whom they had known familiarly all their lives, in the village or on the farm. It is quite within the probabilities that this same thing was happening all over the South. James Redpath recognized the justice of this assumption, and furnished the following instance in support of it. During a short stay in East Tennessee he was in a citizen colonel's tent one day talking, when a big private appeared at the door, and, without salute or other circumlocution, said to the colonel:

" Say, Jim, I'm a-goin' home for a few days."

" What for?"

" Well, I hain't b'en there for a right smart while, and I'd like to see how things is comin' on."

" How long are you going to be gone?"

" 'Bout two weeks."

" Well, don't be gone longer than that; and get back sooner if you can."

That was all, and the citizen officer resumed his conversation where the private had broken it off. This was in the first months of the war, of course. The camps in our part of Missouri were under Brigadier-General Thomas H. Harris. He was a townsman of ours, a first-rate fellow, and well liked; but we had all familiarly known him as the sole and modest-salaried operator in our telegraph office, where he had to send about one dispatch a week in ordinary times, and two when there was a rush of business; consequently, when he appeared in our midst one day, on the wing, and delivered a military command of some sort, in a large military fashion, nobody was surprised at the response which he got from the assembled soldiery:

" Oh, now, what'll you take to *don't*, Tom Harris?"

It was quite the natural thing. One might justly imagine that we were hopeless material for war. And so we seemed, in our ignorant state; but there were those among us who afterwards learned the grim trade; learned to obey like machines; became valuable soldiers; fought all through the war, and came out at the end with excellent records. One of the very boys who refused to go out on picket duty that night, and called me an ass for thinking he would expose himself to danger in such a foolhardy way, had become distinguished for intrepidity before he was a year older.

I did secure my picket that night — not by authority, but by diplomacy. I got Bowers to go by agreeing to exchange ranks with him for the time being, and go along and stand the watch with him as his subordinate. We stayed out there a couple of dreary hours in the pitchy darkness and the rain, with nothing to modify the dreariness but Bowers's monotonous growlings at the war and the weather; then we began to nod, and presently found it next to impossible to stay in the saddle; so we gave up the tedious job, and went back to the camp without waiting for the relief guard. We rode into camp without interruption or objection from anybody, and the enemy could have done the same, for there were no sentries. Everybody was asleep; at midnight there was nobody to send out another picket, so none was sent. We never tried to establish a watch at night again, as far as I remember, but we generally kept a picket out in the daytime.

In that camp the whole command slept on the corn in the big corn-crib; and there was usually a general row before morning, for the place was full of rats, and they would scramble over the boys' bodies and faces, annoying and irritating everybody; and now and then they would bite some one's toe, and the person who owned the toe would start up and magnify his English and begin to throw corn in the dark. The ears were half as heavy as bricks, and when they struck they hurt. The persons struck would respond, and inside of five minutes every man would be locked in a death-grip with his neighbor. There was a grievous deal of blood shed in the corn-crib, but this was all that was spilt while I was in the war. No, that is not quite true. But for one circumstance it would have been all. I will come to that now.

Our scares were frequent. Every few days rumors would come that the enemy were approaching. In these cases we always fell back on some other camp of ours; we never stayed where we were. But the rumors always turned out to be false; so at last even we began to grow indifferent to them. One night a negro was sent to our corn-crib with the same old warning: the enemy was hovering in our neighborhood. We all said

let him hover. We resolved to stay still and be comfortable. It was a fine warlike resolution, and no
doubt we all felt the stir of it in our veins — for a
moment. We had been having a very jolly time, that
was full of horse-play and school-boy hilarity; but
that cooled down now, and presently the fast-waning
fire of forced jokes and forced laughs died out altogether, and the company became silent. Silent and
nervous. And soon uneasy — worried — apprehensive. We had said we would stay, and we were committed. We could have been persuaded to go, but
there was nobody brave enough to suggest it. An
almost noiseless movement presently began in the dark
by a general but unvoiced impulse. When the movement was completed each man knew that he was not
the only person who had crept to the front wall and
had his eye at a crack between the logs. No, we were
all there; all there with our hearts in our throats, and
staring out towards the sugar-troughs where the forest
footpath came through. It was late, and there was a
deep woodsy stillness everywhere. There was a veiled
moonlight, which was only just strong enough to enable
us to mark the general shape of objects. Presently a
muffled sound caught our ears, and we recognized it as
the hoof-beats of a horse or horses. And right away
a figure appeared in the forest path; it could have
been made of smoke, its mass had so little sharpness
of outline. It was a man on horseback, and it seemed
to me that there were others behind him. I got hold
of a gun in the dark, and pushed it through a crack
between the logs, hardly knowing what I was doing, I
was so dazed with fright. Somebody said " Fire!" I
pulled the trigger. I seemed to see a hundred flashes
and hear a hundred reports; then I saw the man fall
down out of the saddle. My first feeling was of surprised gratification; my first impulse was an apprentice-

17A

sportsman's impulse to run and pick up his game. Somebody said, hardly audibly, "Good — we've got him! — wait for the rest." But the rest did not come. We waited — listened — still no more came. There was not a sound, not the whisper of a leaf; just perfect stillness; an uncanny kind of stillness, which was all the more uncanny on account of the damp, earthy, late-night smells now rising and pervading it. Then, wondering, we crept stealthily out, and approached the man. When we got to him the moon revealed him distinctly. He was lying on his back, with his arms abroad; his mouth was open and his chest heaving with long gasps, and his white shirt-front was all splashed with blood. The thought shot through me that I was a murderer; that I had killed a man — a man who had never done me any harm. That was the coldest sensation that ever went through my marrow. I was down by him in a moment, helplessly stroking his forehead; and I would have given anything then — my own life freely — to make him again what he had been five minutes before. And all the boys seemed to be feeling in the same way; they hung over him, full of pitying interest, and tried all they could to help him, and said all sorts of regretful things. They had forgotten all about the enemy; they thought only of this one forlorn unit of the foe. Once my imagination persuaded me that the dying man gave me a reproachful look out of his shadowy eyes, and it seemed to me that I could rather he had stabbed me than done that. He muttered and mumbled like a dreamer in his sleep about his wife and his child; and I thought with a new despair, "This thing that I have done does not end with him; it falls upon *them* too, and they never did me any harm, any more than he."

In a little while the man was dead. He was killed in war; killed in fair and legitimate war; killed in battle, as you may say; and yet he was as sincerely mourned by the opposing force as if he had been their brother. The boys stood there a half-hour sorrowing over him, and recalling the details of the tragedy, and wondering who he might be, and if he were a spy, and saying that if it were to do over again they would not hurt him unless he attacked them first. It soon came out that mine was not the only shot fired; there were five others — a division of the guilt which was a great relief to me, since it in some degree lightened and diminished the burden I was carrying. There were six shots fired at once; but I was not in my right mind at the time, and my heated imagination had magnified my one shot into a volley.

The man was not in uniform, and was not armed. He was a stranger in the country; that was all we ever found out about him. The thought of him got to preying upon me every night; I could not get rid of it. I could not drive it away, the taking of that un-offending life seemed such a wanton thing. And it seemed an epitome of war; that all war must be just that — the killing of strangers against whom you feel no personal animosity; strangers whom, in other circumstances, you would help if you found them in trouble, and who would help you if you needed it. My campaign was spoiled. It seemed to me that I was not rightly equipped for this awful business; that war was intended for men, and I for a child's nurse. I resolved to retire from this avocation of sham soldiership while I could save some remnant of my self-respect. These morbid thoughts clung to me against reason; for at bottom I did not believe I had touched that man. The law of probabilities decreed me guiltless of his blood; for in all my small experience with guns I had never hit anything I had tried to hit, and I knew I had done my best to hit him. Yet there was no solace in the thought. Against a diseased imagination demonstration goes for nothing.

The rest of my war experience was of a piece with what I have already told of it. We kept monotonously falling back upon one camp or another, and eating up the country. I marvel now at the patience of the farmers and their families. They ought to have shot us; on the contrary, they were as hospitably kind and courteous to us as if we had deserved it. In one of these camps we found Ab Grimes, an Upper Mississippi pilot, who afterwards became famous as a dare-devil rebel spy, whose career bristled with desperate adventures. The look and style of his comrades suggested that they had not come into the war to play, and their deeds made good the conjecture later. They were fine horsemen and good revolver shots; but their favorite arm was the lasso. Each had one at his pommel, and could snatch a man out of the saddle with it every time, on a full gallop, at any reasonable distance.

In another camp the chief was a fierce and profane old blacksmith of sixty, and he had furnished his twenty recruits with gigantic home-made bowie-knives, to be swung with two hands, like the *machetes* of the Isthmus. It was a grisly spectacle to see that earnest band practicing their murderous cuts and slashes under the eye of that remorseless old fanatic.

The last camp which we fell back upon was in a hollow near the village of Florida, where I was born — in Monroe County. Here we were warned one day that a Union colonel was sweeping down on us with a whole regiment at his heel. This looked decidedly serious. Our boys went apart and consulted; then we went back and told the other companies present that the war was a disappointment to us, and we were going to disband. They were getting ready themselves to fall back on some place or other, and were only waiting for General Tom Harris, who was expected to arrive at any moment; so they tried to persuade us to wait a little while, but the majority of us said no, we were accustomed to falling back, and didn't need any of Tom Harris's help; we could get along perfectly well without him — and save time, too. So about half of our fifteen, including myself, mounted and left on the instant; the others yielded to persuasion and stayed — stayed through the war.

An hour later we met General Harris on the road, with two or three people in his company — his staff, probably, but we could not tell; none of them were in uniform; uniforms had not come into vogue among us yet. Harris ordered us back; but we told him there was a Union colonel coming with a whole regiment in his wake, and it looked as if there was going to be a disturbance; so we had concluded to go home. He raged a little, but it was of no use; our minds were made up. We had done our share; had killed one man, exterminated one army, such as it was; let him go and kill the rest, and that would end the war. I did not see that brisk young general again until last year; then he was wearing white hair and whiskers.

In time I came to know that Union colonel whose coming frightened me out of the war and crippled the Southern cause to that extent — General Grant. I came within a few hours of seeing him when he was as unknown as I was myself; at a time when anybody could have said, "Grant? — Ulysses S. Grant? I do not remember hearing the name before." It seems difficult to realize that there was once a time when such a remark could be rationally made; but there *was*, and I was within a few miles of the place and the occasion, too, though proceeding in the other direction.

The thoughtful will not throw this war paper of mine lightly aside as being valueless. It has this value: it

17***

is a not unfair picture of what went on in many and
many a militia camp in the first months of the rebellion,
when the green recruits were without discipline, without
the steadying and heartening influence of trained lead-
ers; when all their circumstances were new and strange,
and charged with exaggerated terrors, and before the
invaluable experience of actual collision in the field
had turned them from rabbits into soldiers. If this
side of the picture of that early day has not before
been put into history, then history has been to that
degree incomplete, for it had and has its rightful place
there. There was more Bull Run material scattered
through the early camps of this country than exhibited
itself at Bull Run. And yet it learned its trade presently, and helped to fight the great battles later. I
could have become a soldier myself if I had waited
I had got part of it learned; I knew more about retreating than the man that invented retreating.

LUCK

IT was at a banquet in London in honor of one of the
two or three conspicuously illustrious English military names of this generation.   For reasons which will
presently appear, I will withhold his real name and
titles and call him Lieutenant-General Lord Arthur
Scoresby, Y.C., K.C.B., etc., etc., etc.   What a fascination there is in a renowned name!   There sat the
man, in actual flesh, whom I had heard of so many
thousands of times since that day, thirty years before,
when his name shot suddenly to the zenith from a
Crimean battlefield, to remain forever celebrated.   It
was food and drink to me to look, and look, and look
at that demi-god; scanning, searching, noting: the
quietness, the reserve, the noble gravity of his countenance; the simple honesty that expressed itself all
over him; the sweet unconsciousness of his greatness
— unconsciousness of the hundreds of admiring eyes
fastened upon him, unconsciousness of the deep,
loving, sincere worship welling out of the breasts of
those people and flowing towards him.

The clergyman at my left was an old acquaintance
of mine — clergyman now, but had spent the first half
of his life in the camp and field and as an instructor in
the military school at Woolwich.   Just at the moment
I have been talking about, a veiled and singular light

[NOTE.—This is not a fancy sketch.   I got it from a clergyman who
was an instructor at Woolwich forty years ago, and who vouched for its
truth.— M. T.]

Q***

glimmered in his eyes and he leaned down and muttered confidentially to me — indicating the hero of the banquet with a gesture:

" Privately — he's an absolute fool."

This verdict was a great surprise to me. If its subject had been Napoleon, or Socrates, or Solomon, my astonishment could not have been greater. Two things I was well aware of: that the Reverend was a man of strict veracity and that his judgment of men was good. Therefore I knew, beyond doubt or question, that the world was mistaken about this hero: he *was* a fool. So I meant to find out, at a convenient moment, how the Reverend, all solitary and alone, had discovered the secret.

Some days later the opportunity came, and this is what the Reverend told me:

About forty years ago I was an instructor in the military academy at Woolwich. I was present in one of the sections when young Scoresby underwent his preliminary examination. I was touched to the quick with pity, for the rest of the class answered up brightly and handsomely, while he — why, dear me, he didn't know *anything*, so to speak. He was evidently good, and sweet, and lovable, and guileless; and so it was exceedingly painful to see him stand there, as serene as a graven image, and deliver himself of answers which were veritably miraculous for stupidity and ignorance. All the compassion in me was aroused in his behalf. I said to myself, when he comes to be examined again he will be flung over, of course; so it will be simply a harmless act of charity to ease his fall as much as I can. I took him aside and found that he knew a little of Cæsar's history; and as he didn't know anything else, I went to work and drilled him like a galley-slave on a certain line of stock questions concerning Cæsar which I knew would be used. If you'll believe me, he went through with flying colors on examination day! He went through on that purely superficial "cram," and got compliments too, while others, who knew a thousand times more than he, got plucked. By some strangely lucky accident — an accident not likely to happen twice in a century — he was asked no question outside of the narrow limits of his drill.

It was stupefying. Well, all through his course I stood by him, with something of the sentiment which a mother feels for a crippled child; and he always saved himself — just by miracle, apparently.

Now, of course, the thing that would expose him and kill him at last was mathematics. I resolved to make his death as easy as I could; so I drilled him and crammed him, and crammed him and drilled him, just on the line of questions which the examiners would be most likely to use, and then launched him on his fate. Well, sir, try to conceive of the result: to my consternation, he took the first prize! And with it he got a perfect ovation in the way of compliments.

Sleep? There was no more sleep for me for a week. My conscience tortured me day and night. What I had done I had done purely through charity, and only to ease the poor youth's fall. I never had dreamed of any such preposterous results as the thing that had hapened. I felt as guilty and miserable as Frankenstein. Here was a wooden-head whom I had put in the way of glittering promotions and prodigious responsibilities, and but one thing could happen: he and his responsibilities would all go to ruin together at the first opportunity.

The Crimean War had just broken out. Of course there had to be a war, I said to myself. We couldn't

have peace and give this donkey a chance to die before
he is found out. I waited for the earthquake. It
came. And it made me reel when it did come. He
was actually gazetted to a captaincy in a marching
regiment! Better men grow old and gray in the service
before they climb to a sublimity like that. And who
could ever have foreseen that they would go and put
such a load of responsibility on such green and inadequate shoulders? I could just barely have stood it if
they had made him a cornet; but a captain — think of
it! I thought my hair would turn white.

Consider what I did — I who so loved repose and
inaction. I said to myself, I am responsible to the
country for this, and I must go along with him and
protect the country against him as far as I can. So I
took my poor little capital that I had saved up through
years of work and grinding economy, and went with a
sigh and bought a cornetcy in his regiment, and away
we went to the field.

And there — oh, dear, it was awful. Blunders? —
why, he never did anything *but* blunder. But, you
see, nobody was in the fellow's secret. Everybody
had him focused wrong, and necessarily misinterpreted
his performance every time. Consequently they took
his idiotic blunders for inspirations of genius. They
did, honestly! His mildest blunders were enough to
make a man in his right mind cry; and they did make
me cry — and rage and rave, too, privately. And the
thing that kept me always in a sweat of apprehension
was the fact that every fresh blunder he made increased
the luster of his reputation! I kept saying to myself,
he'll get so high, that when discovery does finally
come, it will be like the sun falling out of the sky.

He went right along up, from grade to grade, over
the dead bodies of his superiors, until at last, in the
hottest moment of the battle of......down went our

colonel, and my heart jumped into my mouth, for Scoresby was next in rank! Now for it, said I; we'll all land in Sheol in ten minutes, sure.

The battle was awfully hot; the allies were steadily giving way all over the field. Our regiment occupied a position that was vital; a blunder now must be destruction. At this crucial moment, what does this immortal fool do but detach the regiment from its place and order a charge over a neighboring hill where there wasn't a suggestion of an enemy! "There you go!" I said to myself; "this *is* the end at last."

And away we did go, and were over the shoulder of the hill before the insane movement could be discovered and stopped. And what did we find? An entire and unsuspected Russian army in reserve! And what happened? We were eaten up? That is necessarily what would have happened in ninety-nine cases out of a hundred. But no; those Russians argued that no single regiment would come browsing around there at such a time. It must be the entire English army, and that the sly Russian game was detected and blocked; so they turned tail, and away they went, pell-mell, over the hill and down into the field, in wild confusion, and we after them; they themselves broke the solid Russian center in the field, and tore through, and in no time there was the most tremendous rout you ever saw, and the defeat of the allies was turned into a sweeping and splendid victory! Marshal Canrobert looked on, dizzy with astonishment, admiration, and delight; and sent right off for Scoresby, and hugged him, and decorated him on the field, in presence of all the armies!

And what was Scoresby's blunder that time? Merely the mistaking his right hand for his left — that was all. An order had come to him to fall back and support our right; and instead, he fell *forward* and went over

the hill to the left. But the name he won that day as
a marvelous military genius filled the world with his
glory, and that glory will never fade while history
books last.

He is just as good and sweet and lovable and unpre-
tending as a man can be, but he doesn't know enough
to come in when it rains. Now that is absolutely true.
He is the supremest ass in the universe; and until half
an hour ago nobody knew it but himself and me. He
has been pursued, day by day and year by year, by a
most phenomenal and astonishing luckiness. He has
been a shining soldier in all our wars for a generation;
he has littered his whole military life with blunders,
and yet has never committed one that didn't make him
a knight or a baronet or a lord or something. Look
at his breast; why, he is just clothed in domestic and
foreign decorations. Well, sir, every one of them is
the record of some shouting stupidity or other; and
taken together, they are proof that the very best thing
in all this world that can befall a man is to be born
lucky. I say again, as I said at the banquet, Scoresby's
an absolute fool.

A CURIOUS EXPERIENCE

THIS is the story which the Major told me, as nearly as I can recall it:

In the winter of 1862–3 I was commandant of Fort Trumbull, at New London, Conn. Maybe our life there was not so brisk as life at " the front "; still it was brisk enough, in its way — one's brains didn't cake together there for lack of something to keep them stirring. For one thing, all the Northern atmosphere at that time was thick with mysterious rumors — rumors to the effect that rebel spies were flitting everywhere, and getting ready to blow up our Northern forts, burn our hotels, send infected clothing into our towns, and all that sort of thing. You remember it. All this had a tendency to keep us awake, and knock the traditional dullness out of garrison life. Besides, ours was a recruiting station — which is the same as saying we hadn't any time to waste in dozing, or dreaming, or fooling around. Why, with all our watchfulness, fifty per cent. of a day's recruits would leak out of our hands and give us the slip the same night. The bounties were so prodigious that a recruit could pay a sentinel three or four hundred dollars to let him escape, and still have enough of his bounty-money left to constitute a fortune for a poor man. Yes, as I said before, our life was not drowsy.

Well, one day I was in my quarters alone, doing

some writing, when a pale and ragged lad of fourteen or fifteen entered, made a neat bow, and said:

" I believe recruits are received here?"

" Yes."

" Will you please enlist me, sir?"

" Dear me, no! You are too young, my boy, and too small."

A disappointed look came into his face, and quickly deepened into an expression of despondency. He turned slowly away, as if to go; hesitated, then faced me again, and said, in a tone that went to my heart:

" I have no home, and not a friend in the world. If you *could* only enlist me!"

But of course the thing was out of the question, and I said so as gently as I could. Then I told him to sit down by the stove and warm himself, and added:

" You shall have something to eat, presently. You are hungry?"

He did not answer; he did not need to: the gratitude in his big, soft eyes was more eloquent than any words could have been. He sat down by the stove, and I went on writing. Occasionally I took a furtive glance at him. I noticed that his clothes and shoes, although soiled and damaged, were of good style and material. This fact was suggestive. To it I added the facts that his voice was low and musical; his eyes deep and melancholy; his carriage and address gentlemanly; evidently the poor chap was in trouble. As a result, I was interested.

However, I became absorbed in my work by and by, and forgot all about the boy. I don't know how long this lasted; but, at length, I happened to look up. The boy's back was towards me, but his face was turned in such a way that I could see one of his cheeks — and down that cheek a rill of noiseless tears was flowing.

"God bless my soul!" I said to myself; "I forgot the poor rat was starving." Then I made amends for my brutality by saying to him, "Come along, my lad; you shall dine with *me;* I am alone to-day."

He gave me another of those grateful looks, and a happy light broke in his face. At the table he stood with his hand on his chair-back until I was seated, then seated himself. I took up my knife and fork and — well, I simply held them, and kept still; for the boy had inclined his head and was saying a silent grace. A thousand hallowed memories of home and my childhood poured in upon me, and I sighed to think how far I had drifted from religion and its balm for hurt minds, its comfort and solace and support.

As our meal progressed I observed that young Wicklow — Robert Wicklow was his full name — knew what to do with his napkin; and — well, in a word, I observed that he was a boy of good breeding; never mind the details. He had a simple frankness, too, which won upon me. We talked mainly about himself, and I had no difficulty in getting his history out of him. When he spoke of his having been born and reared in Louisiana, I warmed to him decidedly, for I had spent some time down there. I knew all the "coast" region of the Mississippi, and loved it, and had not been long enough away from it for my interest in it to begin to pale. The very names that fell from his lips sounded good to me — so good that I steered the talk in directions that would bring them out. Baton Rouge, Plaquemine, Donaldsonville, Sixty-mile Point, Bonnet-Carré, the Stock Landing, Carrollton, the Steamship Landing, the Steamboat Landing, New Orleans, Tchoupitoulas Street, the Esplanade, the Rue des Bons Enfants, the St. Charles Hotel, the Tivoli Circle, the Shell Road, Lake Pontchartrain; and it was particularly delightful to me to hear once more of the *R. E.*

Lee, the *Natchez*, the *Eclipse*, the *General Quitman*, the *Duncan F. Kenner*, and other old familiar steamboats. It was almost as good as being back there, these names so vividly reproduced in my mind the look of the things they stood for. Briefly, this was little Wicklow's history:

When the war broke out, he and his invalid aunt and his father were living near Baton Rouge, on a great and rich plantation which had been in the family for fifty years. The father was a Union man. He was persecuted in all sorts of ways, but clung to his principles. At last one night masked men burned his mansion down, and the family had to fly for their lives. They were hunted from place to place, and learned all there was to know about poverty, hunger, and distress. The invalid aunt found relief at last: misery and exposure killed her; she died in an open field, like a tramp, the rain beating upon her and the thunder booming overhead. Not long afterwards the father was captured by an armed band; and while the son begged and pleaded, the victim was strung up before his face. [At this point a baleful light shone in the youth's eyes, and he said, with the manner of one who talks to himself: "If I cannot be enlisted, no matter — I shall find a way — I shall find a way."] As soon as the father was pronounced dead, the son was told that if he was not out of that region within twenty-four hours it would go hard with him. That night he crept to the riverside and hid himself near a plantation landing. By and by the *Duncan F. Kenner* stopped there, and he swam out and concealed himself in the yawl that was dragging at her stern. Before daylight the boat reached the Stock Landing and he slipped ashore. He walked the three miles which lay between that point and the house of an uncle of his in Good-Children street, in New Orleans, and then his

troubles were over for the time being. But this uncle was a Union man, too, and before very long he concluded that he had better leave the South. So he and young Wicklow slipped out of the country on board a sailing vessel, and in due time reached New York. They put up at the Astor House. Young Wicklow had a good time of it for a while, strolling up and down Broadway, and observing the strange Northern sights; but in the end a change came — and not for the better. The uncle had been cheerful at first, but now he began to look troubled and despondent; moreover, he became moody and irritable; talked of money giving out, and no way to get more —" not enough left for one, let alone two." Then, one morning, he was missing — did not come to breakfast. The boy inquired at the office, and was told that the uncle had paid his bill the night before and gone away — to Boston, the clerk believed, but was not certain.

The lad was alone and friendless. He did not know what to do, but concluded he had better try to follow and find his uncle. He went down to the steamboat landing: learned that the trifle of money in his pocket would not carry him to Boston; however, it would carry him to New London; so he took passage for that port, resolving to trust to Providence to furnish him means to travel the rest of the way. He had now been wandering about the streets of New London three days and nights, getting a bite and a nap here and there for charity's sake. But he had given up at last; courage and hope were both gone. If he could enlist, nobody could be more thankful; if he could not get in as a soldier, couldn't he be a drummer boy? Ah, he would work *so* hard to please, and would be so grateful!

Well, there's the history of young Wicklow, just as he told it to me, barring details. I said:

" My boy, you are among friends now — don't you

18A

be troubled any more." How his eyes glistened! I called in Sergeant John Rayburn — he was from Hartford; lives in Hartford yet; maybe you know him — and said, " Rayburn, quarter this boy with the musicians. I am going to enroll him as a drummer boy, and I want you to look after him and see that he is well treated."

Well, of course, intercourse between the commandant of the post and the drummer boy came to an end now; but the poor little friendless chap lay heavy on my heart just the same. I kept on the lookout, hoping to see him brighten up and begin to be cheery and gay; but no, the days went by, and there was no change. He associated with nobody; he was always absent-minded, always thinking; his face was always sad. One morning Rayburn asked leave to speak to me privately. Said he:

" I hope I don't offend, sir; but the truth is, the musicians are in such a sweat it seems as if somebody's *got* to speak."

" Why, what is the trouble?"

" It's the Wicklow boy, sir. The musicians are down on him to an extent you can't imagine."

" Well, go on, go on. What has he been doing?"

" Prayin', sir."

" Praying!"

" Yes, sir; the musicians haven't any peace of their life for that boy's prayin'. First thing in the morning he's at it; noons he's at it; and nights — well, *nights* he just lays into 'em like all possessed! Sleep? Bless you, they *can't* sleep: he's got the floor, as the sayin' is, and then when he once gets his supplication-mill agoin' there just simply ain't any let-up *to* him. He starts in with the band master, and he prays for him; next he takes the head bugler, and he prays for him; next the bass drum, and he scoops *him* in; and so on, right straight through the band, givin' them all a show, and takin' that amount of interest in it which would make you think he thought he warn't but a little while for this world, and believed he couldn't be happy in heaven without he had a brass band along, and wanted to pick 'em out for himself, so he could depend on 'em to do up the national tunes in a style suitin' to the place. Well, sir, heavin' boots at him don't have no effect; it's dark in there; and, besides, he don't pray fair, anyway, but kneels down behind the big drum; so it don't make no difference if they *rain* boots at him, *he* don't give a dern — warbles right along, same as if it was applause. They sing out, ' Oh, dry up !' ' Give us a rest !' ' Shoot him !' ' Oh, take a walk !' and all sorts of such things. But what of it? It don't phase him. *He* don't mind it." After a pause : " Kind of a good little fool, too; gits up in the mornin' and carts all that stock of boots back, and sorts 'em out and sets each man's pair where they belong. And they've been throwed at him so much now that he knows every boot in the band — can sort 'em out with his eyes shut."

After another pause, which I forbore to interrupt:

" But the roughest thing about it is that when he's done prayin'— when he ever *does* get done — he pipes up and begins to *sing*. Well, you know what a honey kind of a voice he's got when he talks; you know how it would persuade a cast-iron dog to come down off of a doorstep and lick his hand. Now if you'll take my word for it, sir, it ain't a circumstance to his singin' ! Flute music is harsh to that boy's singin'. Oh, he just gurgles it out so soft and sweet and low, there in the dark, that it makes you think you are in heaven."

" What is there ' rough ' about that?"

" Ah, that's just it, sir. You hear him sing

" ' Just as I am — poor, wretched, blind '—

just you hear him sing that once, and see if you don't
melt all up and the water come into your eyes! I
don't care *what* he sings, it goes plum straight home
to you — it goes deep down to where you *live* — and
it fetches you every time! Just you hear him sing

> " 'Child of sin and sorrow, filled with dismay,
>   Wait not till to-morrow, yield thee to-day;
>   Grieve not that love
>   Which, from above '—

and so on. It makes a body feel like the wickedest,
ungratefulest brute that walks. And when he sings
them songs of his about home, and mother, and childhood, and old memories, and things that's vanished,
and old friends dead and gone, it fetches everything
before your face that you've ever loved and lost in all
your life — and it's just beautiful, it's just divine to
listen to, sir — but, Lord, Lord, the heart-break of it!
The band — well, they all cry — every rascal of them
blubbers, and don't try to hide it, either; and first you
know, that very gang that's been slammin' boots at
that boy will skip out of their bunks all of a sudden,
and rush over in the dark and hug him! Yes, they
do — and slobber all over him, and call him pet names,
and beg him to forgive them. And just at that time,
if a regiment was to offer to hurt a hair of that cub's
head, they'd go for that regiment, if it was a whole
army corps!"

Another pause.

"Is that all?" said I.

"Yes, sir."

"Well, dear me, what is the complaint? What do
they want done?"

"Done? Why, bless you, sir, they want you to
stop him from *singin'*."

"What an idea! You said his music was divine."

"That's just it. It's *too* divine. Mortal man can't stand it. It stirs a body up so; it turns a body inside out; it racks his feelin's all to rags; it makes him feel bad and wicked, and not fit for any place but perdition. It keeps a body in such an everlastin' state of repentin', that nothin' don't taste good and there ain't no comfort in life. And then the *cryin'*, you see — every mornin' they are ashamed to look one another in the face."

"Well, this is an odd case, and a singular complaint. So they really want the singing stopped?"

"Yes, sir, that is the idea. They don't wish to ask too much; they would like powerful well to have the prayin' shut down on, or leastways trimmed off around the edges; but the main thing's the singin'. If they can only get the singin' choked off, they think they can stand the prayin', rough as it is to be bullyragged so much that way."

I told the sergeant I would take the matter under consideration. That night I crept into the musicians' quarters and listened. The sergeant had not overstated the case. I heard the praying voice pleading in the dark; I heard the execrations of the harassed men; I heard the rain of boots whiz through the air, and bang and thump around the big drum. The thing touched me, but it amused me, too. By and by, after an impressive silence, came the singing. Lord, the pathos of it, the enchantment of it! Nothing in the world was ever so sweet, so gracious, so tender, so holy, so moving. I made my stay very brief; I was beginning to experience emotions of a sort not proper to the commandant of a fortress.

Next day I issued orders which stopped the praying and singing. Then followed three or four days which were so full of bounty-jumping excitements and irritations that I never once thought of my drummer boy.

18***

But now comes Sergeant Rayburn, one morning, and says:

" That new boy acts mighty strange, sir."

" How?"

" Well, sir, he's all the time writing."

" Writing?   What does he write — letters?"

" I don't know, sir; but whenever he's off duty, he is always poking and nosing around the fort, all by himself — blest if I think there's a hole or corner in it he hasn't been into — and every little while he outs with pencil and paper and scribbles something down."

This gave me a most unpleasant sensation. I wanted to scoff at it, but it was not a time to scoff at *anything* that had the least suspicious tinge about it.   Things were happening all around us, in the North, then, that warned us to be always on the alert, and always suspecting.   I recalled to mind the suggestive fact that this boy was from the South — the extreme South, Louisiana — and the thought was not of a reassuring nature, under the circumstances.   Nevertheless, it cost me a pang to give the orders which I now gave to Rayburn.   I felt like a father who plots to expose his own child to shame and injury.   I told Rayburn to keep quiet, bide his time, and get me some of those writings whenever he could manage it without the boy's finding it out.   And I charged him not to do anything which might let the boy discover that he was being watched.   I also ordered that he allow the lad his usual liberties, but that he be followed at a distance when he went out into the town.

During the next two days Rayburn reported to me several times.   No success.   The boy was still writing, but he always pocketed his paper with a careless air whenever Rayburn appeared in the vicinity.   He had gone twice to an old deserted stable in the town, remained a minute or two, and come out again.   One could not pooh-pooh these things — they had an evil look. I was obliged to confess to myself that I was getting uneasy. I went into my private quarters and sent for my second in command — an officer of intelligence and judgment, son of General James Watson Webb. He was surprised and troubled. We had a long talk over the matter, and came to the conclusion that it would be worth while to institute a secret search. I determined to take charge of that myself. So I had myself called at two in the morning; and, pretty soon after, I was in the musicians' quarters, crawling along the floor on my stomach among the snorers. I reached my slumbering waif's bunk at last, without disturbing anybody, captured his clothes and kit, and crawled stealthily back again. When I got to my own quarters, I found Webb there, waiting and eager to know the result. We made search immediately. The clothes were a disappointment. In the pockets we found blank paper and a pencil; nothing else, except a jackknife and such queer odds and ends and useless trifles as boys hoard and value. We turned to the kit hopefully. Nothing there but a rebuke for us! — a little Bible with this written on the fly-leaf: "Stranger, be kind to my boy, for his mother's sake."

I looked at Webb — he dropped his eyes; he looked at me — I dropped mine. Neither spoke. I put the book reverently back in its place. Presently Webb got up and went away, without remark. After a little I nerved myself up to my unpalatable job, and took the plunder back to where it belonged, crawling on my stomach as before. It seemed the peculiarly appropriate attitude for the business I was in.

I was most honestly glad when it was over and done with.

About noon next day Rayburn came, as usual, to report. I cut him short. I said:

R***

"Let this nonsense be dropped. We are making a bugaboo out of a poor little cub who has got no more harm in him than a hymn-book."

The sergeant looked surprised, and said:

"Well, you know it was your orders, sir, and I've got some of the writing."

"And what does it amount to? How did you get it?"

"I peeped through the key-hole, and see him writing. So, when I judged he was about done, I made a sort of a little cough, and I see him crumple it up and throw it in the fire, and look all around to see if anybody was coming. Then he settled back as comfortable and careless as anything. Then I comes in, and passes the time of day pleasantly, and sends him of an errand. He never looked uneasy, but went right along. It was a coal fire and new built; the writing had gone over behind a chunk, out of sight; but I got it out; there it is; it ain't hardly scorched, you see."

I glanced at the paper and took in a sentence or two. Then I dismissed the sergeant and told him to send Webb to me. Here is the paper in full:

"FORT TRUMBULL, the 8th.

"COLONEL,— I was mistaken as to the calibre of the three guns I ended my list with. They are 18-pounders; all the rest of the armament is as I stated. The garrison remains as before reported, except that the two light infantry companies that were to be detached for service at the front are to stay here for the present — can't find out for how long, just now, but will soon. We are satisfied that, all things considered, matters had better be postponed un—"

There it broke off — there is where Rayburn coughed and interrupted the writer. All my affection for the boy, all my respect for him and charity for his forlorn condition, withered in a moment under the blight of this revelation of cold-blooded baseness.

But never mind about that.   Here was business —
business that required profound and immediate attention, too.   Webb and I turned the subject over and
over, and examined it all around.   Webb said:

"What a pity he was interrupted!   Something is
going to be postponed until — when?   And what *is*
the something?   Possibly he would have mentioned it,
the pious little reptile!"

"Yes," I said, "we have missed a trick.   And
who is ' *we* ' in the letter?   Is it conspirators inside
the fort or outside?"

That " we " was uncomfortably suggestive.   However, it was not worth while to be guessing around
that, so we proceeded to matters more practical.   In
the first place, we decided to double the sentries and
keep the strictest possible watch.   Next, we thought
of calling Wicklow in and making him divulge everything; but that did not seem wisest until other methods
should fail.   We must have some more of the writings;
so we began to plan to that end.   And now we had an
idea: Wicklow never went to the post-office — perhaps
the deserted stable was his post-office.   We sent for
my confidential clerk — a young German named Sterne,
who was a sort of natural detective — and told him all
about the case, and ordered him to go to work on it.
Within the hour we got word that Wicklow was writing
again.   Shortly afterwards word came that he had
asked leave to go out into the town.   He was detained
a while, and meantime Sterne hurried off and concealed
himself in the stable.   By and by he saw Wicklow
saunter in, look about him, then hide something under
some rubbish in a corner, and take leisurely leave
again.   Sterne pounced upon the hidden article — a
letter — and brought it to us.   It had no superscription and no signature.   It repeated what we had
already read, and then went on to say:

"We think it best to postpone till the two companies are gone. I mean the four inside think so; have not communicated with the others — afraid of attracting attention. I say four because we have lost two; they had hardly enlisted and got inside when they were shipped off to the front. It will be absolutely necessary to have two in their places. The two that went were the brothers from Thirty-mile Point. I have something of the greatest importance to reveal, but must not trust it to this method of communication; will try the other."

"The little scoundrel!" said Webb; "who *could* have supposed he was a spy? However, never mind about that; let us add up our particulars, such as they are, and see how the case stands to date. First, we've got a rebel spy in our midst, whom we know; secondly, we've got three more in our midst whom we don't know; thirdly, these spies have been introduced among us through the simple and easy process of enlisting as soldiers in the Union army — and evidently two of them have got sold at it, and been shipped off to the front; fourthly, there are assistant spies ' outside '— number indefinite; fifthly, Wicklow has very important matter which he is afraid to communicate by the ' present method '— will ' try the other.' That is the case, as it now stands. Shall we collar Wicklow and make him confess? Or shall we catch the person who removes the letters from the stable and make *him* tell? Or shall we keep still and find out more?"

We decided upon the last course. We judged that we did not need to proceed to summary measures now, since it was evident that the conspirators were likely to wait till those two light infantry companies were out of the way. We fortified Sterne with pretty ample powers, and told him to use his best endeavors to find out Wicklow's " other method " of communication. We meant to play a bold game; and to this end we proposed to keep the spies in an unsuspecting state as long as possible. So we ordered Sterne to return to the stable immediately, and, if he found the coast clear, to conceal Wicklow's letter where it was before, and leave it there for the conspirators to get.

The night closed down without further event. It was cold and dark and sleety, with a raw wind blowing; still I turned out of my warm bed several times during the night, and went the rounds in person, to see that all was right and that every sentry was on the alert. I always found them wide awake and watchful; evidently whispers of mysterious dangers had been floating about, and the doubling of the guards had been a kind of indorsement of those rumors. Once towards morning, I encountered Webb, breasting his way against the bitter wind, and learned then that he, also, had been the rounds several times to see that all was going right.

Next day's events hurried things up somewhat. Wicklow wrote another letter; Sterne preceded him to the stable and saw him deposit it; captured it as soon as Wicklow was out of the way, then slipped out and followed the little spy at a distance, with a detective in plain clothes at his own heels, for we thought it judicious to have the law's assistance handy in case of need. Wicklow went to the railway station, and waited around till the train from New York came in, then stood scanning the faces of the crowd as they poured out of the cars. Presently an aged gentleman, with green goggles and a cane, came limping along, stopped in Wicklow's neighborhood, and began to look about him expectantly. In an instant Wicklow darted forward, thrust an envelope into his hand, then glided away and disappeared in the throng. The next instant Sterne had snatched the letter; and as he hurried past the detective, he said: "Follow the old gentleman — don't lose sight of him." Then Sterne skurried out with the crowd, and came straight to the fort.

We sat with closed doors, and instructed the guard outside to allow no interruption.

First we opened the letter captured at the stable. It read as follows:

"HOLY ALLIANCE,— Found, in the usual gun, commands from the Master, left there last night, which set aside the instructions heretofore received from the subordinate quarter. Have left in the gun the usual indication that the commands reached the proper hand—"

Webb, interrupting: "Isn't the boy under constant surveillance now?"

I said yes; he had been under strict surveillance ever since the capturing of his former letter.

"Then how could he put anything into a gun, or take anything out of it, and not get caught?"

"Well," I said, "I don't like the look of that very well."

"I don't, either," said Webb. "It simply means that there are conspirators among the very sentinels. Without their connivance in some way or other, the thing couldn't have been done."

I sent for Rayburn, and ordered him to examine the batteries and see what he could find. The reading of the letter was then resumed:

"The new commands are peremptory, and require that the MMMM shall be FFFFF at 3 o'clock to-morrow morning. Two hundred will arrive, in small parties, by train and otherwise, from various directions, and will be at appointed place at right time. I will distribute the sign to-day. Success is apparently sure, though something must have got out, for the sentries have been doubled, and the chiefs went the rounds last night several times. W. W. comes from southerly to-day and will receive secret orders — by the other method. All six of you must be in 166 at sharp 2 A. M. You will find B. B. there, who will give you detailed instructions. Password same as last time, only reversed — put first syllable last and last syllable first. REMEMBER XXXX. Do not forget. Be of good heart; before the next sun rises you will be heroes; your fame will be permanent; you will have added a deathless page to history. AMEN."

"Thunder and Mars," said Webb, "but we are getting into mighty hot quarters, as I look at it!"

I said there was no question but that things were beginning to wear a most serious aspect.   Said I:

"A desperate enterprise is on foot, that is plain enough.   To-night is the time set for it — that, also, is plain.   The exact nature of the enterprise — I mean the manner of it — is hidden away under those blind bunches of M's and F's, but the end and aim, I judge, is the surprise and capture of the post.   We must move quick and sharp now.   I think nothing can be gained by continuing our clandestine policy as regards Wicklow.   We *must* know, and as soon as possible, too, where ' 166 ' is located, so that we can make a descent upon the gang there at 2 A. M.; and doubtless the quickest way to get that information will be to force it out of that boy.   But first of all, and before we make any important move, I must lay the facts before the War Department, and ask for plenary powers."

The dispatch was prepared in cipher to go over the wires; I read it, approved it, and sent it along.

We presently finished discussing the letter which was under consideration, and then opened the one which had been snatched from the lame gentleman.   It contained nothing but a couple of perfectly blank sheets of note paper!   It was a chilly check to our hot eagerness and expectancy.   We felt as blank as the paper, for a moment, and twice as foolish.   But it was for a moment only; for, of course, we immediately afterwards thought of "sympathetic ink."   We held the paper close to the fire and watched for the characters to come out, under the influence of the heat; but nothing appeared but some faint tracings, which we could make nothing of.   We then called in the surgeon, and sent him off with orders to apply every test he was acquainted with till he got the right one, and report the contents of the letter to me the instant he brought them to the surface. This check was a confounded annoyance, and we naturally chafed under the delay; for we had fully expected to get out of that letter some of the most important secrets of the plot.

Now appeared Sergeant Rayburn, and drew from his pocket a piece of twine string about a foot long, with three knots tied in it, and held it up.

" I got it out of a gun on the water-front," said he. " I took the tompions out of all the guns and examined close; this string was the only thing that was in any gun."

So this bit of string was Wicklow's " sign " to signify that the " Master's " commands had not miscarried. I ordered that every sentinel who had served near that gun during the past twenty-four hours be put in confinement at once and separately, and not allowed to communicate with any one without my privity and consent.

A telegram now came from the Secretary of War. It read as follows:

" Suspend *habeas corpus.* Put town under martial law. Make necessary arrests. Act with vigor and promptness. Keep the Department informed."

We were now in shape to go to work. I sent out and had the lame gentleman quietly arrested and as quietly brought into the fort; I placed him under guard, and forbade speech to him or from him. He was inclined to bluster at first, but he soon dropped that.

Next came word that Wicklow had been seen to give something to a couple of our new recruits; and that, as soon as his back was turned, these had been seized and confined. Upon each was found a small bit of paper, bearing these words and signs in pencil:

> EAGLE'S THIRD FLIGHT.
>
> REMEMBER XXXX.
>
> 166.

In accordance with instructions, I telegraphed to the Department, in cipher, the progress made, and also described the above ticket. We seemed to be in a strong enough position now to venture to throw off the mask as regarded Wicklow; so I sent for him. I also sent for and received back the letter written in sympathetic ink, the surgeon accompanying it with the information that thus far it had resisted his tests, but that there were others he could apply when I should be ready for him to do so.

Presently Wicklow entered. He had a somewhat worn and anxious look, but he was composed and easy, and if he suspected anything it did not appear in his face or manner. I allowed him to stand there a moment or two; then I said, pleasantly:

"My boy, why do you go to that old stable so much?"

He answered, with simple demeanor and without embarrassment:

"Well, I hardly know, sir; there isn't any particular reason, except that I like to be alone, and I amuse myself there."

"You amuse yourself there, do you?"

"Yes, sir," he replied, as innocently and simply as before.

"Is that all you do there?"

"Yes, sir," he said, looking up with childlike wonderment in his big, soft eyes.

"You are *sure ?*"

"Yes, sir, sure."

After a pause I said:

"Wicklow, why do you write so much?"

"I? I do not write much, sir."

"You don't?"

"No, sir. Oh, if you mean scribbling, I *do* scribble some, for amusement."

"What do you do with your scribblings?"

"Nothing, sir — throw them away."

"Never send them to anybody?"

"No, sir."

I suddenly thrust before him the letter to the "Colonel." He started slightly, but immediately composed himself. A slight tinge spread itself over his cheek.

"How came you to send *this* piece of scribbling, then?"

"I nev — never meant any harm, sir!"

"Never meant any harm! You betray the armament and condition of the post, and mean no harm by it?"

He hung his head and was silent.

"Come, speak up, and stop lying. Whom was this letter intended for?"

He showed signs of distress now; but quickly collected himself, and replied, in a tone of deep earnestness:

"I will tell you the truth, sir — the whole truth. The letter was never intended for anybody at all. I wrote it only to amuse myself. I see the error and foolishness of it now; but it is the only offense, sir, upon my honor."

"Ah, I am glad of that. It is dangerous to be writing such letters. I hope you are sure this is the only one you wrote?"

"Yes, sir, perfectly sure."

His hardihood was stupefying. He told that lie with as sincere a countenance as any creature ever wore. I waited a moment to soothe down my rising temper, and then said:

"Wicklow, jog your memory now, and see if you can help me with two or three little matters which I wish to inquire about."

"I will do my very best, sir."

"Then, to begin with — who is ' the Master?' "

It betrayed him into darting a startled glance at our faces, but that was all. He was serene again in a moment, and tranquilly answered:

"I do not know, sir."

"You do not know?"

"I do not know."

"You are *sure* you do not know?"

He tried hard to keep his eyes on mine, but the strain was too great; his chin sunk slowly towards his breast and he was silent; he stood there nervously fumbling with a button, an object to command one's pity, in spite of his base acts. Presently I broke the stillness with the question:

"Who are the ' Holy Alliance '?"

His body shook visibly, and he made a slight random gesture with his hands, which to me was like the appeal of a despairing creature for compassion. But he made no sound. He continued to stand with his face bent towards the ground. As we sat gazing at him, waiting for him to speak, we saw the big tears begin to roll down his cheeks. But he remained silent. After a little, I said:

"You must answer me, my boy, and you must tell me the truth. Who are the Holy Alliance?"

He wept on in silence. Presently I said, somewhat sharply:

"Answer the question!"

19A

He struggled to get command of his voice; and then, looking up appealingly, forced the words out between his sobs:

"Oh, have pity on me, sir! I cannot answer it, for I do not know."

"What!"

"Indeed, sir, I am telling the truth. I never have heard of the Holy Alliance till this moment. On my honor, sir, this is so."

"Good heavens! Look at this second letter of yours; there, do you see those words, '*Holy Alliance*'? What do you say now?"

He gazed up into my face with the hurt look of one upon whom a great wrong had been wrought, then said, feelingly:

"This is some cruel joke, sir; and how could they play it upon me, who have tried all I could to do right, and have never done harm to anybody? Some one has counterfeited my hand; I never wrote a line of this; I have never seen this letter before!"

"Oh, you unspeakable liar! Here, what do you say to *this?*"— and I snatched the sympathetic-ink letter from my pocket and thrust it before his eyes.

His face turned white! — as white as a dead person's. He wavered slightly in his tracks, and put his hand against the wall to steady himself. After a moment he asked, in so faint a voice that it was hardly audible:

"Have you — read it?"

Our faces must have answered the truth before my lips could get out a false "yes," for I distinctly saw the courage come back into that boy's eyes. I waited for him to say something, but he kept silent. So at last I said:

"Well, what have you to say as to the revelations in this letter?"

He answered, with perfect composure:

"Nothing, except that they are entirely harmless and innocent; they can hurt nobody."

I was in something of a corner now, as I couldn't disprove his assertion. I did not know exactly how to proceed. However, an idea came to my relief, and I said:

"You are sure you know nothing about the Master and the Holy Alliance, and did not write the letter which you say is a forgery?"

"Yes, sir — sure."

I slowly drew out the knotted twine string and held it up without speaking. He gazed at it indifferently, then looked at me inquiringly. My patience was sorely taxed. However, I kept my temper down, and said, in my usual voice:

"Wicklow, do you see this?"

"Yes, sir."

"What is it?"

"It seems to be a piece of string."

"*Seems?* It *is* a piece of string. Do you recognize it?"

"No, sir," he replied, as calmly as the words could be uttered.

His coolness was perfectly wonderful! I paused now for several seconds, in order that the silence might add impressiveness to what I was about to say; then I rose and laid my hand on his shoulder, and said, gravely:

"It will do you no good, poor boy, none in the world. This sign to the ' Master,' this knotted string, found in one of the guns on the water front —"

"Found *in* the gun! Oh, no, no, no! do not say *in* the gun, but in a crack in the tompion! — it *must* have been in the crack!" and down he went on his knees and clasped his hands and lifted up a face that was pitiful to see, so ashy it was, and wild with terror.

" No, it was *in* the gun."

" Oh, something has gone wrong! My God, I am lost!" and he sprang up and darted this way and that, dodging the hands that were put out to catch him, and doing his best to escape from the place. But of course escape was impossible. Then he flung himself on his knees again, crying with all his might, and clasped me around the legs; and so he clung to me and begged and pleaded, saying, " Oh, have pity on me! Oh, be merciful to me! Do not betray me; they would not spare my life a moment! Protect me, save me. I will confess everything!"

It took us some time to quiet him down and modify his fright, and get him into something like a rational frame of mind. Then I began to question him, he answering humbly, with downcast eyes, and from time to time swabbing away his constantly flowing tears:

" So you are at heart a rebel?"

" Yes, sir."

" And a spy?"

" Yes, sir."

" And have been acting under distinct orders from outside?"

" Yes, sir."

" Willingly?"

" Yes, sir."

" *Gladly*, perhaps?"

" Yes, sir; it would do no good to deny it. The South is my country; my heart is Southern, and it is all in her cause."

" Then the tale you told me of your wrongs and the persecution of your family was made up for the occasion?"

" They — they told me to say it, sir."

" And you would betray and destroy those who

pitied and sheltered you. Do you comprehend how base you are, you poor misguided thing?"

He replied with sobs only.

"Well, let that pass. To business. Who is the 'Colonel,' and where is he?"

He began to cry hard, and tried to beg off from answering. He said he would be killed if he told. I threatened to put him in the dark cell and lock him up if he did not come out with the information. At the same time I promised to protect him from all harm if he made a clean breast. For all answer, he closed his mouth firmly and put on a stubborn air which I could not bring him out of. At last I started with him; but a single glance into the dark cell converted him. He broke into a passion of weeping and supplicating, and declared he would tell everything.

So I brought him back, and he named the "Colonel," and described him particularly. Said he would be found at the principal hotel in the town, in citizen's dress. I had to threaten him again, before he would describe and name the "Master." Said the Master would be found at No. 15 Bond street, New York, passing under the name of R. F. Gaylord. I telegraphed name and description to the chief of police of the metropolis, and asked that Gaylord be arrested and held till I could send for him.

"Now," said I, "it seems that there are several of the conspirators 'outside,' presumably in New London. Name and describe them."

He named and described three men and two women — all stopping at the principal hotel. I sent out quietly, and had them and the "Colonel" arrested and confined in the fort.

"Next, I want to know all about your three fellow-conspirators who are here in the fort."

He was about to dodge me with a falsehood, I

19***

thought; but I produced the mysterious bits of paper which had been found upon two of them, and this had a salutary effect upon him. I said we had possession of two of the men, and he must point out the third. This frightened him badly, and he cried out:

" Oh, please don't make me; he would kill me on the spot!"

I said that that was all nonsense; I would have somebody near by to protect him, and, besides, the men should be assembled without arms. I ordered all the raw recruits to be mustered, and then the poor, trembling little wretch went out and stepped along down the line, trying to look as indifferent as possible. Finally he spoke a single word to one of the men, and before he had gone five steps the man was under arrest.

As soon as Wicklow was with us again, I had those three men brought in. I made one of them stand forward, and said:

" Now Wicklow, mind, not a shade's divergence from the exact truth. Who is this man, and what do you know about him?"

Being " in for it," he cast consequences aside, fastened his eyes on the man's face, and spoke straight along without hesitation — to the following effect:

" His real name is George Bristow. He is from New Orleans; was second mate of the coast-packet *Capitol* two years ago; is a desperate character, and has served two terms for manslaughter — one for killing a deck-hand named Hyde with a capstan bar, and one for killing a roustabout for refusing to heave the lead, which is no part of a roustabout's business. He is a spy, and was sent here by the Colonel to act in that capacity. He was third mate of the *St. Nicholas* when she blew up in the neighborhood of Memphis, in '58, and came near being lynched for robbing the dead and wounded while they were being taken ashore in an empty wood-boat.''

And so forth and so on — he gave the man's biography in full. When he had finished, I said to the man:

'' What have you to say to this?''

'' Barring your presence, sir, it is the infernalist lie that ever was spoke!''

I sent him back into confinement, and called the others forward in turn. Same result. The boy gave a detailed history of each, without ever hesitating for a word or a fact; but all I could get out of either rascal was the indignant assertion that it was all a lie. They would confess nothing. I returned them to captivity, and brought out the rest of my prisoners, one by one. Wicklow told all about them — what towns in the South they were from, and every detail of their connection with the conspiracy.

But they all denied his facts, and not one of them confessed a thing. The men raged, the women cried. According to their stories, they were all innocent people from out West, and loved the Union above all things in this world. I locked the gang up, in disgust, and fell to catechising Wicklow once more.

'' Where is No. 166, and who is B. B.?''

But *there* he was determined to draw the line. Neither coaxing nor threats had any effect upon him. Time was flying — it was necessary to institute sharp measures. So I tied him up a-tiptoe by the thumbs. As the pain increased, it wrung screams from him which were almost more than I could bear. But I held my ground, and pretty soon he shrieked out:

'' Oh, *please* let me down, and I will tell!''

'' No — you'll tell *before* I let you down.''

Every instant was agony to him now, so out it came:

8***

"No. 166, Eagle Hotel!"— naming a wretched tavern down by the water, a resort of common laborers, 'longshoremen, and less reputable folk.

So I released him, and then demanded to know the object of the conspiracy.

"To take the fort to-night," said he, doggedly and sobbing.

"Have I got all the chiefs of the conspiracy?"

"No. You've got all except those that are to meet at 166."

"What does 'Remember XXXX' mean?"

No reply.

"What is the password to No. 166?"

No reply.

"What do those bunches of letters mean —'FFFFF' and 'MMMM'? Answer! or you will catch it again."

"I never *will* answer! I will die first. Now do what you please."

"Think what you are saying, Wicklow. Is it final?"

He answered steadily, and without a quiver in his voice:

"It is final. As sure as I love my wronged country and hate everything this Northern sun shines on, I will die before I will reveal those things."

I tied him up by the thumbs again. When the agony was full upon him it was heart-breaking to hear the poor thing's shrieks, but we got nothing else out of him. To every question he screamed the same reply: "I can die, and I *will* die; but I will never tell."

Well, we had to give it up. We were convinced that he certainly would die rather than confess. So we took him down, and imprisoned him under strict guard.

Then for some hours we busied ourselves with sending telegrams to the War Department, and with making preparations for a descent upon No. 166.

It was stirring times, that black and bitter night.

Things had leaked out, and the whole garrison was on the alert. The sentinels were trebled, and nobody could move, outside or in, without being brought to a stand with a musket leveled at his head. However, Webb and I were less concerned now than we had previously been, because of the fact that the conspiracy must necessarily be in a pretty crippled condition, since so many of its principals were in our clutches.

I determined to be at No. 166 in good season, capture and gag B. B., and be on hand for the rest when they arrived. At about a quarter past one in the morning I crept out of the fortress with half a dozen stalwart and gamy U. S. regulars at my heels, and the boy Wicklow, with his hands tied behind him. I told him we were going to No. 166, and that if I found he had lied again and was misleading us, he would have to show us the right place or suffer the consequences.

We approached the tavern stealthily and reconnoitred. A light was burning in the small barroom, the rest of the house was dark. I tried the front door; it yielded, and we softly entered, closing the door behind us. Then we removed our shoes, and I led the way to the barroom. The German landlord sat there, asleep in his chair. I woke him gently, and told him to take off his boots and precede us, warning him at the same time to utter no sound. He obeyed without a murmur, but evidently he was badly frightened. I ordered him to lead the way to 166. We ascended two or three flights of stairs as softly as a file of cats; and then, having arrived near the farther end of a long hall, we came to a door through the glazed transom of which we could discern the glow of a dim light from within. The landlord felt for me in the dark and whispered me that that was 166. I tried the door — it was locked on the inside. I whispered an order to one of my biggest soldiers; we set our ample shoulders

to the door, and with one heave we burst it from its
hinges. I caught a half-glimpse of a figure in a bed —
saw its head dart towards the candle; out went the
light and we were in pitch darkness. With one big
bound I lit on that bed and pinned its occupant down
with my knees. My prisoner struggled fiercely, but I
got a grip on his throat with my left hand, and that
was a good assistance to my knees in holding him
down. Then straightway I snatched out my revolver,
cocked it, and laid the cold barrel warningly against his
cheek.

"Now somebody strike a light!" said I. "I've
got him safe."

It was done. The flame of the match burst up. I
looked at my captive, and, by George, it was a young
woman!

I let go and got off the bed, feeling pretty sheepish.
Everybody stared stupidly at his neighbor. Nobody
had any wit or sense left, so sudden and overwhelming
had been the surprise. The young woman began to
cry, and covered her face with the sheet. The landlord said, meekly:

"My daughter, she has been doing something that
is not right, *nicht wahr ?*"

"Your daughter? Is she your daughter?"

"Oh, yes, she is my daughter. She is just to-night
come home from Cincinnati a little bit sick."

"Confound it, that boy has lied again. This is not
the right 166; this is not B. B. Now, Wicklow, you
will find the correct 166 for us, or — hello! where is
that boy?"

Gone, as sure as guns! And, what is more, we
failed to find a trace of him. Here was an awful pre-
dicament. I cursed my stupidity in not tying him to
one of the men; but it was of no use to bother about
that now. What should I do in the present circum-

stances? — that was the question. That girl *might* be
B. B., after all. I did not believe it, but still it would
not answer to take unbelief for proof. So I finally
put my men in a vacant room across the hall from 166,
and told them to capture anybody and everybody that
approached the girl's room, and to keep the landlord
with them, and under strict watch, until further orders.
Then I hurried back to the fort to see if all was right
there yet.

Yes, all was right. And all remained right. I
stayed up all night to make sure of that. Nothing
happened. I was unspeakably glad to see the dawn
come again, and be able to telegraph the Department
that the Stars and Stripes still floated over Fort Trumbull.

An immense pressure was lifted from my breast.
Still I did not relax vigilance, of course, nor effort,
either; the case was too grave for that. I had up my
prisoners, one by one, and harried them by the hour,
trying to get them to confess, but it was a failure.
They only gnashed their teeth and tore their hair, and
revealed nothing.

About noon came tidings of my missing boy. He
had been seen on the road, tramping westward, some
eight miles out, at six in the morning. I started a
cavalry lieutenant and a private on his track at once.
They came in sight of him twenty miles out. He had
climbed a fence and was wearily dragging himself
across a slushy field towards a large old-fashioned
mansion in the edge of a village. They rode through
a bit of woods, made a detour, and closed upon the
house from the opposite side; then dismounted and
skurried into the kitchen. Nobody there. They
slipped into the next room, which was also unoccu-
pied; the door from that room into the front or sitting
room was open. They were about to step through it

when they heard a low voice; it was somebody praying. So they halted reverently, and the lieutenant put his head in and saw an old man and an old woman kneeling in a corner of that sitting-room. It was the old man that was praying, and just as he was finishing his prayer, the Wicklow boy opened the front door and stepped in. Both of those old people sprang at him and smothered him with embraces, shouting:

"Our boy! our darling! God be praised. The lost is found! He that was dead is alive again!"

Well, sir, what do you think! That young imp was born and reared on that homestead, and had never been five miles away from it in all his life till the fortnight before he loafed into my quarters and gulled me with that maudlin yarn of his! It's as true as gospel. That old man was his father — a learned old retired clergyman; and that old lady was his mother.

Let me throw in a word or two of explanation concerning that boy and his performances. It turned out that he was a ravenous devourer of dime novels and sensation-story papers — therefore, dark mysteries and gaudy heroisms were just in his line. Then he had read newspaper reports of the stealthy goings and comings of rebel spies in our midst, and of their lurid purposes and their two or three startling achievements, till his imagination was all aflame on that subject. His constant comrade for some months had been a Yankee youth of much tongue and lively fancy, who had served for a couple of years as "mud clerk" (that is, subordinate purser) on certain of the packet-boats plying between New Orleans and points two or three hundred miles up the Mississippi — hence his easy facility in handling the names and other details pertaining to that region. Now I had spent two or three months in that part of the country before the war; and I knew just enough about it to be easily taken in by that

boy, whereas a born Louisianian would probably have
caught him tripping before he had talked fifteen minutes. Do you know the reason he said he would rather
die than explain certain of his treasonable enigmas?
Simply because he *couldn't* explain them! — they had
no meaning; he had fired them out of his imagination
without forethought or afterthought; and so, upon
sudden call, he wasn't able to invent an explanation of
them. For instance, he couldn't reveal what was hidden in the " sympathetic ink " letter, for the ample
reason that there wasn't anything hidden in it; it was
blank paper only. He hadn't put anything into a gun,
and had never intended to — for his letters were all
written to imaginary persons, and when he hid one in
the stable he always removed the one he had put there
the day before; so he was not acquainted with that
knotted string, since he was seeing it for the first time
when I showed it to him; but as soon as I had let him
find out where it came from, he straightway adopted
it, in his romantic fashion, and got some fine effects
out of it. He invented Mr. " Gaylord "; there wasn't
any 15 Bond street, just then — it had been pulled
down three months before. He invented the " Colonel "; he invented the glib histories of those unfor-
tunates whom I captured and confronted with him; he
invented " B. B."; he even invented No. 166, one
may say, for he didn't know there *was* such a number
in the Eagle Hotel until we went there. He stood
ready to invent anybody or anything whenever it was
wanted. If I called for " outside " spies, he promptly
described strangers whom he had seen at the hotel, and
whose names he had happened to hear. Ah, he lived
in a gorgeous, mysterious, romantic world during those
few stirring days, and I think it was *real* to him, and
that he enjoyed it clear down to the bottom of his
heart.

But he made trouble enough for us, and just no end of humiliation. You see, on account of him we had fifteen or twenty people under arrest and confinement in the fort, with sentinels before their doors. A lot of the captives were soldiers and such, and to them I didn't have to apologize; but the rest were first-class citizens, from all over the country, and no amount of apologies was sufficient to satisfy them. They just fumed and raged and made no end of trouble! And those two ladies — one was an Ohio Congressman's wife, the other a Western bishop's sister — well, the scorn and ridicule and angry tears they poured out on me made up a keepsake that was likely to make me remember them for a considerable time — and I shall. That old lame gentleman with the goggles was a college president from Philadelphia, who had come up to attend his nephew's funeral. He had never seen young Wicklow before, of course. Well, he not only missed the funeral, and got jailed as a rebel spy, but Wicklow had stood up there in my quarters and coldly described him as a counterfeiter, nigger-trader, horse-thief, and firebug from the most notorious rascal-nest in Galveston; and this was a thing which that poor old gentleman couldn't seem to get over at all.

And the War Department! But, oh, my soul, let's draw the curtain over that part!

Note.— I showed my manuscript to the Major, and he said: "Your unfamiliarity with military matters has betrayed you into some little mistakes. Still, they are picturesque ones — let them go; military men will smile at them, the rest won't detect them. You have got the main facts of the history right, and have set them down just about as they occurred."— M. T.

MRS. McWILLIAMS AND THE LIGHTNING

WELL, sir — continued Mr. McWilliams, for this was not the beginning of his talk — the fear of lightning is one of the most distressing infirmities a human being can be afflicted with. It is mostly confined to women; but now and then you find it in a little dog, and sometimes in a man. It is a particularly distressing infirmity, for the reason that it takes the sand out of a person to an extent which no other fear can, and it can't be *reasoned* with, and neither can it be shamed out of a person. A woman who could face the very devil himself — or a mouse — loses her grip and goes all to pieces in front of a flash of lightning. Her fright is something pitiful to see.

Well, as I was telling you, I woke up, with that smothered and unlocatable cry of " Mortimer! Mortimer!" wailing in my ears; and as soon as I could scrape my faculties together I reached over in the dark and then said:

" Evangeline, is that you calling? What is the matter? Where are you?"

" Shut up in the boot-closet. You ought to be ashamed to lie there and sleep so, and such an awful storm going on."

" Why, how *can* one be ashamed when he is asleep? It is unreasonable; a man *can't* be ashamed when he is asleep, Evangeline."

" You never try, Mortimer — you know very well you never try."

I caught the sound of muffled sobs.

That sound smote dead the sharp speech that was on my lips, and I changed it to —

"I'm sorry, dear — I'm truly sorry. I never meant to act so. Come back and —"

"Mortimer!"

"Heavens! what is the matter, my love?"

"Do you mean to say you are in that bed yet?"

"Why, of course."

"Come out of it instantly. I should think you would take some *little* care of your life, for *my* sake and the children's, if you will not for your own."

"But, my love —"

"Don't talk to me, Mortimer. You *know* there is no place so dangerous as a bed, in such a thunder-storm as this — all the books say that; yet there you would lie, and deliberately throw away your life — for goodness knows what, unless for the sake of arguing, and arguing, and —"

"But, confound it, Evangeline, I'm *not* in the bed *now*. I'm —"

[Sentence interrupted by a sudden glare of lightning, followed by a terrified little scream from Mrs. Mc-Williams and a tremendous blast of thunder.]

"There! You see the result. O, Mortimer, how *can* you be so profligate as to swear at such a time as this?"

"I *didn't* swear. And that *wasn't* a result of it, anyway. It would have come, just the same, if I hadn't said a word; and you know very well, Evan-geline — at least, you ought to know — that when the atmosphere is charged with electricity —"

"Oh, yes; now argue it, and argue it, and argue it! — I don't see how you can act so, when you *know* there is not a lightning-rod on the place, and your poor wife and children are absolutely at the mercy of

Providence.   What *are* you doing? — lighting a match at such a time as this!   Are you stark mad?''

" Hang it, woman, where's the harm?   The place is as dark as the inside of an infidel, and —''

" Put it out! put it out instantly!   Are you determined to sacrifice us all?   You *know* there is nothing attracts lightning like a light.   [*Fzt! — crash! boom — boloom-boom-boom!*]   Oh, just hear it!   Now you see what you've done!''

" No, I *don't* see what I've done.   A match may attract lightning, for all I know, but it don't *cause* lightning — I'll go odds on that.   And it didn't attract it worth a cent this time; for if that shot was leveled at my match, it was blessed poor markmanship — about an average of none out of a possible million, I should say.   Why, at Dollymount such marksmanship as that —''

" For shame, Mortimer!   Here we are standing right in the very presence of death, and yet in so solemn a moment you are capable of using such language as that.   If you have no desire to — Mortimer!''

" Well?''

" Did you say your prayers to-night?''

" I — I — meant to, but I got to trying to cipher out how much twelve times thirteen is, and —''

[*Fzt! — boom-berroom-boom! bumble-umble bang-*SMASH!]

" Oh, we are lost, beyond all help!   How *could* you neglect such a thing at such a time as this?''

" But it *wasn't* ' such a time as this.'   There wasn't a cloud in the sky.   How could *I* know there was going to be all this rumpus and pow-wow about a little slip like that?   And I don't think it's just fair for you to make so much out of it, anyway, seeing it happens so seldom; I haven't missed before since I brought on that earthquake, four years ago.''

20A

" MORTIMER! How you talk! Have you forgotten the yellow-fever?"

" My dear, you are always throwing up the yellow-fever to me, and I think it is perfectly unreasonable. You can't even send a telegraphic message as far as Memphis without relays, so how is a little devotional slip of mine going to carry so far? I'll *stand* the earthquake, because it was in the neighborhood; but I'll be hanged if I'm going to be responsible for every blamed —"

[*Fzt!* — BOOM *beroom*-boom! boom. — BANG!]

" Oh, dear, dear, dear! I *know* it struck something, Mortimer. We never shall see the light of another day; and if it will do you any good to remember, when we are gone, that your dreadful language — *Mortimer!*"

" WELL! What now?"

" Your voice sounds as if — Mortimer, are you actually standing in front of that open fireplace?"

" That is the very crime I am committing."

" Get away from it this moment! You do seem determined to bring destruction on us all. Don't you *know* that there is no better conductor for lightning than an open chimney? *Now* where have you got to?"

" I'm here by the window."

" Oh, for pity's sake! have you lost your mind? Clear out from there, this moment! The very children in arms know it is fatal to stand near a window in a thunder-storm. Dear, dear, I know I shall never see the light of another day! Mortimer!"

" Yes."

" What is that rustling?"

" It's me."

" What are you doing?"

" Trying to find the upper end of my pantaloons."

" Quick! throw those things away! I do believe

you would deliberately put on those clothes at such a time as this; yet you know perfectly well that *all* authorities agree that woolen stuffs attract lightning. Oh, dear, dear, it isn't sufficient that one's life must be in peril from natural causes, but you must do everything you can possibly think of to augment the danger. Oh, *don't* sing! What *can* you be thinking of?"

" Now where's the harm in it?"

" Mortimer, if I have told you once, I have told you a hundred times, that singing causes vibrations in the atmosphere which interrupt the flow of the electric fluid, and — What on *earth* are you opening that door for?"

" Goodness gracious, woman, is there any harm in *that?*"

" *Harm?* There's *death* in it. Anybody that has given this subject any attention knows that to create a draught is to invite the lightning. You haven't half shut it; shut it *tight* — and do hurry, or we are all destroyed. Oh, it is an awful thing to be shut up with a lunatic at such a time as this. Mortimer, what *are* you doing?"

" Nothing. Just turning on the water. This room is smothering hot and close. I want to bathe my face and hands."

" You have certainly parted with the remnant of your mind! Where lightning strikes any other substance once, it strikes water fifty times. Do turn it off. Oh, dear, I am sure that nothing in this world can save us. It does seem to me that — Mortimer, what was that?"

" It was a da — it was a picture. Knocked it down."

" Then you are close to the wall! I never heard of such imprudence! Don't you *know* that there's no better conductor for lightning than a wall? Come away from there! And you came as near as anything to swearing, too. Oh, how can you be so desperately wicked, and your family in such peril? Mortimer, did you order a feather bed, as I asked you to do?"

"No. Forgot it."

"Forgot it! It may cost you your life. If you had a feather bed now, and could spread it in the middle of the room and lie on it, you would be perfectly safe. Come in here — come quick, before you have a chance to commit any more frantic indiscretions."

I tried, but the little closet would not hold us both with the door shut, unless we could be content to smother. I gasped awhile, then forced my way out. My wife called out:

"Mortimer, something *must* be done for your preservation. Give me that German book that is on the end of the mantel-piece, and a candle; but don't light it; give me a match; I will light it in here. That book has some directions in it."

I got the book — at cost of a vase and some other brittle things; and the madam shut herself up with her candle. I had a moment's peace; then she called out:

"Mortimer, what was that?"

"Nothing but the cat."

"The cat! Oh, destruction! Catch her, and shut her up in the washstand. Do be quick, love; cats are *full* of electricity. I just know my hair will turn white with this night's awful perils."

I heard the muffled sobbings again. But for that, I should not have moved hand or foot in such a wild enterprise in the dark.

However, I went at my task — over chairs, and against all sorts of obstructions, all of them hard ones, too, and most of them with sharp edges — and at last I got kitty cooped up in the commode, at an expense of over four hundred dollars in broken furniture and shins. Then these muffled words came from the closet:

"It says the safest thing is to stand on a chair in the middle of the room, Mortimer; and the legs of the chair must be insulated with non-conductors. That is, you must set the legs of the chair in glass tumblers. [*Fzt ! — boom — bang ! — smash !*] Oh, hear that! Do hurry, Mortimer, before you are struck."

I managed to find and secure the tumblers. I got the last four — broke all the rest. I insulated the chair legs, and called for further instructions.

"Mortimer, it says, 'Während eines Gewitters entferne man Metalle, wie z. B., Ringe, Uhren, Schlüssel, etc., von sich und halte sich auch nicht an solchen Stellen auf, wo viele Metalle bei einander liegen, oder mit andern Körpern verbunden sind, wie an Herden, Oefen, Eisengittern u. dgl.' What does that mean, Mortimer? Does it mean that you must keep metals *about* you, or keep them *away* from you?"

"Well, I hardly know. It appears to be a little mixed. All German advice is more or less mixed. However, I think that that sentence is mostly in the dative case, with a little genitive and accusative sifted in, here and there, for luck; so I reckon it means that you must keep some metals *about* you."

"Yes, that must be it. It stands to reason that it is. They are in the nature of lightning-rods, you know. Put on your fireman's helmet, Mortimer; that is mostly metal."

I got it, and put it on — a very heavy and clumsy and uncomfortable thing on a hot night in a close room. Even my nightdress seemed to be more clothing than I strictly needed.

"Mortimer, I think your middle ought to be protected. Won't you buckle on your militia saber, please?"

20***

I complied.

" Now, Mortimer, you ought to have some way to protect your feet.   Do please put on your spurs."

I did it — in silence — and kept my temper as well as I could.

" Mortimer, it says, ' Das Gewitter läuten ist sehr gefährlich, weil die Glocke selbst, sowie der durch das Läuten veranlasste Luftzug und die Höhe des Thurmes den Blitz anziehen könnten.'   Mortimer, does that mean that it is dangerous not to ring the church bells during a thunder-storm?"

" Yes, it seems to mean that — if that is the past participle of the nominative case singular, and I reckon it is.   Yes, I think it means that on account of the height of the church tower and the absence of *Luftzug* it would be very dangerous (*sehr gefährlich*) not to ring the bells in time of a storm; and moreover, don't you see, the very wording —"

" Never mind that, Mortimer; don't waste the precious time in talk.   Get the large dinner-bell; it is right there in the hall.   Quick, Mortimer, dear; we are almost safe.   Oh, dear, I do believe we are going to be saved, at last!"

Our little summer establishment stands on top of a high range of hills, overlooking a valley.   Several farm-houses are in our neighborhood — the nearest some three or four hundred yards away.

When I, mounted on the chair, had been clanging that dreadful bell a matter of seven or eight minutes, our shutters were suddenly torn open from without, and a brilliant bull's-eye lantern was thrust in at the window, followed by a hoarse inquiry:

" What in the nation is the matter here?"

The window was full of men's heads, and the heads were full of eyes that stared wildly at my nightdress and my warlike accoutrements.

"WHAT IS THE MATTER HERE?"

I dropped the bell, skipped down from the chair in confusion, and said:

"There is nothing the matter, friends — only a little discomfort on account of the thunder-storm. I was trying to keep off the lightning."

"Thunder-storm? Lightning? Why, Mr. McWilliams, have you lost your mind? It is a beautiful starlight night; there has been no storm."

I looked out, and I was so astonished I could hardly speak for a while. Then I said:

"I do not understand this. We distinctly saw the glow of the flashes through the curtains and shutters, and heard the thunder."

One after another of those people lay down on the ground to laugh — and two of them died. One of the survivors remarked:

"Pity you didn't think to open your blinds and look over to the top of the high hill yonder. What you heard was cannon; what you saw was the flash. You see, the telegraph brought some news, just at midnight; Garfield's nominated — and that's what's the matter!"

Yes, Mr. Twain, as I was saying in the beginning (said Mr. McWilliams), the rules for preserving people against lightning are so excellent and so innumerable that the most incomprehensible thing in the world to me is how anybody ever manages to get struck.

So saying, he gathered up his satchel and umbrella, and departed; for the train had reached his town.

MEISTERSCHAFT: IN THREE ACTS*

DRAMATIS PERSONÆ:

MR. STEPHENSON.   MARGARET STEPHENSON.
GEORGE FRANKLIN.   ANNIE STEPHENSON.
WILLIAM JACKSON.   MRS. BLUMENTHAL, the Wirthin.
          GRETCHEN, Kellnerin.

ACT I.

SCENE I.

Scene of the play, the parlor of a small private dwelling in a village.

(Margaret discovered crocheting — has a pamphlet.)

MARGARET. (*Solus.*) Dear, dear! it's dreary enough, to have to study this impossible German tongue: to be exiled from home and all human society except a body's sister in order to do it, is just simply abscheulich. Here's only three weeks of the three

---

* EXPLANATORY.   I regard the idea of this play as a valuable invention. I call it the Patent Universally-Applicable Automatically-Adjustable Language Drama.   This indicates that it is adjustable to any tongue, and performable in any tongue.   The English portions of the play are to remain just as they are, permanently; but you change the foreign portions to any language you please, at will.   Do you see?   You at once have the same old play in a new tongue.   And you can keep on changing it from language to language, until your private theatrical pupils have become glib and at

(308)

months gone and it seems like three years. I don't
believe I can live through it, and I'm sure Annie can't.
(*Refers to her book, and rattles through, several times,
like one memorizing :*) Entschuldigen Sie, mein Herr,
können Sie mir vielleicht sagen, um wie viel Uhr der
erste Zug nach Dresden abgeht? (*Makes mistakes and
corrects them.*) I just hate Meisterschaft! We may
see people; we can have society; yes, on condition
that the conversation shall be in German, and in German only — every single word of it! Very kind — oh,
very! when neither Annie nor I can put two words
together, except as they are put together for us in

---

home in the speech of all nations. *Zum Beispiel*, suppose we wish to
adjust the play to the French tongue. First, we give Mrs. Blumenthal and
Gretchen French names. Next, we knock the German Meisterschaft
sentences out of the first scene, and replace them with sentences from the
French Meisterschaft — like this, for instance: "Je voudrais faire des
emplettes ce matin; voulez-vous avoir l'obligeance de venir avec moi chez
le tailleur français?" And so on. Wherever you find German, replace it
with French, leaving the English parts undisturbed. When you come to
the long conversation in the second act, turn to any pamphlet of your
French Meisterschaft, and shovel in as much French talk on *any* subject as
will fill up the gaps left by the expunged German. Example — page 423,
French Meisterschaft:

> On dirait qu'il va faire chaud.
> J'ai chaud.
> J'ai extrêmement chaud.
> Ah! qu'il fait chaud!
> Il fait une chaleur étouffante!
> L'air est brûlant.
> Je meurs de chaleur.
> Il est presque impossible de supporter la chaleur.
> Cela vous fait transpirer.
> Mettons nous à l'ombre.
> Il fait du vent.
> Il fait un vent froid.
> Il fait un temps très-agréable pour se promener aujourd'hui.

And so on, all the way through. It is very easy to adjust the play to
any desired language. Anybody can do it.]

Meisterschaft or that idiotic Ollendorff! (*Refers to book, and memorizes: Mein Bruder hat Ihren Herrn Vater nicht gesehen, als er gestern in dem Laden des deutschen Kaufmannes war.*) Yes, we can have society, provided we talk German. What would such a conversation be like! If you should stick to Meisterschaft, it would change the subject every two minutes; and if you stuck to Ollendorff, it would be all about your sister's mother's good stocking of thread, or your grandfather's aunt's good hammer of the carpenter, and who's got it, and there an end. You couldn't keep up your interest in such topics. (*Memorizing: Wenn irgend möglich — möchte ich noch heute Vormittag dort ankommen, da es mir sehr daran gelegen ist, einen meiner Geschäftsfreunde zu treffen.*) My mind is made up to one thing: I will be an exile, in spirit and in truth; I will see no one during these three months. Father is very ingenious — oh, very! thinks he is, anyway. Thinks he has invented a way to *force* us to learn to speak German. He is a dear good soul, and all that; but invention isn't his fash'. He will see. (*With eloquent energy.*) Why, nothing in the world shall — Bitte, können Sie mir vielleicht sagen, ob Herr Schmidt mit diesem Zuge angekommen ist? Oh, dear, dear George — three weeks! It seems a whole century since I saw him. I wonder if he suspects that I — that I — care for him — j-just a wee, wee bit? I believe he does. And I believe Will suspects that Annie cares for *him* a little, that I do. And I know perfectly well that they care for *us.* They agree with all our opinions, no matter what they are; and if they have a prejudice, they change it, as soon as they see how foolish it is. Dear George! at first he just couldn't abide cats; but now, why now he's just all for cats; he fairly welters in cats. I never saw such a reform. And it's just so with *all* his principles: he hasn't got

one that he had before.   Ah, if all men were like him,
this world would — (*Memorizing: Im Gegentheil,
mein Herr, dieser Stoff ist sehr billig.   Bitte, sehen Sie
sich nur die Qualität an.*)   Yes, and what did *they* go
to studying German for, if it wasn't an inspiration of
the highest and purest sympathy?   Any other explanation is nonsense — why, they'd as soon have thought
of studying American history.   (*Turns her back, buries
herself in her pamphlet, first memorizing aloud, until
Annie enters, then to herself, rocking to and fro, and
rapidly moving her lips, without uttering a sound.*)

(Enter Annie, absorbed in her pamphlet — does not at first see Margaret.)

ANNIE.   (*Memorizing: Er liess mich gestern früh
rufen, und sagte mir dass er einen sehr unangenehmen
Brief von Ihrem Lehrer erhalten hatte.   Repeats twice
aloud, then to herself, briskly moving her lips.*)

M. (*Still not seeing her sister.*)   Wie geht es Ihrem
Herrn Schwiegervater?   Es freut mich sehr dass Ihre
Frau Mutter wieder wohl ist.   (*Repeats.   Then mouths
in silence.*)

A. (*Repeats her sentence a couple of times aloud;
then looks up, working her lips, and discovers Margaret.*)
Oh, you here?   (*Running to her.*)   Oh, lovey-dovey,
dovey-lovey, I've got the gr-reatest news!   Guess,
guess, guess!   You'll never guess in a hundred thousand million years — and more!

M. Oh, tell me, tell me, dearie; don't keep me in
agony.

A. Well, I will.   What — do — you think?   *They're*
here!

M. Wh-a-t!   Who?   When?   Which?   Speak!

A. Will and George!

M. Annie Alexandra Victoria Stephenson, what *do*
you mean?

A. As sure as guns!

M. (*Spasmodically unarming and kissing her.*) Sh'!
don't use such language.   Oh, darling, say it again!

A. As sure as guns!

M. I don't mean that!   Tell me again, that —

A. (*Springing up and waltzing about the room.*)
They're here — in this very village — to learn German
— for three months!   Es sollte mich sehr freuen wenn
Sie —

M. (*Joining in the dance.*)   Oh, it's just too lovely
for anything!   (*Unconsciously memorizing:*) Es wäre
mir lieb wenn Sie morgen mit mir in die Kirche gehen
könnten, aber ich kann selbst nicht gehen, weil ich
Sonntags gewöhnlich krank bin.   Juckhe!

A. (*Finishing some unconscious memorizing.*) —
morgen Mittag bei mir speisen könnten.   Juckhe!   Sit
down and I'll tell you all I've heard.   (*They sit.*)
They're here, and under that same odious law that
fetters us — our tongues, I mean; the metaphor's
faulty, but no matter.   They can go out, and see
people, only on condition that they hear and speak
German, and German only.

M. Isn't — that — too lovely!

A. And they're coming to see us!

M. Darling!   (*Kissing her.*)   But are you sure?

A. Sure as guns — Gatling guns!

M. 'Sh! don't, child, it's schrecklich!   Darling —
you aren't mistaken?

A. As sure as g — batteries!

(They jump up and dance a moment — then —)

M. (*With distress.*)   But, Annie dear! — *we* can't
talk German — and neither can they!

A. (*Sorrowfully.*)   I didn't think of that.

M. How cruel it is!   What can we do?

A. (*After a reflective pause, resolutely.*)   Margaret
— we've *got* to.

M. Got to what?

A. Speak German.

M. Why, how, child?

A. (*Contemplating her pamphlet with earnestness.*)
I can tell you one thing. Just give me the blessed
privilege: just hinsetzen Will Jackson here in front of
me, and I'll talk German to him as long as this Meisterschaft holds out to burn.

M. (*Joyously.*) Oh, what an elegant idea! You
certainly have got a mind that's a mine of resources,
if ever anybody had one.

A. I'll skin this Meisterschaft to the last sentence in
it!

M. (*With a happy idea.*) Why, Annie, it's the
greatest thing in the world. I've been all this time
struggling and despairing over these few little Meisterschaft primers; but as sure as you live, I'll have the
whole fifteen by heart before this time day after to-
morrow. See if I don't.

A. And so will I; and I'll trowel in a layer of
Ollendorff mush between every couple of courses of
Meisterschaft bricks. Juckhe!

M. Hoch! hoch! hoch!

A. Stoss an!

M. Juckhe! Wir werden gleich gute deutsche
Schülerinnen werden! Juck —

A. — he!

M. Annie, when are they coming to see us? To-
night?

A. No.

M. No? Why not? When are they coming? What
are they waiting for? The idea! I hever heard of
such a thing! What do you —

A. (*Breaking in.*) Wait, wait, wait! give a body a
chance. They have their reasons.

M. Reason? What reasons?

A. Well, now, when you stop and think, they're royal good ones. They've got to talk German when they come, haven't they? Of course. Well, they don't *know* any German but Wie befinden Sie sich, and Haben Sie gut geschlafen, and Vater unser, and Ich trinke lieber Bier als Wasser, and a few little parlor things like that; but when it comes to *talking*, why they don't know a hundred and fifty German words, put them all together.

M. Oh, I see.

A. So they're going neither to eat, sleep, smoke, nor speak the truth till they've crammed home the whole fifteen Meisterschafts auswendig!

M. Noble hearts!

A. They're given themselves till day after to-morrow, half-past 7 P. M., and then they'll arrive here loaded.

M. Oh, how lovely, how gorgeous, how beautiful! Some think this world is made of mud; I think it's made of rainbows. (*Memorizing.*) Wenn irgend möglich, so möchte ich noch heute Vormittag dort ankommen, da es mir sehr daran gelegen ist — Annie, I can learn it just like nothing!

A. So can I. Meisterschaft's mere fun — I don't see how it ever could have seemed difficult. Come! We can't be disturbed here; let's give orders that we don't want anything to eat for two days; and are absent to friends, dead to strangers, and not at home even to nougat peddlers —

M. Schön! and we'll lock ourselves into our rooms, and at the end of two days, whosoever may ask us a Meisterschaft question shall get a Meisterschaft answer — and hot from the bat!

BOTH. (*Reciting in unison.*) Ich habe einen Hut für meinen Sohn, ein Paar Handschuhe für meinen Bruder, und einen Kamm für mich selbst gekauft.

(Exeunt.)

(*Enter Mrs. Blumenthal, the Wirthin.*)

WIRTHIN. (*Solus.*) Ach, die armen Mädchen, sie hassen die deutsche Sprache, drum ist es ganz und gar unmöglich dass sie sie je lernen können. Es bricht mir ja mein Herz ihre Kummer über die Studien anzusehen...... Warum haben sie den Entchluss gefasst in ihren Zimmern ein Paar Tage zu bleiben?...... Ja — gewiss — das versteht sich; sie sind entmuthigt — arme Kinder!

(*A knock at the door.*) Herein!

(*Enter Gretchen with card.*)

GR. Er ist schon wieder da, und sagt dass er nur *Sie* sehen will. (*Hands the card.*) Auch —

WIRTHIN. Gott im Himmel — der Vater der Mädchen! (*Puts the card in her pocket.*) Er wünscht die *Töchter* nicht zu treffen? Ganz recht; also, Du schweigst.

GR. Zu Befehl.

WIRTHIN. Lass ihn hereinkommen.

GR. Ja, Frau Wirthin!

(*Exit Gretchen.*)

WIRTHIN. (*Solus.*) Ah — jetzt muss ich ihm die Wahrheit offenbaren.

(*Enter Mr. Stephenson.*)

STEPHENSON. Good morning, Mrs. Blumenthal — keep your seat, keep your seat, please. I'm only here for a moment — merely to get your report, you know. (*Seating himself.*) Don't want to see the girls — poor things, they'd want to go home with me. I'm afraid I couldn't have the heart to say no. How's the German getting along?

WIRTHIN. N-not very well; I was afraid you would ask me that. You see, they hate it, they don't take the least interest in it, and there isn't anything to incite them to an interest, you see. And so they can't talk at all.

S. M-m. That's bad. I had an idea that they'd get lonesome, and have to seek society; and then, of course, my plan would work, considering the cast-iron conditions of it.

WIRTHIN. But it hasn't so far. I've thrown nice company in their way — I've done my very best, in every way I could think of — but it's no use; they won't go out, and they won't receive anybody. And a body can't blame them; they'd be tongue-tied — couldn't do anything with a German conversation. Now, when I started to learn German — such poor German as I know — the case was very different; my intended was a German. I was to live among Germans the rest of my life; and so I *had* to learn. Why, bless my heart! I nearly *lost* the man the first time he asked me — I thought he was talking about the measles. They were very prevalent at the time. Told him I didn't want any in mine. But I found out the mistake, and I was fixed for him next time......Oh, yes, Mr. Stephenson, a sweetheart's a prime incentive!

S. (*Aside.*) Good soul! she doesn't suspect that my plan is a double scheme — includes a speaking knowledge of German, which I am bound they shall have, and the keeping them away from those two young fellows — though if I had known that those boys were going off for a year's foreign travel, I — however, the girls would never learn that language at home; they're here, and I won't relent — they've got to stick the three months out. (*Aloud.*) So they are making poor progress? Now tell me — will they learn it — after a sort of fashion, I mean — in three months?"

WIRTHIN. Well, now, I'll tell you the only chance I see. Do what I will, they won't answer my German with anything but English; if that goes on, they'll stand stock still. Now I'm willing to do this: I'll straighten everything up, get matters in smooth running order, and day after to-morrow I'll go to bed sick, and stay sick three weeks.

S. Good! You are an angel! I see your idea. The servant girl —

WIRTHIN. That's it; that's my project. She doesn't know a word of English. And Gretchen's a real good soul, and can talk the slates off a roof. Her tongue's just a flutter-mill. I'll keep my room — just ailing a little — and they'll never see my face except when they pay their little duty-visits to me, and then I'll say English disorders my mind. They'll be shut up with Gretchen's windmill, and she'll just grind them to powder. Oh, *they'll* get a start in the language — sort of a one, sure's you live. You come back in three weeks.

S. Bless you, my Retterin! I'll be here to the day! Get ye to your sick room — you shall have treble pay. (*Looking at watch.*) Good! I can just catch my train. Leben Sie wohl!

(Exit.)

WIRTHIN. Leben Sie wohl! mein Herr!

ACT II.

SCENE I.

Time, a couple of days later. The girls discovered with their work and primers.

ANNIE. Was felt der Wirthin?

MARGARET. Das weiss ich nicht. Sie ist schon vor zwei Tagen ins Bett gegangen —

A. My! how fliessend you speak!

M. Danke schön — und sagte dass sie nicht wohl sei.

A. Good? Oh, no, I don't mean that! no — only lucky for *us* — glücklich, you know I mean because it'll be so much nicer to have them all to ourselves.

M. Oh, natürlich! Ja! Dass ziehe ich durchaus vor. Do you believe your Meisterschaft will stay with you, Annie?

A. Well, I know it *is* with me — every last sentence of it; and a couple of hods of Ollendorff, too, for emergencies. Maybe they'll refuse to deliver — right off — at first, you know — der Verlegenheit wegen — aber ich will sie später herausholen — when I get my hand in — und vergisst Du das nicht!

M. Sei nicht grob, Liebste. What shall we talk about first — when they come?

A. Well — let me see. There's shopping — and — all that about the trains, you know — and going to church — and — buying tickets to London, and Berlin, and all around — and all that subjunctive stuff about the battle in Afghanistan, and where the American was said to be born, and so on — and — and ah — oh, there's so *many* things — I don't think a body can choose beforehand, because you know the circumstances and the atmosphere always have so much to do in directing a conversation, especially a German conversation, which is only a kind of an insurrection, anyway. I believe it's best to just depend on Prov — (*Glancing at watch, and gasping.*) — half-past — seven!

M. Oh, dear, I'm all of a tremble! Let's get something ready, Annie!

(*Both fall nervously to reciting*) : Entschuldigen Sie, mein Herr, können Sie mir vielleicht sagen wie ich nach dem norddeutschen Bahnhof gehe? (*They repeat it several times, losing their grip and mixing it all up.*)

(A knock.)

BOTH. Herein! Oh, dear! O der heilige —

(*Enter Gretchen.*)

GRETCHEN (*Ruffled and indignant*). Entschuldigen Sie, meine gnädigsten Fräulein, es sind zwei junge rasende Herren draussen, die herein wollen, aber ich habe ihnen geschworen dass — (*Handing the cards.*)

M. Du liebe Zeit, they're here! And of course down goes my back hair! Stay and receive them, dear, while I — (*Leaving.*)

A. I — alone? I won't! I'll go with you! (*To* GR.) Lassen Sie die Herren näher treten; und sagen Sie ihnen dass wir gleich zurückkommen werden. (*Exit.*)

GR. (*Solus.*) Was! Sie freuen sich darüber? Und ich sollte wirklich diese Blödsinnigen, dies grobe Rindvieh hereinlassen? In den hülflosen Umständen meiner gnädigen jungen Damen? — Unsinn! (*Pause — thinking.*) Wohlan! Ich werde sie mal beschützen! Sollte man nicht glauben, dass sie einen Sparren zu viel hätten? (*Tapping her skull significantly.*) Was sie mir doch Alles gesagt haben! Der Eine: "Guten Morgen! wie geht es Ihrem Herrn Schwiegervater?" Du liebe Zeit! Wie sollte ich einen Schwiegervater haben können! Und der Andere: "Es thut mir sehr leid dass Ihrer Herr Vater meinen Bruder nicht gesehen. hat, als er doch gestern in dem Laden des deutschen Kaufmannes war!" Potztausendhimmelsdonnerwetter! Oh, ich war ganz rasend! Wie ich aber rief: "Meine Herren, ich kenne Sie nicht, und Sie kennen meinen Vater nicht, wissen Sie, denn er ist schon lange durchgebrannt, und geht nicht beim Tage in einen Laden hinein, wissen Sie — und ich habe keinen Schwiegervater, Gott sei Dank, werde auch nie einen kriegen, werde ueberhaupt, wissen Sie, ein solches Ding nie haben, nie dulden, nie ausstehen: warum greifen Sie ein Mädchen an, das nur Unschuld kennt, das Ihnen nie Etwas zu Leide gethan hat?'' Dann haben sie sich beide die Finger in die Ohren gesteckt und gebetet: '' Allmächtiger Gott! Erbarme Dich unser!'' (*Pause.*) Nun, ich werde schon diesen Schurken Einlass gönnen, aber ich werde ein Auge mit ihnen haben, damit sie sich nicht wie reine Teufel geberden sollen.

(*Exit, grumbling and shaking her head.*)

(Enter William and George.)

W. My land, what a girl! and what an incredible gift of gabble! — kind of patent climate-proof compensation-balance self-acting automatic Meisterschaft — touch her button, and br-r-r! away she goes!

GEO. Never heard anything like it; tongue journaled on ball-bearings! I wonder what she said; seemed to be swearing, mainly.

W. (*After mumbling Meisterschaft a while.*) Look here, George, this is awful — come to think — this project: *we* can't talk this frantic language.

GEO. I know it, Will, and it *is* awful; but I can't live without seeing Margaret — I've endured it as long as I can. I should die if I tried to hold out longer — and even German is preferable to death.

W. (*Hesitatingly.*) Well, I don't know; it's a matter of opinion.

GEO. (*Irritably.*) It isn't a matter of opinion, either. German *is* preferable to death.

W. (*Reflectively.*) Well, I don't know — the problem is so sudden — but I think you may be right: some kinds of death. It is more than likely that a slow, lingering — well, now, there in Canada in the early times a couple of centuries ago, the Indians would take a missionary and skin him, and get some hot ashes and boiling water and one thing and another, and by and by that missionary — well, yes, I can see that, by and by, talking German could be a pleasant change for him.

GEO. Why, of course. Das versteht sich; but *you* have to always think a thing out, or you're not satisfied. But let's not go to bothering about thinking out this present business; we're here, we're in for it; you are as moribund to see Annie as I am to see Margaret; you know the terms: we've got to speak German. Now stop your mooning and get at your Meisterschaft; we've got nothing else in the world.

W. Do you think that'll see us through?

GEO. Why it's *got* to. Suppose we wandered out of it and took a chance at the language on our own responsibility, where the nation would we be? Up a stump, that's where. Our only safety is in sticking like wax to the text.

W. But what can we talk about?

GEO. Why, anything that Meisterschaft talks about. It ain't our affair.

W. I know; but Meisterschaft talks about everything.

GEO. And yet don't talk about anything long enough for it to get embarrassing. Meisterschaft is just splendid for general conversation.

W. Yes, that's so; but it's so *blamed* general! Won't it sound foolish?

GEO. Foolish? Why, of course; all German sounds foolish.

W. Well, that is true; I didn't think of that.

GEO. Now, don't fool around any more. Load up; load up; get ready. Fix up some sentences; you'll need them in two minutes now.

(*They walk up and down, moving their lips in dumb-show memorizing.*)

W. Look here — when we've said all that's in the book on a topic, and want to change the subject, how can we say so? — how would a German say it?

21***

GEO. Well, I don't know. But you know when they mean "Change cars," they say *Umsteigen*. Don't you reckon that will answer?

W. Tip-top! It's short and goes right to the point: and it's got a business whang to it that's almost American. Umsteigen! — change subject! — why, it's the very thing.

GEO. All right, then, *you* umsteigen — for I hear them coming.

(Enter the girls.)

A. to W. (*With solemnity.*) Guten Morgen, mein Herr, es freut mich sehr, Sie zu sehen.

W. Guten Morgen, mein Fräulein, es freut mich sehr Sie zu sehen.

(*Margaret and George repeat the same sentences. Then, after an embarrassing silence, Margaret refers to her book and says*):

M. Bitte, meine Herrn, setzen Sie sich.

THE GENTLEMEN. Danke schön. (*The four seat themselves in couples, the width of the stage apart, and the two conversations begin. The talk is not flowing — at any rate at first; there are painful silences all along. Each couple worry out a remark and a reply: there is a pause of silent thinking, and then the other couple deliver themselves.*)

W. Haben Sie meinen Vater in dem Laden meines Bruders nicht gesehen?

A. Nein, mein Herr, ich habe Ihren Herrn Vater in dem Laden Ihres Herrn Bruders nicht gesehen.

GEO. Waren Sie gestern Abend im Koncert, oder im Theater?

M. Nein, ich war gestern Abend nicht im Koncert, noch im Theater, ich war gestern Abend zu Hause

(General break-down — long pause.)

W. Ich störe doch nicht etwa?

A. Sie stören mich durchaus nicht.

GEO. Bitte, lassen Sie sich nicht von mir stören.

M. Aber ich bitte Sie, Sie stören mich durchaus nicht.

W. (*To both girls.*)   Wenn wir Sie stören so gehen wir gleich wieder.

A. O, nein! Gewiss, nein!

M. Im Gegentheil, es freut uns sehr, Sie zu sehen — alle beide.

W. Schön!

GEO. Gott sei dank!

M. (*Aside.*)   It's just lovely!

A. (*Aside.*)   It's like a poem.

(Pause.)

W. Umsteigen!

M. Um — welches?

W. Umsteigen.

GEO.   Auf English, change cars — oder subject.

BOTH GIRLS. Wie schön!

W. Wir haben uns die Freiheit genommen, bei Ihnen vorzusprechen.

A. Sie sind sehr gütig.

GEO. Wir wollten uns erkundigen, wie Sie sich befänden.

M. Ich bin Ihnen sehr verbunden — meine Schwester auch.

W. Meine Frau lasst sich Ihnen bestens empfehlen.

A. Ihre *Frau?*

W. (*Examining his book.*) Vielleicht habe ich mich geirrt.   (*Shows the place.*)   Nein, gerade so sagt das Buch.

A. (*Satisfied.*) Ganz recht.   Aber —

W. Bitte empfehlen Sie mich Ihrem Herrn Bruder.

A. Ah, das ist viel besser — viel besser.   (*Aside.*) Wenigstens es wäre viel besser wenn ich einen Bruder hätte.

U***

GEO. Wie ist es Ihnen gegangen, seitdem **ich das** Vergnügen hätte, Sie anderswo zu sehen?

M. Danke bestens, ich befinde mich gewöhnlich ziemlich wohl.

(Gretchen slips in with a gun, and listens.)

GEO. (*Still to Margaret.*)   Befindet sich Ihre Frau Gemahlin wohl?

GR. (*Raising hands and eyes.*)   Frau Gemahlin— heiliger Gott! (*Is like to betray herself with her smothered laughter, and glides out.*)

M. Danke sehr, meine Frau ist ganz wohl.

(Pause.)

W. Dürfen wir vielleicht — umsteigen?

THE OTHERS. Gut!

GEO. (*Aside.*)   I feel better now. I'm beginning to catch on. (*Aloud.*) Ich möchte gern morgen früh einige Einkäufe machen und würde Ihnen sehr verbunden sein, wenn Sie mir den Gefallen thäten, mir die Namen der besten hiesigen Firmen aufzuschreiben.

M. (*Aside.*)   How sweet!

W. (*Aside.*)   Hang it, *I* was going to say that! That's one of the noblest things in the book.

A. Ich möchte Ihnen gern begleiten, aber es ist mir wirklich heute Morgen ganz unmöglich auszugehen. (*Aside.*)   It's getting as easy as 9 times 7 is 46.

M. Sagen Sie dem Brieftäger, wenn's gefällig ist, er möchte Ihnen den eingeschriebenen Brief geben lassen.

W. Ich würde Ihnen sehr verbunden sein, wenn Sie diese Schachtel für mich nach der Post tragen würden, da mir sehr daran liegt einen meiner Geschäftsfreunde in dem Laden des deutschen Kaufmanns heute Abend treffen zu können. (*Aside.*)   All down but nine; set 'm up on the other alley

A. Aber Herr Jackson! Sie haben die Sätze gemischt. Es ist unbegreiflich wie Sie das haben thun können. Zwischen Ihrem ersten Theil und Ihrem letzten Theil haben Sie ganze fünfzig Seiten übergeschlagen! Jetzt bin ich ganz verloren. Wie kann man reden, wenn man seinen Platz durchaus nicht wieder finden kann?

W. Oh, bitte, verzeihen Sie; ich habe das wirklich nicht beabsichtigt.

A. (*Mollified.*) Sehr wohl, lassen Sie gut sein. Aber thun Sie es nicht wieder. Sie müssen ja doch einräumen, dass solche Dinge unerträgliche Verwirrung mit sich führen.

(Gretchen slips in again with her gun.)

W. Unzweifelhaft haben Sie Recht, meine holdselige Landsmännin......Umsteigen!

(As George gets fairly into the following, Gretchen draws a bead on him, and lets drive at the close, but the gun snaps.)

GEO. Glauben Sie das ich ein hübsches Wohnzimmer für mich selbst und ein kleines Schlafzimmer für meinen Sohn in diesem Hotel für fünfzehn Mark die Woche bekommen kann, oder würden Sie mir rathen, in einer Privatwohnung Logis zu nehmen? (*Aside.*) That's a daisy!

GR. (*Aside.*) Schade! (*She draws her charge and reloads.*)

M. Glauben Sie nicht Sie werden besser thun bei diesem Wetter zu Hause zu bleiben?

A. Freilich glaube ich, Herr Franklin, Sie werden sich erkälten, wenn Sie bei diesem unbeständigen Wetter ohne Ueberrock ausgehen.

GR. (*Relieved — aside.*) So? Man redet von Ausgehen. Das klingt schon besser. (*Sits.*)

W. (*To A.*) Wie theuer haben Sie das gekauft? (*Indicating a part of her dress.*)

A. Das hat achtzehn Mark gekostet.

W. Das ist sehr theuer.

GEO. Ja, obgleich dieser Stoff wunderschön ist und das Muster sehr geschmackvoll und auch das Vorzüglichste dass es in dieser Art gibt, so ist es doch furchtbar theuer für einen solchen Artikel.

M. (*Aside.*) How sweet is this communion of soul with soul !

A. Im Gegentheil, mein Herr, das ist sehr billig. Sehen Sie sich nur die Qualität an.

(They all examine it.)

GEO. Möglicherweise ist es das allerneuste das man in diesem Stoff hat; aber das Muster gefällt mir nicht.

(Pause.)

W. Umsteigen !

A. Welchen Hund haben Sie? Haben Sie den hubschen Hund des Kaufmanns, oder den hässlichen Hund der Urgrossmutter des Lehrlings des bogenbeinigen Zimmermanns?

W. (*Aside.*) Oh, come, she's ringing in a cold deck on us : that's Ollendorff.

GEO. Ich habe nicht den Hund des — des — (*Aside.*) Stuck ! That's no Meisterschaft; they don't play fair. (*Aloud.*) Ich habe nicht den Hund des — des — In unserem Buche leider, gibt es keinen Hund; daher, ob ich auch gern von solchen Thieren sprechen möchte, ist es mir doch unmöglich, weil ich nicht vorbereitet bin. Entschuldigen Sie, meine Damen.

GR. (*Aside.*) Beim Teufel, sie sind *alle* blödsinnig geworden. In meinem Leben habe ich nie ein so närrisches, verfluchtes, verdammtes Gespräch gehört.

W. Bitte, umsteigen.

(Run the following rapidly through.)

M. (*Aside.*) Oh, I've flushed an easy batch !

(*Aloud.*) Würden Sie mir erlauben meine Reisetasche hier hinzustellen?

GR. (*Aside.*) Wo ist seine Reisetasche? Ich sehe keine.

W. Bitte sehr.

GEO. Ist meine Reisetasche Ihnen im Wege?

GR. (*Aside.*) Und wo ist *seine* Reisetasche?

A. Erlauben Sie mir Sie von meiner Reisetasche zu befreien.

GR. (*Aside.*) Du Esel!

W. Ganz und gar nicht. (*To Geo.*) Es ist sehr schwül in diesem Coupé.

GR. (*Aside.*) Coupè.

Geo. Sie haben Recht. Erlauben Sie mir, gefälligst, das Fenster zu öffnen. Ein wenig Luft würde uns got thun.

M. Wir fahren sehr rasch.

A. Haben Sie den Namen jener Station gehört?

W. Wie lange halten wir auf dieser Station an?

GEO. Ich reise nach Dresden, Schaffner. Wo muss ich umsteigen?

A. Sie steigen nicht um, Sie bleiben sitzen.

GR. (*Aside.*) Sie sind ja alle ganz und gar verrückt! Man denke sich sie glauben dass sie auf der Eisenbahn reisen.

GEO. (*Aside, to William.*) Now brace up; pull all your confidence together, my boy, and we'll try that lovely good-bye business a flutter. I think it's about the gaudiest thing in the book, if you boom it right along and don't get left on a base. It'll impress the girls. (*Aloud.*) Lassen Sie uns gehen: es ist schon sehr spät, und ich muss morgen ganz früh aufstehen.

GR. (*Aside — grateful.*) Gott sei Dank dass sie endlich gehen. (*Sets her gun aside.*)

W. (*To Geo.*) Ich danke Ihnen höflichst für die Ehre die sie mir erweisen, aber ich kann nicht länger bleiben.

GEO. (*To W.*) Entschuldigen Sie mich gütigst, aber ich kann wirklich nicht länger bleiben.

(Gretchen looks on stupefied.)

W. (*To Geo.*)   Ich habe schon eine Einladung angenommen; ich kann wirklich nicht länger bleiben.

(Gretchen fingers her gun again.)

GEO. (*To W.*)   Ich muss gehen.

W. (*To Geo.*) Wie! Sie wollen schon wieder gehen? Sie sind ja eben erst gekommen.

M. (*Aside.*)   It's just music!

A. (*Aside.*)   Oh, how lovely they do it!

GEO. (*To W.*) Also denken sie doch noch nicht an's Gehen.

W. (*To Geo.*) Es thut mir unendlich leid, aber ich muss nach Hause. Meine Frau wird sich wundern, was aus mir geworden ist.

GEO. (*To W.*) Meine Frau hat keine Ahnung wo ich bin: ich muss wirklich jetzt fort.

W. (*To Geo.*) Dann will ich Sie nicht länger aufhalten; ich bedaure sehr dass Sie uns einen so kurzen Besuch gemacht haben.

GEO. (*To W.*)   Adieu — auf recht baldiges Wiedersehen.

W. UMSTEIGEN!

(Great hand-clapping from the girls.)

M. (*Aside.*)   Oh, how perfect! how elegant!

A. (*Aside.*)   Per-fectly enchanting!

JOYOUS CHORUS. (*All.*) Ich habe gehabt, du hast gehabt, er hat gehabt, wir haben gehabt, ihr habet gehabt, sie haben gehabt.

(Gretchen faints, and tumbles from her chair, and the gun goes off with a crash. Each girl, frightened, seizes the protecting hand of her sweetheart. Gretchen scrambles up. Tableau.)

W. (*Takes out some money — beckons Gretchen to him. George adds money to the pile.*) Hübsches Mädchen (*giving her some of the coins*), hast Du etwas gesehen?

GR. (*Courtesy — aside.*) Der Engel! (*Aloud — impressively.*) Ich habe nichts gesehen.

W. (*More money.*) Hast Du etwas gehört?

GR. Ich habe nichts gehört.

W. (*More money.*) Und Morgen?

GR. Morgen — wäre es nöthig — bin ich taub und blind.

W. Unvergleichbares Mädchen! Und (*giving the rest of the money*) darnach?

GR. (*Deep courtesy — aside.*) Erzengel! (*Aloud.*) Darnach, mein gnädgister, betrachten Sie mich also *taub — blind — todt !*

ALL. (*In chorus — with reverent joy.*) Ich habe gehabt, du hast gehabt, er hat gehabt, wir haben gehabt, ihr habet gehabt, sie haben gehabt!

ACT III.

Three weeks later.

SCENE I.

(Enter Gretchen, and puts her shawl on a chair. Brushing around with the traditional feather duster of the drama. Smartly dressed, for she is prosperous.)

GR. Wie hätte man sich das vorstellen können! In nur drei Wochen bin ich schon reich geworden! (*Gets out of her pocket handful after handful of silver, which she piles on the table, and proceeds to repile and count, occasionally ringing or biting a piece to try its quality.*) Oh, dass (*with a sigh*) die Frau Wirthin nur

ewig krank bliebe!......Diese edlen jungen Männer
— sie sind ja so liebenswürdig! Und so fleissig! —
und so treu! Jeden Morgen kommen sie gerade um
drei Viertel auf neun; und plaudern und schwatzen,
und plappern, und schnattern, die jungen Damen auch;
um Schlage zwölf nehmen sie Abschied; um Schlage
eins kommen sie schon wieder, und plaudern und
schwatzen und plappern und schnattern; gerade um
sechs Uhr nehmen sie wiederum Abschied; um halb
acht kehren sie noche'mal zurück, und plaudern und
schwatzen und plappern und schnattern bis zehn Uhr,
oder vielleicht ein Viertel nach, falls ihre Uhren nach
gehen (und stets gehen sie nach am Ende des Besuchs,
aber stets vor Beginn desselben), und zuweilen unter-
halten sich die jungen Leute beim Spazierengehen; und
jeden Sonntag gehen sie dreimal in die Kirche; und
immer plaudern sie, und schwatzen und plappern
und schnattern bis ihnen die Zähne aus dem Munde
fallen. Und *ich?* Durch Mangel an Uebung, ist mir
die Zunge mit Moos belegt worden! Freilich ist's mir
eine dumme Zeit gewesen. Aber — um Gotteswillen,
was geht das mir an? Was soll ich daraus machen?
Täglich sagt die Frau Wirthin " Gretchen " (*dumb-
show of paying a piece of money into her hand*), " du
bist eine der besten Sprach-Lehrerinnen der Welt!"
Ach, Gott! Und täglich sagen die edlen jungen
Männer, "Gretchen, liebes Kind " (*money-paying again
in dumb-show — three coins*), " bleib' taub — blind —
todt!" und so bleibe ich......Jetzt wird es ungefähr
neun Uhr sein; bald kommen sie vom Spaziergehen
zurück. Also, es wäre gut dass ich meinem eigenen
Schatz einen Besuch abstatte und spazieren gehe.
(*Dons her shawl.*)

(Exit. L.)

(Enter Wirthin. R.)

WIRTHIN. That was Mr. Stephenson's train that

just came in.   Evidently the girls are out walking with
Gretchen; — can't find *them*, and *she* doesn't seem to
be around.   (*A ring at the door.*)   That's him.   I'll
go see.

(Exit. R.)

(Enter Stephenson and Wirthin. R.)

S. Well, how does sickness seem to agree with you?

WIRTHIN. So well that I've never been out of my
room since, till I heard your train come in.

S. Thou miracle of fidelity!   Now I argue from
that, that the new plan is working.

WIRTHIN. Working?   Mr. Stephenson, you never
saw anything like it in the whole course of your life!
It's absolutely wonderful the way it works.

S. Succeeds?   No — you don't mean it.

WIRTHIN. Indeed, I do mean it.   I tell you, Mr.
Stephenson, that plan was just an inspiration — that's
what it was.   You could teach a cat German by it.

S. Dear me, this is noble news!   Tell me about it.

WIRTHIN. Well, it's all Gretchen — ev-ery bit of it.
I told you she was a jewel.   And then the sagacity of
that child — why, I never dreamed it was in her.   Sh-
she, "Never you ask the young ladies a question —
never let on — just keep mum — leave the whole thing
to me," sh-she.

S. Good!   And she justified, did she?

WIRTHIN.   Well, sir, the amount of German gabble
that that child crammed into those two girls inside the
next forty-eight hours — well, *I* was satisfied!   So I've
never asked a question — never *wanted* to ask any.
I've just lain curled up there, happy.   The little dears!
they've flitted in to see me a moment, every morning
and noon and supper-time; and as sure as I'm sitting
here, inside of six days they were clattering German to
me like a house afire!

S. Sp-lendid, splendid!

WIRTHIN. Of course it ain't grammatical — the inventor of the language can't talk grammatical; if the
dative didn't fetch him the accusative would; but it's
German all the same, and don't you forget it!

S. Go on — go on — this is delicious news —

WIRTHIN. Gretchen, she says to me at the start,
" Never you mind about company for 'em," sh-she —
" I'm company enough." And I says, " All right
—fix it your own way, child;" and that she *was*
right is shown by the fact that to this day they don't
care a straw for any company but hers.

S. Dear me; why, it's admirable!

WIRTHIN. Well, I should think so! They just dote
on that hussy — can't seem to get enough of her.
Gretchen tells me so herself. And the care she takes
of them! She tells me that every time there's a moonlight night she coaxes them out for a walk; and if a
body can believe her, she actually bullies them off to
church three times every Sunday!

S. Why, the little dev — missionary! Really, she's
a genius!

WIRTHIN. She's a bud, *I* tell you! Dear me, how
she's brought those girls' health up! Cheeks? — just
roses. Gait? — they walk on watch-springs! And
happy? — by the bliss in their eyes, you'd think
they're in Paradise! Ah, that Gretchen! Just you
imagine *our* trying to achieve these marvels!

S. You're right — every time. Those girls — why,
all they'd have wanted to know was what we wanted
done, and then they wouldn't have *done* it — the mis-
chievous young rascals!

WIRTHIN. Don't tell *me?* Bless you, I found that
out early — when *I* was bossing.

S. Well, I'm im-mensely pleased. *Now* fetch them
down. I'm not afraid now. They won't want to go
home.

WIRTHIN. Home! I don't believe you could drag them away from Gretchen with nine span of horses. But if you want to see them, put on your hat and come along; they're out somewhere trapesing along with Gretchen. (*Going.*)

S. I'm with you — lead on.

WIRTHIN. We'll go out the side door. It's towards the Anlage.

(Exit both. L.)

(Enter George and Margaret, R. Her head lies upon his shoulder, his arm is about her waist; they are steeped in sentiment.)

M. (*Turning a fond face up at him.*)   Du Engel!

GEO. Liebste! (*Kiss.*)

M. Oh, das Liedchen dass Du mir gewidmet hast — es ist so schön, so wunderschön. Wie hätte ich je geahnt dass Du ein Poët wärest!

GEO. Mein Schätzchen! — es ist mir lieb wenn Dir die Kleinigkeit gefällt.

M. Ah, es ist mit der zärtlichsten Musik gefüllt — klingt ja so süss und selig — wie das Flüstern des Sommerwindes die Abenddämmerung hindurch. Wieder — Theuerste! — sag' es wieder.

GEO.   Du bist wie eine Blume! —
              So schön und hold und rein —
          Ich schau Dich an, und Wehmuth
              Schleicht mir ins Herz hinein.
          Mir ist als ob ich die Hände
              Aufs Haupt Dir legen sollt,
          Betend, dass Gott Dich erhalte,
              So rein und schön und hold.

M. A-ch! (*Dumb-show sentimentalisms.*) **Georgie** —

GEO. Kindchen!

M. Warum kommen sie nicht?

GEO. Das weiss ich gar nicht. Sie waren —

M. Es wird spät. Wir müssen sie antreiben. Komm!

22A

GEO. Ich glaube sie werden recht bald ankommen, aber —

(Exit both. L.)

(Enter Gretchen, R., in a state of mind. Slumps into a chair limp with despair.)

GR. Ach! was wird jetzt aus mir werden! Zufällig habe ich in der Ferne den verdammten Papa gesehen! — und die Frau Wirthin auch! Oh, diese Erscheinung —die hat mir beinahe das Leben genommen. Sie suchen die jungen Damen — das weiss ich wenn sie diese und die jungen Herren zusammen fänden — du heiliger Gott! Wenn das gescheiht, wären wir Alle ganz und gar verloren! Ich muss sie gleich finden, und ihr eine Warnung geben!

(Exit. L.)

(Enter Annie and Will, R., posed like the former couple and sentimental.)

A. Ich liebe sich schon so sehr — Deiner edlen Natur wegen. Dass du dazu auch ein Dichter bist! — ach, mein Leben ist übermässig reich geworden! Wer hätte sich doch einbilden können dass ich einen Mann zu einem so wunderschönen Gedicht hätte begeistern können?

W. Liebste! Es ist nur eine Kleinigkeit.

A. Nein, nein, es ist ein echtes Wunder! Sage es noch einmal — ich flehe Dich an.

W.   Du bist wie eine Blume! —
             So schön und hold und rein —
           Ich schau' Dich an, und Wehmuth
             Schleicht mir ins Herz hinein.
           Mir ist als ob ich die Hände
             Aufs Haupt Dir legen sollt',
           Betend, dass Gott Dich erhalte.
             So rein und schön und hold.

A. Ach, es ist himmlisch — einfach himmlisch.
(*Kiss.*) Schreibt auch George Gedichte?

W. Oh, ja — zuweilen.

A. Wie schön!

W. (*Aside.*) Smouches 'em, same as I do! It was a noble good idea to play that little thing on her. George wouldn't ever think of that — somehow he never had any invention.

A. (*Arranging chairs.*) Jetzt will ich bei Dir sitzen bleiben, und Du —

W. (*They sit.*) Ja — und ich —

A. Du wirst mir die alte Geschichte, die immer neu bleibt, noch wieder erzählen.

W. Zum Beispiel, dass ich Dich liebe!

A. Wieder!

W. Ich — sie kommen!

(Enter George and Margaret.)

A. Das macht nichts. Fortan!

(George unties M.'s bonnet. She reties his cravat — interspersings of love-pats, etc., and dumb-show of love-quarrellings.)

W. Ich lieb Dich.

A. Ach! Noch einmal!

W. Ich habe Dich vom Herzen lieb.

A. Ach! Abermals!

W. Bist Du denn noch nicht satt?

A. Nein. (*The other couple sit down, and Margaret begins a retying of the cravat. Enter the Wirthin and Stephenson, he imposing silence with a sign.*) Mich hungert sehr, ich verhungre!

W. Oh, Du armes Kind! (*Lays her head on his shoulder. Dumb-show between Stephenson and Wirthin.*) Und hungert es nicht mich? Du hast mir nicht einmal gesagt —

A. Dass ich Dich liebe? Mein Eigener! (*Frau*

Wirthin threatens to faint — is supported by Stephenson.)
Höre mich nur an: Ich liebe Dich, ich liebe Dich —

(*Enter Gretchen.*)

GR. (*Tears her hair.*) Oh, dass ich in der Hölle wäre!

M. Ich liebe Dich, ich liebe Dich! Ah, ich bin so glücklich dass ich nicht schlafen kann, nicht lesen kann, nicht reden kann, nicht —

A. Und ich! Ich bin auch so glücklich dass ich nicht speisen kann, nicht studieren, arbeiten, denken, schreiben —

S. (*To Wirthin — aside.*) Oh, there isn't any mistake about it — Gretchen's just a rattling teacher!

WIRTHIN (*To Stephenson — aside.*) I'll skin her alive when I get my hands on her!

M. Komm, alle Verliebte! (*They jump up, join hands, and sing in chorus*) :

> Du, Du, wie ich Dich liebe,
> Du, Du, liebst auch mich!
> Die, die zärtlichsten Triebe —

S. (*Stepping forward.*) Well!

(The girls throw themselves upon his neck with enthusiasm.)

THE GIRLS. Why, father!
S. My darlings!

(The young men hesitate a moment, then they add their embrace, flinging themselves on Stephenson's neck, along with the girls.)

THE YOUNG MEN. Why, father!
S. (*Struggling.*) Oh, come, this is too thin! — too quick, I mean. Let go, you rascals!

GEO. We'll never let go till you put us on the family list.

M. Right! hold to him!
A. Cling to him, Will!

(Gretchen rushes in and joins the general embrace, but is snatched away by the Wirthin, crushed up against the wall, and threatened with destruction.)

S. (*Suffocating.*) All right, all right — have it your own way, you quartette of swindlers!

W. He's a darling! Three cheers for papa!

EVERYBODY. (*Except Stephenson, who bows with hand on heart.*) Hip — hip — hip: hurrah, hurrah, hurrah!

GR. Der Tiger — ah-h-h!

WIRTHIN. Sei ruhig, you hussy!

S. Well, I've lost a couple of precious daughters, but I've gained a couple of precious scamps to fill up the gap with; so it's all right. I'm satisfied, and everybody's forgiven — (*With mock threats at Gretchen.*)

W. Oh, wir werden für Dich sorgen — du herrliches Gretchen!

GR. Danke schön!

M. (*To Wirthin.*) Und für Sie auch; denn wenn Sie nicht so freundlich gewesen wären, krank zu werden, wie wären wir je so glücklich geworden wie jetzt?

WIRTHIN. Well, dear, I *was* kind, but I didn't mean it. But I ain't sorry — not one bit — that I ain't.

(Tableau.)

S. Come, now, the situation is full of hope, and grace, and tender sentiment. If I had in the least the poetic gift, I know I could improvise under such an inspiration (*each girl nudges her sweetheart*) something worthy to — to — Is there no poet among us?

(Each youth turns solemnly his back upon the other, and raises his hands in benediction over his sweetheart's bowed head.)

BOTH YOUTHS AT ONCE:

> Mir ist als ob ich die Hände
> Aus Haupt Dir legen sollt —

22***

(*They* turn and look reproachfully at each other — the girls contemplate them with injured surprise.)

S. (*Reflectively.*) I think I've heard that before somewhere.

WIRTHIN. (*Aside.*) Why, the very cats in Germany know it!

(*Curtain.*)

THE £1,000,000 BANK-NOTE

WHEN I was twenty-seven years old, I was a mining-broker's clerk in San Francisco, and an expert in all the details of stock traffic. I was alone in the world, and had nothing to depend upon but my wits and a clean reputation; but these were setting my feet in the road to eventual fortune, and I was content with the prospect.

My time was my own after the afternoon board, Saturdays, and I was accustomed to put it in on a little sail-boat on the bay. One day I ventured too far, and was carried out to sea. Just at nightfall, when hope was about gone, I was picked up by a small brig which was bound for London. It was a long and stormy voyage, and they made me work my passage without pay, as a common sailor. When I stepped ashore in London my clothes were ragged and shabby, and I had only a dollar in my pocket. This money fed and sheltered me twenty-four hours. During the next twenty-four I went without food and shelter.

About ten o'clock on the following morning, seedy and hungry, I was dragging myself along Portland Place, when a child that was passing, towed by a nurse-maid, tossed a luscious big pear — minus one bite — into the gutter. I stopped, of course, and fastened my desiring eye on that muddy treasure. My mouth watered for it, my stomach craved it, my whole being begged for it. But every time I made a move to

v***   (339) get it some passing eye detected my purpose, and of course I straightened up then, and looked indifferent, and pretended that I hadn't been thinking about the pear at all. This same thing kept happening and happening, and I couldn't get the pear. I was just getting desperate enough to brave all the shame, and to seize it, when a window behind me was raised, and a gentleman spoke out of it, saying:

"Step in here, please."

I was admitted by a gorgeous flunkey, and shown into a sumptuous room where a couple of elderly gentlemen were sitting. They sent away the servant, and made me sit down. They had just finished their breakfast, and the sight of the remains of it almost overpowered me. I could hardly keep my wits together in the presence of that food, but as I was not asked to sample it, I had to bear my trouble as best I could.

Now, something had been happening there a little before, which I did not know anything about until a good many days afterwards, but I will tell you about it now. Those two old brothers had been having a pretty hot argument a couple of days before, and had ended by agreeing to decide it by a bet, which is the English way of settling everything.

You will remember that the Bank of England once issued two notes of a million pounds each, to be used for a special purpose connected with some public transaction with a foreign country. For some reason or other only one of these had been used and canceled; the other still lay in the vaults of the Bank. Well, the brothers, chatting along, happened to get to wondering what might be the fate of a perfectly honest and intelligent stranger who should be turned adrift in London without a friend, and with no money but that million-pound bank-note, and no way to account for his being in possession of it. Brother A said he would starve to death; Brother B said he wouldn't. Brother A said he couldn't offer it at a bank or anywhere else, because he would be arrested on the spot. So they went on disputing till Brother B said he would bet twenty thousand pounds that the man would live thirty days, *anyway*, on that million, and keep out of jail, too. Brother A took him up. Brother B went down to the Bank and bought that note. Just like an Englishman, you see; pluck to the backbone. Then he dictated a letter, which one of his clerks wrote out in a beautiful round hand, and then the two brothers sat at the window a whole day watching for the right man to give it to.

They saw many honest faces go by that were not intelligent enough; many that were intelligent, but not honest enough; many that were both, but the possessors were not poor enough, or, if poor enough, were not strangers. There was always a defect, until I came along; but they agreed that I filled the bill all around; so they elected me unanimously, and there I was now waiting to know why I was called in. They began to ask me questions about myself, and pretty soon they had my story. Finally they told me I would answer their purpose. I said I was sincerely glad, and asked what it was. Then one of them handed me an envelope, and said I would find the explanation inside. I was going to open it, but he said no; take it to my lodgings, and look it over carefully, and not be hasty or rash. I was puzzled, and wanted to discuss the matter a little further, but they didn't; so I took my leave, feeling hurt and insulted to be made the butt of what was apparently some kind of a practical joke, and yet obliged to put up with it, not being in circumstances to resent affronts from rich and strong folk.

I would have picked up the pear now and eaten it

before all the world, but it was gone; so I had lost
that by this unlucky business, and the thought of it did
not soften my feeling towards those men.   As soon as
I was out of sight of that house I opened my envelope,
and saw that it contained money!   My opinion of
those people changed, I can tell you!   I lost not a
moment, but shoved note and money into my vest
pocket, and broke for the nearest cheap eating house.
Well, how I did eat!   When at last I couldn't hold
any more, I took out my money and unfolded it, took
one glimpse and nearly fainted.   Five millions of dollars!   Why, it made my head swim.

I must have sat there stunned and blinking at the
note as much as a minute before I came rightly to
myself again.   The first thing I noticed, then, was the
landlord.   His eye was on the note, and he was petrified.   He was worshiping, with all his body and soul,
but he looked as if he couldn't stir hand or foot.   I
took my cue in a moment, and did the only rational
thing there was to do.   I reached the note towards
him, and said, carelessly:

" Give me the change, please."

Then he was restored to his normal condition, and
made a thousand apologies for not being able to break
the bill, and I couldn't get him to touch it.   He
wanted to look at it, and keep on looking at it; he
couldn't seem to get enough of it to quench the thirst
of his eye, but he shrank from touching it as if it had
been something too sacred for poor common clay to
handle.   I said:

" I am sorry if it is an inconvenience, but I must
insist.   Please change it; I haven't anything else."

But he said that wasn't any matter; he was quite
willing to let the trifle stand over till another time.   I
said I might not be in his neighborhood again for a
good while; but he said it was of no consequence, he

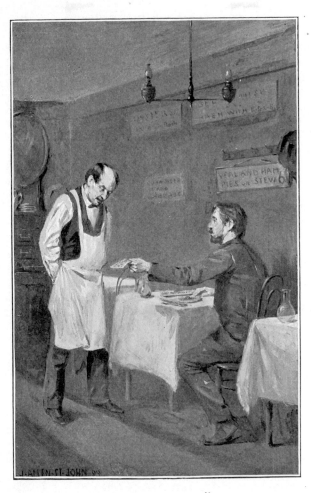

" CHANGE, PLEASE "

could wait, and, moreover, I could have anything I wanted, any time I chose, and let the account run as long as I pleased. He said he hoped he wasn't afraid to trust as rich a gentleman as I was, merely because I was of a merry disposition, and chose to play larks on the public in the matter of dress. By this time another customer was entering, and the landlord hinted to me to put the monster out of sight; then he bowed me all the way to the door, and I started straight for that house and those brothers, to correct the mistake which had been made before the police should hunt me up, and help me do it. I was pretty nervous; in fact, pretty badly frightened, though, of course, I was no way in fault; but I knew men well enough to know that when they find they've given a tramp a million-pound bill when they thought it was a one-pounder, they are in a frantic rage against *him* instead of quarreling with their own near-sightedness, as they ought. As I approached the house my excitement began to abate, for all was quiet there, which made me feel pretty sure the blunder was not discovered yet. I rang. The same servant appeared. I asked for those gentlemen.

"They are gone." This in the lofty, cold way of that fellow's tribe.

"Gone? Gone where?"

"On a journey."

"But whereabouts?"

"To the Continent, I think."

"The Continent?"

"Yes, sir."

"Which way — by what route?"

"I can't say, sir."

"When will they be back?"

"In a month, they said."

"A month! Oh, this is awful! Give me *some* sort

of idea of how to get a word to them. It's of the last importance."

" I can't, indeed. I've no idea where they've gone, sir."

" Then I must see some member of the family."

" Family's away, too; been abroad months — in Egypt and India, I think."

" Man, there's been an immense mistake made. They'll be back before night. Will you tell them I've been here, and that I will keep coming till it's all made right, and they needn't be afraid?"

" I'll tell them, if they come back, but I am not expecting them. They said you would be here in an hour to make inquiries, but I must tell you it's all right, they'll be here on time and expect you."

So I had to give it up and go away. What a riddle it all was! I was like to lose my mind. They would be here " on time." What could that mean? Oh, the letter would explain, maybe. I had forgotten the letter; I got it out and read it. This is what it said:

"You are an intelligent and honest man, as one may see by your face. We conceive you to be poor and a stranger. Enclosed you will find a sum of money. It is lent to you for thirty days, without interest. Report at this house at the end of that time. I have a bet on you. If I win it you shall have any situation that is in my gift — any, that is, that you shall be able to prove yourself familiar with and competent to fill."

No signature, no address, no date.

Well, here was a coil to be in! You are posted on what had preceded all this, but I was not. It was just a deep, dark puzzle to me. I hadn't the least idea what the game was, nor whether harm was meant me or a kindness. I went into a park, and sat down to try to think it out, and to consider what I had best do.

At the end of an hour my reasonings had crystallized into this verdict.

Maybe those men mean me well, maybe they mean

me ill; no way to decide that — let it go. They've got a game, or a scheme, or an experiment, of some kind on hand; no way to determine what it is — let it go. There's a bet on me; no way to find out what it is — let it go. That disposes of the indeterminable quantities; the remainder of the matter is tangible, solid, and may be classed and labeled with certainty. If I ask the Bank of England to place this bill to the credit of the man it belongs to, they'll do it, for they know him, although I don't; but they will ask me how I came in possession of it, and if I tell the truth, they'll put me in the asylum, naturally, and a lie will land me in jail. The same result would follow if I tried to bank the bill anywhere or to borrow money on it. I have got to carry this immense burden around until those men come back, whether I want to or not. It is useless to me, as useless as a handful of ashes, and yet I must take care of it, and watch over it, while I beg my living. I couldn't *give* it away, if I should try, for neither honest citizen nor highwayman would accept it or meddle with it for anything. Those brothers are safe. Even if I lose their bill, or burn it, they are still safe, because they can stop payment, and the Bank will make them whole; but meantime I've got to do a month's suffering without wages or profit — unless I help win that bet, whatever it may be, and get that situation that I am promised. I *should* like to get that; men of their sort have situations in their gift that are worth having.

I got to thinking a good deal about that situation. My hopes began to rise high. Without doubt the salary would be large. It would begin in a month; after that I should be all right. Pretty soon I was feeling first-rate. By this time I was tramping the streets again. The sight of a tailor-shop gave me a sharp longing to shed my rags, and to clothe myself decently once more.   Could I afford it?   No; I had nothing in the world but a million pounds.   So I forced myself to go on by.   But soon I was drifting back again.   The temptation persecuted me cruelly.   I must have passed that shop back and forth six times during that manful struggle.   At last I gave in; I had to.   I asked if they had a misfit suit that had been thrown on their hands. The fellow I spoke to nodded his head towards another fellow, and gave me no answer.   I went to the indicated fellow, and he indicated another fellow with *his* head, and no words.   I went to him, and he said:

"'Tend to you presently."

I waited till he was done with what he was at, then he took me into a back room, and overhauled a pile of rejected suits, and selected the rattiest one for me.   I put it on.   It didn't fit, and wasn't in any way attractive, but it was new, and I was anxious to have it; so I didn't find any fault, but said, with some diffidence:

"It would be an accommodation to me if you could wait some days for the money.   I haven't any small change about me."

The fellow worked up a most sarcastic expression of countenance, and said:

"Oh, you haven't?   Well, of course, I didn't expect it.   I'd only expect gentlemen like you to carry large change."

I was nettled, and said:

"My friend, you shouldn't judge a stranger always by the clothes he wears.   I am quite able to pay for this suit; I simply didn't wish to put you to the trouble of changing a large note."

He modified his style a little at that, and said, though still with something of an air:

"I didn't mean any particular harm, but as long as rebukes are going, I might say it wasn't quite your affair to jump to the conclusion that we couldn't change any note that you might happen to be carrying around. On the contrary, we *can.*"

I handed the note to him, and said:

"Oh, very well; I apologize."

He received it with a smile, one of those large smiles which goes all around over, and has folds in it, and wrinkles, and spirals, and looks like the place where you have thrown a brick in a pond; and then in the act of his taking a glimpse of the bill this smile froze solid, and turned yellow, and looked like those wavy, wormy spreads of lava which you find hardened on little levels on the side of Vesuvius. I never before saw a smile caught like that, and perpetuated. The man stood there holding the bill, and looking like that, and the proprietor hustled up to see what was the matter, and said, briskly:

"Well, what's up? what's the trouble? what's wanting?"

I said: "There isn't any trouble. I'm waiting for my change."

"Come, come; get him his change, Tod; get him his change."

Tod retorted: "Get him his change! It's easy to say, sir; but look at the bill yourself."

The proprietor took a look, gave a low, eloquent whistle, then made a dive for the pile of rejected clothing, and began to snatch it this way and that, talking all the time excitedly, and as if to himself:

"Sell an eccentric millionaire such an unspeakable suit as that! Tod's a fool — a born fool. Always doing something like this. Drives every millionaire away from this place, because he can't tell a millionaire from a tramp, and never could. Ah, here's the thing I am after. Please get those things off, sir, and throw them in the fire. Do me the favor to put on this shirt and this suit; it's just the thing, the very thing —

plain, rich, modest, and just ducally nobby; made to order for a foreign prince — you may know him, sir, his Serene Highness the Hospodar of Halifax; had to leave it with us and take a mourning-suit because his mother was going to die — which she didn't. But that's all right; we can't always have things the way we — that is, the way they — there! trousers all right, they fit you to a charm, sir; now the waistcoat; aha, right again! now the coat — lord! look at that, now! Perfect — the whole thing! I never saw such a triumph in all my experience."

I expressed my satisfaction.

"Quite right, sir, quite right; it'll do for a make-shift, I'm bound to say. But wait till you see what we'll get up for you on your own measure. Come, Tod, book and pen; get at it. Length of leg, 32 "— and so on. Before I could get in a word he had measured me, and was giving orders for dress-suits, morning suits, shirts, and all sorts of things. When I got a chance I said:

"But, my dear sir, I *can't* give these orders, unless you can wait indefinitely, or change the bill."

"Indefinitely! It's a weak word, sir, a weak word. Eternally — *that's* the word, sir. Tod, rush these things through, and send them to the gentleman's address without any waste of time. Let the minor customers wait. Set down the gentleman's address and —"

"I'm changing my quarters. I will drop in and leave the new address."

"Quite right, sir, quite right. One moment — let me show you out, sir. There — good day, sir, good day."

Well, don't you see what was bound to happen? I drifted naturally into buying whatever I wanted, and asking for change. Within a week I was sumptuously equipped with all needful comforts and luxuries, and was housed in an expensive private hotel in Hanover Square. I took my dinners there, but for breakfast I stuck by Harris's humble feeding house, where I had got my first meal on my million-pound bill. I was the making of Harris. The fact had gone all abroad that the foreign crank who carried million-pound bills in his vest pocket was the patron saint of the place. That was enough. From being a poor, struggling, little hand-to-mouth enterprise, it had become celebrated, and overcrowded with customers. Harris was so grateful that he forced loans upon me, and would not be denied; and so, pauper as I was, I had money to spend, and was living like the rich and the great. I judged that there was going to be a crash by and by, but I was in now and must swim across or drown. You see there was just that element of impending disaster to give a serious side, a sober side, yes, a tragic side, to a state of things which would otherwise have been purely ridiculous. In the night, in the dark, the tragedy part was always to the front, and always warning, always threatening; and so I moaned and tossed, and sleep was hard to find. But in the cheerful daylight the tragedy element faded out and disappeared, and I walked on air, and was happy to giddiness, to intoxication, you may say.

And it was natural; for I had become one of the notorieties of the metropolis of the world, and it turned my head, not just a little, but a good deal. You could not take up a newspaper, English, Scotch, or Irish, without finding in it one or more references to the "vest-pocket million-pounder" and his latest doings and sayings. At first, in these mentions, I was at the bottom of the personal-gossip column; next, I was listed above the knights, next above the baronets, next above the barons, and so on, and so on, climbing steadily, as my notoriety augmented, until I reached

23A

the highest altitude possible, and there I remained, taking precedence of all dukes not royal, and of all ecclesiastics except the primate of all England. But mind, this was not fame; as yet I had achieved only notoriety. Then came the climaxing stroke — the accolade, so to speak — which in a single instant transmuted the perishable dross of notoriety into the enduring gold of fame: *Punch* caricatured me! Yes, I was a made man now; my place was established. I might be joked about still, but reverently, not hilariously, not rudely; I could be smiled at, but not laughed at. The time for that had gone by. *Punch* pictured me all a-flutter with rags, dickering with a beef-eater for the Tower of London. Well, you can imagine how it was with a young fellow who had never been taken notice of before, and now all of a sudden couldn't say a thing that wasn't taken up and repeated everywhere; couldn't stir abroad without constantly overhearing the remark flying from lip to lip, " There he goes; that's him!" couldn't take his breakfast without a crowd to look on; couldn't appear in an opera-box without concentrating there the fire of a thousand lorgnettes. Why, I just swam in glory all day long — that is the amount of it.

You know, I even kept my old suit of rags, and every now and then appeared in them, so as to have the old pleasure of buying trifles, and being insulted, and then shooting the scoffer dead with the million-pound bill. But I couldn't keep that up. The illustrated papers made the outfit so familiar that when I went out in it I was at once recognized and followed by a crowd, and if I attempted a purchase the man would offer me his whole shop on credit before I could pull my note on him.

About the tenth day of my fame I went to fulfil my duty to my flag by paying my respects to the American minister.   He received me with the enthusiasm proper in my case, upbraided me for being so tardy in my duty, and said that there was only one way to get his forgiveness, and that was to take the seat at his dinner-party that night made vacant by the illness of one of his guests.   I said I would, and we got to talking.   It turned out that he and my father had been schoolmates in boyhood, Yale students together later, and always warm friends up to my father's death.   So then he required me to put in at his house all the odd time I might have to spare, and I was very willing, of course.

In fact, I was more than willing; I was glad.   When the crash should come, he might somehow be able to save me from total destruction; I didn't know how, but he might think of a way, maybe.   I couldn't venture to unbosom myself to him at this late date, a thing which I would have been quick to do in the beginning of this awful career of mine in London.   No, I couldn't venture it now; I was in too deep; that is, too deep for me to be risking revelations to so new a friend, though not clear beyond my depth, as *I* looked at it.   Because, you see, with all my borrowing, I was carefully keeping within my means — I mean within my salary.   Of course, I couldn't *know* what my salary was going to be, but I had a good enough basis for an estimate in the fact, that if I won the bet I was to have *choice* of any situation in that rich old gentleman's gift provided I was competent — and I should certainly prove competent; I hadn't any doubt about that. And as to the bet, I wasn't worrying about that; I had always been lucky.   Now my estimate of the salary was six hundred to a thousand a year; say, six hundred for the first year, and so on up year by year, till I struck the upper figure by proved merit.   At present I was only in debt for my first year's salary.

Everybody had been trying to lend me money, but I had fought off the most of them on one pretext or another; so this indebtedness represented only £300 borrowed money, the other £300 represented my keep and my purchases. I believed my second year's salary would carry me through the rest of the month if I went on being cautious and economical, and I intended to look sharply out for that. My month ended, my employer back from his journey, I should be all right once more, for I should at once divide the two years' salary among my creditors by assignment, and get right down to my work.

It was a lovely dinner-party of fourteen. The Duke and Duchess of Shoreditch, and their daughter the Lady Anne-Grace-Eleanor-Celeste-and-so-forth-and-so-forth-de-Bohun, the Earl and Countess of Newgate, Viscount Cheapside, Lord and Lady Blatherskite, some untitled people of both sexes, the minister and his wife and daughter, and his daughter's visiting friend, an English girl of twenty-two, named Portia Langham, whom I fell in love with in two minutes, and she with me — I could see it without glasses. There was still another guest, an American — but I am a little ahead of my story. While the people were still in the drawing-room, whetting up for dinner, and coldly inspecting the late comers, the servant announced:

" Mr. Lloyd Hastings."

The moment the usual civilities were over, Hastings caught sight of me, and came straight with cordially outstretched hand; then stopped short when about to shake, and said, with an embarrassed look:

" I beg your pardon, sir, I thought I knew you."

" Why, you do know me, old fellow."

" No. Are *you* the — the —"

" Vest-pocket monster? I am, indeed. Don't be afraid to call me by my nickname; I'm used to it."

" Well, well, well, this is a surprise.   Once or twice
I've seen your own name coupled with the nickname,
but it never occurred to me that *you* could be the
Henry Adams referred to.   Why, it isn't six months
since you were clerking away for Blake Hopkins in
Frisco on a salary, and sitting up nights on an extra
allowance, helping me arrange and verify the Gould
and Curry Extension papers and statistics.   The idea
of your being in London, and a vast millionaire, and a
colossal celebrity !   Why, it's the Arabian Nights come
again.   Man, I can't take it in at all; can't realize it;
give me time to settle the whirl in my head."

" The fact is, Lloyd, you are no worse off than I
am.   I can't realize it myself."

" Dear me, it *is* stunning, now isn't it?   Why, it's
just three months to-day since we went to the Miners'
restaurant —"

" No; the What Cheer."

" Right, it *was* the What Cheer; went there at two
in the morning, and had a chop and coffee after a hard
six-hours grind over those Extension papers, and I
tried to persuade you to come to London with me, and
offered to get leave of absence for you and pay all
your expenses, and give you something over if I succeeded in making the sale; and you would not listen
to me, said I wouldn't succeed, and you couldn't afford
to lose the run of business and be no end of time getting the hang of things again when you got back home.
And yet here you are.   How odd it all is !   How did
you happen to come, and whatever *did* give you this
incredible start?"

" Oh, just an accident.   It's a long story — a
romance, a body may say.   I'll tell you all about it,
but not now."

" When?"

" The end of this month."

23***

"That's more than a fortnight yet. It's too much of a strain on a person's curiosity. Make it a week."

"I can't. You'll know why, by and by. But how's the trade getting along?"

His cheerfulness vanished like a breath, and he said with a sigh:

"You were a true prophet, Hal, a true prophet. I wish I hadn't come. I don't want to talk about it."

"But you must. You must come and stop with me to-night, when we leave here, and tell me all about it."

"Oh, may I? Are you in earnest?" and the water showed in his eyes.

"Yes; I want to hear the whole story, every word."

"I'm so grateful! Just to find a human interest once more, in some voice and in some eye, in me and affairs of mine, after what I've been through here — lord! I could go down on my knees for it!"

He gripped my hand hard, and braced up, and was all right and lively after that for the dinner — which didn't come off. No; the usual thing happened, the thing that is always happening under that vicious and aggravating English system — the matter of precedence couldn't be settled, and so there was no dinner. Englishmen always eat dinner before they go out to dinner, because *they* know the risks they are running; but nobody ever warns the stranger, and so he walks placidly into the trap. Of course, nobody was hurt this time, because we had all been to dinner, none of us being novices excepting Hastings, and he having been informed by the minister at the time that he invited him that in deference to the English custom he had not provided any dinner. Everybody took a lady and processioned down to the dining-room, because it is usual to go through the motions; but there the dispute began. The Duke of Shoreditch wanted to take precedence, and sit at the head of the table, holding that he outranked a minister who represented merely a nation and not a monarch; but I stood for my rights, and refused to yield. In the gossip column I ranked all dukes not royal, and said so, and claimed precedence of this one. It couldn't be settled, of course, struggle as we might and did, he finally (and injudiciously) trying to play birth and antiquity, and I "seeing" his Conqueror and "raising" him with Adam, whose direct posterity I was, as shown by my name, while *he* was of a collateral branch, as shown by *his*, and by his recent Norman origin; so we all processioned back to the drawing-room again and had a perpendicular lunch — plate of sardines and a strawberry, and you group yourself and stand up and eat it. Here the religion of precedence is not so strenuous; the two persons of highest rank chuck up a shilling, the one that wins has first go at his strawberry, and the loser gets the shilling. The next two chuck up, then the next two, and so on. After refreshment, tables were brought, and we all played cribbage, sixpence a game. The English never play any game for amusement. If they can't make something or lose something — they don't care which — they won't play.

We had a lovely time; certainly two of us had, Miss Langham and I. I was so bewitched with her that I couldn't count my hands if they went above a double sequence; and when I struck home I never discovered it, and started up the outside row again, and would have lost the game every time, only the girl did the same, she being in just my condition, you see; and consequently neither of us ever got out, or cared to wonder why we didn't; we only just knew we were happy, and didn't wish to know anything else, and didn't want to be interrupted. And I *told* her — I did, indeed — told her I loved her; and she — well, she blushed till her hair turned red, but she liked it;

W***

she *said* she did. Oh, there was never such an evening! Every time I pegged I put on a postscript;
every time she pegged she acknowledged receipt of it,
counting the hands the same. Why, I couldn't even
say "Two for his heels" without adding, "*My*, how
sweet you do look!" and she would say, "Fifteen
two, fifteen four, fifteen six, and a pair are eight, and
eight are sixteen — *do* you think so?"— peeping out
aslant from under her lashes, you know, so sweet and
cunning. Oh, it was just *too*-too!

Well, I was perfectly honest and square with her;
told her I hadn't a cent in the world but just the
million-pound note she'd heard so much talk about,
and *it* didn't belong to me, and that started her curiosity; and then I talked low, and told her the whole
history right from the start, and it nearly killed her
laughing. What in the nation she could find to laugh
about *I* couldn't see, but there it was; every half-
minute some new detail would fetch her, and I would
have to stop as much as a minute and a half to give
her a chance to settle down again. Why, she laughed
herself lame — she did, indeed; I never saw anything
like it. I mean I never saw a painful story — a story
of a person's troubles and worries and fears — produce
just *that* kind of effect before. So I loved her all the
more, seeing she could be so cheerful when there
wasn't anything to be cheerful about; for I might
soon need that kind of wife, you know, the way things
looked. Of course, I told her we should have to wait
a couple of years, till I could catch up on my salary;
but she didn't mind that, only she hoped I would be as
careful as possible in the matter of expenses, and not
let them run the least risk of trenching on our third
year's pay. Then she began to get a little worried,
and wondered if we were making any mistake, and
starting the salary on a higher figure for the first year

than I would get. This was good sense, and it made me feel a little less confident than I had been feeling before; but it gave me a good business idea, and I brought it frankly out.

"Portia, dear, would you mind going with me that day, when I confront those old gentlemen?"

She shrank a little, but said:

"N-o; if my being with you would help hearten you. But — would it be quite proper, do you think?"

"No, I don't know that it would — in fact, I'm afraid it wouldn't; but, you see, there's so *much* dependent upon it that —"

"Then I'll go anyway, proper or improper," she said, with a beautiful and generous enthusiasm. "Oh, I shall be so happy to think I'm helping!"

"Helping, dear? Why, you'll be doing it all. You're so beautiful and so lovely and so winning, that with you there I can pile our salary up till I break those good old fellows, and they'll never have the heart to struggle."

Sho! you should have seen the rich blood mount, and her happy eyes shine!

"You wicked flatterer! There isn't a word of truth in what you say, but still I'll go with you. Maybe it will teach you not to expect other people to look with your eyes."

Were my doubts dissipated? Was my confidence restored? You may judge by this fact: privately I raised my salary to twelve hundred the first year on the spot. But I didn't tell her; I saved it for a surprise.

All the way home I was in the clouds, Hastings talking, I not hearing a word. When he and I entered my parlor, he brought me to myself with his fervent appreciations of my manifold comforts and luxuries.

"Let me just stand here a little and look my fill.

Dear me! it's a palace — it's just a palace! And in it everything a body *could* desire, including cosey coal fire and supper standing ready. Henry, it doesn't merely make me realize how rich you are; it makes me realize, to the bone, to the marrow, how poor I am — how poor I am, and how miserable, how defeated, routed, annihilated!"

Plague take it! this language gave me the cold shudders. It scared me broad awake, and made me comprehend that I was standing on a half-inch crust, with a crater underneath. *I* didn't know I had been dreaming — that is, I hadn't been allowing myself to know it for a while back; but *now* — oh, dear! Deep in debt, not a cent in the world, a lovely girl's happiness or woe in my hands, and nothing in front of me but a salary which might never — oh, *would* never — materialize! Oh, oh, oh! I am ruined past hope! nothing can save me!

" Henry, the mere unconsidered drippings of your daily income would —"

" Oh, my daily income! Here, down with this hot Scotch, and cheer up your soul. Here's with you! Or, no — you're hungry; sit down and —"

" Not a bite for me; I'm past it. I can't eat, these days; but I'll drink with you till I drop. Come!"

" Barrel for barrel, I'm with you! Ready? Here we go! Now, then, Lloyd, unreel your story while I brew."

" Unreel it? What, again?"

" Again? What do you mean by that?"

" Why, I mean do you want to hear it *over* again?"

" Do I want to hear it *over* again? This *is* a puzzler. Wait; don't take any more of that liquid. You don't need it."

" Look here, Henry, you alarm me. Didn't I tell you the whole story on the way here?"

" You?"

" Yes, I."

" I'll be hanged if I heard a word of it."

" Henry, this is a serious thing. It troubles me. What did you take up yonder at the minister's?"

Then it all flashed on me, and I owned up like a man.

" I took the dearest girl in this world — prisoner!"

So then he came with a rush, and we shook, and shook, and shook till our hands ached; and he didn't blame me for not having heard a word of a story which had lasted while we walked three miles. He just sat down then, like the patient, good fellow he was, and told it all over again. Synopsized, it amounted to this: He had come to England with what he thought was a grand opportunity; he had an " option " to sell the Gould and Curry Extension for the " locators " of it, and keep all he could get over a million dollars. He had worked hard, had pulled every wire he knew of, had left no honest expedient untried, had spent nearly all the money he had in the world, had not been able to get a solitary capitalist to listen to him, and his option would run out at the end of the month. In a word, he was ruined. Then he jumped up and cried out:

" Henry, you can save me! You can save me, and you're the only man in the universe that can. Will you do it? *Won't* you do it?"

" Tell me how. Speak out, my boy."

" Give me a million and my passage home for my ' option '! Don't, *don't* refuse!"

I was in a kind of agony. I was right on the point of coming out with the words, " Lloyd, I'm a pauper myself — absolutely penniless, and in *debt!*" But a white-hot idea came flaming through my head, and I gripped my jaws together, and calmed myself down till

I was as cold as a capitalist. Then I said, in a commercial and self-possessed way:

"I will save you, Lloyd —"

"Then I'm already saved! God be merciful to you forever! If ever I —"

"Let me finish, Lloyd. I will save you, but not in that way; for that would not be fair to you, after your hard work, and the risks you've run. I don't need to buy mines; I can keep my capital moving, in a commercial center like London, without that; it's what I'm at, all the time; but here is what I'll do. I know all about that mine, of course; I know its immense value, and can swear to it if anybody wishes it. You shall sell out inside of the fortnight for three millions cash, using my name freely, and we'll divide, share and share alike."

Do you know, he would have danced the furniture to kindling-wood in his insane joy, and broken everything on the place, if I hadn't tripped him up and tied him.

Then he lay there, perfectly happy, saying:

"I may use your name! Your name — think of it! Man, they'll flock in droves, these rich Londoners; they'll *fight* for that stock! I'm a made man, I'm a made man forever, and I'll never forget you as long as I live!"

In less than twenty-four hours London was abuzz! I hadn't anything to do, day after day, but sit at home, and say to all comers:

"Yes; I told him to refer to me. I know the man, and I know the mine. His character is above reproach, and the mine is worth far more than he asks for it."

Meantime I spent all my evenings at the minister's with Portia. I didn't say a word to her about the mine; I saved it for a surprise. We talked salary; never anything but salary and love; sometimes love, sometimes salary, sometimes love and salary together. And my! the interest the minister's wife and daughter took in our little affair, and the endless ingenuities they invented to save us from interruption, and to keep the minister in the dark and unsuspicious — well, it was just lovely of them!

When the month was up at last, I had a million dollars to my credit in the London and County Bank, and Hastings was fixed in the same way. Dressed at my level best, I drove by the house in Portland Place, judged by the look of things that my birds were home again, went on towards the minister's and got my precious, and we started back, talking salary with all our might. She was so excited and anxious that it made her just intolerably beautiful. I said:

"Dearie, the way you're looking it's a crime to strike for a salary a single penny under three thousand a year."

"Henry, Henry, you'll ruin us!"

"Don't you be afraid. Just keep up those looks, and trust to me. It'll all come out right."

So, as it turned out, I had to keep bolstering up *her* courage all the way. She kept pleading with me, and saying:

"Oh, please remember that if we ask for too much we may get no salary at all; and then what will become of us, with no way in the world to earn our living?"

We were ushered in by that same servant, and there they were, the two old gentlemen. Of course, they were surprised to see that wonderful creature with me, but I said:

"It's all right, gentlemen; she is my future stay and helpmate."

And I introduced them to her, and called them by name. It didn't surprise them; they knew I would know enough to consult the directory. They seated us, and were very polite to me, and very solicitous to relieve her from embarrassment, and put her as much at her ease as they could.   Then I said:

"Gentlemen, I am ready to report."

"We are glad to hear it," said *my* man, "for now we can decide the bet which my brother Abel and I made.   If you have won for me, you shall have any situation in my gift.   Have you the million-pound note?"

"Here it is, sir," and I handed it to him.

"I've won!" he shouted, and slapped Abel on the back.   "*Now* what do you say, brother?"

"I say he *did* survive, and I've lost twenty thousand pounds.   I never would have believed it."

"I've a further report to make," I said, "and a pretty long one.   I want you to let me come soon, and detail my whole month's history; and I promise you it's worth hearing.   Meantime, take a look at that."

"What, man!   Certificate of deposit for £200,000. Is it yours?"

"Mine.   I earned it by thirty days' judicious use of that little loan you let me have.   And the only use I made of it was to buy trifles and offer the bill in change."

"Come, this is astonishing!   It's incredible, man!"

"Never mind, I'll prove it.   Don't take my word unsupported."

But now Portia's turn was come to be surprised. Her eyes were spread wide, and she said:

"Henry, is that really your money?   Have you been fibbing to me?"

"I have, indeed, dearie.   But you'll forgive me, *I* know."

She put up an arch pout, and said:

"Don't you be so sure.   You are a naughty thing to deceive me so!"

" Oh, you'll get over it, sweetheart, you'll get over it; it was only fun, you know. Come, let's be going."

" But wait, wait! The situation, you know. I want to give you the situation," said my man.

" Well," I said, " I'm just as grateful as I can be, but really I don't want one."

" But you can have the very choicest one in my gift."

" Thanks again, with all my heart; but I don't even want *that* one."

" Henry, I'm ashamed of you. You don't half thank the good gentleman. May I do it for you?"

" Indeed, you shall, dear, if you can improve it. Let us see you try."

She walked to my man, got up in his lap, put her arm round his neck, and kissed him right on the mouth. Then the two old gentlemen shouted with laughter, but I was dumfounded, just petrified, as you may say. Portia said:

" Papa, he has said you haven't a situation in your gift that he'd take; and I feel just as hurt as —"

" My darling, is that your papa?"

" Yes; he's my step-papa, and the dearest one that ever was. You understand now, don't you, why I was able to laugh when you told me at the minister's, not knowing my relationships, what trouble and worry papa's and Uncle Abel's scheme was giving you?"

Of course, I spoke right up now, without any fooling, and went straight to the point.

" Oh, my dearest dear sir, I want to take back what I said. You *have* got a situation open that I want."

" Name it."

" Son-in-law."

" Well, well, well! But you know, if you haven't ever served in that capacity, you, of course, can't furnish recommendations of a sort to satisfy the conditions of the contract, and so —"

" Try me — oh, do, I beg of you! Only just try me thirty or forty years, and if —''

" Oh, well, all right; it's but a little thing to ask, take her along.''

Happy, we two? There are not words enough in the unabridged to describe it. And when London got the whole history, a day or two later, of my month's adventures with that bank-note, and how they ended, did London talk, and have a good time? Yes.

My Portia's papa took that friendly and hospitable bill back to the Bank of England and cashed it; then the Bank canceled it and made him a present of it, and he gave it to us at our wedding, and it has always hung in its frame in the sacredest place in our home ever since. For it gave me my Portia. But for it I could not have remained in London, would not have appeared at the minister's, never should have met her. And so I always say, " Yes, it's a million-pounder, as you see; but it never made but one purchase in its life, and *then* got the article for only about a tenth part of its value.''

MENTAL TELEGRAPHY

A MANUSCRIPT WITH A HISTORY

NOTE TO THE EDITOR.— By glancing over the enclosed bundle of rusty old manuscript, you will perceive that I once made a great discovery: the discovery that certain sorts of thing which, from the beginning of the world, had always been regarded as merely "curious coincidences"— that is to say, accidents— were no more accidental than is the sending and receiving of a telegram an accident. I made this discovery sixteen or seventeen years ago, and gave it a name —"Mental Telegraphy." It is the same thing around the outer edges of which the Psychical Society of England began to group (and play with) four or five years ago, and which they named "Telepathy." Within the last two or three years they have penetrated towards the heart of the matter, however, and have found out that mind can act upon mind in a quite detailed and elaborate way over vast stretches of land and water. And they have succeeded in doing, by their great credit and influence, what I could never have done — they have convinced the world that mental telegraphy is not a jest, but a fact, and that it is a thing not rare, but exceedingly common. They have done our age a service — and a very great service, I think.

In this old manuscript you will find mention of an extraordinary experience of mine in the mental telegraphic line, of date about the year 1874 or 1875 — the one concerning the Great Bonanza book. It was this experience that called my attention to the matter under consideration. I began to keep a record, after that, of such experiences of mine as seemed explicable by the theory that minds telegraph thoughts to each other. In 1878 I went to Germany and began to write the book called *A Tramp Abroad*. The bulk of this old batch of manuscript was written at that time and for that book. But I removed it when I came to revise the volume for the press; for I feared that the public would treat the thing as a joke and throw it aside, whereas I was in earnest.

At home, eight or ten years ago, I tried to creep in under shelter of an authority grave enough to protect the article from ridicule — the *North American Review*. But Mr. Metcalf was too wary for me. He said that to treat these mere "coincidences" seriously was a thing which the *Review* couldn't dare to do; that I must put either my name or my *nom de plume* to the article, and thus save the *Review* from harm. But I couldn't consent to that; it would be the surest possible way to defeat my desire that the public should receive the thing seriously, and be willing to stop and give it some fair degree of attention. So I pigeon-holed the MS., because I could not get it published anonymously.

Now see how the world has moved since then. These small experiences of mine, which were too formidable at that time for admission to a grave magazine — if the magazine must allow them to appear as something above and beyond "accidents" and "coincidences"— are trifling and common-place now, since the flood of light recently cast upon mental telegraphy by the intelligent labors of the Psychical Society. But I think they are worth publishing, just to show what harmless and ordinary matters were considered dangerous and incredible eight or ten years ago.

As I have said, the bulk of this old manuscript was written in 1878; a later part was written from time to time two, three, and four years after-wards. The "Postscript" I add to-day.

MAY, '78.— Another of those apparently trifling things has happened to me which puzzle and per-plex all men every now and then, keep them think-ing an hour or two, and leave their minds barren of explanation or solution at last. Here it is — and it looks inconsequential enough, I am obliged to say. A few days ago I said: "It must be that Frank Millet doesn't know we are in Germany, or he would have written long before this. I have been on the point of dropping him a line at least a dozen times during the past six weeks, but I always decided to wait a day or two longer, and see if we shouldn't hear from him. But now I *will* write." And so I did. I directed the letter to Paris, and thought, "*Now* we shall hear from him before this letter is fifty miles from Heidelberg — it always happens so."

True enough; but *why* should it? That is the puzzling part of it. We are always talking about letters "crossing" each other, for that is one of the very commonest accidents of this life. We call it "accident," but perhaps we misname it. We have the instinct a dozen times a year that the letter we are writing is going to "cross" the other person's letter; and if the reader will rack his memory a little he will recall the fact that this presentiment had strength enough to it to make him cut his letter down to a decided briefness, because it would be a waste of time to write a letter which was going to "cross," and hence be a useless letter. I think that in my experience this instinct has generally come to me in cases where I had put off my letter a good while in the hope that the other person would write.

Yes, as I was saying, I had waited five or six weeks; then I wrote but three lines, because I felt and seemed to know that a letter from Millet would cross mine. And so it did. He wrote the same day that I wrote. The letters crossed each other. His letter went to Berlin, care of the American minister, who sent it to me. In this letter Millet said he had been trying for six weeks to stumble upon somebody who knew my German address, and at last the idea had occurred to him that a letter sent to the care of the embassy at Berlin might possibly find me.

Maybe it was an "accident" that he finally determined to write me at the same moment that I finally determined to write him, but I think not.

With me the most irritating thing has been to wait a tedious time in a purely business matter, hoping that the other party will do the writing, and then sit down and do it myself, perfectly satisfied that that other man is sitting down at the same moment to write a letter which will "cross" mine. And yet one must go on writing, just the same; because if you get up from your table and postpone, that other man will do the same thing, exactly as if you two were harnessed together like the Siamese twins, and must duplicate each other's movements.

Several months before I left home a New York firm did some work about the house for me, and did not make a success of it, as it seemed to me. When the bill came, I wrote and said I wanted the work perfected before I paid. They replied that they were very busy, but that as soon as they could spare the proper man the thing should be done. I waited more than two months, enduring as patiently as possible the companionship of bells which would fire away of their own accord sometimes when nobody was touching them, and at other times wouldn't ring though you struck the button with a sledge hammer. Many a time I got ready to write and then postponed it; but at last I sat down one evening and poured out my grief to the extent of a page or so, and then cut my letter suddenly short, because a strong instinct told me that the firm had begun to move in the matter. When I came down to breakfast next morning the postman had not yet taken my letter away, but the electrical man had been there, done his work, and was gone again! He had received his orders the previous evening from his employers, and had come up by the night train.

If that was an "accident," it took about three months to get it up in good shape.

One evening last summer I arrived in Washington, registered at the Arlington Hotel, and went to my room. I read and smoked until ten o'clock; then, finding I was not yet sleepy, I thought I would take a breath of fresh air. So I went forth in the rain, and tramped through one street after another in an aimless and enjoyable way. I knew that Mr. O——, a friend

of mine, was in town, and I wished I might run across
him; but I did not propose to hunt for him at midnight, especially as I did not know where he was stopping.   Towards twelve o'clock the streets had become
so deserted that I felt lonesome; so I stepped into a
cigar shop far up the avenue, and remained there
fifteen minutes, listening to some bummers discussing
national politics.   Suddenly the spirit of prophecy
came upon me, and I said to myself, " Now I will go
out at this door, turn to the left, walk ten steps, and
meet Mr. O—— face to face."   I did it, too! I could
not see his face, because he had an umbrella before it,
and it was pretty dark anyhow, but he interrupted the
man he was walking and talking with, and I recognized
his voice and stopped him.

That I should step out there and stumble upon Mr.
O—— was nothing, but that I should know beforehand that I was going to do it was a good deal.   It is
a very curious thing when you come to look at it.   I
stood far within the cigar shop when I delivered my
prophecy; I walked about five steps to the door,
opened it, closed it after me, walked down a flight of
three steps to the sidewalk, then turned to the left and
walked four or five more, and found my man.   I repeat
that in itself the thing was nothing; but to know it
would happen so *beforehand*, wasn't that really curious?

I have criticised absent people so often, and then
discovered, to my humiliation, that I was talking with
their relatives, that I have grown superstitious about
that sort of thing and dropped it.   How like an idiot
one feels after a blunder like that!

We are always mentioning people, and in that very
instant they appear before us.   We laugh, and say,
" Speak of the devil," and so forth, and there we
drop it, considering it an " accident."   It is a cheap
and convenient way of disposing of a grave and very

24***

puzzling mystery.   The fact is, it does seem to happen too often to be an accident.

Now I come to the oddest thing that ever happened to me.   Two or three years ago I was lying in bed, idly musing, one morning — it was the 2d of March — when suddenly a red-hot new idea came whistling down into my camp, and exploded with such comprehensive effectiveness as to sweep the vicinity clean of rubbishy reflections, and fill the air with their dust and flying fragments.   This idea, stated in simple phrase, was that the time was ripe and the market ready for a certain book: a book which ought to be written at once; a book which must command attention and be of peculiar interest — to wit, a book about the Nevada silver mines.   The " Great Bonanza " was a new wonder then, and everybody was talking about it.   It seemed to me that the person best qualified to write this book was Mr. William H. Wright, a journalist of Virginia, Nevada, by whose side I had scribbled many months when I was a reporter there ten or twelve years before.   He might be alive still; he might be dead; I could not tell; but I would write him, anyway.   I began by merely and modestly suggesting that he make such a book; but my interest grew as I went on, and I ventured to map out what I thought ought to be the plan of the work, he being an old friend, and not given to taking good intentions for ill.   I even dealt with details, and suggested the order and sequence which they should follow.   I was about to put the manuscript in an envelope, when the thought occurred to me that if this book should be written at my suggestion, and then no publisher happened to want it, I should feel uncomfortable; so I concluded to keep my letter back until I should have secured a publisher.   I pigeon-holed my document, and dropped a note to my own publisher, asking him to name a day for a business consultation. He was out of town on a far journey.

My note remained unanswered, and at the end of three or four days the whole matter had passed out of my mind. On the 9th of March the postman brought three or four letters, and among them a thick one whose superscription was in a hand which seemed dimly familiar to me. I could not " place " it at first, but presently I succeeded. Then I said to a visiting relative who was present:

" Now I will do a miracle. I will tell you everything this letter contains — date, signature, and all — without breaking the seal. It is from a Mr. Wright, of Virginia, Nevada, and is dated the 2d of March — seven days ago. Mr. Wright proposes to make a book about the silver mines and the Great Bonanza, and asks what I, as a friend, think of the idea. He says his subjects are to be so and so, their order and sequence so and so, and he will close with a history of the chief feature of the book, the Great Bonanza."

I opened the letter, and showed that I had stated the date and the contents correctly. Mr. Wright's letter simply contained what my own letter, written on the same date, contained, and mine still lay in its pigeon-hole, where it had been lying during the seven days since it was written.

There was no clairvoyance about this, if I rightly comprehend what clairvoyance is. I think the clairvoyant professes to actually *see* concealed writing, and read it off word for word. This was not my case. I only seemed to know, and to know absolutely, the contents of the letter in detail and due order, but I had to *word* them myself. I translated them, so to speak, out of Wright's language into my own.

Wright's letter and the one which I had written to him but never sent were in substance the same.

x***

Necessarily this could not come by accident; such elaborate accidents cannot happen. Chance might have duplicated one or two of the details, but she would have broken down on the rest. I could not doubt — there was no tenable reason for doubting — that Mr. Wright's mind and mine had been in close and crystal-clear communication with each other across three thousand miles of mountain and desert on the morning of the 2d of March. I did not consider that both minds *originated* that succession of ideas, but that one mind originated it, and simply telegraphed it to the other. I was curious to know which brain was the telegrapher and which the receiver, so I wrote and asked for particulars. Mr. Wright's reply showed that his mind had done the originating and telegraphing, and mine the receiving. Mark that significant thing now; consider for a moment how many a splendid " original " idea has been unconsciously stolen from a man three thousand miles away! If one should question that this is so, let him look into the cyclopædia and con once more that curious thing in the history of inventions which has puzzled every one so much — that is, the frequency with which the same machine or other contrivance has been invented at the same time by several persons in different quarters of the globe. The world was without an electric telegraph for several thousand years; then Professor Henry, the American, Wheatstone in England, Morse on the sea, and a German in Munich, all invented it at the same time. The discovery of certain ways of applying steam was made in two or three countries in the same year. Is it not possible that inventors are constantly and unwittingly stealing each other's ideas whilst they stand thousands of miles asunder?

Last spring a literary friend of mine,* who lived a

---

* W. D. Howells.

hundred miles away, paid me a visit, and in the course of our talk he said he had made a discovery — conceived an entirely new idea — one which certainly had never been used in literature. He told me what it was. I handed him a manuscript, and said he would find substantially the same idea in that — a manuscript which I had written a week before. The idea had been in my mind since the previous November; it had only entered his while I was putting it on paper, a week gone by. He had not yet written his; so he left it unwritten, and gracefully made over all his right and title in the idea to me.

The following statement, which I have clipped from a newspaper, is true. I had the facts from Mr. Howells's lips when the episode was new:

"A remarkable story of a literary coincidence is told of Mr. Howells's *Atlantic Monthly* serial 'Dr. Breen's Practice.' A lady of Rochester, New York, contributed to the magazine, after 'Dr. Breen's Practice' was in type, a short story which so much resembled Mr. Howells's that he felt it necessary to call upon her and explain the situation of affairs in order that no charge of plagiarism might be preferred against him. He showed her the proof-sheets of his story, and satisfied her that the similarity between her work and his was one of those strange coincidences which have from time to time occurred in the literary world."

I had read portions of Mr. Howells's story, both in MS. and in proof, before the lady offered her contribution to the magazine.

Here is another case. I clip it from a newspaper:

"The republication of Miss Alcott's novel 'Moods' recalls to a writer in the Boston *Post* a singular coincidence which was brought to light before the book was first published: 'Miss Anna M. Crane, of Baltimore, published 'Emily Chester,' a novel which was pronounced a very striking and strong story. A comparison of this book with 'Moods' showed that the two writers, though entire strangers to each other, and living hundreds of miles apart, had both chosen the same subject for their novels, had followed almost the same line of treatment up to a certain point, where the parallel ceased, and the denouéments were entirely opposite. And even more curious, the leading characters in both books had identically the same names, so that the names in Miss Alcott's novel had to be changed. Then the book was published by Loring.' "

Four or five times within my recollection there has been a lively newspaper war in this country over poems whose authorship was claimed by two or three different people at the same time. There was a war of this kind over "Nothing to Wear," "Beautiful Snow," "Rock me to Sleep, Mother," and also over one of Mr. Will Carleton's early ballads, I think. These were all blameless cases of unintentional and unwitting mental telegraphy, I judge.

A word more as to Mr. Wright. He had had his book in mind some time; consequently he, and not I, had originated the idea of it. The subject was entirely foreign to my thoughts; I was wholly absorbed in other things. Yet this friend, whom I had not seen and had hardly thought of for eleven years, was able to shoot his thoughts at me across three thousand miles of country, and fill my head with them, to the exclusion of every other interest, in a single moment. He had begun his letter after finishing his work on the morning paper — a little after three o'clock, he said. When it was three in the morning in Nevada it was about six in Hartford, where I lay awake thinking about nothing in particular; and just about that time his ideas came pouring into my head from across the continent, and I got up and put them on paper, under the impression that they were my own original thoughts.

I have never seen any mesmeric or clairvoyant performances or spiritual manifestations which were in the least degree convincing — a fact which is not of consequence, since my opportunities have been meager; but I am forced to believe that one human mind (still inhabiting the flesh) can communicate with another, over any sort of a distance, and without any *artificial* preparation of " sympathetic conditions " to act as a transmitting agent. I suppose that when the sympathetic conditions happen to exist the two minds communicate with each other, and that otherwise they don't; and I suppose that if the sympathetic conditions could be kept up right along, the two minds would continue to correspond without limit as to time.

Now there is that curious thing which happens to everybody: suddenly a succession of thoughts or sensations flocks in upon you, which startles you with the weird idea that you have ages ago experienced just this succession of thoughts or sensations in a previous existence. The previous existence is possible, no doubt, but I am persuaded that the solution of this hoary mystery lies not there, but in the fact that some far-off stranger has been telegraphing his thoughts and sensations into your consciousness, and that he stopped because some counter-current or other obstruction intruded and broke the line of communication. Perhaps they seem repetitions to you because they *are* repetitions, got at second hand from the other man. Possibly Mr. Brown, the " mind-reader," reads other people's minds, possibly he does not; but I know of a surety that I have read another man's mind, and therefore I do not see why Mr. Brown shouldn't do the like also.

I wrote the foregoing about three years ago, in Heidelberg, and laid the manuscript aside, purposing to add to it instances of mind-telegraphing from time to time as they should fall under my experience. Meantime the " crossing " of letters has been so frequent as to become monotonous. However, I have managed to get something useful out of this hint; for now, when I get tired of waiting upon a man whom I very much wish to hear from, I sit down and *compel* him to write, whether he wants to or not; that is to say, I sit down and write him, and then tear my letter up, satisfied that my act has forced him to write me at the same moment. I do not need to mail my letter — the writing it is the only essential thing.

Of course I have grown superstitious about this letter-crossing business — this was natural. We stayed awhile in Venice after leaving Heidelberg. One day I was going down the Grand Canal in a gondola, when I heard a shout behind me, and looked around to see what the matter was; a gondola was rapidly following, and the gondolier was making signs to me to stop. I did so, and the pursuing boat ranged up alongside. There was an American lady in it — a resident of Venice. She was in a good deal of distress. She said:

" There's a New York gentleman and his wife at the Hotel Britannia who arrived a week ago, expecting to find news of their son, whom they have heard nothing about during eight months. There was no news. The lady is down sick with despair; the gentleman can't sleep or eat. Their son arrived at San Francisco eight months ago, and announced the fact in a letter to his parents the same day. That is the last trace of him. The parents have been in Europe ever since; but their trip has been spoiled, for they have occupied their time simply in drifting restlessly from place to place, and writing letters everywhere and to everybody, begging for news of their son; but the mystery remains as dense as ever. Now the gentleman wants to stop writing and go to cabling. He wants to cable San Francisco. He has never done it before, because he is afraid of — of he doesn't know what — death of his son, no doubt. But he wants somebody to *advise* him to cable; wants me to do it. Now I simply can't; for if no news came, that mother yonder would die. So I have chased you up in order to get you to support me in urging him to be patient, and put the thing off a week or two longer; it may be the saving of this lady. Come along; let's not lose any time.''

So I went along, but I had a programme of my own. When I was introduced to the gentleman I said: '' I have some superstitions, but they are worthy of respect. If you will cable San Francisco immediately, you will hear news of your son inside of twenty-four hours. I don't know that you will get the news from San Francisco, but you will get it from somewhere. The only necessary thing is to *cable* — that is all. The news will come within twenty-four hours. Cable Peking, if you prefer; there is no choice in this matter. This delay is all occasioned by your not cabling long ago, when you were first moved to do it.''

It seems absurd that this gentleman should have been cheered up by this nonsense, but he was; he brightened up at once, and sent his cablegram; and next day, at noon, when a long letter arrived from his lost son, the man was as grateful to me as if I had really had something to do with the hurrying up of that letter. The son had shipped from San Francisco in a sailing vessel, and his letter was written from the first port he touched at, months afterwards.

This incident argues nothing, and is valueless. I insert it only to show how strong is the superstition which '' letter-crossing '' has bred in me. I was so sure that a cablegram sent to any place, no matter where, would defeat itself by '' crossing '' the incoming news, that my confidence was able to raise up a hopeless man, and make him cheery and hopeful.

But here are two or three incidents which come strictly under the head of mind-telegraphing. One Monday morning, about a year ago, the mail came in, and I picked up one of the letters and said to a friend: '' Without opening this letter I will tell you what it says. It is from Mrs. ————, and she says she was in New York last Saturday, and was purposing to run up here in the afternoon train and surprise us, but at the last moment changed her mind and returned westward to her home."

I was right; my details were exactly correct. Yet we had had no suspicion that Mrs. —————— was coming to New York, or that she had even a remote intention of visiting us.

I smoke a good deal — that is to say, all the time — so, during seven years, I have tried to keep a box of matches handy, behind a picture on the mantel-piece; but I have had to take it out in trying, because George (colored), who makes the fires and lights the gas, always uses my matches, and never replaces them. Commands and persuasions have gone for nothing with him all these seven years. One day last summer, when our family had been away from home several months, I said to a member of the household:

" Now, with all this long holiday, and nothing in the way to interrupt —"

" I can finish the sentence for you," said the member of the household.

" Do it, then," said I.

" George ought to be able, by practicing, to learn to let those matches alone."

It was correctly done. That was what I was going to say. Yet until that moment George and the matches had not been in my mind for three months, and it is plain that the part of the sentence which I uttered offers not the least cue or suggestion of what I was purposing to follow it with.

My mother* is descended from the younger of two English brothers named Lambton, who settled in this country a few generations ago. The tradition goes that the elder of the two eventually fell heir to a certain

* She was still living when this was written.

estate in England (now an earldom), and died right away. This has always been the way with our family. They always die when they could make anything by not doing it. The two Lambtons left plenty of Lambtons behind them; and when at last, about fifty years ago, the English baronetcy was exalted to an earldom, the great tribe of American Lambtons began to bestir themselves — that is, those descended from the elder branch. Ever since that day one or another of these has been fretting his life uselessly away with schemes to get at his " rights." The present " rightful earl " — I mean the American one — used to write me occasionally, and try to interest me in his projected raids upon the title and estates by offering me a share in the latter portion of the spoil; but I have always managed to resist his temptations.

Well, one day last summer I was lying under a tree, thinking about nothing in particular, when an absurd idea flashed into my head, and I said to a member of the household, " Suppose I should live to be ninety-two, and dumb and blind and toothless, and just as I was gasping out what was left of me on my deathbed —"

" Wait, I will finish the sentence," said a member of the household.

" Go on," said I.

" Somebody should rush in with a document, and say, ' All the other heirs are dead, and you are the Earl of Durham!' "

That is truly what I was going to say. Yet until that moment the subject had not entered my mind or been referred to in my hearing for months before. A few years ago this thing would have astounded me, but the like could not much surprise me now, though it happened every week; for I think I *know* now that mind can communicate accurately with mind without the aid of the slow and clumsy vehicle of speech.

This age does seem to have exhausted invention nearly; still, it has one important contract on its hands yet — the invention of the *phrenophone ;* that is to say, a method whereby the communicating of mind with mind may be brought under command and reduced to certainty and system. The telegraph and the telephone are going to become too slow and wordy for our needs. We must have the *thought* itself shot into our minds from a distance; then, if we need to put it into words, we can do that tedious work at our leisure. Doubtless the something which conveys our thoughts through the air from brain to brain is a finer and subtler form of electricity, and all we need do is to find out how to capture it and how to force it to do its work, as we have had to do in the case of the electric currents. Before the day of telegraphs neither one of these marvels would have seemed any easier to achieve than the other.

While I am writing this, doubtless somebody on the other side of the globe is writing it, too. The question is, am I inspiring him or is he inspiring me? I cannot answer that; but that these thoughts have been passing through somebody else's mind all the time I have been setting them down I have no sort of doubt.

I will close this paper with a remark which I found some time ago in Boswell's *Johnson :*

" Voltaire's *Candide* is wonderfully similar in its plan and conduct to Johnson's *Rasselas ;* insomuch that I have heard Johnson say that if they had not been published so closely one after the other that there was not time for imitation, *it would have been in vain to deny that the scheme of that which came latest was taken from the other.*"

The two men were widely separated from each other at the time, and the sea lay between them.

POSTSCRIPT.

In the *Atlantic* for June, 1882, Mr. John Fiske refers to the often-quoted Darwin-and-Wallace "coincidence":

"I alluded, just now, to the 'unforeseen circumstance' which led Mr. Darwin in 1859 to break his long silence, and to write and publish the *Origin of Species*. This circumstance served, no less than the extraordinary success of his book, to show how ripe the minds of men had become for entertaining such views as those which Mr. Darwin propounded. In 1858 Mr. Wallace, who was then engaged in studying the natural history of the Malay Archipelago, sent to Mr. Darwin (as the man most likely to understand him) a paper in which he sketched the outlines of a theory identical with that upon which Mr. Darwin had so long been at work. The same sequence of observed facts and inferences that had led Mr. Darwin to the discovery of natural selection and its consequences had led Mr. Wallace to the very threshold of the same discovery; but in Mr. Wallace's mind the theory had by no means been wrought out to the same degree of completeness to which it had been wrought in the mind of Mr. Darwin. In the preface to his charming book on Natural Selection, Mr. Wallace, with rare modesty and candor, acknowledges that whatever value his speculations may have had, they have been utterly surpassed in richness and cogency of proof by those of Mr. Darwin. This is no doubt true, and Mr. Wallace has done such good work in further illustration of the theory that he can well afford to rest content with the second place in the first announcement of it.

"The coincidence, however, between Mr. Wallace's conclusions and those of Mr. Darwin was very remarkable. But, after all, coincidences of this sort have not been uncommon in the history of scientific inquiry. Nor is it at all surprising that they should occur now and then, when we remember that a great and pregnant discovery must always be concerned with some question which many of the foremost minds in the world are busy thinking about. It was so with the discovery of the differential calculus, and again with the discovery of the planet Neptune. It was so with the interpretation of the Egyptian hieroglyphics, and with the establishment of the undulatory theory of light. It was so, to a considerable extent, with the introduction of the new chemistry, with the discovery of the mechanical equivalent of heat, and the whole doctrine of the correlation of forces. It was so with the invention of the electric telegraph and with the discovery of

25A

spectrum analysis. And it is not at all strange that it should have been so with the doctrine of the origin of species through natural selection.''

He thinks these '' coincidences '' were apt to happen because the matters from which they sprang were matters which many of the foremost minds in the world were busy thinking about. But perhaps *one* man in each case did the telegraphing to the others. The aberrations which gave Leverrier the idea that there must be a planet of such and such mass and such and such orbit hidden from sight out yonder in the remote abysses of space were not new; they had been noticed by astronomers for generations. Then why should it happen to occur to three people, widely separated — Leverrier, Mrs. Somerville, and Adams — to suddenly go to worrying about those aberrations all at the same time, and set themselves to work to find out what caused them, and to measure and weigh an invisible planet, and calculate its orbit, and hunt it down and catch it? — a strange project which nobody but they had ever thought of before. If one astronomer had invented that odd and happy project fifty years before, don't you think he would have telegraphed it to several others without knowing it?

But now I come to a puzzler. How is it that *inanimate* objects are able to affect the mind? They seem to do that. However, I wish to throw in a parenthesis first — just a reference to a thing everybody is familiar with — the experience of receiving a clear and particular *answer* to your telegram before your telegram has reached the sender of the answer. That is a case where your telegram has gone straight from your brain to the man it was meant for, far outstripping the wire's slow electricity, and it is an exercise of mental telegraphy which is as common as dining. To return to the influence of inanimate things. In the cases of non-professional clairvoyance examined by the Psychical Society the clairvoyant has usually been blindfolded, then some object which has been touched or worn by a person is placed in his hand; the clairvoyant immediately describes that person, and goes on and gives a history of some event with which the text object has been connected. If the inanimate object is able to affect and inform the clairvoyant's mind, maybe it can do the same when it is working in the interest of mental telegraphy. Once a lady in the West wrote me that her son was coming to New York to remain three weeks, and would pay me a visit if invited, and she gave me his address. I mislaid the letter, and forgot all about the matter till the three weeks were about up. Then a sudden and fiery irruption of remorse burst up in my brain that illuminated all the region round about, and I sat down at once and wrote to the lady and asked for that lost address. But, upon reflection, I judged that the stirring up of my recollection had not been an accident, so I added a postscript to say, never mind, I should get a letter from her son before night. And I did get it; for the letter was already in the town, although not delivered yet. It had influenced me somehow. I have had so many experiences of this sort — a dozen of them at least — that I am nearly persuaded that inanimate objects do not confine their activities to helping the clairvoyant, but do every now and then give the mental telegraphist a lift.

The case of mental telegraphy which I am coming to now comes under I don't exactly know what head. I clipped it from one of our local papers six or eight years ago. I know the details to be right and true, for the story was told to me in the same form by one of the two persons concerned (a clergyman of Hartford) at the time that the curious thing happened:

"A REMARKABLE COINCIDENCE.— Strange coincidences make the most interesting of stories and most curious of studies. Nobody can quite say how they come about, but everybody appreciates the fact when they do come, and it is seldom that any more complete and curious coincidence is recorded of minor importance than the following, which is absolutely true and occurred in this city:

"At the time of the building of one of the finest residences of Hartford, which is still a very new house, a local firm supplied the wall-paper for certain rooms, contracting both to furnish and to put on the paper. It happened that they did not calculate the size of one room exactly right, and the paper of the design selected for it fell short just half a roll. They asked for delay enough to send on to the manufacturers for what was needed, and were told that there was no especial hurry. It happened that the manufacturers had none on hand, and had destroyed the blocks from which it was printed. They wrote that they had a full list of the dealers to whom they had sold that paper, and that they would write to each of these, and get from some of them a roll. It might involve a delay of a couple of weeks, but they would surely get it.

"In the course of time came a letter saying that, to their great surprise, they could not find a single roll. Such a thing was very unusual, but in this case it had so happened. Accordingly the local firm asked for further time, saying they would write to their own customers who had bought of that pattern, and would get the piece from them. But to their surprise, this effort also failed. A long time had now elapsed, and there was no use of delaying any longer. They had contracted to paper the room, and their only course was to take off that which was insufficient and put on some other of which there was enough to go around. Accordingly at length a man was sent out to remove the paper. He got his apparatus ready, and was about to begin to work, under the direction of the owner of the building, when the latter was for the moment called away. The house was large and very interesting, and so many people had rambled about it that finally admission had been refused by a sign at the door. On the occasion, however, when a gentleman had knocked and asked for leave to look about, the owner, being on the premises, had been sent for to reply to the request in person. That was the call that for the moment delayed the final preparations. The gentleman went to the door and admitted the stranger, saying he would show him about the house, but first must return for a moment to that room to finish his directions there, and he told the curious story about the paper as they went on. They entered the room together, and the first thing the stranger, who lived fifty miles away, said on looking about was,

'Why, I have that very paper on a room in my house, and I have an extra roll of it laid away, which is at your service.' In a few days the wall was papered according to the original contract. Had not the owner been at the house, the stranger would not have been admitted; had he called a day later, it would have been too late; had not the facts been almost accidentally told to him, he would probably have said nothing of the paper, and so on. The exact fitting of all the circumstances is something very remarkable, and makes one of those stories that seem hardly accidental in their nature."

Something that happened the other day brought my hoary MS. to mind, and that is how I came to dig it out from its dusty pigeon-hole grave for publication. The thing that happened was a question. A lady asked it: "Have you ever had a vision — when awake?" I was about to answer promptly, when the last two words of the question began to grow and spread and swell, and presently they attained to vast dimensions. She did not know that they were important; and I did not at first, but I soon saw that they were putting me on the track of the solution of a mystery which had perplexed me a good deal. You will see what I mean when I get down to it. Ever since the English Society for Psychical Research began its investigations of ghost stories, haunted houses, and apparitions of the living and the dead, I have read their pamphlets with avidity as fast as they arrived. Now one of their commonest inquiries of a dreamer or a vision-seer is, "Are you sure you were awake at the time?" If the man can't say he is sure he was awake, a doubt falls upon his tale right there. But if he is positive he was awake, and offers reasonable evidence to substantiate it, the fact counts largely for the credibility of this story. It does with the society, and it did with me until that lady asked me the above question the other day.

The question set me to considering, and brought me to the conclusion that you can be asleep — at least, wholly unconscious — for a time, and not suspect that

25***

it has happened, and not have any way to prove that it *has* happened. A memorable case was in my mind. About a year ago I was standing on the porch one day, when I saw a man coming up the walk. He was a stranger, and I hoped he would ring and carry his business into the house without stopping to argue with me; he would have to pass the front door to get to me, and I hoped he wouldn't take the trouble; to help, I tried to look like a stranger myself — it often works. I was looking straight at that man; he had got to within ten feet of the door and within twenty-five feet of me — and suddenly he disappeared. It was as astounding as if a church should vanish from before your face and leave nothing behind it but a vacant lot. I was unspeakably delighted. I had seen an apparition at last, with my own eyes, in broad daylight. I made up my mind to write an account of it to the society. I ran to where the specter had been, to make sure he was playing fair, then I ran to the other end of the porch, scanning the open grounds as I went. No, everything was perfect; he couldn't have escaped without my seeing him; he was an apparition, without the slightest doubt, and I would write him up before he was cold. I ran, hot with excitement, and let myself in with a latch-key. When I stepped into the hall my lungs collapsed and my heart stood still. For there sat that same apparition in a chair all alone, and as quiet and reposeful as if he had come to stay a year! The shock kept me dumb for a moment or two, then I said, "Did you come in at that door?"

"Yes."

"Did *you* open it, or did you ring?"

"I rang, and the colored man opened it."

I said to myself: "This is astonishing. It takes George all of two minutes to answer the door-bell when he is in a hurry, and I have never see him in a hurry.   How *did* this man stand two minutes at that door, within five steps of me, and I did not see him?"

I should have gone to my grave puzzling over that riddle but for that lady's chance question last week: " Have you ever had a vision — when awake?" It stands explained now.   During at least sixty seconds that day I was asleep, or at least totally unconscious, without suspecting it.   In that interval the man came to my immediate vicinity, rang, stood there and waited, then entered and closed the door, and I did not see him and did not hear the door slam.

If he had slipped around the house in that interval and gone into the cellar — he had time enough — I should have written him up for the society, and magnified him, and gloated over him, and hurrahed about him, and thirty yoke of oxen could not have pulled the belief out of me that I was of the favored ones of the earth, and had seen a vision — while wide awake.

Now how are you to tell when you are awake? What are you to go by?   People bite their fingers to find out.   Why, you can do that in a dream

A CURE FOR THE BLUES

B^Y courtesy of Mr. Cable I came into possession of a singular book eight or ten years ago. It is likely that mine is now the only copy in existence. Its title-page, unabbreviated, reads as follows:

"The Enemy Conquered; or, Love Triumphant. By G. Ragsdale McClintock,* author of ' An Address,' etc., delivered at Sunflower Hill, South Carolina, and member of the Yale Law School. New Haven: published by T. H. Pease, 83 Chapel street, 1845."

No one can take up this book, and lay it down again unread. Whoever reads one line of it is caught, is chained; he has become the contented slave of its fascinations; and he will read and read, devour and devour, and will not let it go out of his hand till it is finished to the last line, though the house be on fire over his head. And after a first reading he will not throw it aside, but will keep it by him, with his Shakespeare and his Homer, and will take it up many and many a time, when the world is dark and his spirits are low, and be straightway cheered and refreshed. Yet this work has been allowed to lie wholly neglected, unmentioned, and apparently unregretted, for nearly half a century.

The reader must not imagine that he is to find in it wisdom, brilliancy, fertility of invention, ingenuity of

---

* The name here given is a substitute for the one actually attached to the pamphlet.

construction, excellence of form, purity of style, perfection of imagery, truth to nature, clearness of statement, humanly possible situations, humanly possible people, fluent narrative, connected sequence of events — or philosophy, or logic, or sense. No; the rich, deep, beguiling charm of the book lies in the total and miraculous *absence* from it of all these qualities — a charm which is completed and perfected by the evident fact that the author, whose naïve innocence easily and surely wins our regard, and almost our worship, does not know that they are absent, does not even suspect that they are absent. When read by the light of these helps to an understanding of the situation, the book is delicious — profoundly and satisfyingly delicious.

I call it a book because the author calls it a book, I call it a work because he calls it a work; but, in truth, it is merely a duodecimo pamphlet of thirty-one pages. It was written for fame and money, as the author very frankly — yes, and very hopefully, too, poor fellow — says in his preface. The money never came — no penny of it ever came; and how long, how pathetically long, the fame has been deferred — forty-seven years! He was young then, it would have been so much to him then; but will he care for it now?

As time is measured in America, McClintock's epoch is antiquity. In his long-vanished day the Southern author had a passion for "eloquence"; it was his pet, his darling. He would be eloquent, or perish. And he recognized only one kind of eloquence — the lurid, the tempestuous, the volcanic. He liked words — big words, fine words, grand words, rumbling, thundering, reverberating words; with sense attaching if it could be got in without marring the sound, but not otherwise. He loved to stand up before a dazed world, and pour forth flame and smoke and lava and pumice stone into the skies, and work his subterranean

thunders, and shake himself with earthquakes, and
stench himself with sulphur fumes. If he consumed
his own fields and vineyards, that was a pity, yes; but
he would have his eruption at any cost. Mr. Mc-
Clintock's eloquence — and he is always eloquent, his
crater is always spouting — is of the pattern common
to his day, but he departs from the custom of the time
in one respect: his brethren allowed sense to intrude
when it did not mar the sound, but he does not allow
it to intrude at all. For example, consider this figure,
which he uses in the village "Address" referred to
with such candid complacency in the title-page above
quoted — "like the topmost topaz of an ancient
tower." Please read it again; contemplate it; measure it; walk around it; climb up it; try to get at an
approximate realization of the size of it. Is the fellow
to that to be found in literature, ancient or modern,
foreign or domestic, living or dead, drunk or sober?
One notices how fine and grand it sounds. We know
that if it was loftily uttered, it got a noble burst of applause from the villagers; yet there isn't a ray of sense
in it, or meaning to it.

McClintock finished his education at Yale in 1843,
and came to Hartford on a visit that same year. I
have talked with men who at that time talked with him,
and felt of him, and knew he was real. One needs to
remember that fact and to keep fast hold of it; it is
the only way to keep McClintock's book from undermining one's faith in McClintock's actuality.

As to the book. The first four pages are devoted
to an inflamed eulogy of Woman — simply Woman in
general, or perhaps as an Institution — wherein, among
other compliments to her details, he pays a unique one
to her voice. He says it "fills the breast with fond
alarms, echoed by every rill." It sounds well enough,
but it is not true. After the eulogy he takes up his

real work and the novel begins. It begins in the woods, near the village of Sunflower Hill.

Brightening clouds seemed to rise from the mist of the fair Chatta-hoochee, to spread their beauty over the thick forest, to guide the hero whose bosom beats with aspirations to conquer the enemy that would tarnish his name, and to win back the admiration of his long-tried friend.

It seems a general remark, but it is not general; the hero mentioned is the to-be hero of the book; and in this abrupt fashion, and without name or description, he is shoveled into the tale. "With aspirations to conquer the enemy that would tarnish his name" is merely a phrase flung in for the sake of the sound — let it not mislead the reader. No one is trying to tarnish this person; no one has thought of it. The rest of the sentence is also merely a phrase; the man has no friend as yet, and of course has had no chance to try him, or win back his admiration, or disturb him in any other way.

The hero climbs up over "Sawney's Mountain," and down the other side, making for an old Indian "castle"— which becomes "the red man's hut" in the next sentence; and when he gets there at last, he "surveys with wonder and astonishment" the invisible structure, "which time had buried in the dust; and thought to himself his happiness was not yet complete." One doesn't know why it wasn't, nor how near it came to being complete, nor what was still wanting to round it up and make it so. Maybe it was the Indian; but the book does not say. At this point we have an episode:

Beside the shore of the brook sat a young man, about eighteen or twenty, who seemed to be reading some favorite book, and who had a remarkably noble countenance — eyes which betrayed more than a common mind. This of course made the youth a welcome guest, and gained him friends in whatever condition of life he might be placed. The traveler observed that he was a well-built figure which showed strength and grace in every move-ment. He accordingly addressed him in quite a gentlemanly manner, and inquired of him the way to the village. After he had received the desired information, and was about taking his leave, the youth said, "Are you not Major Elfonzo, the great musician *— the champion of a noble cause — the modern Achilles, who gained so many victories in the Florida War?" "I bear that name," said the Major, "and those titles, trusting at the same time that the ministers of grace will carry me triumphantly through all my laudable undertakings, and if," continued the Major, "you, sir, are the patronizer of noble deeds, I should like to make you my confidant, and learn your address." The youth looked somewhat amazed, bowed low, mused for a moment, and began: "My name is Roswell. I have been recently admitted to the bar, and can only give a faint outline of my future success in that honorable profession; but I trust, sir, like the Eagle, I shall look down from lofty rocks upon the dwellings of man, and shall ever be ready to give you any assistance in my official capacity, and whatever this muscular arm of mine can do, whenever it shall be called from its buried greatness." The major grasped him by the hand, and exclaimed: "O! thou exalted spirit of inspiration — thou flame of burning prosperity, may the Heaven-directed blaze be the glare of thy soul, and battle down every rampart that seems to impede your progress!"

There is a strange sort of originality about Mc-Clintock; he imitates other people's styles, but no-body can imitate his, not even an idiot. Other people can be windy, but McClintock blows a gale; other people can blubber sentiment, but McClintock spews it; other people can mishandle metaphors, but only McClintock knows how to make a business of it. Mc-Clintock is always McClintock, he is always consistent, his style is always his own style. He does not make the mistake of being relevant on one page and irrelevant on another; he is irrelevant on all of them. He does not make the mistake of being lucid in one place and obscure in another; he is obscure all the time. He does not make the mistake of slipping in a name

---

* Further on it will be seen that he is a country expert on the fiddle, and has a three-township fame.

here and there that is out of character with his work;
he always uses names that exactly and fantastically fit his
lunatics.   In the matter of undeviating consistency he
stands alone in authorship.   It is this that makes his
style unique, and entitles it to a name of its own —
McClintockian.   It is this that protects it from being
mistaken for anybody else's.   Uncredited quotations
from other writers often leave a reader in doubt as to
their authorship, but McClintock is safe from that accident; an uncredited quotation from him would always
be recognizable.   When a boy nineteen years old, who
had just been admitted to the bar, says, "I trust, sir,
like the Eagle, I shall look down from lofty rocks upon
the dwellings of man," we know who is speaking
through that boy; we should recognize that note anywhere.   There be myriads of instruments in this world's
literary orchestra, and a multitudinous confusion of
sounds that they make, wherein fiddles are drowned,
and guitars smothered, and one sort of drum mistaken
for another sort; but whensoever the brazen note of
the McClintockian trombone breaks through that fog
of music, that note is recognizable, and about it there
can be no blur of doubt.

The novel now arrives at the point where the Major
goes home to see his father.   When McClintock wrote
this interview, he probably believed it was pathetic.

The road which led to the town presented many attractions.   Elfonzo
had bid farewell to the youth of deep feeling, and was now wending his way
to the dreaming spot of his fondness.   The south winds whistled through
the woods, as the waters dashed against the banks, as rapid fire in the pent
furnace roars.   This brought him to remember while alone, that he quietly
left behind the hospitality of a father's house, and gladly entered the world,
with higher hopes than are often realized.   But as he journeyed onward,
he was mindful of the advice of his father, who had often looked sadly on
the ground, when tears of cruelly deceived hope moistened his eyes.   Elfonzo
had been somewhat of a dutiful son; yet fond of the amusements of life —

— had been in distant lands — had enjoyed the pleasure of the world, and had frequently returned to the scenes of his boyhood, almost destitute of many of the comforts of life. In this condition, he would frequently say to his father, " Have I offended you, that you look upon me as a stranger, and frown upon me with stinging looks? Will you not favor me with the sound of your voice? If I have trampled upon your veneration, or have spread a humid veil of darkness around your expectations, send me back into the world, where no heart beats for me — where the foot of man has never yet trod; but give me at least one kind word — allow me to come into the presence sometimes of thy winter-worn locks." " Forbid it, Heaven, that I should be angry with thee," answered the father, "my son, and yet I send thee back to the children of the world — to the cold charity of the combat, and to a land of victory. I read another destiny in thy counte- nance — I learn thy inclinations from the flame that has already kindled in my soul a strange sensation. It will seek thee, my dear Elfonzo, it will find thee — thou canst not escape that lighted torch, which shall blot out from the remembrance of men a long train of prophecies which they have fore- told against thee. I once thought not so. Once, I was blind; but now the path of life is plain before me, and my sight is clear; yet Elfonzo, return to thy worldly occupation — take again in thy hand, that chord of sweet sounds — struggle with the civilized world, and with your own heart; fly swiftly to the enchanted ground — let the night-owl send forth its screams from the stubborn oak — let the sea sport upon the beach, and the stars sing together; but learn of these, Elfonzo, thy doom, and thy hiding-place. Our most innocent as well as our most lawful desires must often be denied us, that we may learn to sacrifice them to a Higher will."

Remembering such admonitions with gratitude, Elfonzo was immediately urged by the recollection of his father's family to keep moving.

McClintock has a fine gift in the matter of surprises; but as a rule they are not pleasant ones, they jar upon the feelings. His closing sentence in the last quotation is of that sort. It brings one down out of the tinted clouds in too sudden and collapsed a fashion. It in- censes one against the author for a moment. It makes the reader want to take him by his winter-worn locks, and trample on his veneration, and deliver him over to the cold charity of combat, and blot him out with his own lighted torch. But the feeling does not last. The master takes again in his hand that concord of sweet sounds of his, and one is reconciled, pacified.

His steps became quicker and quicker — he hastened through the piny woods, dark as the forest was, and with joy he very soon reached the little village of repose, in whose bosom rested the boldest chivalry. His close attention to every important object — his modest questions about whatever was new to him — his reverence for wise old age, and his ardent desire to learn many of the fine arts, soon brought him into respectable notice.

One mild winter day, as he walked along the streets towards the Academy, which stood upon a small eminence, surrounded by native growth — some venerable in its appearance, others young and prosperous — all seemed inviting, and seemed to be the very place for learning as well as for genius to spend its research beneath its spreading shades. He entered its classic walls in the usual mode of southern manners.

The artfulness of this man! None knows so well as he how to pique the curiosity of the reader — and how to disappoint it. He raises the hope, here, that he is going to tell all about how one enters a classic wall in the usual mode of Southern manners; but does he? No; he smiles in his sleeve, and turns aside to other matters.

The principal of the Institution begged him to be seated, and listen to the recitations that were going on. He accordingly obeyed the request, and seemed to be much pleased. After the school was dismissed, and the young hearts regained their freedom, with the songs of the evening, laughing at the anticipated pleasures of a happy home, while others tittered at the actions of the past day, he addressed the teacher in a tone that indicated a resolution — with an undaunted mind. He said he had determined to become a student, if he could meet with his approbation. "Sir," said he, "I have spent much time in the world. I have traveled among the uncivilized inhabitants of America. I have met with friends, and combated with foes; but none of these gratify my ambition, or decide what is to be my destiny. I see the learned world have an influence with the voice of the people themselves. The despoilers of the remotest kingdoms of the earth, refer their differences to this class of persons. This the illiterate and inexperienced little dream of; and now if you will receive me as I am, with these deficiencies — with all my misguided opinions, I will give you my honor, sir, that I will never disgrace the Institution, or those who have placed you in this honorable station." The instructor, who had met with many disappointments, knew how to feel for a stranger who had been thus turned upon the charities of an unfeeling community. He looked at him earnestly, and said: "Be of good cheer — look forward, sir, to the high destination you may attain. Remember, the more elevated the mark at which you aim, the more sure, the more glorious, the more magnificent the prize." From wonder to wonder, his encouragement led the impatient listener. A strange nature bloomed before him — giant streams promised him success — gardens of hidden treasures opened to his view. All this, so vividly described, seemed to gain a new witchery from his glowing fancy.

It seems to me that this situation is new in romance. I feel sure it has not been attempted before. Military celebrities have been disguised and set at lowly occupations for dramatic effect, but I think McClintock is the first to send one of them to school. Thus, in this book, you pass from wonder to wonder, through gardens of hidden treasure, where giant streams bloom before you, and behind you, and all around, and you feel as happy, and groggy, and satisfied, with your quart of mixed metaphor aboard, as you would if it had been mixed in a sample-room, and delivered from a jug.

Now we come upon some more McClintockian surprises — a sweetheart who is sprung upon us without any preparation, along with a name for her which is even a little more of a surprise than she herself is.

In 1842 he entered the class, and made rapid progress in the English and Latin departments. Indeed, he continued advancing with such rapidity that he was like to become the first in his class, and made such unexpected progress, and was so studious, that he had almost forgotten the pictured saint of his affections. The fresh wreaths of the pine and cypress had waited anxiously to drop once more the dews of Heaven upon the heads of those who had so often poured forth the tender emotions of their souls under its boughs. He was aware of the pleasure that he had seen there. So one evening, as he was returning from his reading, he concluded he would pay a visit to this enchanting spot. Little did he think of witnessing a shadow of his former happiness, though no doubt, he wished it might be so. He continued sauntering by the roadside, meditating on the past. The nearer he approached the spot, the more anxious he became. At that moment, a tall female figure flitted across his path, with a bunch of roses in her hand; her countenance showed uncommon vivacity, with a resolute spirit; her ivory teeth already appeared as she smiled beautifully, promenading,—while her ringlets of hair, dangled unconsciously around her snowy neck. Nothing was wanting to complete her beauty. The tinge of the rose was in full bloom upon her cheek; the charms of sensibility and tenderness were always her associates. In Ambulinia's bosom dwelt a noble soul — one that never faded — one that never was conquered.

Ambulinia! It can hardly be matched in fiction. The full name is Ambulinia Valeer. Marriage will presently round it out and perfect it. Then it will be Mrs. Ambulinia Valeer Elfonzo. It takes the chromo.

Her heart yielded to no feeling but the love of Elfonzo, on whom she gazed with intense delight, and to whom she felt herself more closely bound, because he sought the hand of no other. Elfonzo was roused from his apparent reverie. His books no longer were his inseparable companions — his thoughts arrayed themselves to encourage him to the field of victory. He endeavored to speak to his supposed Ambulinia, but his speech appeared not in words. No, his effort was a stream of fire, that kindled his soul into a flame of admiration, and carried his senses away captive. Ambulinia had disappeared, to make him more mindful of his duty. As she walked speedily away through the piny woods, she calmly echoed: "O! Elfonzo, thou wilt now look from thy sunbeams. Thou shalt now walk in a new path — perhaps thy way leads though darkness; but fear not, the stars foretell happiness."

To McClintock that jingling jumble of fine words meant something, no doubt, or seemed to mean something; but it is useless for us to try to divine what it was. Ambulinia comes — we don't know whence nor why; she mysteriously intimates — we don't know what; and then she goes echoing away — we don't know whither; and down comes the curtain. McClintock's art is subtle; McClintock's art is deep.

26A

Not many days afterwards, as surrounded by fragrant flowers, she sat one evening at twilight, to enjoy the cool breeze that whispered notes of melody along the distant groves, the little birds perched on every side, as if to watch the movements of their new visitor. The bells were tolling, when Elfonzo silently stole along by the wild wood flowers, holding in his hand his favorite instrument of music — his eye continually searching for Ambulinia, who hardly seemed to perceive him, as she played carelessly with the songsters that hopped from branch to branch. Nothing could be more striking than the difference between the two. Nature seemed to have given the more tender soul to Elfonzo, and the stronger and more courageous to Ambulinia. A deep feeling spoke from the eyes of Elfonzo — such a feeling as can only be expressed by those who are blessed as admirers, and by those who are able to return the same with sincerity of heart. He was a few years older than Ambulinia: she had turned a little into her seventeenth. He had almost grown up in the Cherokee country, with the same equal proportions as one of the natives. But little intimacy had existed between them until the year forty-one — because the youth felt that the character of such a lovely girl was too exalted to inspire any other feeling than that of quiet reverence. But as lovers will not always be insulted, at all times and under all circumstances, by the frowns and cold looks of crabbed old age, which should continually reflect dignity upon those around, and treat the unfortunate as well as the fortunate with a graceful mien, he continued to use diligence and perseverance. All this lighted a spark in his heart that changed his whole character, and like the unyielding Deity that follows the storm to check its rage in the forest, he resolves for the first time to shake off his embarrassment, and return where he had before only worshiped.

At last we begin to get the Major's measure. We are able to put this and that casual fact together, and build the man up before our eyes, and look at him. And after we have got him built, we find him worth the trouble. By the above comparison between his age and Ambulinia's, we guess the war-worn veteran to be twenty-two; and the other facts stand thus: he had grown up in the Cherokee country with the same equal proportions as one of the natives — how flowing and graceful the language, and yet how tantalizing as to meaning! — he had been turned adrift by his father, to whom he had been " somewhat of a dutiful son "; he

wandered in distant lands; came back frequently " to
the scenes of his boyhood, almost destitute of many of
the comforts of life," in order to get into the presence
of his father's winter-worn locks, and spread a humid
veil of darkness around his expectations; but he was
always promptly sent back to the cold charity of the
combat again; he learned to play the fiddle, and made
a name for himself in that line; he had dwelt among
the wild tribes; he had philosophized about the despoilers of the kingdoms of the earth, and found out —
the cunning creature —that they refer their differences
to the learned for settlement; he had achieved a vast
fame as a military chieftain, the Achilles of the Florida
campaigns, and then had got him a spelling-book and
started to school; he had fallen in love with Ambulinia
Valeer while she was teething, but had kept it to himself a while, out of the reverential awe which he felt
for the child; but now at last, like the unyielding Deity
who follows the storm to check its rage in the forest,
he resolves to shake off his embarrassment, and to
return where before he had only worshiped. The
Major, indeed, has made up his mind to rise up and
shake his faculties together, and to see if *he* can't do
that thing himself. This is not clear. But no matter
about that: there stands the hero, compact and visible;
and he is no mean structure, considering that his
creator had never created anything before, and hadn't
anything but rags and wind to build with this time. It
seems to me that no one can contemplate this odd
creature, this quaint and curious blatherskite, without
admiring McClintock, or, at any rate, loving him and
feeling grateful to him; for McClintock made him, he
gave him to us; without McClintock we could not
have had him, and would now be poor.

But we must come to the feast again. Here is a
courtship scene, down there in the romantic glades

among the raccoons, alligators, and things, that has merit, peculiar literary merit. See how Achilles woos. Dwell upon the second sentence (particularly the close of it) and the beginning of the third. Never mind the new personage, Leos, who is intruded upon us unheralded and unexplained. That is McClintock's way; it is his habit; it is a part of his genius; he cannot help it; he never interrupts the rush of his narrative to make introductions.

It could not escape Ambulinia's penetrating eye that he sought an interview with her, which she as anxiously avoided, and assumed a more distant calmness than before, seemingly to destroy all hope. After many efforts and struggles with his own person, with timid steps the Major approached the damsel, with the same caution as he would have done in a field of battle. "Lady Ambulinia," said he, trembling, "I have long desired a moment like this. I dare not let it escape. I fear the consequences; yet I hope your indulgence will at least hear my petition. Can you not anticipate what I would say, and what I am about to express? Will you not, like Minerva, who sprung from the brain of Jupiter, release me from thy winding chains or cure me—" "Say no more, Elfonzo," answered Ambulinia, with a serious look, raising her hand as if she intended to swear eternal hatred against the whole world; "another lady in my place would have perhaps answered your question in bitter coldness. I know not the little arts of my sex. I care but little for the vanity of those who would chide me, and am unwilling as well as ashamed to be guilty of anything that would lead you to think 'all is not gold that glitters'; so be not rash in your resolution. It is better to repent now, than to do it in a more solemn hour. Yes, I know what you would say. I know you have a costly gift for me — the noblest that man can make — your heart! you should not offer it to one so unworthy. Heaven, you know, has allowed my father's house to be made a house of solitude, a home of silent obedience, which my parents say is more to be admired than big names and high-sounding titles. Notwithstanding all this, let me speak the emotions of an honest heart — allow me to say in the fullness of my hopes that I anticipate better days. The bird may stretch its wings towards the sun, which it can never reach; and flowers of the field appear to ascend in the same direction, because they cannot do otherwise; but man confides his complaints to the saints in whom he believes; for in their abodes of light they know no more sorrow.

From your confession and indicative looks, I must be that person; if so deceive not yourself."

Elfonzo replied, " Pardon me, my dear madam, for my frankness. I have loved you from my earliest days — everything grand and beautiful hath borne the image of Ambulinia; while precipices on every hand surrounded me, your guardian angel stood and beckoned me away from the deep abyss. In every trial, in every misfortune, I have met with your helping hand; yet I never dreamed or dared to cherish thy love, till a voice impaired with age encouraged the cause, and declared they who acquired thy favor should win a victory. I saw how Leos worshiped thee. I felt my own unworthiness. I began to know jealousy, a strong guest indeed, in my bosom, yet I could see if I gained your admiration Leos was to be my rival. I was aware that he had the influence of your parents, and the wealth of a deceased relative, which is too often mistaken for permanent and regular tranquillity; yet I have determined by your permission to beg an interest in your prayers — to ask you to animate my drooping spirits by your smiles and your winning looks; for, if you but speak, I shall be conqueror, my enemies shall stagger like Olympus shakes. And though earth and sea may tremble, and the charioteer of the sun may forget his dashing steed, yet I am assured that it is only to arm me with divine weapons, which will enable me to complete my long-tried intention." " Return to yourself, Elfonzo," said Ambulinia, pleasantly; " a dream of vision has disturbed your intellect; you are above the atmosphere, dwelling in the celestial regions; nothing is there that urges or hinders, nothing that brings discord into our present litigation. I entreat you to condescend a little, and be a man, and forget it all. When Homer describes the battle of the gods and noble men, fighting with giants and dragons, they represent under this image our struggles with the delusions of our passions. You have exalted me, an unhappy girl, to the skies; you have called me a saint, and portrayed in your imagination an angel in human form. Let her remain such to you, let her continue to be as you have supposed, and be assured that she will consider a share in your esteem as her highest treasure. Think not that I would allure you from the path in which your conscience leads you; for you know I respect the conscience of others, as I would die for my own. Elfonzo, if I am worthy of thy love, let such conversation never again pass between us. Go, seek a nobler theme ! we will seek it in the stream of time, as the sun set in the Tigris." As she spake these words she grasped the hand of Elfonzo, saying at the same time —" Peace and prosperity attend you, my hero; be up and doing." Closing her remarks with this expression, she walked slowly away, leaving Elfonzo

26***

astonished and amazed.   He ventured not to follow or detain her.   Here
he stood alone, gazing at the stars; confounded as he was, here he stood.

Yes; there he stood.   There seems to be no doubt
about that.   Nearly half of this delirious story has now
been delivered to the reader.   It seems a pity to reduce
the other half to a cold synopsis.   Pity! it is more
than a pity, it is a crime; for to synopsize McClintock
is to reduce a sky-flushing conflagration to dull embers,
it is to reduce barbaric splendor to ragged poverty.
McClintock never wrote a line that was not precious;
he never wrote one that could be spared; he never
framed one from which a word could be removed without damage.   Every sentence that this master has produced may be likened to a perfect set of teeth, white,
uniform, beautiful.   If you pull one, the charm is
gone.

Still, it is now necessary to begin to pull, and to
keep it up; for lack of space requires us to synopsize.

We left Elfonzo standing there amazed.   At what,
we do not know.   Not at the girl's speech.   No; we
ourselves should have been amazed at it, of course, for
none of us has ever heard anything resembling it; but
Elfonzo was used to speeches made up of noise and
vacancy, and could listen to them with undaunted mind
like the " topmost topaz of an ancient tower "; he
was used to making them himself; he — but let it go,
it cannot be guessed out; we shall never know what it
was that astonished him.   He stood there awhile; then
he said, " Alas! am I now Grief's disappointed son at
last?"   He did not stop to examine his mind, and to
try to find out what he probably meant by that, because, for one reason, " a mixture of ambition and
greatness of soul moved upon his young heart," and
started him for the village.   He resumed his bench in
school, " and reasonably progressed in his education."
His heart was heavy, but he went into society, and

sought surcease of sorrow in its light distractions. He
made himself popular with his violin, "which seemed
to have a thousand chords — more symphonious than
the Muses of Apollo, and more enchanting than the
ghost of the Hills." This is obscure, but let it go.

During this interval Leos did some unencouraged
courting, but at last, "choked by his undertaking,"
he desisted.

Presently "Elfonzo again wends his way to the
stately walls and new-built village." He goes to the
house of his beloved; she opens the door herself. To
my surprise — for Ambulinia's heart had still seemed
free at the time of their last interview — love beamed
from the girl's eyes. One sees that Elfonzo was surprised, too; for when he caught that light, "a halloo
of smothered shouts ran through every vein." A neat
figure — a very neat figure, indeed! Then he kissed
her. "The scene was overwhelming." They went
into the parlor. The girl said it was safe, for her
parents were abed, and would never know. Then we
have this fine picture — flung upon the canvas with
hardly an effort, as you will notice.

> Advancing towards him she gave a bright display of her rosy neck, and
> from her head the ambrosial locks breathed divine fragrance; her robe hung
> waving to his view, while she stood like a goddess confessed before him.

There is nothing of interest in the couple's interview.
Now at this point the girl invites Elfonzo to a village
show, where jealousy is the motive of the play, for she
wants to teach him a wholesome lesson, if he is a jealous person. But this is a sham, and pretty shallow.
McClintock merely wants a pretext to drag in a
plagiarism of his upon a scene or two in "Othello."

The lovers went to the play. Elfonzo was one of
the fiddlers. He and Ambulinia must not be seen
together, lest trouble follow with the girl's malignant

z***

father; we are made to understand that clearly. So the two sit together in the orchestra, in the midst of the musicians. This does not seem to be good art. In the first place, the girl would be in the way, for orchestras are always packed closely together, and there is no room to spare for people's girls; in the next place, one cannot conceal a girl in an orchestra without everybody taking notice of it. There can be no doubt, it seems to me, that this is bad art.

Leos is present. Of course, one of the first things that catches his eye is the maddening spectacle of Ambulinia "leaning upon Elfonzo's chair." This poor girl does not seem to understand even the rudiments of concealment. But she is "in her seventeenth," as the author phrases it, and that is her justification.

Leos meditates, constructs a plan — with personal violence as a basis, of course. It was their way down there. It is a good plain plan, without any imagination in it. He will go out and stand at the front door, and when these two come out he will "arrest Ambulinia from the hands of the insolent Elfonzo," and thus make for himself a "more prosperous field of immortality than ever was decreed by Omnipotence, or ever pencil drew or artist imagined." But, dear me, while he is waiting there the couple climb out at the back window and scurry home! This is romantic enough, but there is a lack of dignity in the situation.

At this point McClintock puts in the whole of his curious play — which we skip.

Some correspondence follows now. The bitter father and the distressed lovers write the letters. Elopements are attempted. They are idiotically planned, and they fail. Then we have several pages of romantic powwow and confusion signifying nothing. Another elopement is planned; it is to take place on Sunday, when everybody is at church. But the " hero " cannot keep the secret; he tells everybody. Another author would have found another instrument when he decided to defeat this elopement; but that is not McClintock's way. He uses the person that is nearest at hand.

The evasion failed, of course. Ambulinia, in her flight, takes refuge in a neighbor's house. Her father drags her home. The villagers gather, attracted by the racket.

Elfonzo was moved at this sight. The people followed on to see what was going to become of Ambulinia, while he, with downcast looks, kept at a distance, until he saw them enter the abode of the father, thrusting her, that was the sigh of his soul, out of his presence into a solitary apartment, when she exclaimed, "Elfonzo! Elfonzo! oh, Elfonzo! where art thou, with all thy heroes? haste, oh! haste, come thou to my relief. Ride on the wings of the wind! Turn thy force loose like a tempest, and roll on thy army like a whirlwind, over this mountain of trouble and confusion. Oh, friends! if any pity me, let your last efforts throng upon the green hills, and come to the relief of Ambulinia, who is guilty of nothing but innocent love." Elfonzo called out with a loud voice, "My God, can I stand this! arouse up, I beseech you, and put an end to this tyranny. Come, my brave boys," said he, "are you ready to go forth to your duty?" They stood around him. "Who," said he, "will call us to arms? Where are my thunderbolts of war? Speak ye, the first who will meet the foe! Who will go forth with me in this ocean of grievous temptation? If there is one who desires to go, let him come and shake hands upon the altar of devotion, and swear that he will be a hero; yes, a Hector in a cause like this, which calls aloud for a speedy remedy." "Mine be the deed," said a young lawyer, "and mine alone; Venus alone shall quit her station before I will forsake one jot or tittle of my promise to you; what is death to me? what is all this warlike army, if it is not to win a victory? I love the sleep of the lover and the mighty; nor would I give it over till the blood of my enemies should wreak with that of my own. But God forbid that our fame should soar on the blood of the slumberer." Mr. Valeer stands at his door with the frown of a demon upon his brow, with his dangerous weapon* ready to strike the first man who should enter his door. "Who will arise

---

* It is a crowbar.

and go forward through blood and carnage to the rescue of my Ambulinia?"
said Elfonzo. "All," exclaimed the multitude; and onward they went,
with their implements of battle. Others, of a more timid nature, stood
among the distant hills to see the result of the contest.

It will hardly be believed that after all this thunder
and lightning not a drop of rain fell; but such is the
fact. Elfonzo and his gang stood up and blackguarded
Mr. Valeer with vigor all night, getting their outlay
back with interest; then in the early morning the army
and its general retired from the field, leaving the victory
with their solitary adversary and his crowbar. This is
the first time this has happened in romantic literature.
The invention is original. Everything in this book is
original; there is nothing hackneyed about it anywhere. Always, in other romances, when you find the
author leading up to a climax, you know what is going
to happen. But in this book it is different; the thing
which seems inevitable and unavoidable never happens;
it is circumvented by the art of the author every time.

Another elopement was attempted. It failed.

We have now arrived at the end. But it is not exciting. McClintock thinks it is; but it isn't. One day
Elfonzo sent Ambulinia another note — a note proposing elopement No. 16. This time the plan is admirable; admirable, sagacious, ingenious, imaginative,
deep — oh, everything, and perfectly easy. One wonders why it was never thought of before. This is the
scheme. Ambulinia is to leave the breakfast table,
ostensibly to "attend to the placing of those flowers,
which ought to have been done a week ago"— artificial ones, of course; the others wouldn't keep so long
— and then, instead of fixing the flowers, she is to
walk out to the grove, and go off with Elfonzo. The
invention of this plan overstrained the author, that is
plain, for he straightway shows failing powers. The
details of the plan are not many or elaborate. The

author shall state them himself — this good soul, whose intentions are always better than his English:

> You walk carelessly towards the academy grove, where you will find me with a lightning steed, elegantly equipped to bear you off where we shall be joined in wedlock with the first connubial rights.

Last scene of all, which the author, now much enfeebled, tries to smarten up and make acceptable to his spectacular heart by introducing some new properties — silver bow, golden harp, olive branch — things that can all come good in an elopement, no doubt, yet are not to be compared to an umbrella for real handiness and reliability in an excursion of that kind.

> And away she ran to the sacred grove, surrounded with glittering pearls, that indicated her coming. Elfonzo hails her with his silver bow and his golden harp. They meet — Ambulinia's countenance brightens — Elfonzo leads up the winged steed. "Mount," said he, "ye true hearted, ye fearless soul — the day is ours." She sprang upon the back of the young thunderbolt, a brilliant star sparkles upon her head, with one hand she grasps the reins, and with the other she holds an olive branch. "Lend thy aid, ye strong winds," they exclaimed, "ye moon, ye sun, and all ye fair host of heaven, witness the enemy conquered." "Hold," said Elfonzo, "thy dashing steed." "Ride on," said Ambulinia, "the voice of thunder is behind us." And onward they went, with such rapidity, that they very soon arrived at Rural Retreat, where they dismounted, and were united with all the solemnities that usually attend such divine operations.

There is but one Homer, there is but one Shakespeare, there is but one McClintock — and his immortal book is before you. Homer could not have written this book, Shakespeare could not have written it, I could not have done it myself. There is nothing just like it in the literature of any country or of any epoch. It stands alone; it is monumental. It adds G. Ragsdale McClintock's to the sum of the republic's imperishable names.

THE CURIOUS BOOK

COMPLETE

[The foregoing review of the great work of G. Ragsdale McClintock is liberally illuminated with sample extracts, but these cannot appease the appetite. Only the complete book, unabridged, can do that. Therefore it is here printed.— M. T.]

THE ENEMY CONQUERED; OR, LOVE TRIUMPHANT

> Sweet girl, thy smiles are full of charms,
>   Thy voice is sweeter still,
> It fills the breast with fond alarms,
>   Echoed by every rill.

BEGIN this little work with an eulogy upon woman, who has ever been distinguished for her perseverance, her constancy, and her devoted attention to those upon whom she has been pleased to place her *affections*. Many have been the themes upon which writers and public speakers have dwelt with intense and increasing interest. Among these delightful themes stands that of woman, the balm to all our sighs and disappointments, and the most pre-eminent of all other topics. Here the poet and orator have stood and gazed with wonder and with admiration; they have dwelt upon her innocence, the ornament of all her virtues. First viewing her external charms, such as are set forth in her form and her benevolent countenance, and then passing to the deep hidden springs of loveliness and disinterested devotion. In every clime,

(408)

and in every age, she has been the pride of her *nation*. Her watchfulness is untiring; she who guarded the sepulchre was the first to approach it, and the last to depart from its awful yet sublime scene. Even here, in this highly-favored land, we look to her for the security of our institutions, and for our future greatness as a nation. But, strange as it may appear, woman's charms and virtues are but slightly appreciated by thousands. Those who should raise the standard of female worth, and paint her value with her virtues, in living colors, upon the banners that are fanned by the zephyrs of heaven, and hand them down to posterity as emblematical of a rich inheritance, do not properly estimate them.

Man is not sensible, at all times, of the nature and the emotions which bear that name; he does not understand, he will not comprehend; his intelligence has not expanded to that degree of glory which drinks in the vast revolution of humanity, its end, its mighty destination, and the causes which operated, and are still operating, to produce a more elevated station, and the objects which energize and enliven its consummation. This he is a stranger to; he is not aware that woman is the recipient of celestial love, and that man is dependent upon her to perfect his character; that without her, philosophically and truly speaking, the brightest of his intelligence is but the coldness of a winter moon, whose beams can produce no fruit, whose solar light is not its own, but borrowed from the great dispenser of effulgent beauty. We have no disposition in the world to flatter the fair sex, we would raise them above those dastardly principles which only exist in little souls, contracted hearts, and a distracted brain. Often does she unfold herself in all her fascinating loveliness, presenting the most captivating charms; yet we find man frequently treats such purity of purpose

with indifference.   Why does he do it?   Why does he
baffle that which is inevitably the source of his better
days?   Is he so much of a stranger to those excellent
qualities as not to appreciate woman, as not to have
respect to her dignity?   Since her art and beauty first
captivated man, she has been his delight and his comfort; she has shared alike in his misfortunes and in his
prosperity.

Whenever the billows of adversity and the tumultuous waves of trouble beat high, her smiles subdue their
fury.   Should the tear of sorrow and the mournful
sigh of grief interrupt the peace of his mind, her voice
removes them all, and she bends from her circle to
encourage him onward.   When darkness would obscure
his mind, and a thick cloud of gloom would bewilder
its operations, her intelligent eye darts a ray of streaming light into his heart.   Mighty and charming is that
disinterested devotion which she is ever ready to exercise towards man, not waiting till the last moment of
his danger, but seeks to relieve him in his early afflic-
tions.   It gushes forth from the expansive fullness of a
tender and devoted heart, where the noblest, the purest,
and the most elevated and refined feelings are matured
and developed in those many kind offices which invariably make her character.

In the room of sorrow and sickness, this unequaled
characteristic may always be seen, in the performance
of the most charitable acts; nothing that she can do to
promote the happiness of him who she claims to be
her protector, will be omitted; all is invigorated by the
animating sunbeams which awaken the heart to songs
of gayety.   Leaving this point, to notice another
prominent consideration, which is generally one of
great moment and of vital importance.   Invariably she
is firm and steady in all her pursuits and aims.   There
is required a combination of forces and extreme oppo-

sition to drive her from her position; she takes her stand, not to be moved by the sound of Apollo's lyre, or the curved bow of pleasure.

Firm and true to what she undertakes, and that which she requires by her own aggrandizement, and regards as being within the strict rules of propriety, she will remain stable and unflinching to the last. A more genuine principle is not to be found in the most determined, resolute heart of man. For this she deserves to be held in the highest commendation, for this she deserves the purest of all other blessings, and for this she deserves the most laudable reward of all others. It is a noble characteristic, and is worthy the imitation of any age. And when we look at it in one particular aspect, it is still magnified, and grows brighter and brighter the more we reflect upon its eternal duration. What will she not do, when her word as well as her affections and *love* are pledged to her lover? Everything that is dear to her on earth, all the hospitalities of kind and loving parents, all the sincerity and loveliness of sisters, and the benevolent devotion of brothers, who have surrounded her with every comfort; she will forsake them all, quit the harmony and sweet sound of the lute and the harp, and throw herself upon the affections of some devoted admirer, in whom she fondly hopes to find more than she has left behind, which is not often realized by many. Truth and virtue all combined! How deserving our admiration and love! Ah! cruel would it be in man, after she has thus manifested such an unshaken confidence in him, and said by her determination to abandon all the endearments and blandishments of home, to act a villainous part, and prove a traitor in the revolution of his mission, and then turn Hector over the innocent victim whom he swore to protect, in the presence of Heaven, recorded by the pen of an angel.

Striking as this trait may unfold itself in her character, and as pre-eminent as it may stand among the
fair display of her other qualities, yet there is another,
which struggles into existence, and adds an additional
lustre to what she already possesses. I mean that disposition in woman which enables her, in sorrow, in
grief, and in distress, to bear all with enduring patience.
This she has done, and can and will do, amid the din
of war and clash of arms. Scenes and occurrences
which, to every appearance, are calculated to rend the
heart with the profoundest emotions of trouble, do
not fetter that exalted principle imbued in her very
nature. It is true, her tender and feeling heart may
often be moved (as she is thus constituted), but still
she is not conquered, she has not given up to the
harlequin of disappointments, her energies have not
become clouded in the last moment of misfortune, but
she is continually invigorated by the archetype of her
affections. She may bury her face in her hands, and
let the tear of anguish roll, she may promenade the
delightful walks of some garden, decorated with all the
flowers of nature, or she may steal out along some
gently rippling stream, and there, as the silver waters
uninterruptedly move forward, shed her silent tears;
they mingle with the waves, and take a last farewell of
their agitated home, to seek a peaceful dwelling among
the rolling floods; yet there is a voice rushing from
her breast, that proclaims *victory* along the whole line
and battlement of her affections. That voice is the
voice of patience and resignation; that voice is one
that bears everything calmly and dispassionately, amid
the most distressing scenes, when the fates are arrayed
against her peace, and apparently plotting for her
destruction, still she is resigned.

Woman's affections are deep, consequently her
troubles may be made to sink deep. Although you

may not be able to mark the traces of her grief and the furrowings of her anguish upon her winning countenance, yet be assured they are nevertheless preying upon her inward person, sapping the very foundation of that heart which alone was made for the weal and not the woe of man. The deep recesses of the soul are fields for their operation. But they are not destined simply to take the regions of the heart for their dominion, they are not satisfied merely with interrupting her better feelings; but after a while you may see the blooming cheek beginning to droop and fade, her intelligent eye no longer sparkles with the starry light of heaven, her vibrating pulse long since changed its regular motion, and her palpitating bosom beats once more for the mid-day of her glory. Anxiety and care ultimately throw her into the arms of the haggard and grim monster death. But, oh, how patient, under every pining influence! Let us view the matter in bolder colors; see her when the dearest object of her affections recklessly seeks every bacchanalian pleasure, contents himself with the last rubbish of creation. With what solicitude she awaits his return! Sleep fails to perform its office — she weeps while the nocturnal shades of the night triumph in the stillness. Bending over some favorite book, whilst the author throws before her mind the most beautiful imagery, she startles at every sound. The midnight silence is broken by the solemn announcement of the return of another morning. He is still absent; she listens for that voice which has so often been greeted by the melodies of her own; but, alas! stern silence is all that she receives for her vigilance.

Mark her unwearied watchfulness, as the night passes away. At last, brutalized by the accursed thing, he staggers along with rage, and, shivering with cold, he makes his appearance. Not a murmur is heard from

27A

her lips. On the contrary, she meets him with a smile — she caresses him with her tender arms, with all the gentleness and softness of her sex. Here, then, is seen her disposition, beautifully arrayed. Woman, thou art more to be admired than the spicy gales of Arabia, and more sought for than the gold of Golconda. We believe that Woman should associate freely with man, and we believe that it is for the preservation of her rights. She should become acquainted with the metaphysical designs of those who condescend to sing the siren song of flattery. This, we think, should be according to the unwritten law of decorum, which is stamped upon every innocent heart. The precepts of prudery are often steeped in the guilt of contamination, which blasts the expectations of better moments. Truth, and beautiful dreams — loveliness, and delicacy of character, with cherished affections of the ideal woman — gentle hopes and aspirations, are enough to uphold her in the storms of darkness, without the transferred colorings of a stained sufferer. How often have we seen it in our public prints, that woman occupies a false station in the world! and some have gone so far as to say it was an unnatural one. So long has she been regarded a weak creature, by the rabble and illiterate — they have looked upon her as an insufficient actress on the great stage of human life — a mere puppet, to fill up the drama of human existence — a thoughtless, inactive being — that she has too often come to the same conclusion herself, and has sometimes forgotten her high destination, in the meridian of her glory. We have but little sympathy or patience for those who treat her as a mere Rosy Melindi — who are always fishing for pretty compliments — who are satisfied by the gossamer of Romance, and who can be allured by the verbosity of high-flown words, rich in language, but poor and barren in sentiment. Beset, as she has been, by the intellectual vulgar, the selfish, the designing, the cunning, the hidden, and the artful — no wonder she has sometimes folded her wings in despair, and forgotten her *heavenly* mission in the delirium of imagination; no wonder she searches out some wild desert, to find a peaceful home. But this cannot always continue. A new era is moving gently onward, old things are rapidly passing away; old superstitions, old prejudices, and old notions are now bidding farewell to their old associates and companions, and giving way to one whose wings are plumed with the light of heaven, and tinged by the dews of the morning. There is a remnant of blessedness that clings to her in spite of all evil influence, there is enough of the Divine Master left, to accomplish the noblest work ever achieved under the canopy of the vaulted skies; and that time is fast approaching, when the picture of the true woman will shine from its frame of glory, to captivate, to win back, to restore, and to call into being once more, *the object of her mission.*

> Star of the brave! thy glory shed,
> O'er all the earth, thy army led —
> Bold meteor of immortal birth!
> Why come from Heaven to dwell on Earth?

Mighty and glorious are the days of youth; happy the moments of the *lover*, mingled with smiles and tears of his devoted, and long to be remembered are the achievements which he gains with a palpitating heart and a trembling hand. A bright and lovely dawn, the harbinger of a fair and prosperous day, had arisen over the beautiful little village of Cumming, which is surrounded by the most romantic scenery in the Cherokee country. Brightening clouds seemed to rise from the mist of the fair Chattahoochee, to spread their beauty over the thick forest, to guide the hero whose bosom beats with aspirations to conquer the enemy that would tarnish his name, and to win back the admiration of his long-tried friend. He endeavored to make his way through Sawney's Mountain, where many meet to catch the gales that are continually blowing for the refreshment of the stranger and the traveler. Surrounded as he was by hills on every side, naked rocks dared the efforts of his energies. Soon the sky became overcast, the sun buried itself in the clouds, and the fair day gave place to gloomy twilight, which lay heavily on the Indian Plains. He remembered an old Indian Castle, that once stood at the foot of the mountain. He thought if he could make his way to this, he would rest contented for a short time. The mountain air breathed fragrance — a rosy tinge rested on the glassy waters that murmured at its base. His resolution soon brought him to the remains of the red man's hut; he surveyed with wonder and astonishment the decayed building, which time had buried in the dust, and thought to himself, his happiness was not yet complete. Beside the shore of the brook sat a young man, about eighteen or twenty, who seemed to be reading some favorite book, and who had a remarkably noble countenance — eyes which betrayed more than a common mind. This of course made the youth a welcome guest, and gained him friends in whatever condition of life he might be placed. The traveler observed that he was a well-built figure, which showed strength and grace in every movement. He accordingly addressed him in quite a gentlemanly manner, and inquired of him the way to the village. After he had received the desired information, and was about taking his leave, the youth said, " Are you not Major Elfonzo, the great musician — the champion of a noble cause — the modern Achilles, who gained so many victories in the Florida War?" " I bear that

name," said the Major, " and those titles, trusting at
the same time that the ministers of grace will carry
me triumphantly through all my laudable undertakings, and if," continued the Major, " you, sir, are the
patronizer of noble deeds, I should like to make you
my confidant, and learn your address." The youth
looked somewhat amazed, bowed low, mused for a
moment, and began: " My name is Roswell. I have
been recently admitted to the bar, and can only give a
faint outline of my future success in that honorable
profession; but I trust, sir, like the Eagle, I shall look
down from lofty rocks upon the dwellings of man, and
shall ever be ready to give you any assistance in my
official capacity, and whatever this muscular arm of
mine can do, whenever it shall be called from its buried
greatness." The Major grasped him by the hand, and
exclaimed: "O! thou exalted spirit of inspiration —
thou flame of burning prosperity, may the Heaven-
directed blaze be the glare of thy soul, and battle down
every rampart that seems to impede your progress !'

The road which led to the town, presented many
attractions. Elfonzo had bid farewell to the youth of
deep feeling, and was now wending his way to the
dreaming spot of his fondness. The south winds
whistled through the woods, as the waters dashed
against the banks, as rapid fire in the pent furnace
roars. This brought him to remember while alone,
that he quietly left behind the hospitality of a father's
house, and gladly entered the world, with higher hopes
than are often realized. But as he journeyed onward,
he was mindful of the advice of his father, who had
often looked sadly on the ground, when tears of cruelly
deceived hope, moistened his eye. Elfonzo had been
somewhat of a dutiful son; yet fond of the amusements of life — had been in distant lands — had enjoyed the pleasure of the world, and had frequently

27****

returned to the scenes of his boyhood, almost destitute of many of the comforts of life. In this condition, he would frequently say to his father, " Have I offended you, that you look upon me as a stranger, and frown upon me with stinging looks? Will you not favor me with the sound of your voice? If I have trampled upon your veneration, or have spread a humid veil of darkness around your expectations, send me back into the world where no heart beats for me — where the foot of man has never yet trod; but give me at least one kind word — allow me to come into the presence sometimes of thy winterworn locks." " Forbid it, Heaven, that I should be angry with thee," answered the father, " my son, and yet I send thee back to the children of the world — to the cold charity of the combat, and to a land of victory. I read another destiny in thy countenance — I learn thy inclinations from the flame that has already kindled in my soul a strange sensation. It will seek thee, my dear *Elfonzo*, it will find thee — thou canst not escape that lighted torch, which shall blot out from the remembrance of men a long train of prophecies which they have foretold against thee. I once thought not so. Once, I was blind; but now the path of life is plain before me, and my sight is clear; yet Elfonzo, return to thy worldly occupation — take again in thy hand that chord of sweet sounds — struggle with the civilized world, and with your own heart; fly swiftly to the enchanted ground — let the night-*Owl* send forth its screams from the stubborn oak — let the sea sport upon the beach, and the stars sing together; but learn of these, Elfonzo, thy doom, and thy hiding-place. Our most innocent as well as our most lawful *desires* must often be denied us, that we may learn to sacrifice them to a Higher will."

Remembering such admonitions with gratitude, Elfonzo was immediately urged by the recollection of his father's family to keep moving. His steps became quicker and quicker — he hastened through the *piny* woods, dark as the forest was, and with joy he very soon reached the little village of repose, in whose bosom rested the boldest chivalry. His close attention to every important object — his modest questions about whatever was new to him — his reverence for wise old age, and his ardent desire to learn many of the fine arts, soon brought him into respectable notice.

One mild winter day as he walked along the streets towards the Academy, which stood upon a small eminence, surrounded by native growth — some venerable in its appearance, others young and prosperous — all seemed inviting, and seemed to be the very place for learning as well as for genius to spend its research beneath its spreading shades. He entered its classic walls in the usual mode of southern manners. The principal of the Institution begged him to be seated, and listen to the recitations that were going on. He accordingly obeyed the request, and seemed to be much pleased. After the school was dismissed, and the young hearts regained their freedom, with the songs of the evening, laughing at the anticipated pleasures of a happy home, while others tittered at the actions of the past day, he addressed the teacher in a tone that indicated a resolution — with an undaunted mind. He said he had determined to become a student, if he could meet with his approbation. " Sir," said he, " I have spent much time in the world. I have traveled among the uncivilized inhabitants of America. I have met with friends, and combated with foes; but none of these gratify my ambition, or decide what is to be my destiny. I see the learned world have an influence with the voice of the people themselves. The despoilers of the remotest kingdoms of the earth, refer their differ-

AA***

ences to this class of persons. This the illiterate and inexperienced little dream of; and now if you will receive me as I am, with these deficiencies — with all my misguided opinions, I will give you my honor, sir, that I will never disgrace the Institution, or those who have placed you in this honorable station." The instructor, who had met with many disappointments, knew how to feel for a stranger who had been thus turned upon the charities of an unfeeling community. He looked at him earnestly, and said: "Be of good cheer — look forward, sir, to the high destination you may attain. Remember, the more elevated the mark at which you aim, the more sure, the more glorious, the more magnificent the prize." From wonder to wonder, his encouragement led the impatient listener. A strange nature bloomed before him — giant streams promised him success — gardens of hidden treasures opened to his view. All this, so vividly described, seemed to gain a new witchery from his glowing fancy.

In 1842, he entered the class, and made rapid progress in the English and Latin departments. Indeed, he continued advancing with such rapidity that he was like to become the first in his class, and made such unexpected progress, and was so studious, that he had almost forgotten the pictured saint of his affections. The fresh wreaths of the pine and cypress, had waited anxiously to drop once more the dews of Heaven upon the heads of those who had so often poured forth the tender emotions of their souls under its boughs. He was aware of the pleasure that he had seen there. So one evening, as he was returning from his reading, he concluded he would pay a visit to this enchanting spot. Little did he think of witnessing a shadow of his former happiness, though no doubt, he wished it might be so. He continued sauntering by the road-side, meditating on the past. The nearer he approached the spot, the more anxious he became. At that moment, a tall female figure flitted across his path, with a bunch of roses in her hand; her countenance showed uncommon vivacity, with a resolute spirit; her ivory teeth already appeared as she smiled beautifully, promenading,— while her ringlets of hair dangled unconsciously around her snowy neck. Nothing was wanting to complete her beauty. The tinge of the rose was in full bloom upon her cheek; the charms of sensibility and tenderness were always her associates. In Ambulinia's bosom dwelt a noble soul — one that never faded — one that never was conquered. Her heart yielded to no feeling but the love of Elfonzo, on whom she gazed with intense delight, and to whom she felt herself more closely bound, because he sought the hand of no other. Elfonzo was roused from his apparent reverie. His books no longer were his inseparable companions — his thoughts arrayed themselves to encourage him to the field of victory. He endeavored to speak to his supposed Ambulinia, but his speech appeared not in words. No, his effort was a stream of fire, that kindled his soul into a flame of admiration, and carried his senses away captive. Ambulinia had disappeared, to make him more mindful of his duty. As she walked speedily away through the piny woods, she calmly echoed: "O! Elfonzo, thou wilt now look from thy sunbeams. Thou shalt now walk in a new path — perhaps thy way leads through darkness; but fear not, the stars foretell happiness."

Not many days afterwards, as surrounded by fragrant flowers, she sat one evening at twilight, to enjoy the cool breeze that whispered notes of melody along the distant groves, the little birds perched on every side, as if to watch the movements of their new visitor. The bells were tolling, when Elfonzo silently stole along by the wild wood flowers, holding in his hand his favorite instrument of music — his eye continually searching for Ambulinia, who hardly seemed to perceive him, as she played carelessly with the songsters that hopped from branch to branch. Nothing could be more striking than the difference between the two. Nature seemed to have given the more tender soul to Elfonzo, and the stronger and more courageous to Ambulinia. A deep feeling spoke from the eyes of Elfonzo,— such a feeling as can only be expressed by those who are blessed as admirers, and by those who are able to return the same with sincerity of heart. He was a few years older than Ambulinia; she had turned a little into her seventeenth. He had almost grown up in the Cherokee country, with the same equal proportions as one of the natives. But little intimacy had existed between them until the year forty-one — because the youth felt that the character of such a lovely girl was too exalted to inspire any other feeling than that of quiet reverence. But as lovers will not always be insulted, at all times and under all circumstances, by the frowns and cold looks of crabbed old age, which should continually reflect dignity upon those around, and treat the unfortunate as well as the fortunate with a graceful mien, he continued to use diligence and perseverance. All this lighted a spark in his heart that changed his whole character, and like the unyielding Deity that follows the storm to check its rage in the forest, he resolves for the first time to shake off his embarrassment, and return where he had before only worshiped.

It could not escape Ambulinia's penetrating eye that he sought an interview with her, which she as anxiously avoided, and assumed a more distant calmness than before, seemingly to destroy all hope. After many efforts and struggles with his own person, with timid steps the Major approached the damsel, with the same

caution as he would have done in a field of battle.
"Lady Ambulinia," said he, trembling, "I have long
desired a moment like this. I dare not let it escape.
I fear the consequences; yet I hope your indulgence
will at least hear my petition. Can you not anticipate
what I would say, and what I am about to express?
Will not you, like Minerva, who sprung from the brain
of Jupiter, release me from thy winding chains or cure
me —" "Say no more, Elfonzo," answered Ambulinia, with a serious look, raising her hand as if she
intended to swear eternal hatred against the whole
world; "another lady in my place would have perhaps
answered your question in bitter coldness. I know
not the little arts of my sex. I care but little for the
vanity of those who would chide me, and am unwilling
as well as ashamed to be guilty of anything that would
lead you to think ' all is not gold that glitters '; so be
not rash in your resolution. It is better to repent now,
than to do it in a more solemn hour. Yes, I know
what you would say. I know you have a costly gift
for me — the noblest that man can make — *your heart !*
you should not offer it to one so unworthy. Heaven,
you know, has allowed my father's house to be made a
house of solitude, a home of silent obedience, which
my parents say is more to be admired than big names
and high-sounding titles. Notwithstanding all this, let
me speak the emotions of an honest heart; allow me
to say in the fullness of my hopes that I anticipate
better days. The bird may stretch its wings towards
the sun, which it can never reach; and flowers of the
field appear to ascend in the same direction, because
they cannot do otherwise; but man confides his complaints to the saints in whom he believes; for in their
abodes of light they know no more sorrow. From
your confession and indicative looks, I must be that
person; if so, deceive not yourself."

Elfonzo replied, "Pardon me, my dear madam, for my frankness. I have loved you from my earliest days; everything grand and beautiful hath borne the image of Ambulinia; while precipices on every hand surrounded me, your *guardian angel* stood and beckoned me away from the deep abyss. In every trial, in every misfortune, I have met with your helping hand; yet I never dreamed or dared to cherish thy love till a voice impaired with age encouraged the cause, and declared they who acquired thy favor should win a victory. I saw how Leos worshiped thee. I felt my own unworthiness. I began to *know jealousy* — a strong guest, indeed, in my bosom — yet I could see if I gained your admiration Leos was to be my rival. I was aware that he had the influence of your parents, and the wealth of a deceased relative, which is too often mistaken for permanent and regular tranquillity; yet I have determined by your permission to beg an interest in your prayers — to ask you to animate my drooping spirits by your smiles and your winning looks; for if you but speak I shall be conqueror, my enemies shall stagger like Olympus shakes. And though earth and sea may tremble, and the charioteer of the sun may forget his dashing steed, yet I am assured that it is only to arm me with divine weapons which will enable me to complete my long-tried intention." "Return to yourself, Elfonzo," said Ambulinia, pleasantly; "a dream of vision has disturbed your intellect; you are above the atmosphere, dwelling in the celestial regions; nothing is there that urges or hinders, nothing that brings discord into our present litigation. I entreat you to condescend a little, and be a man, and forget it all. When Homer describes the battle of the gods and noble men fighting with giants and dragons, they represent under this image our struggles with the delusions of our passions. You

have exalted me, an unhappy girl, to the skies; you
have called me a saint, and portrayed in your imagination an angel in human form.   Let her remain such to
you, let her continue to be as you have supposed, and
be assured that she will consider a share in your esteem
as her highest treasure.   Think not that I would allure
you from the path in which your conscience leads you;
for you know I respect the conscience of others, as I
would die for my own.   Elfonzo, if I am worthy of
thy love, let such conversation never again pass between us.   Go, seek a nobler theme! we will seek it in
the stream of time, as the sun set in the Tigris."   As
she spake these words she grasped the hand of Elfonzo,
saying at the same time, "Peace and prosperity attend
you, my hero: be up and doing!"   Closing her remarks with this expression, she walked slowly away,
leaving Elfonzo astonished and amazed.   He ventured
not to follow or detain her.   Here he stood alone,
gazing at the stars; confounded as he was, here he
stood.   The rippling stream rolled on at his feet.
Twilight had already begun to draw her sable mantle
over the earth, and now and then the fiery smoke
would ascend from the little town which lay spread out
before him.   The citizens seemed to be full of life and
good-humor; but poor Elfonzo saw not a brilliant
scene.   No; his future life stood before him, stripped
of the hopes that once adorned all his sanguine desires.
"Alas!" said he, "am I now Grief's disappointed
son at last."   Ambulinia's image rose before his fancy.
A mixture of ambition and greatness of soul moved
upon his young heart, and encouraged him to bear all
his crosses with the patience of a Job, notwithstanding
he had to encounter with so many obstacles.   He still
endeavored to prosecute his studies, and reasonably
progressed in his education.   Still, he was not content;
there was something yet to be done before his happi-

ness was complete. He would visit his friends and acquaintances. They would invite him to social parties, insisting that he should partake of the amusements that were going on. This he enjoyed tolerably well. The ladies and gentlemen were generallly well pleased with the Major; as he delighted all with his violin, which seemed to have a thousand chords — more symphonious than the Muses of Apollo, and more enchanting than the ghost of the Hills. He passed some days in the country. During that time Leos had made many calls upon Ambulinia, who was generally received with a great deal of courtesy by the family. They thought him to be a young man worthy of attention, though he had but little in his soul to attract the attention or even win the affections of her whose graceful manners had almost made him a slave to every bewitching look that fell from her eyes. Leos made several attempts to tell her of his fair prospects — how much he loved her, and how much it would add to his bliss if he could but think she would be willing to share these blessings with him; but, choked by his undertaking, he made himself more like an inactive drone, than he did like one who bowed at beauty's shrine.

Elfonzo again wends his way to the stately walls and new-built village. He now determines to see the end of the prophecy which had been foretold to him. The clouds burst from his sight; he believes if he can but see his Ambulinia, he can open to her view the bloody altars that have been misrepresented to stigmatize his name. He knows that her breast is transfixed with the sword of reason, and ready at all times to detect the hidden villainy of her enemies. He resolves to see her in her own home, with the consoling theme: " ' I can but perish if I go.' Let the consequences be what they may," said he, " if I die, it shall be contending and struggling for my own rights."

Night had almost overtaken him when he arrived in town. Colonel Elder, a noble-hearted, high-minded, and independent man, met him at his door as usual, and seized him by the hand. "Well, Elfonzo," said the Colonel, "how does the world use you in your efforts?" "I have no objection to the world," said Elfonzo, "but the people are rather singular in some of their opinions." "Aye, well," said the Colonel, "you must remember that creation is made up of many mysteries; just take things by the right handle; be always sure you know which is the smooth side before you attempt your polish; be reconciled to your fate, be it what it may; and never find fault with your condition, unless your complaining will benefit it. Perseverance is a principle that should be commendable in those who have judgment to govern it. I should never have been so successful in my hunting excursions had I waited till the deer, by some magic dream, had been drawn to the muzzle of the gun before I made an attempt to fire at the game that dared my boldness in the wild forest. The great mystery in hunting seems to be — a good marksman, a resolute mind, a fixed determination, and my word for it, you will never return home without sounding your horn with the breath of a new victory. And so with every other undertaking. Be confident that your ammunition is of the right kind — always pull your trigger with a steady hand, and so soon as you perceive a calm, touch her off, and the spoils are yours."

This filled him with redoubled vigor, and he set out with a stronger anxiety than ever to the home of Ambulinia. A few short steps soon brought him to the door, half out of breath. He rapped gently. Ambulinia, who sat in the parlor alone, suspecting Elfonzo was near, ventured to the door, opened it, and beheld the hero, who stood in an humble attitude,

bowed gracefully, and as they caught each other's
looks, the light of peace beamed from the eyes of
Ambulinia.   Elfonzo caught the expression; a halloo
of smothered shouts ran through every vein, and for
the first time he dared to impress a kiss upon her
cheek.   The scene was overwhelming; had the temptation been less animating, he would not have ventured
to have acted so contrary to the desired wish of his
Ambulinia; but who could have withstood the irresisti-
ble temptation!   What society condemns the practice,
but a cold, heartless, uncivilized people, that know
nothing of the warm attachments of refined society?
Here the dead was raised to his long cherished hopes,
and the lost was found.   Here all doubt and danger
were buried in the vortex of oblivion; sectional differences no longer disunited their opinions; like the freed
bird from the cage, sportive claps its rustling wings,
wheels about to heaven in a joyful strain, and raises its
notes to the upper sky.   Ambulinia insisted upon Elfonzo to be seated, and give her a history of his
unnecessary absence; assuring him the family had retired, consequently they would ever remain ignorant of
his visit.   Advancing towards him, she gave a bright
display of her rosy neck, and from her head the am-
brosial locks breathed divine fragrance; her robe hung
waving to his view, while she stood like a goddess
confessed before him.

" It does seem to me, my dear sir," said Ambulinia,
" that you have been gone an age.   Oh, the restless
hours I have spent since I last saw you, in yon beautiful grove.   There is where I trifled with your feelings
for the express purpose of trying your attachment for
me.   I now find you are devoted; but ah! I trust you
live not unguarded by the powers of Heaven.   Though
oft did I refuse to join my hand with thine, and as oft
did I cruelly mock thy entreaties with borrowed

shapes: yes, I feared to answer thee by terms, in words sincere and undissembled. O! could I pursue, and you had leisure to hear the annals of my woes, the evening star would shut Heaven's gates upon the impending day, before my tale would be finished, and this night would find me soliciting your forgiveness.'' '' Dismiss thy fears and thy doubts,'' replied Elfonzo. '' Look, O! look: that angelic look of thine,—bathe not thy visage in tears; banish those floods that are gathering; let my confession and my presence bring thee some relief.'' '' Then, indeed, I will be cheerful,'' said Ambulinia, '' and I think if we will go to the exhibition this evening, we certainly will see something worthy of our attention. One of the most tragical scenes is to be acted that has ever been witnessed, and one that every jealous-hearted person should learn a lesson from. It cannot fail to have a good effect, as it will be performed by those who are young and vigorous, and learned as well as enticing. You are aware, Major Elfonzo, who are to appear on the stage, and what the characters are to represent.'' '' I am acquainted with the circumstances,'' replied Elfonzo, '' and as I am to be one of the musicians upon that interesting occasion, I should be much gratified if you would favor me with your company during the hours of the exercises.''

'' What strange notions are in your mind?'' inquired Ambulinia. '' Now I know you have something in view, and I desire you to tell me why it is that you are so anxious that I should continue with you while the exercises are going on; though if you think I can add to your happiness and predilections, I have no particular objection to acquiesce in your request. Oh, I think I foresee, now, what you anticipate.'' '' And will you have the goodness to tell me what you think it to be?'' inquired Elfonzo. '' By all means,'' an-

28A

swered Ambulinia; " a rival, sir, you would fancy in your own mind; but let me say to you, fear not! fear not! I will be one of the last persons to disgrace my sex, by thus encouraging every one who may feel disposed to visit me, who may honor me with their graceful bows and their choicest compliments. It is true, that young men too often mistake civil politeness for the finer emotions of the heart, which is tantamount to courtship; but, ah! how often are they deceived, when they come to test the weight of sunbeams, with those on whose strength hangs the future happiness of an untried life."

The people were now rushing to the Academy with impatient anxiety; the band of music was closely followed by the students; then the parents and guardians; nothing interrupted the glow of spirits which ran through every bosom, tinged with the songs of a Virgil and the tide of a Homer. Elfonzo and Ambulinia soon repaired to the scene, and fortunately for them both the house was so crowded that they took their seats together in the music department, which was not in view of the auditory. This fortuitous circumstance added more to the bliss of the Major than a thousand such exhibitions would have done. He forgot that he was man; music had lost its charms for him; whenever he attempted to carry his part, the string of the instrument would break, the bow became stubborn, and refused to obey the loud calls of the audience. Here, he said, was the paradise of his home, the long-sought-for opportunity; he felt as though he could send a million supplications to the throne of Heaven, for such an exalted privilege. Poor Leos, who was somewhere in the crowd, looking as attentively as if he was searching for a needle in a haystack; here he stood, wondering to himself why Ambulinia was not there. "Where can she be? Oh! if she was only here, how I could relish the scene! Elfonzo is certainly not in town; but what if he is?   I have got the wealth, if I have not the dignity, and I am sure that the squire and his lady have always been particular friends of mine, and I think with this assurance I shall be able to get upon the blind side of the rest of the family, and make the heaven-born Ambulinia the mistress of all I possess.'' Then, again, he would drop his head, as if attempting to solve the most difficult problem in Euclid.   While he was thus conjecturing in his own mind, a very interesting part of the exhibition was going on, which called the attention of all present. The curtains of the stage waved continually by the repelled forces that were given to them, which caused Leos to behold Ambulinia leaning upon the chair of Elfonzo.   Her lofty beauty, seen by the glimmering of the chandelier, filled his heart with rapture, he knew not how to contain himself; to go where they were, would expose him to ridicule; to continue where he was, with such an object before him, without being allowed an explanation in that trying hour, would be to the great injury of his mental as well as of his physical powers; and, in the name of high heaven, what must he do?   Finally, he resolved to contain himself as well as he conveniently could, until the scene was over, and then he would plant himself at the door, to arrest Ambulinia from the hands of the insolent Elfonzo, and thus make for himself a more prosperous field of immortality than ever was decreed by Omnipotence, or ever pencil drew or artist imagined.   Accordingly he made himself sentinel, immediately after the performance of the evening,— retained his position apparently in defiance of all the world, he waited, he gazed at every lady, his whole frame trembled; here he stood, until everything like human shape had disappeared from the institution, and he had done nothing; he had failed to accomplish that which he so eagerly sought for. Poor, unfortunate creature! he had not the eyes of an Argus, or he might have seen his Juno and Elfonzo, assisted by his friend Sigma, make their escape from the window, and, with the rapidity of a race-horse, hurry through the blast of the storm, to the residence of her father, without being recognized. He did not tarry long, but assured Ambulinia the endless chain of their existence was more closely connected than ever, since he had seen the virtuous, innocent, imploring, and the constant Amelia murdered by the jealous-hearted Farcillo, the accursed of the land.

The following is the tragical scene, which is only introduced to show the subject matter that enabled Elfonzo to come to such a determinate resolution, that nothing of the kind should ever dispossess him of his true character, should he be so fortunate as to succeed in his present undertaking.

Amelia was the wife of Farcillo, and a virtuous woman; Gracia, a young lady, was her particular friend and confidant. Farcillo grew jealous of Amelia, murders her, finds out that he was deceived, *and stabs himself*. Amelia appears alone, talking to herself.

A. Hail, ye solitary ruins of antiquity, ye sacred tombs and silent walks! it is your aid I invoke; it is to you, my soul, wrapt in deep meditation, pours forth its prayer. Here I wander upon the stage of mortality, since the world hath turned against me. Those whom I believed to be my friends, alas! are now my enemies, planting thorns in all my paths, poisoning all my pleasures, and turning the past to pain. What a lingering catalogue of sighs and tears lies just before me, crowding my aching bosom with the fleeting dream of humanity, which must shortly terminate. And to what purpose will all this bustle of life, these agitations and emotions of the heart have conduced, if it leave behind it nothing of utility, if it leave no traces of improvement? Can it be that I am deceived in my conclusions? No, I see that I have nothing to hope for, but everything to fear, which tends to drive me from the walks of time.

> Oh! in this dead night, if loud winds arise,
> To lash the surge and bluster in the skies,
> May the west its furious rage display,
> Toss me with storms in the watery way.

(Enter Gracia.)

G. Oh, Amelia, is it you, the object of grief, the daughter of opulence, of wisdom and philosophy, that thus complaineth? It cannot be you are the child of misfortune, speaking of the monuments of former ages, which were allotted not for the reflection of the distressed, but for the fearless and bold.

A. Not the child of poverty, Gracia, or the heir of glory and peace, but of fate. Remember, I have wealth more than wit can number; I have had power more than kings could encompass; yet the world seems a desert; all nature appears an afflictive spectacle of warring passions. This blind fatality, that capriciously sports with the rules and lives of mortals, tells me that the mountains will never again send forth the water of their springs to my thirst. Oh, that I might be freed and set at liberty from wretchedness! But I fear, I fear this will never be.

G. Why, Amelia, this untimely grief? What has caused the sorrows that bespeak better and happier days, to thus lavish out such heaps of misery? You are aware that your instructive lessons embellish the mind with holy truths, by wedding its attention to none but great and noble affections.

A. This, of course, is some consolation. I will ever love my own species with feelings of a fond recollec-

28***

tion, and while I am studying to advance the universal philanthropy, and the spotless name of my own sex, I will try to build my own upon the pleasing belief that I have accelerated the advancement of one who whispers of departed confidence.

> And I, like some poor peasant fated to reside
> Remote from friends, in a forest wide.
> Oh, see what woman's woes and human wants require,
> Since that great day hath spread the seed of sinful fire.

G. Look up, thou poor disconsolate; you speak of quitting earthly enjoyments.   Unfold thy bosom to a friend, who would be willing to sacrifice every enjoyment for the restoration of that dignity and gentleness of mind which used to grace your walks, and which is so natural to yourself; not only that, but your paths were strewed with flowers of every hue and of every order.

> With verdant green the mountains glow,
> For thee, for thee, the lilies grow;
> Far stretched beneath the tented hills,
> A fairer flower the valley fills.

A. Oh, would to Heaven I could give you a short narrative of my former prospects for happiness, since you have acknowledged to be an unchangeable confidant — the richest of all other blessings.   Oh, ye names forever glorious, ye celebrated scenes, ye renowned spot of my hymeneal moments; how replete is your chart with sublime reflections! How many profound vows, decorated with immaculate deeds, are written upon the surface of that precious spot of earth where I yielded up my life of celibacy, bade youth with all its beauties a final adieu, took a last farewell of the laurels that had accompanied me up the hill of my juvenile career.   It was then I began to descend towards the valley of disappointment and sorrow; it was then I cast my little bark upon a mysterious ocean of wedlock, with him who then smiled and caressed me, but, alas! now frowns with bitterness, and has grown jealous and cold towards me, because the ring he gave me is misplaced or lost. Oh, bear me, ye flowers of memory, softly through the eventful history of past times; and ye places that have witnessed the progression of man in the circle of so many societies, aid, oh, aid my recollection, while I endeavor to trace the vicissitudes of a life devoted in endeavoring to comfort him that I claim as the object of my wishes.

> Ah! ye mysterious men, of all the world, how few
> Act just to Heaven and to your promise true!
> But He who guides the stars with a watchful eye,
> The deeds of men lay open without disguise;
> Oh, this alone will avenge the wrongs I bear,
> For all the oppressed are his peculiar care.

(F. makes a slight noise.)

A. Who is there — Farcillo?

G. Then I must be gone. Heaven protect you. Oh, Amelia, farewell, be of good cheer.

> May you stand, like Olympus' towers,
> Against earth and all jealous powers!
> May you, with loud shouts ascend on high
> Swift as an eagle in the upper sky.

A. Why so cold and distant to-night, Farcillo? Come, let us each other greet, and forget all the past, and give security for the future.

F. Security! talk to me about giving security for the future — what an insulting requisition! Have you said your prayers to-night, Madam Amelia?

A. Farcillo, we sometimes forget our duty, particularly when we expect to be caressed by others.

F. If you bethink yourself of any crime, or of any fault, that is yet concealed from the courts of Heaven

BB***

and the thrones of grace, I bid you ask and solicit forgiveness for it now.

A. Oh, be kind, Farcillo, don't treat me so. What do you mean by all this?

F. Be kind, you say; you, madam, have forgot that kindness you owe to me, and bestowed it upon another; you shall suffer for your conduct when you make your peace with your God. I would not slay thy unprotected spirit. I call to Heaven to be my guard and my watch — I would not kill thy soul, in which all once seemed just, right, and perfect; but I must be brief, woman.

A. What, talk you of killing? Oh. Farcillo, Farcillo, what is the matter?

F. Aye, I do, without doubt; mark what I say, Amelia.

A. Then, O God, O Heaven, and Angels, be propitious, and have mercy upon me.

F. Amen to that, madam, with all my heart, and with all my soul.

A. Farcillo, listen to me one moment; I hope you will not kill me.

F. Kill you, aye, that I will; attest it, ye fair host of light, record it, ye dark imps of hell!

A. Oh, I fear you — you are fatal when darkness covers your brow; yet I know not why I should fear, since I never wronged you in all my life. I stand, sir, guiltless before you.

F. You pretend to say you are guiltless! Think of thy sins, Amelia; think, oh, think, hidden woman.

A. Wherein have I not been true to you? That death is unkind, cruel, and unnatural, that kills for loving.

F. Peace, and be still while I unfold to thee.

A. I will, Farcillo, and while I am thus silent, tell me the cause of such cruel coldness in an hour like this.

F. That *ring*, oh, that ring I so loved, and gave thee as the ring of my heart; the allegiance you took to be faithful, when it was presented; the kisses and smiles with which you honored it. You became tired of the donor, despised it as a plague, and finally gave it to Malos, the hidden, the vile traitor.

A. No, upon my word and honor, I never did; I appeal to the Most High to bear me out in this matter. Send for Malos, and ask him.

F. Send for Malos, aye! Malos you wish to see; I thought so. I knew you could not keep his name concealed. Amelia, sweet Amelia, take heed, take heed of perjury; you are on the stage of death, to suffer for *your sins*.

A. What, not to die I hope, my Farcillo, my ever beloved.

F. Yes, madam, to die a traitor's death. Shortly your spirit shall take its exit; therefore confess freely thy sins, for to deny tends only to make me groan under the bitter cup thou hast made for me. Thou art to die with the name of traitor on thy brow!

A. Then, O Lord, have mercy upon me; give me courage, give me grace and fortitude to stand this hour of trial.

F. Amen, I say, with all my heart.

A. And, oh, Farcillo, will you have mercy, too? I never intentionally offended you in all my life; never *loved* Malos, never gave him cause to think so, as the high court of Justice will acquit me before its tribunal.

F. Oh, false, perjured woman, thou dost chill my blood, and makest me a demon like thyself. I saw the ring.

A. He found it, then, or got it clandestinely; send for him, and let him confess the truth; let his confession be sifted.

F. And you still wish to see him! I tell you,

madam, he hath already confessed, and thou knowest the darkness of thy heart.

A. What, my deceived Farcillo, that I gave him the ring, in which all my affections were concentrated? Oh, surely not.

F. Aye, he did. Ask thy conscience, and it will speak with a voice of thunder to thy soul.

A. He will not say so, he dare not, he cannot.

F. No, he will not say so now, because his mouth, I trust, is hushed in death, and his body stretched to the four winds of heaven, to be torn to pieces by carnivorous birds.

A. What, is he dead, and gone to the world of spirits with that declaration in his mouth? Oh, unhappy man! Oh, insupportable hour!

F. Yes, and had all his sighs and looks and tears been lives, my great revenge could have slain them all, without the least condemnation.

A. Alas! he is ushered into eternity without testing the matter for which I am abused and sentenced and condemned to die.

F. Cursed, infernal woman! Weepest thou for him to my face? He that hath robbed me of my peace, my energy, the whole love of my life? Could I call the fabled Hydra, I would have him live and perish, survive and die, until the sun itself would grow dim with age. I would make him have the thirst of a Tantalus, and roll the wheel of an Ixion, until the stars of heaven should quit their brilliant stations.

A. Oh, invincible God, save me! Oh, unsupportable moment! Oh, heavy hour! Banish me, Farcillo — send me where no eye can ever see me, where no sound shall ever greet my ear; but, oh, slay me not, Farcillo; vent thy rage and thy spite upon this emaciated frame of mine, only spare my life.

F. Your petitions avail nothing, cruel Amelia.

A. Oh, Farcillo, perpetrate the dark deed to-morrow; let me live till then, for my past kindness to you, and it may be some kind angel will show to you that I am not only the object of innocence, but one who never loved another but your noble self.

F. Amelia, the decree has gone forth, it is to be done, and that quickly; thou art to die, madam.

A. But half an hour allow me, to see my father and my only child, to tell her the treachery and vanity of this world.

F. There is no alternative, there is no pause: my daughter shall not see its deceptive mother die; your father shall not know that his daughter fell disgraced, despised by all but her enchanting Malos.

A. Oh, Farcillo, put up thy threatening dagger into its scabbard; let it rest and be still, just while I say one prayer for thee and for my child.

F. It is too late, thy doom is fixed, thou hast not confessed to Heaven or to me, my child's protector — thou art to die. Ye powers of earth and heaven, protect and defend me in this alone. (*Stabs her while imploring for mercy.*)

A. Oh, Farcillo, Farcillo, a guiltless death I die.

F. Die! die! die!

(Gracia enters running, falls on her knees weeping, and kisses Amelia.)

G. Oh, Farcillo, Farcillo! oh, Farcillo!

F. I am here, the genius of the age, and the avenger of my wrongs.

G. Oh, lady, speak once more; sweet Amelia, oh, speak again. Gone, gone — yes, forever gone! Farcillo, oh, cold-hearted Farcillo, some evil fiend hath urged you to do this, Farcillo.

F. Say not so again, or you shall receive the same fate. I did the glorious deed, madam — beware, then, how you talk.

G. I fear not your implements of war; I will let you know you have not the power to do me harm. If you have a heart of triple brass, it shall be reached and melted, and thy blood shall chill thy veins and grow stiff in thy arteries. Here is the ring of the virtuous and innocent murdered Amelia; I obtained it from Malos, who yet lives, in hopes that he will survive the wound given him, and says he got it clandestinely — declares Amelia to be the princess of truth and virtue, invulnerable to anything like forgetting her first devotion to thee. The world has heard of your conduct and your jealousy, and with one universal voice declares her to be the best of all in piety; that she is the star of this great universe, and a more virtuous woman never lived since the wheels of time began. Oh, had you waited till to-morrow, or until I had returned, some kind window would have been opened to her relief. But, alas! she is gone — yes, forever gone, to try the realities of an unknown world!

(Farcillo leaning over the body of Amelia.)

F. Malos not dead, and here is my ring! Oh, Amelia! falsely, falsely murdered! Oh, bloody deed! Oh, wretch that I am! Oh, angels forgive me! Oh, God, withhold thy vengeance! Oh, Amelia! if Heaven would make a thousand worlds like this, set with diamonds, and all of one perfect chrysolite, I would not have done this for them all, I would not have frowned and cursed as I did. Oh, she was heavenly true, nursed in the very lap of bright angels! Cursed slave that I am! Jealousy, oh! thou infernal demon! Lost, lost to every sense of honor! Oh! Amelia — heaven-born Amelia — dead, dead! Oh! oh! oh! — then let me die with thee. Farewell! farewell! ye world that deceived me! (*Stabs himself.*)

Soon after the excitement of this tragical scene was over, and the enlisted feeling for Amelia had grown more buoyant with Elfonzo and Ambulinia, he determined to visit his retired home, and make the necessary improvements to enjoy a better day; consequently he conveyed the following lines to Ambulinia:

> Go tell the world that hope is glowing,
>   Go bid the rocks their silence break,
> Go tell the stars that love is glowing,
>   Then bid the hero his lover take.

In the region where scarcely the foot of man hath ever trod, where the woodman hath not found his way, lies a blooming grove, seen only by the sun when he mounts his lofty throne, visited only by the light of the stars, to whom are intrusted the guardianship of earth, before the sun sinks to rest in his rosy bed. High cliffs of rocks surround the romantic place, and in the small cavity of the rocky wall grows the daffodil clear and pure; and as the wind blows along the enchanting little mountain which surrounds the lonely spot, it nourishes the flowers with the dewdrops of heaven. Here is the seat of Elfonzo; darkness claims but little victory over this dominion, and in vain does she spread out her gloomy wings. Here the waters flow perpetually, and the trees lash their tops together to bid the welcome visitor a happy muse. Elfonzo, during his short stay in the country, had fully persuaded himself that it was his duty to bring this solemn matter to an issue. A duty that he individually owed, as a gentleman, to the parents of Ambulinia, a duty in itself involving not only his own happiness and his own standing in society, but one that called aloud the act of the parties to make it perfect and complete. How he should communicate his intentions to get a favorable reply, he was at a loss to know; he knew not whether to address Esq. Valeer in prose or in poetry, in a jocular or an argumentative manner, or whether he should use moral suasion, legal injunction, or seize and take by reprisal; if it was to do the latter, he would have no difficulty in deciding in his own mind, but his gentlemanly honor was at stake; so he concluded to address the following letter to the father and mother of Ambulinia, as his address in person he knew would only aggravate the old gentleman, and perhaps his lady.

CUMMING, GA., January 22, 1844.

MR. AND MRS. VALEER—

Again, I resume the pleasing task of addressing you, and once more beg an immediate answer to my many salutations. From every circumstance that has taken place, I feel in duty bound to comply with my obligations; to forfeit my word would be more than I dare do; to break my pledge, and my vows that have been witnessed, sealed, and delivered in the presence of an unseen Deity, would be disgraceful on my part, as well as ruinous to Ambulinia. I wish no longer to be kept in suspense about this matter. I wish to act gentlemanly in every particular. It is true, the promises I have made are unknown to any but Ambulinia, and I think it unnecessary to here enumerate them, as they who promise the most, generally perform the least. Can you for a moment doubt my sincerity, or my character? My only wish is, sir, that you may calmly and dispassionately look at the situation of the case, and if your better judgment should dictate otherwise, my obligations may induce me to pluck the flower that you so diametrically opposed. We have sworn by the saints — by the gods of battle, and by that faith whereby just men are made perfect — to be united. I hope, my dear sir, you will find it convenient as well as agreeable, to give me a favorable answer, with the signature of Mrs. Valeer, as well as yourself.

With very great esteem,

your humble servant,

J. I. ELFONZO.

The moon and stars had grown pale when Ambulinia had retired to rest. A crowd of unpleasant thoughts passed through her bosom. Solitude dwelt in her chamber — no sound from the neighboring world penetrated its stillness; it appeared a temple of silence, of repose, and of mystery. At that moment she heard a still voice calling her father. In an instant, like the flash of lightning, a thought ran through her mind, that it must be the bearer of Elfonzo's communication. "It is not a dream!" she said, "no, I cannot read dreams. Oh! I would to Heaven I was near that glowing eloquence — that poetical language — it charms the mind in an inexpressible manner, and warms the coldest heart." While consoling herself with this strain, her father rushed into her room almost frantic with rage, exclaiming: "Oh, Ambulinia! Ambulinia!! undutiful, ungrateful daughter! What does this mean? Why does this letter bear such heartrending intelligence? Will you quit a father's house with this debased wretch, without a place to lay his distracted head; going up and down the country, with every novel object that may chance to wander through this region. He is a pretty man to make love known to his superiors, and you, Ambulinia, have done but little credit to yourself by honoring his visits. Oh, wretchedness! can it be, that my hopes of happiness are forever blasted! Will you not listen to a father's entreaties, and pay some regard to a mother's tears. I know, and I do pray that God will give me fortitude to bear with this sea of troubles, and rescue my daughter, my Ambulinia, as a brand from the eternal burning." "Forgive me, father, oh! forgive thy child," replied Ambulinia. "My heart is ready to break, when I see you in this grieved state of agitation. Oh! think not so meanly of me, as that I mourn for my own danger. Father, I am only woman. Mother, I am only the templement of thy youthful years, but will suffer courageously whatever punishment you think proper to inflict upon me, if you will but allow me to comply with my most sacred promises — if you will but give me my personal right, and my personal liberty. Oh, father! if your generosity will but give me these, I ask nothing more. When Elfonzo offered me his heart, I gave him my hand, never to forsake him, and now may the mighty God banish me, before I leave him in adversity. What a heart must I have to rejoice in prosperity with him whose offers I have accepted, and then, when poverty comes, haggard as it may be — for me to trifle with the oracles of Heaven, and change with every fluctuation that may interrupt our happiness — like the politician who runs the political gantlet for office one day, and the next day, because the horizon is darkened a little, he is seen running for his life, for fear he might perish in its ruins. Where is the philosophy; where is the consistency; where is the charity; in conduct like this? Be happy then, my beloved father, and forget me; let the sorrow of parting break down the wall of separation and make us equal in our feeling; let me now say how ardently I love you; let me kiss that age-worn cheek, and should my tears bedew thy face, I will wipe them away. Oh, I never can forget you; no, never, never!''

"Weep not," said the father "Ambulinia. I will forbid Elfonzo my house, and desire that you may keep retired a few days. I will let him know that my friendship for my family is not linked together by cankered chains; and if he ever enters upon my premises again, I will send him to his long home.'' "Oh, father! let me entreat you to be calm upon this occasion, and though Elfonzo may be the sport of the clouds and winds, yet I feel assured that no fate will send him to the silent tomb, until the God of the Universe calls him hence with a triumphant voice.''

Here the father turned away, exclaiming: "I will answer his letter in a very few words, and you, madam, will have the goodness to stay at home with your mother; and remember, I am determined to protect you from the consuming fire that looks so fair to your view."

CUMMING, January 22, 1844.

SIR — In regard to your request, I am as I ever have been, utterly opposed to your marrying into my family; and if you have any regard for yourself, or any gentlemanly feeling, I hope you will mention it to me no more; but seek some other one who is not so far superior to you in standing.

W. W. VALEER.

When Elfonzo read the above letter, he became so much depressed in spirits that many of his friends thought it advisable to use other means to bring about the happy union. "Strange," said he, "that the contents of this diminutive letter should cause me to have such depressed feelings; but there is a nobler theme that this. I know not why my *military title* is not as great as that of *Squire Valeer*. For my life I cannot see that my ancestors are inferior to those who are so bitterly opposed to my marriage with Ambulinia. I know I have seen huge mountains before me, yet, when I think that I know gentlemen will insult me upon this delicate matter, should I become angry at fools and babblers, who pride themselves in their impudence and ignorance. No. My equals! I know not where to find them. My inferiors! I think it beneath me; and my superiors! I think it presumption; therefore, if this youthful heart is protected by any of the divine rights, I never will betray my trust."

He was aware that Ambulinia had a confidence that was, indeed, as firm and as resolute as she was beautiful and interesting. He hastened to the cottage of Louisa, who received him in her usual mode of pleasantness, and informed him that Ambulinia had just that moment left. "Is it possible?" said Elfonzo. "Oh, murdered hour! Why did she not remain and be the guardian of my secrets? But hasten and tell me how

29A

she has stood this trying scene, and what are her future determinations." "You know," said Louisa, "Major Elfonzo, that you have Ambulinia's first love, which is of no small consequence. She came here about twilight, and shed many precious tears in consequence of her own fate with yours. We walked silently in yon little valley you see, where we spent a 'momentary repose. She seemed to be quite as determined as ever, and before we left that beautiful spot she offered up a prayer to Heaven for thee." "I will see her then," replied Elfonzo, "though legions of enemies may oppose. She is mine by foreordination — she is mine by prophecy — she is mine by her own free will, and I will rescue her from the hands of her oppressors. Will you not, Miss Louisa, assist me in my capture?" "I will certainly, by the aid of Divine Providence," answered Louisa, "endeavor to break those slavish chains that bind the richest of prizes; though allow me, Major, to entreat you to use no harsh means on this important occasion; take a decided stand, and write freely to Ambulinia upon this subject, and I will see that no intervening cause hinders its passage to her. God alone will save a mourning people. Now is the day, and now is the hour to obey a command of such valuable worth." The Major felt himself grow stronger after this short interview with Louisa. He felt as if he could whip his weight in wildcats — he knew he was master of his own feelings, and could now write a letter that would bring this litigation to *an issue*.

CUMMING, January 24, 1844.

DEAR AMBULINIA—

We have now reached the most trying moment of our lives; we are pledged not to forsake our trust; we have waited for a favorable hour to come, thinking your friends would settle the matter agreeably among themselves, and finally be reconciled to our marriage; but as I have waited in vain, and looked in vain, I have determined in my own mind to make a proposition to you, though you may think it not in accord with your station, or compatible with your rank; yet, "sub hoc signo vinces." You know I cannot resume my visits, in consequence of the utter hostility that your father has to me; therefore the consummation of our union will have to be sought for in a more sublime sphere, at the residence of a respectable friend of this village. You cannot have any scruples upon this mode of proceeding, if you will but remember it emanates from one who loves you better than his own life — who is more than anxious to bid you welcome to a new and happy home. Your warmest associates say come; the talented, the learned, the wise, and the experienced say come;— all these with their friends say, come. Viewing these, with many other inducements, I flatter myself that you will come to the embraces of your Elfonzo; for now is the time of your acceptance and the day of your liberation. You cannot be ignorant, Ambulinia, that thou art the desire of my heart; its thoughts are too noble, and too pure, to conceal themselves from you. I shall wait for your answer to this impatiently, expecting that you will set the time to make your departure, and to be in readiness at a moment's warning to share the joys of a more preferable life. This will be handed to you by Louisa, who will take a pleasure in communicating anything to you that may relieve your dejected spirits, and will assure you that I now stand ready, willing, and waiting to make good my vows.

I am, dear Ambulinia, yours

truly, and forever,

J. I. ELFONZO.

Louisa made it convenient to visit Mr. Valeer's, though they did not suspect her in the least the bearer of love epistles; consequently, she was invited in the room to console Ambulinia, where they were left alone. Ambulinia was seated by a small table — her head resting on her hand — her brilliant eyes were bathed in tears. Louisa handed her the letter of Elfonzo, when another spirit animated her features — the spirit of renewed confidence that never fails to strengthen the female character in an hour of grief and sorrow like this, and as she pronounced the last accent of his name, she exclaimed, "And does he love me yet! I never will forget your generosity, Louisa. Oh, unhappy and yet blessed Louisa! may you never feel what I have felt — may you never know the pangs of love. Had I never loved, I never would have been unhappy; but I turn to Him who can save, and if His wisdom does not will my expected union, I know He will give me strength to bear my lot. Amuse yourself with this little book, and take it as an apology for my silence," said Ambulinia, "while I attempt to answer this volume of consolation." "Thank you," said Louisa, "you are excusable upon this occasion; but I pray you, Ambulinia, to be expert upon this momentous subject, that there may be nothing mistrustful upon my part." "I will," said Ambulinia, and immediately resumed her seat and addressed the following to Elfonzo:

CUMMING, GA., January 28, 1844.

DEVOTED ELFONZO —

I hail your letter as a welcome messenger of faith, and can now say truly and firmly that my feelings correspond with yours. Nothing shall be wanting on my part to make my obedience your fidelity. Courage and perseverance will accomplish success. Receive this as my oath, that while I grasp your hand in my own imagination, we stand united before a higher tribunal than any on earth. All the powers of my life, soul, and body, I devote to thee. Whatever dangers may threaten me, I fear not to encounter them. Perhaps I have determined upon my own destruction, by leaving the house of the best of parents; be it so, I flee to you; I share your destiny, faithful to the end. The day that I have concluded upon for this task, is *Sabbath* next, when the family with the citizens are generally at church. For Heaven's sake let not that day pass unimproved: trust not till to-morrow, it is the cheat of life — the future that never comes — the grave of many noble births — the cavern of ruined enterprise: which like the lightning's flash is born, and dies, and perishes, ere the voice of him who sees, can cry, *behold! behold!!* You may trust to what I say, no power shall tempt me to betray confidence. Suffer me to add one word more.

> I will soothe thee, in all thy grief,
>   Beside the gloomy river;
> And though thy love may yet be brief;
>   Mine is fixed forever.

Receive the deepest emotions of my heart for thy constant love, and may the power of inspiration be thy guide, thy portion, and thy all. In great haste,   Yours faithfully,

AMBULINIA.

" I now take my leave of you, sweet girl," said Louisa, " sincerely wishing you success on Sabbath next." When Ambulinia's letter was handed to Elfonzo, he perused it without doubting its contents. Louisa charged him to make but few confidants; but like most young men who happened to win the heart of a beautiful girl, he was so elated with the idea that he felt as a commanding general on parade, who had confidence in all, consequently gave orders to all. The appointed Sabbath, with a delicious breeze and cloudless sky, made its appearance. The people gathered in crowds to the church — the streets were filled with the neighboring citizens, all marching to the house of worship. It is entirely useless for me to attempt to describe the feelings of Elfonzo and Ambulinia, who were silently watching the movements of the multitude, apparently counting them as they entered the house of God, looking for the last one to darken the door. The impatience and anxiety with which they waited, and the bliss they anticipated on the eventful day, is altogether indescribable. Those that have been so fortunate as to embark in such a noble enterprise, know all its realities; and those who have not had this inestimable privilege, will have to taste its sweets before they can tell to others its joys, its comforts, and its Heavenborn worth. Immediately after Ambulinia had assisted the family off to church, she took the advantage of that opportunity to make good her promises. She left a home of enjoyment to be wedded to one whose love had been justifiable. A few short steps brought her to the presence of Louisa, who urged her to make good use of her time, and not to delay a moment, but to go

29***

with her to her brother's house, where Elfonzo would
forever make her happy. With lively speed, and yet
a graceful air, she entered the door and found herself
protected by the champion of her confidence. The
necessary arrangements were fast making to have the
two lovers united — everything was in readiness except
the parson; and as they are generally very sanctimoni-
ous on such occasions, the news got to the parents of
Ambulinia before the everlasting knot was tied, and
they both came running, with uplifted hands and injured feelings, to arrest their daughter from an unguarded and hasty resolution. Elfonzo desired to
maintain his ground, but Ambulinia thought it best
for him to leave, to prepare for a greater contest. He
accordingly obeyed, as it would have been a vain endeavor for him to have battled against a man who was
armed with deadly weapons; and besides, he could not
resist the request of such a pure heart. Ambulinia
concealed herself in the upper story of the house, fear-
ing the rebuke of her father; the door was locked, and
no chastisement was now expected. Esquire Valeer,
whose pride was already touched, resolved to preserve
the dignity of his family. He entered the house almost
exhausted, looking wildly for Ambulinia. "Amazed
and astonished indeed I am," said he, "at a people
who call themselves civilized, to allow such behavior as
this. Ambulinia, Ambulinia!" he cried, "come to
the calls of your first, your best, and your only friend.
I appeal to you, sir," turning to the gentleman of the
house, "to know where Ambulinia has gone, or where
is she?" "Do you mean to insult me, sir, in my
own house?" inquired the confounded gentleman. "I
will burst," said Mr. V., "asunder every door in your
dwelling, in search of my daughter, if you do not
speak quickly, and tell me where she is. I care nothing about that outcast rubbish of creation, that mean,

low-lived Elfonzo, if I can but obtain Ambulinia.   Are
you not going to open this door?'' said he.   '' By the
Eternal that made Heaven and earth! I will go about
the work instantly, if it is not done.''   The confused
citizens gathered from all parts of the village, to know
the cause of this commotion.   Some rushed into the
house; the door that was locked flew open, and there
stood Ambulinia, weeping.   '' Father, be still,'' said
she, '' and I will follow thee home.''   But the agitated
man seized her, and bore her off through the gazing
multitude.   '' Father!'' she exclaimed, '' I humbly beg
your pardon — I will be dutiful — I will obey thy commands.   Let the sixteen years I have lived in obedience
to thee, be my future security.''   '' I don't like to be
always giving credit, when the old score is not paid up,
madam;'' said the father.   The mother followed almost
in a state of derangement, crying and imploring her to
think beforehand, and ask advice from experienced
persons, and they would tell her it was a rash undertaking.   '' Oh!'' said she, '' Ambulinia, my daughter,
did you know what I have suffered — did you know
how many nights I have whiled away in agony, in pain,
and in fear, you would pity the sorrows of a heart-
broken mother.''

'' Well, mother,'' replied Ambulinia, '' I know I
have been disobedient; I am aware that what I have
done might have been done much better; but oh!
what shall I do with my honor? it is so dear to me; I
am pledged to Elfonzo.   His high moral worth is certainly worth some attention; moreover, my vows, I
have no doubt, are recorded in the book of life, and
must I give these all up? must my fair hopes be forever blasted?   Forbid it father, oh! forbid it mother,
forbid it heaven.''   '' I have seen so many beautiful
skies overclouded,'' replied the mother, '' so many
blossoms nipped by the frost, that I am afraid to trust

cc***

you to the care of those fair days, which may be interrupted by thundering and tempestuous nights. You
no doubt think as I did — life's devious ways were
strewed with sweet scented flowers, but ah! how long
they have lingered around me and took their flight in
the vivid hope that laughs at the drooping victims it
has murdered." Elfonzo was moved at this sight.
The people followed on to see what was going to
become of Ambulinia, while he, with downcast looks,
kept at a distance, until he saw them enter the abode
of the father, thrusting her, that was the sigh of his
soul, out of his presence into a solitary apartment,
when she exclaimed, "Elfonzo! Elfonzo! oh, Elfonzo! where art thou, with all thy heroes? haste,
oh! haste, come thou to my relief. Ride on the wings
of the wind! Turn thy force loose like a tempest, and
roll on thy army like a whirlwind, over this mountain
of trouble and confusion. Oh, friends! if any pity
me, let your last efforts throng upon the green hills,
and come to the relief of Ambulinia, who is guilty of
nothing but innocent love." Elfonzo called out with
a loud voice, "My God, can I stand this! arouse up,
I beseech you, and put an end to this tyranny. Come,
my brave boys," said he, "are you ready to go forth
to your duty?" They stood around him. "Who,"
said he, "will call us to arms? Where are my thunderbolts of war? Speak ye, the first who will meet the
foe! Who will go forward with me in this ocean of
grievous temptation? If there is one who desires to
go, let him come and shake hands upon the altar of
devotion, and swear that he will be a hero; yes, a
Hector in a cause like this, which calls aloud for a
speedy remedy." "Mine be the deed," said a young
lawyer, "and mine alone; Venus alone shall quit her
station before I will forsake one jot or tittle of my
promise to you; what is death to me? what is all this

warlike army, if it is not to win a victory? I love the sleep of the lover and the mighty; nor would I give it over till the blood of my enemies should wreak with that of my own. But God forbid that our fame should soar on the blood of the slumberer." Mr. Valeer stands at his door with the frown of a demon upon his brow, with his dangerous weapon ready to strike the first man who should enter his door. "Who will arise and go forward through blood and carnage to the rescue of my Ambulinia?" said Elfonzo. "All," exclaimed the multitude; and onward they went, with their implements of battle. Others, of a more timid nature, stood among the distant hills to see the result of the contest.

Elfonzo took the lead of his band. Night arose in clouds; darkness concealed the heavens; but the blazing hopes that stimulated them gleamed in every bosom. All approached the anxious spot; they rushed to the front of the house and, with one exclamation, demanded Ambulinia. "Away, begone, and disturb my peace no more," said Mr. Valeer. "You are a set of base, insolent, and infernal rascals. Go, the northern star points your path through the dim twilight of the night; go, and vent your spite upon the lonely hills; pour forth your love, you poor, weak-minded wretch, upon your idleness and upon your guitar, and your fiddle; they are fit subjects for your admiration, for let me assure you, though this sword and iron lever are cankered, yet they frown in sleep, and let one of you dare to enter my house this night and you shall have the contents and the weight of these instruments." "Never yet did base dishonor blur my name," said Elfonzo: "mine is a cause of renown; here are my warriors, fear and tremble, for this night, though hell itself should oppose, I will endeavor to avenge her whom thou hast banished in solitude. The

voice of Ambulinia shall be heard from that dark
dungeon.'' At that moment Ambulinia appeared at
the window above, and with a tremulous voice said,
'' live, Elfonzo! oh! live to raise my stone of moss!
why should such language enter your heart? why
should thy voice rend the air with such agitation? I
bid thee live, once more remembering these tears of
mine are shed alone for thee, in this dark and gloomy
vault, and should I perish under this load of trouble,
join the song of thrilling accents with the raven above
my grave, and lay this tattered frame beside the banks
of the Chattahoochee, or the stream of Sawney's
brook; sweet will be the song of death to your Ambulinia. My ghost shall visit you in the smiles of Paradise, and tell your high fame to the minds of that
region, which is far more preferable than this lonely
cell. My heart shall speak for thee till the latest hour;
I know faint and broken are the sounds of sorrow, yet
our souls, Elfonzo, shall hear the peaceful songs
together. One bright name shall be ours on high, if
we are not permitted to be united here; bear in mind
that I still cherish my old sentiments, and the poet will
mingle the names of Elfonzo and Ambulinia in the tide
of other days.'' ''Fly, Elfonzo,'' said the voices of
his united band, ''to the wounded heart of your beloved. All enemies shall fall beneath thy sword. Fly
through the clefts, and the dim spark shall sleep
in death.'' Elfonzo rushes forward and strikes his
shield against the door, which was barricaded, to prevent any intercourse. His brave sons throng around
him. The people pour along the streets, both male
and female, to prevent or witness the melancholy
scene.

''To arms, to arms!'' cried Elfonzo, ''here is a
victory to be won, a prize to be gained that is more to
me than the whole world beside.'' ''It cannot be

done to-night," said Mr. Valeer. " I bear the clang of death; my strength and armor shall prevail. My Ambulinia shall rest in this hall until the break of another day, and if we fall, we fall together. If we die, we die clinging to our tattered rights, and our blood alone shall tell the mournful tale of a murdered daughter and a ruined father." Sure enough, he kept watch all night, and was successful in defending his house and family. The bright morning gleamed upon the hills, night vanished away, the Major and his associates felt somewhat ashamed that they had not been as fortunate as they expected to have been; however, they still leaned upon their arms in dispersed groups; some were walking the streets, others were talking in the Major's behalf. Many of the citizens suspended business, as the town presented nothing but consternation. A novelty that might end in the destruction of some worthy and respectable citizens. Mr. Valeer ventured in the streets, though not without being well armed. Some of his friends congratulated him on the decided stand he had taken, and hoped he would settle the matter amicably with Elfonzo, without any serious injury. " Me," he replied, " what, me, condescend to fellowship with a coward, and a low-live, lazy, undermining villain? no, gentlemen, this cannot be; I had rather be borne off, like the bubble upon the dark blue ocean, with Ambulinia by my side, than to have him in the ascending or descending line of relationship. Gentlemen," continued he, " if Elfonzo is so much of a distinguished character, and is so learned in the fine arts, why do you not patronize such men? why not introduce him into your families, as a gentleman of taste and of unequaled magnanimity? why are you so very anxious that he should become a relative of mine? Oh, gentlemen, I fear you yet are tainted with the curiosity of our first parents, who were beguiled by the poisonous kiss of an old ugly serpent, and who, for one *apple*, *damned* all mankind. I wish to divest myself, as far as possible, of that untutored custom. I have long since learned that the perfection of wisdom, and the end of true philosophy is to proportion our wants to our possessions, our ambition to our capacities; we will then be a happy and a virtuous people.'' Ambulinia was sent off to prepare for a long and tedious journey. Her new acquaintances had been instructed by her father how to treat her, and in what manner, and to keep the anticipated visit entirely secret. Elfonzo was watching the movements of everybody; some friends had told him of the plot that was laid to carry off Ambulinia. At night, he rallied some two or three of his forces, and went silently along to the stately mansion; a faint and glimmering light showed through the windows; lightly he steps to the door, there were many voices rallying fresh in fancy's eye; he tapped the shutter, it was opened instantly and he beheld once more seated beside several ladies, the hope of all his toils; he rushed towards her, she rose from her seat, rejoicing; he made one mighty grasp, when Ambulinia exclaimed, '' huzza for Major Elfonzo! I will defend myself and you, too, with this conquering instrument I hold in my hand; huzza, I say, I now invoke time's broad wing to shed around us some dewdrops of verdant spring.''

But the hour had not come for this joyous reunion; her friends struggled with Elfonzo for some time, and finally succeeded in arresting her from his hands. He dared not injure them, because they were matrons whose courage needed no spur; she was snatched from the arms of Elfonzo, with so much eagerness, and yet with such expressive signification, that he calmly withdrew from this lovely enterprise, with an ardent hope that he should be lulled to repose by the zephyrs which whispered peace to his soul.   Several long days and nights passed unmolested, all seemed to have grounded their arms of rebellion, and no callidity appeared to be going on with any of the parties.   Other arrangements were made by Ambulinia; she feigned herself to be entirely the votary of a mother's care, and said, by her graceful smiles, that manhood might claim his stern dominion in some other region, where such boisterous love was not so prevalent.   This gave the parents a confidence that yielded some hours of sober joy; they believed that Ambulinia would now cease to love Elfonzo, and that her stolen affections would now expire with her misguided opinions.   They therefore declined the idea of sending her to a distant land.   But oh! they dreamed not of the rapture that dazzled the fancy of Ambulinia, who would say, when alone, youth should not fly away on his rosy pinions, and leave her to grapple in the conflict with unknown admirers.

> No frowning age shall control
> The constant current of my soul,
> Nor a tear from pity's eye
> Shall check my sympathetic sigh.

With this resolution fixed in her mind, one dark and dreary night, when the winds whistled and the tempest roared, she received intelligence that Elfonzo was then waiting, and every preparation was then ready, at the residence of Dr. Tully, and for her to make a quick escape while the family were reposing.   Accordingly she gathered her books, went to the wardrobe supplied with a variety of ornamental dressing, and ventured alone in the streets to make her way to Elfonzo, who was near at hand, impatiently looking and watching her arrival.   "What forms," said she, "are those rising before me?   What is that dark spot on the clouds?   I do wonder what frightful ghost that is, gleaming on the red tempest? Oh, be merciful and tell me what region you are from. Oh, tell me, ye strong spirits, or ye dark and fleeting clouds, that I yet have a friend." "A friend," said a low, whispering voice. "I am thy unchanging, thy aged, and thy disappointed mother. Oh, Ambulinia, why hast thou deceived me? Why brandish in that hand of thine a javelin of pointed steel? Why suffer that lip I have kissed a thousand times, to equivocate? My daughter, let these tears sink deep into thy soul, and no longer persist in that which may be your destruction and ruin. Come, my dear child, retract your steps, and bear me company to your welcome home." Without one retorting word, or frown from her brow, she yielded to the entreaties of her mother, and with all the mildness of her former character she went along with the silver lamp of age, to the home of candor and benevolence. Her father received her cold and formal politeness —"Where has Ambulinia been, this blustering evening, Mrs. Valeer?" inquired he. "Oh, she and I have been taking a solitary walk," said the mother; "all things, I presume, are now working for the best."

Elfonzo heard this news shortly after it happened. "What," said he, "has heaven and earth turned against me? I have been disappointed times without number. Shall I despair? — must I give it over? Heaven's decrees will not fade; I will write again — I will try again; and if it traverses a gory field, I pray forgiveness at the altar of justice."

DESOLATE HILL, CUMMING, GEO., 1844.

UNCONQUERED AND BELOVED AMBULINIA —

I have only time to say to you, not to despair; thy fame shall not perish; my visions are brightening before me. The whirlwind's rage is past, and we now shall subdue our enemies without doubt. On Monday morning, when your friends are at breakfast, they will not suspect your departure, or even mistrust me being in town, as it has been reported advantageously, that I have left for the west. You walk carelessly towards the academy grove, where you will find me with a lightning steed, elegantly equipped to bear you off where we shall be joined in wedlock with the first connubial rights. Fail not to do this — think not of the tedious relations of our wrongs — be invincible. You alone occupy all my ambition, and I alone will make you my happy spouse, with the same unimpeached veracity. I remain, forever, your devoted friend and admirer,   J. I. Elfonzo.

The appointed day ushered in undisturbed by any clouds; nothing disturbed Ambulinia's soft beauty. With serenity and loveliness she obeys the request of Elfonzo. The moment the family seated themselves at the table —" Excuse my absence for a short time," said she, "while I attend to the placing of those flowers, which should have been done a week ago." And away she ran to the sacred grove, surrounded with glittering pearls, that indicated her coming. Elfonzo hails her with his silver bow and his golden harp. They meet — Ambulinia's countenance brightens — Elfonzo leads up his winged steed. " Mount," said he, " ye true-hearted, ye fearless soul — the day is ours." She sprang upon the back of the young thunderbolt, a brilliant star sparkles upon her head, with one hand she grasps the reins, and with the other she holds an olive branch. " Lend thy aid, ye strong winds," they exclaimed, " ye moon, ye sun, and all ye fair host of heaven, witness the enemy conquered." " Hold," said Elfonzo, " thy dashing steed." " Ride on," said Ambulinia, " the voice of thunder is behind us." And onward they went, with such rapidity that they very soon arrived at Rural Retreat, where they dismounted, and were united with all the solemnities that usually attend such divine operations. They passed the day in thanksgiving and great rejoicing, and on that evening they visited their uncle, where many of their friends and acquaintances had gathered to congratulate them in the field of untainted bliss.

The kind old gentleman met them in the yard: "Well," said he, "I wish I may die, Elfonzo, if you and Ambulinia haven't tied a knot with your tongue that you can't untie with your teeth. But come in, come in, never mind, all is right — the world still moves on, and no one has fallen in this great battle."

Happy now is their lot! Unmoved by misfortune, they live among the fair beauties of the South. Heaven spreads their peace and fame upon the arch of the rainbow, and smiles propitously at their triumph, *through the tears of the storm.*

ABOUT ALL KINDS OF SHIPS

THE MODERN STEAMER AND THE OBSOLETE STEAMER

WE are victims of one common superstition — the superstition that we realize the changes that are daily taking place in the world because we read about them and know what they are. I should not have supposed that the modern ship could be a surprise to me, but it is. It seems to be as much of a surprise to me as it could have been if I had never read anything about it. I walk about this great vessel, the *Havel*, as she plows her way through the Atlantic, and every detail that comes under my eye brings up the miniature counterpart of it as it existed in the little ships I crossed the ocean in fourteen, seventeen, eighteen, and twenty years ago.

In the *Havel* one can be in several respects more comfortable than he can be in the best hotels on the continent of Europe. For instance, she has several bathrooms, and they are as convenient and as nicely equipped as the bathrooms in a fine private house in America; whereas in the hotels of the continent one bathroom is considered sufficient, and it is generally shabby and located in some out-of-the-way corner of the house; moreover, you need to give notice so long beforehand that you get over wanting a bath by the time you get it. In the hotels there are a good many different kinds of noises, and they spoil sleep; in my room in the ship I hear no sounds. In the hotels they usually shut off the electric light at midnight; in the ship one may burn it in one's room all night.

In the steamer *Batavia*, twenty years ago, one candle, set in the bulkhead between two staterooms, was there to light both rooms, but did not light either of them. It was extinguished at 11 at night, and so were all the saloon lamps except one or two, which were left burning to help the passenger see how to break his neck trying to get around in the dark. The passengers sat at table on long benches made of the hardest kind of wood; in the *Havel* one sits on a swivel chair with a cushioned back to it. In those old times the dinner bill of fare was always the same: a pint of some simple, homely soup or other, boiled codfish and potatoes, slab of boiled beef, stewed prunes for dessert — on Sundays " dog in a blanket," on Thursdays " plum duff." In the modern ship the *menu* is choice and elaborate, and is changed daily. In the old times dinner was a sad occasion; in our day a concealed orchestra enlivens it with charming music. In the old days the decks were always wet; in our day they are usually dry, for the promenade-deck is roofed over, and a sea seldom comes aboard. In a moderately disturbed sea, in the old days, a landsman could hardly keep his legs, but in such a sea in our day the decks are as level as a table. In the old days the inside of a ship was the plainest and barrenest thing, and the most dismal and uncomfortable that ingenuity could devise; the modern ship is a marvel of rich and costly decoration and sumptuous appointment, and is equipped with every comfort and convenience that money can buy. The old ships had no place of assembly but the dining-room, the new ones have several spacious and beautiful drawing-rooms. The old ships offered the passenger no chance to smoke except in the place that was called the "fiddle." It was a repulsive den made of rough boards (full of cracks) and its office was to protect the main hatch. It was grimy and dirty; there were no seats; the only light was a lamp of the rancid-oil-and-rag kind; the place was very cold, and never dry, for the seas broke in through the cracks every little while and drenched the cavern thoroughly. In the modern ship there are three or four large smoking-rooms, and they have card tables and cushioned sofas, and are heated by steam and lighted by electricity. There are few European hotels with such smoking-rooms.

The former ships were built of wood, and had two or three water-tight compartments in the hold with doors in them which were often left open, particularly when the ship was going to hit a rock. The modern leviathan is built of steel, and the water-tight bulkheads have no doors in them; they divide the ship into nine or ten water-tight compartments and endow her with as many lives as a cat. Their complete efficiency was established by the happy results following the memorable accident to the *City of Paris* a year or two ago.

One curious thing which is at once noticeable in the great modern ship is the absence of hubbub, clatter, rush of feet, roaring of orders. That is all gone by. The elaborate maneuvers necessary in working the vessel into her dock are conducted without sound; one sees nothing of the processes, hears no commands. A Sabbath stillness and solemnity reign, in place of the turmoil and racket of the earlier days. The modern ship has a spacious bridge fenced chin-high with sail-cloth, and floored with wooden gratings; and this bridge, with its fenced fore-and-aft annexes, could accommodate a seated audience of a hundred and fifty men. There are three steering equipments, each competent if the others should break. From the bridge the ship is steered, and also handled. The handling is not done by shout or whistle, but by signaling with patent automatic gongs. There are three tell-tales, with plainly lettered dials — for steering, handling the engines, and for communicating orders to the invisible mates who are conducting the landing of the ship or casting off. The officer who is astern is out of sight and too far away to hear trumpet calls; but the gongs near him tell him to haul in, pay out, make fast, let go, and so on; he hears, but the passengers do not, and so the ship seems to land herself without human help.

This great bridge is thirty or forty feet above the water, but the sea climbs up there sometimes; so there is another bridge twelve or fifteen feet higher still, for use in these emergencies. The force of water is a strange thing. It slips between one's fingers like air, but upon occasion it acts like a solid body and will bend a thin iron rod. In the *Havel* it has splintered a heavy oaken rail into broom-straws instead of merely breaking it in two, as would have been the seemingly natural thing for it to do. At the time of the awful Johnstown disaster, according to the testimony of several witnesses, rocks were carried some distance on the surface of the stupendous torrent; and at St. Helena, many years ago, a vast sea wave carried a battery of cannon forty feet up a steep slope and deposited the guns there in a row. But the water has done a still stranger thing, and it is one which is credibly vouched for. A marlinspike is an implement about a foot long which tapers from its butt to the other extremity and ends in a sharp point. It is made of iron and is heavy. A wave came aboard a ship in a storm and raged aft, breast high, carrying a marlin-spike point first with it, and with such lightning-like swiftness and force as to drive it three or four inches into a sailor's body and kill him.

In all ways the ocean greyhound of to-day is im·
posing and impressive to one who carries in his head
no ship pictures of a recent date.   In bulk she comes
near to rivaling the Ark; yet this monstrous mass of
steel is driven five hundred miles through the waves in
twenty-four hours.   I remember the brag run of a
steamer which I traveled in once on the Pacific — it
was two hundred and nine miles in twenty-four hours;
a year or so later I was a passenger in the excursion
tub *Quaker City*, and on one occasion in a level and
glassy sea, it was claimed that she reeled off two hundred and eleven miles between noon and noon, but it
was probably a campaign lie.   That little steamer had
seventy passengers, and a crew of forty men, and
seemed a good deal of a beehive.   But in this present
ship we are living in a sort of solitude, these soft
summer days, with sometimes a hundred passengers
scattered about the spacious distances, and sometimes
nobody in sight at all; yet, hidden somewhere in the
vessel's bulk, there are (including crew) near eleven
hundred people.

The stateliest lines in the literature of the sea are these :

" Britannia needs no bulwarks, no towers along the steep —
   Her march is o'er the mountain waves, her home is on the deep ! "

There it is.   In those old times the little ships
climbed over the waves and wallowed down into the
trough on the other side; the giant ship of our day
does not climb over the waves, but crushes her way
through them.   Her formidable weight and mass and
impetus give her mastery over any but extraordinary
storm waves.

The ingenuity of man!   I mean in this passing
generation.   To-day I found in the chart-room a frame
of removable wooden slats on the wall, and on the slats
was painted uninforming information like this:

30***

Trim-Tank,	.	.	.	.	.	.	Empty
Double-Bottom No. 1,	.	.	.	.	.		Full
Double-Bottom No. 2,	.	.	.	.	.		Full
Double-Bottom No. 3,	.	.	.	.	.		Full
Double-Bottom No. 4,	.	.	.	.	.		Full

While I was trying to think out what kind of a game this might be and how a stranger might best go to work to beat it, a sailor came in and pulled out the "Empty" end of the first slat and put it back with its reverse side to the front, marked "Full." He made some other change, I did not notice what. The slat-frame was soon explained. Its function was to indicate how the ballast in the ship was distributed. The striking thing was that the ballast was water. I did not know that a ship had ever been ballasted with water. I had merely read, some time or other, that such an experiment was to be tried. But that is the modern way; between the experimental trial of a new thing and its adoption, there is no wasted time, if the trial proves its value.

On the wall, near the slat-frame, there was an outline drawing of the ship, and this betrayed the fact that this vessel has twenty-two considerable lakes of water in her. These lakes are in her bottom; they are imprisoned between her real bottom and a false bottom. They are separated from each other, thwartships, by water-tight bulkheads, and separated down the middle by a bulkhead running from the bow four-fifths of the way to the stern. It is a chain of lakes four hundred feet long and from five to seven feet deep. Fourteen of the lakes contain fresh water brought from shore, and the aggregate weight of it is four hundred tons. The rest of the lakes contain salt water — six hundred and eighteen tons. Upwards of a thousand tons of water, altogether.

Think how handy this ballast is. The ship leaves

port with the lakes all full.   As she lightens forward through consumption of coal, she loses trim — her head rises, her stern sinks down.   Then they spill one of the sternward lakes into the sea, and the trim is restored.   This can be repeated right along as occasion may require.   Also, a lake at one end of the ship can be moved to the other end by pipes and steam pumps. When the sailor changed the slat-frame to-day, he was posting a transference of that kind.   The seas had been increasing, and the vessel's head needed more weighting, to keep it from rising on the waves instead of plowing through them; therefore, twenty-five tons of water had been transferred to the bow from a lake situated well towards the stern.

A water compartment is kept either full or empty. The body of water must be compact, so that it cannot slosh around.   A shifting ballast would not do, of course.

The modern ship is full of beautiful ingenuities, but it seems to me that this one is the king.   I would rather be the originator of that idea than of any of the others.   Perhaps the trim of a ship was never perfectly ordered and preserved until now.   A vessel out of trim will not steer, her speed is maimed, she strains and labors in the seas.   Poor creature, for six thousand years she has had no comfort until these latest days. For six thousand years she swam through the best and cheapest ballast in the world, the only perfect ballast, but she couldn't tell her master and he had not the wit to find it out for himself.   It is odd to reflect that there is nearly as much water inside of this ship as there is outside, and yet there is no danger.

DD***

NOAH'S ARK

THE progress made in the great art of ship-building since Noah's time is quite noticeable. Also, the looseness of the navigation laws in the time of Noah is in quite striking contrast with the strictness of the navigation laws of our time. It would not be possible for Noah to do in our day what he was permitted to do in his own. Experience has taught us the necessity of being more particular, more conservative, more careful of human life. Noah would not be allowed to sail from Bremen in our day. The inspectors would come and examine the Ark, and make all sorts of objections. A person who knows Germany can imagine the scene and the conversation without difficulty and without missing a detail. The inspector would be in a beautiful military uniform; he would be respectful, dignified, kindly, the perfect gentleman, but steady as the north star to the last requirement of his duty. He would make Noah tell him where he was born, and how old he was, and what religious sect he belonged to, and the amount of his income, and the grade and position he claimed socially, and the name and style of his occupation, and how many wives and children he had, and how many servants, and the name, sex, and age of the whole of them; and if he hadn't a passport he would be courteously required to get one right away. Then he would take up the matter of the Ark:

" What is her length?"

" Six hundred feet."

" Depth?"

" Sixty-five."

" Beam?"

" Fifty or sixty."

" Built of —"

" Wood."

" What kind?"

" Shittim and gopher."

" Interior and exterior decorations?"

" Pitched within and without."

." Passengers?"

" Eight."

" Sex?"

" Half male, the others female."

" Ages?"

" From a hundred years up."

" Up to where?"

" Six hundred."

" Ah — going to Chicago; good idea, too. Surgeon's name?"

" We have no surgeon."

" Must provide a surgeon. Also an undertaker — particularly the undertaker. These people must not be left without the necessities of life at their age. Crew?"

" The same eight."

" The same eight?"

" The same eight."

" And half of them women?"

" Yes, sir."

" Have they ever served as seamen?"

" No, sir."

" Have the men?"

" No, sir."

" Have any of you ever been to sea?"

" No, sir."

" Where were you reared?'

" On a farm — all of us."

" This vessel requires a crew of eight hundred men, she not being a steamer. You must provide them. She must have four mates and nine cooks. Who is captain?"

" I am, sir."

" You must get a captain. Also a chambermaid.
Also sick nurses for the old people. Who designed
this vessel?"

" I did, sir."

" Is it your first attempt?"

" Yes, sir."

" I partly suspected it.   Cargo?"

" Animals."

" Kind?"

" All kinds."

" Wild, or tame?"

" Mainly wild."

" Foreign or domestic?"

" Mainly foreign."

" Principal wild ones?"

" Megatherium, elephant, rhinoceros, lion, tiger,
wolf, snakes — all the wild things of all climes — two
of each."

" Securely caged?"

" No, not caged."

" They must have iron cages. Who feeds and waters
the menagerie?"

" We do."

" The old people?"

" Yes, sir."

" It is dangerous — for both.   The animals must be
cared for by a competent force.   How many animals
are there?"

" Big ones, seven thousand; big and little together,
ninety-eight thousand."

" You must provide twelve hundred keepers.   How
is the vessel lighted?"

" By two windows."

" Where are they?"

" Up under the eaves."

" Two windows for a tunnel six hundred feet long and sixty-five feet deep? You must put in the electric light — a few arc lights and fifteen hundred incandescents. What do you do in case of leaks? How many pumps have you?"

" None, sir."

" You must provide pumps. How do you get water for the passengers and the animals?"

" We let down the buckets from the windows."

" It is inadequate. What is your motive power?"

" What is my which?"

" Motive power. What power do you use in driving the ship?"

" None."

" You must provide sails or steam. What is the nature of your steering apparatus?"

" We haven't any."

" Haven't you a rudder?"

" No, sir."

" How do you steer the vessel?"

" We don't."

" You must provide a rudder, and properly equip it. How many anchors have you?"

" None."

" You must provide six. One is not permitted to sail a vessel like this without that protection. How many life-boats have you?"

" None, sir."

" Provide twenty-five. How many life-preservers?"

" None."

" You will provide two thousand. How long are you expecting your voyage to last?"

" Eleven or twelve months."

" Eleven or twelve months. Pretty slow — but you will be in time for the Exposition. What is your ship sheathed with — copper?"

" Her hull is bare — not sheathed at all."

" Dear man, the wood-boring creatures of the sea would riddle her like a sieve and send her to the bottom in three months. She *cannot* be allowed to go away in this condition; she must be sheathed. Just a word more: Have you reflected that Chicago is an inland city and not reachable with a vessel like this?"

" Shecargo? What is Shecargo? I am not going to Shecargo."

" Indeed? Then may I ask what the animals are for?"

" Just to breed others from."

" Others? Is it possible that you haven't enough?"

" For the present needs of civilization, yes; but the rest are going to be drowned in a flood, and these are to renew the supply."

" A flood?"

" Yes, sir."

" Are you sure of that?"

" Perfectly sure. It is going to rain forty days and forty nights."

" Give yourself no concern about that, dear sir, it often does that here."

" Not this kind of rain. This is going to cover the mountain tops, and the earth will pass from sight."

" Privately — but of course not officially — I am sorry you revealed this, for it compels me to withdraw the option I gave you as to sails or steam. I must require you to use steam. Your ship cannot carry the hundredth part of an eleven-months water supply for the animals. You will have to have condensed water."

" But I tell you I am going to dip water from outside with buckets."

" It will not answer. Before the flood reaches the mountain tops the fresh waters will have joined the salt seas, and it will all be salt. You must put in steam and condense your water. I will now bid you good day, sir: Did I understand you to say that this was your very first attempt at ship building?"

" My very first, sir, I give you the honest truth. I built this Ark without having ever had the slightest training or experience or instruction in marine architecture."

" It is a remarkable work, sir, a most remarkable work. I consider that it contains more features that are new — absolutely new and unhackneyed — than are to be found in any other vessel that swims the seas."

" This compliment does me infinite honor, dear sir, infinite; and I shall cherish the memory of it while life shall last. Sir, I offer my duty and most grateful thanks. Adieu."

No, the German inspector would be limitlessly courteous to Noah, and would make him feel that he was among friends, but he wouldn't let him go to sea with that Ark.

COLUMBUS'S CRAFT

BETWEEN Noah's time and the time of Columbus naval architecture underwent some changes, and from being unspeakably bad was improved to a point which may be described as less unspeakably bad. I have read somewhere, some time or other, that one of Columbus's ships was a ninety-ton vessel. By comparing that ship with the ocean greyhounds of our time one is able to get down to a comprehension of how small that Spanish bark was, and how little fitted she would be to run opposition in the Atlantic passenger trade to-day. It would take seventy-four of her to match the tonnage of the *Havel* and carry the *Havel's* trip. If I remember rightly, it took her ten weeks to make the passage. With our ideas this would now be considered an objectionable gait. She probably had a captain, a mate, and a crew consisting of four seamen and a boy. The crew of a modern greyhound numbers two hundred and fifty persons.

Columbus's ship being small and very old, we know that we may draw from these two facts several absolute certainties in the way of minor details which history has left unrecorded. For instance: being small, we know that she rolled and pitched and tumbled in any ordinary sea, and stood on her head or her tail, or lay down with her ear in the water, when storm seas ran high; also, that she was used to having billows plunge aboard and wash her decks from stem to stern; also, that the storm racks were on the table all the way over, and that nevertheless a man's soup was oftener landed in his lap than in his stomach; also, that the dining-saloon was about ten feet by seven, dark, airless, and suffocating with oil-stench; also, that there was only about one stateroom, the size of a grave, with a tier of two or three berths in it of the dimensions and comfortableness of coffins, and that when the light was out the darkness in there was so thick and real that you could bite into it and chew it like gum; also, that the only promenade was on the lofty poop-deck astern (for the ship was shaped like a high-quarter shoe) — a streak sixteen feet long by three feet wide, all the rest of the vessel being littered with ropes and flooded by the seas.

We know all these things to be true, from the mere fact that we know the vessel was small. As the vessel was old, certain other truths follow, as matters of course. For instance: she was full of rats; she was full of cockroaches; the heavy seas made her seams open and shut like your fingers, and she leaked like a basket; where leakage is, there also, of necessity, is bilgewater; and where bilgewater is, only the dead can enjoy life. This is on account of the smell. In the presence of bilgewater, Limburger cheese becomes odorless and ashamed.

From these absolutely sure data we can competently picture the daily life of the great discoverer. In the early morning he paid his devotions at the shrine of the Virgin. At eight bells he appeared on the poop-deck promenade. If the weather was chilly he came up clad from plumed helmet to spurred heel in magnificent plate armor inlaid with arabesques of gold, having previously warmed it at the galley fire. If the weather was warm he came up in the ordinary sailor toggery of the time — great slouch hat of blue velvet with a flowing brush of snowy ostrich plumes, fastened on with a flashing cluster of diamonds and emeralds; gold-embroidered doublet of green velvet with slashed sleeves exposing under-sleeves of crimson satin; deep collar and cuff ruffles of rich limp lace; trunk hose of pink velvet, with big knee-knots of brocaded yellow ribbon; pearl-tinted silk stockings, clocked and daintily embroidered; lemon-colored buskins of unborn kid, funnel-topped, and drooping low to expose the pretty stockings; deep gauntlets of finest white heretic skin, from the factory of the Holy Inquisition, formerly part of the person of a lady of rank; rapier with sheath crusted with jewels, and hanging from a broad baldric upholstered with rubies and sapphires.

He walked the promenade thoughtfully, he noted the aspects of the sky and the course of the wind; he kept an eye out for drifting vegetation and other signs of land; he jawed the man at the wheel for pastime; he got out an imitation egg and kept himself in practice on his old trick of making it stand on its end; now and then he hove a life-line below and fished up a sailor

who was drowning on the quarter-deck; the rest of his
watch he gaped and yawned and stretched, and said he
wouldn't make the trip again to discover six Americas.
For that was the kind of natural human person Columbus was when not posing for posterity.

At noon he took the sun and ascertained that the
good ship had made three hundred yards in twenty-
four hours, and this enabled him to win the pool.
Anybody can win the pool when nobody but himself
has the privilege of straightening out the ship's run and
getting it right.

The Admiral has breakfasted alone, in state: bacon,
beans, and gin; at noon he dines alone, in state: bacon,
beans, and gin; at six he sups alone, in state: bacon,
beans, and gin; at eleven P. M. he takes a night
relish alone, in state: bacon, beans, and gin. At none
of these orgies is there any music; the ship orchestra
is modern. After his final meal he returned thanks for
his many blessings, a little overrating their value, perhaps, and then he laid off his silken splendors or his
gilded hardware, and turned in, in his little coffin-bunk,
and blew out his flickering stencher and began to re-
fresh his lungs with inverted sighs freighted with the
rich odors of rancid oil and bilgewater. The sighs
returned as snores, and then the rats and the cockroaches swarmed out in brigades and divisions and
army corps and had a circus all over him. Such was
the daily life of the great discoverer in his marine
basket during several historic weeks; and the difference
between his ship and his comforts and ours is visible
almost at a glance.

When he returned, the King of Spain, marveling,
said — as history records:

"This ship seems to be leaky. Did she leak
badly?"

"You shall judge for yourself, sire. I pumped the

Atlantic Ocean through her sixteen times on the passage."

This is General Horace Porter's account. Other authorities say fifteen.

It can be shown that the differences between that ship and the one I am writing these historical contributions in are in several respects remarkable. Take the matter of decoration, for instance. I have been looking around again, yesterday and to-day, and have noted several details which I conceive to have been absent from Columbus's ship, or at least slurred over and not elaborated and perfected. I observe stateroom doors three inches thick, of solid oak and polished. I note companion-way vestibules with walls, doors, and ceilings paneled in polished hardwoods, some light, some dark, all dainty and delicate joiner-work, and yet every joint compact and tight; with beautiful pictures inserted, composed of blue tiles — some of the pictures containing as many as sixty tiles — and the joinings of those tiles perfect. These are daring experiments. One would have said that the first time the ship went straining and laboring through a storm-tumbled sea those tiles would gape apart and drop out. That they have not done so is evidence that the joiner's art has advanced a good deal since the days when ships were so shackly that when a giant sea gave them a wrench the doors came unbolted. I find the walls of the dining-saloon upholstered with mellow pictures wrought in tapestry and the ceiling aglow with pictures done in oil. In other places of assembly I find great panels filled with embossed Spanish leather, the figures rich with gilding and bronze. Everywhere I find sumptuous masses of color — color, color, color — color all about, color of every shade and tint and variety; and, as a result, the ship is bright and cheery to the eye, and this cheeriness invades one's spirit and contents it.

To fully appreciate the force and spritual value of this radiant and opulent dream of color, one must stand outside at night in the pitch dark and the rain, and look in through a port, and observe it in the lavish splendor of the electric lights. The old-time ships were dull, plain, graceless, gloomy, and horribly depressing. They compelled the blues; one could not escape the blues in them. The modern idea is right: to surround the passenger with conveniences, luxuries, and abundance of inspiriting color. As a result, the ship is the pleasantest place one can be in, except, perhaps, one's home.

A VANISHED SENTIMENT

ONE thing is gone, to return no more forever — the romance of the sea. Soft sentimentality about the sea has retired from the activities of this life, and is but a memory of the past, already remote and much faded. But within the recollection of men still living, it was in the breast of every individual; and the further any individual lived from salt water the more of it he kept in stock. It was as pervasive, as universal, as the atmosphere itself. The mere mention of the sea, the romantic sea, would make any company of people sentimental and mawkish at once. The great majority of the songs that were sung by the young people of the back settlements had the melancholy wanderer for subject and his mouthings about the sea for refrain. Picnic parties paddling down a creek in a canoe when the twilight shadows were gathering always sang:

> Homeward bound, homeward bound
> From a foreign shore;

and this was also a favorite in the West with the

passengers on sternwheel steamboats.   There was another:

> My boat is by the shore
>   And my bark is on the sea,
> But before I go, Tom Moore,
>   Here's a double health to thee.

And this one, also:

> O pilot, 'tis a fearful night,
> There's danger on the deep.

And this:

> A life on the ocean wave
>   And a home on the rolling deep,
> Where the scattered waters rave
>   And the winds their revels keep!

And this:

> A wet sheet and a flowing sea,
>   And a wind that follows fair.

And this:

> My foot is on my gallant deck,
> Once more the rover is free!

And the "Larboard Watch"— the person referred to below is at the masthead, or somewhere up there:

> Oh, who can tell what joy he feels,
> As o'er the foam his vessel reels,
> And his tired eyelids slumb'ring fall,
> He rouses at the welcome call
>   Of "Larboard watch — ahoy!"

Yes, and there was forever and always some jackass-voiced person braying out:

> Rocked in the cradle of the deep,
> I lay me down in peace to sleep!

Other favorites had these suggestive titles: "The Storm at Sea;" "The Bird at Sea;" "The Sailor

Boy's Dream;" "The Captive Pirate's Lament;"
"We are far from Home on the Stormy Main"—
and so on, and so on, the list is endless. Everybody
on a farm lived chiefly amid the dangers of the deep in
those days, in fancy.

But all that is gone now. Not a vestige of it is left.
The iron-clad, with her unsentimental aspect and frigid
attention to business, banished romance from the war
marine, and the unsentimental steamer has banished it
from the commercial marine. The dangers and uncertainties which made sea life romantic have disappeared
and carried the poetic element along with them. In
our day the passengers never sing sea-songs on board
a ship, and the band never plays them. Pathetic songs
about the wanderer in strange lands far from home,
once so popular and contributing such fire and color to
the imagination by reason of the rarity of that kind of
wanderer, have lost their charm and fallen silent, because everybody is a wanderer in the far lands now,
and the interest in that detail is dead. Nobody is
worried about the wanderer; there are no perils of the
sea for him, there are no uncertainties. He is safer in
the ship than he would probably be at home, for there
he is always liable to have to attend some friend's
funeral and stand over the grave in the sleet, bare-
headed — and that means pneumonia for him, if he
gets his deserts; and the uncertainties of his voyage
are reduced to whether he will arrive on the other side
in the appointed afternoon, or have to wait till morning.

The first ship I was ever in was a sailing vessel. She
was twenty-eight days going from San Francisco to the
Sandwich Islands. But the main reason for this particularly slow passage was, that she got becalmed and
lay in one spot fourteen days in the center of the
Pacific two thousand miles from land. I hear no sea-
songs in this present vessel, but I heard the entire lay-

out in that one. There were a dozen young people —
they are pretty old now, I reckon — and they used to
group themselves on the stern, in the starlight or the
moonlight, every evening, and sing sea-songs till after
midnight, in that hot, silent, motionless calm. They
had no sense of humor, and they always sang " Homeward Bound," without reflecting that that was practically ridiculous, since they were standing still and not
proceeding in any direction at all; and they often
followed that song with " ' Are we almost there, are we
almost there,' said the dying girl as she drew near
home?"

It was a very pleasant company of young people,
and I wonder where they are now. Gone, oh, none
knows whither; and the bloom and grace and beauty
of their youth, where is that? Among them was a
liar; all tried to reform him, but none could do it.
And so, gradually, he was left to himself; none of us
would associate with him. Many a time since I have
seen in fancy that forsaken figure, leaning forlorn
against the taffrail, and have reflected that perhaps if
we had tried harder, and been more patient, we might
have won him from his fault and persuaded him to
relinquish it. But it is hard to tell; with him the vice
was extreme, and was probably incurable. I like to
think — and, indeed, I do think — that I did the best
that in me lay to lead him to higher and better ways.

There was a singular circumstance. The ship lay
becalmed that entire fortnight in exactly the same spot.
Then a handsome breeze came fanning over the sea,
and we spread our white wings for flight. But the
vessel did not budge. The sails bellied out, the gale
strained at the ropes, but the vessel moved not a hair's
breadth from her place. The captain was surprised.
It was some hours before we found out what the cause
of the detention was. It was barnacles. They collect

31***

very fast in that part of the Pacific. They had fastened themselves to the ship's bottom; then others had fastened themselves to the first bunch, others to these, and so on, down and down and down, and the last bunch had glued the column hard and fast to the bottom of the sea, which is five miles deep at that point. So the ship was simply become the handle of a walking cane five miles long — yes, and no more movable by wind and sail than a continent is. It was regarded by every one as remarkable.

Well, the next week — however, Sandy Hook is in sight.

PLAYING COURIER

A TIME would come when we must go from Aix-
les-Bains to Geneva, and from thence, by a series
of day-long and tangled journeys, to Bayreuth in
Bavaria. I should have to have a courier, of course, to
take care of so considerable a party as mine.

But I procrastinated. The time slipped along, and
at last I woke up one day to the fact that we were
ready to move and had no courier. I then resolved
upon what I felt was a foolhardy thing, but I was in
the humor of it. I said I would make the first stage
without help — I did it.

I brought the party from Aix to Geneva by myself
— four people. The distance was two hours and more,
and there was one change of cars. There was not an
accident of any kind, except leaving a valise and some
other matters on the platform — a thing which can
hardly be called an accident, it is so common. So I
offered to conduct the party all the way to Bayreuth.

This was a blunder, though it did not seem so at the
time. There was more detail than I thought there
would be: 1, two persons whom we had left in a
Genevan pension some weeks before must be collected
and brought to the hotel; 2, I must notify the people
on the Grand Quay who store trunks to bring seven of
our stored trunks to the hotel and carry back seven
which they would find piled in the lobby; 3, I must
find out what part of Europe Bayreuth was in and buy
seven railway tickets for that point; 4, I must send a

telegram to a friend in the Netherlands; 5, it was now
two in the afternoon, and we must look sharp and be
ready for the first night train and make sure of sleeping-
car tickets; 6, I must draw money at the bank.

It seemed to me that the sleeping-car tickets must
be the most important thing, so I went to the station
myself to make sure; hotel messengers are not always
brisk people. It was a hot day and I ought to have
driven, but it seemed better economy to walk. It did
not turn out so, because I lost my way and trebled the
distance. I applied for the tickets, and they asked me
which route I wanted to go by, and that embarrassed
me and made me lose my head, there were so many
people standing around, and I not knowing anything
about the routes and not supposing there were going
to be two; so I judged it best to go back and map out
the road and come again.

I took a cab this time, but on my way upstairs at
the hotel I remembered that I was out of cigars, so I
thought it would be well to get some while the matter
was in my mind. It was only round the corner and I
didn't need the cab. I asked the cabman to wait
where he was. Thinking of the telegram and trying to
word it in my head, I forgot the cigars and the cab,
and walked on indefinitely. I was going to have the
hotel people send the telegram, but as I could not be
far from the post-office by this time, I thought I would
do it myself. But it was further than I had supposed.
I found the place at last and wrote the telegram and
handed it in. The clerk was a severe-looking, fidgety
man, and he began to fire French questions at me in
such a liquid form that I could not detect the joints
between his words, and this made me lose my head
again. But an Englishman stepped up and said the
clerk wanted to know where he was to send the telegram. I could not tell him, because it was not my

telegram, and I explained that I was merely sending it for a member of my party. But nothing would pacify the clerk but the address; so I said that if he was so particular I would go back and get it.

However, I thought I would go and collect those lacking two persons first, for it would be best to do everything systematically and in order, and one detail at a time. Then I remembered the cab was eating up my substance down at the hotel yonder; so I called another cab and told the man to go down and fetch it to the post-office and wait till I came.

I had a long hot walk to collect those people, and when I got there they couldn't come with me because they had heavy satchels and must have a cab. I went away to find one, but before I ran across any I noticed that I had reached the neighborhood of the Grand Quay — at least I thought I had — so I judged I could save time by stepping around and arranging about the trunks. I stepped around about a mile, and although I did not find the Grand Quay, I found a cigar shop, and remembered about the cigars. I said I was going to Bayreuth, and wanted enough for the journey. The man asked me which route I was going to take. I said I did not know. He said he would recommend me to go by Zurich and various other places which he named, and offered to sell me seven second-class through tickets for $22 apiece, which would be throwing off the discount which the railroads allowed him. I was already tired of riding second-class on first-class tickets, so I took him up.

By and by I found Natural & Co.'s storage office, and told them to send seven of our trunks to the hotel and pile them up in the lobby. It seemed to me that I was not delivering the whole of the message, still it was all I could find in my head.

Next I found the bank and asked for some money,

but I had left my letter of credit somewhere and was not able to draw. I remembered now that I must have left it lying on the table where I wrote my telegram; so I got a cab and drove to the post-office and went upstairs, and they said that a letter of credit had indeed been left on the table, but that it was now in the hands of the police authorities, and it would be necessary for me to go there and prove property. They sent a boy with me, and we went out the back way and walked a couple of miles and found the place; and then I remembered about my cabs, and asked the boy to send them to me when he got back to the post-office. It was nightfall now, and the Mayor had gone to dinner. I thought I would go to dinner myself, but the officer on duty thought differently, and I stayed. The Mayor dropped in at half-past ten, but said it was too late to do anything to-night — come at 9:30 in the morning. The officer wanted to keep me all night, and said I was a suspicious looking person, and probably did not own the letter of credit, and didn't know what a letter of credit was, but merely saw the real owner leave it lying on the table, and wanted to get it because I was probably a person that would want anything he could get, whether it was valuable or not. But the Mayor said he saw nothing suspicious about me, and that I seemed a harmless person and nothing the matter with me but a wandering mind, and not much of that. So I thanked him and he set me free, and I went home in my three cabs.

As I was dog-tired and in no condition to answer questions with discretion, I thought I would not disturb the Expedition at that time of night, as there was a vacant room I knew of at the other end of the hall; but I did not quite arrive there, as a watch had been set, the Expedition being anxious about me. I was placed in a galling situation. The Expedition sat stiff and forbidding on four chairs in a row, with shawls and things all on, satchels and guide-books in lap. They had been sitting like that for four hours, and the glass going down all the time. Yes, and they were waiting — waiting for me. It seemed to me that nothing but a sudden, happily contrived, and brilliant *tour de force* could break this iron front and make a diversion in my favor; so I shied my hat into the arena and followed it with a skip and a jump, shouting blithely:

" Ha, ha, here we all are, Mr. Merryman!"

Nothing could be deeper or stiller than the absence of applause which followed. But I kept on; there seemed no other way, though my confidence, poor enough before, had got a deadly check and was in effect gone.

I tried to be jocund out of a heavy heart, I tried to touch the other hearts there and soften the bitter resentment in those faces by throwing off bright and airy fun and making of the whole ghastly thing a joyously humorous incident, but this idea was not well conceived. It was not the right atmosphere for it. I got not one smile; not one line in those offended faces relaxed; I thawed nothing of the winter that looked out of those frosty eyes. I started one more breezy, poor effort, but the head of the Expedition cut into the center of it and said:

" Where have you been?"

I saw by the manner of this that the idea was to get down to cold business now. So I began my travels, but was cut short again.

" Where are the two others? We have been in frightful anxiety about them."

" Oh, they're all right. I was to fetch a cab. I will go straight off, and —"

" Sit down! Don't you know it is eleven o'clock? Where did you leave them?"

" At the pension."

" Why didn't you bring them?"

" Because we couldn't carry the satchels. And so I thought —"

" Thought! You should not try to think. One cannot think without the proper machinery. It is two miles to that pension. Did you go there without a cab?"

" I — well I didn't intend to; it only happened so."

" How did it happen so?"

" Because I was at the post-office and I remembered that I had left a cab waiting here, and so, to stop that expense, I sent another cab to — to —"

" To what?"

" Well, I don't remember now, but I think the new cab was to have the hotel pay the old cab, and send it away."

" What good would that do?"

" What good would it do? It would stop the expense, wouldn't it?"

" By putting the new cab in its place to continue the expense?"

I didn't say anything.

" Why didn't you have the new cab come back for you?"

" Oh, that is what I did. I remember now. Yes, that is what I did. Because I recollect that when I —"

" Well, then, why didn't it come back for you?"

" To the post-office? Why, it did."

" Very well, then, how did you come to walk to the pension?"

" I — I don't quite remember how that happened. Oh, yes, I do remember now. I wrote the dispatch to send to the Netherlands, and —"

" Oh, thank goodness, you did accomplish something! I wouldn't have had you fail to send — what

makes you look like that! You are trying to avoid
my eye. That dispatch is the most important thing
that — You haven't sent that dispatch!''

'' I haven't said I didn't send it.''

'' You don't need to. Oh, dear, I wouldn't have
had that telegram fail for anything. Why didn't you
send it?''

'' Well, you see, with so many things to do and
think of, I — they're very particular there, and after I
had written the telegram —''

'' Oh, never mind, let it go, explanations can't help
the matter now — what will he think of us?''

'' Oh, that's all right, that's all right, he'll think
we gave the telegram to the hotel people, and that
they —''

'' Why, certainly! Why didn't you do that? There
was no other rational way.''

'' Yes, I know, but then I had it on my mind that I
must be sure and get to the bank and draw some
money —''

'' Well, you are entitled to some credit, after all, for
thinking of that, and I don't wish to be too hard on
you, though you must acknowledge yourself that you
have cost us all a good deal of trouble, and some of it
not necessary. How much did you draw?''

'' Well, I — I had an idea that — that —''

'' That what?''

'' That — well, it seems to me that in the circumstances — so many of us, you know, and — and —''

'' What are you mooning about? Do turn your face
this way and let me — why, you haven't drawn any
money!''

'' Well, the banker said —''

'' Never mind what the banker said. You must
have had a reason of your own. Not a reason, exactly,
but something which —''

"Well, then, the simple fact was that I hadn't my letter of credit."

"Hadn't your letter of credit?"

"Hadn't my letter of credit."

"Don't repeat me like that. Where was it?"

"At the post-office."

"What was it doing there?"

"Well, I forgot it and left it there."

"Upon my word, I've seen a good many couriers, but of all the couriers that ever I —"

"I've done the best I could."

"Well, so you have, poor thing, and I'm wrong to abuse you so when you've been working yourself to death while we've been sitting here only thinking of our vexations instead of feeling grateful for what you were trying to do for us. It will all come out right. We can take the 7.30 train in the morning just as well. You've bought the tickets?"

"I have — and it's a bargain, too. Second class."

"I'm glad of it. Everybody else travels second class, and we might just as well save that ruinous extra charge. What did you pay?"

"Twenty-two dollars apiece — through to Bayreuth."

"Why, I didn't know you could buy through tickets anywhere but in London and Paris."

"Some people can't, maybe; but some people can — of whom I am one of which, it appears."

"It seems a rather high price."

"On the contrary, the dealer knocked off his commission."

"Dealer?"

"Yes — I bought them at a cigar shop."

"That reminds me. We shall have to get up pretty early, and so there should be no packing to do. Your umbrella, your rubbers, your cigars — what is the matter?"

" Hang it, I've left the cigars at the bank."

" Just think of it! Well, your umbrella?"

" I'll have that all right. There's no hurry."

" What do you mean by that?"

" Oh, that's all right; I'll take care of —"

" Where is that umbrella?"

" It's just the merest step — it won't take me —"

" Where is it?"

" Well, I think I left it at the cigar shop; but anyway —"

" Take your feet out from under that thing. It's just as I expected! Where are your rubbers?"

" They — well —"

" Where are your rubbers?"

" It's got so dry now — well, everybody says there's not going to be another drop of —"

" Where — are — your — rubbers?"

" Well, you see — well, it was this way. First, the officer said —"

" What officer?"

" Police officer; but the Mayor, he

" What Mayor?"

" Mayor of Geneva; but I said —"

" Wait. What is the matter with you?"

" Who, me? Nothing. They both tried to persuade me to stay, and —"

" Stay where?"

" Well — the fact is —"

" Where have you been? What's kept you out till half-past ten at night?"

" Oh, you see, after I lost my letter of credit, I —"

" You are beating around the bush a good deal. Now, answer the question in just one straightforward word. Where are those rubbers?"

" They — well; they're in the county jail."

I started a placating smile, but it petrified. The

climate was unsuitable. Spending three or four hours
in jail did not seem to the Expedition humorous.
Neither did it to me, at bottom.

I had to explain the whole thing, and, of course, it
came out then that we couldn't take the early train,
because that would leave my letter of credit in hock
still. It did look as if we had all got to go to bed
estranged and unhappy, but by good luck that was
prevented. There happened to be mention of the
trunks, and I was able to say I had attended to that
feature.

"There, you are just as good and thoughtful and
painstaking and intelligent as you can be, and it's a
shame to find so much fault with you, and there sha'n't
be another word of it. You've done beautifully, admirably, and I'm sorry I ever said one ungrateful word
to you."

This hit deeper than some of the other things and
made me uncomfortable, because I wasn't feeling as
solid about that trunk errand as I wanted to. There
seemed somehow to be a defect about it somewhere,
though I couldn't put my finger on it, and didn't like
to stir the matter just now, it being late and maybe well
enough to let well enough alone.

Of course there was music in the morning, when it
was found that we couldn't leave by the early train.
But I had no time to wait; I got only the opening bars
of the overture, and then started out to get my letter
of credit.

It seemed a good time to look into the trunk business
and rectify it if it needed it, and I had a suspicion that
it did. I was too late. The concierge said he had
shipped the trunks to Zurich the evening before. I
asked him how he could do that without exhibiting
passage tickets.

"Not necessary in Switzerland. You pay for your

trunks and send them where you please. Nothing goes free but your hand baggage."

" How much did you pay on them?"

" A hundred and forty francs."

" Twenty-eight dollars. There's something wrong about that trunk business, sure."

Next I met the porter. He said:

" You have not slept well, is it not. You have the worn look. If you would like a courier, a good one has arrived last night, and is not engaged for five days already, by the name of Ludi. We recommend him; das heisst, the Grand Hôtel Beau Rivage recommends him."

I declined with coldness. My spirit was not broken yet. And I did not like having my condition taken notice of in this way. I was at the county jail by nine o'clock, hoping that the Mayor might chance to come before his regular hour; but he didn't. It was dull there. Every time I offered to touch anything, or look at anything, or do anything, or refrain from doing anything, the policeman said it was " défendu." I thought I would practice my French on him, but he wouldn't have that either. It seemed to make him particularly bitter to hear his own tongue.

The Mayor came at last, and then there was no trouble; for the minute he had convened the Supreme Court — they always do whenever there is valuable property in dispute — and got everything shipshape and sentries posted, and had prayer by the chaplain; my unsealed letter was brought and opened, and there wasn't anything in it but some photographs; because, as I remembered now, I had taken out the letter of credit so as to make room for the photographs, and had put the letter in my other pocket, which I proved to everybody's satisfaction by fetching it out and show-ing it with a good deal of exultation. So then the

32A

court looked at each other in a vacant kind of way, and then at me, and then at each other again, and finally let me go, but said it was imprudent for me to be at large, and asked me what my profession was. I said I was a courier. They lifted up their eyes in a kind of reverent way and said, " Du lieber Gott!" and I said a word of courteous thanks for their apparent admiration, and hurried off to the bank.

However, being a courier was already making me a great stickler for order and system and one thing at a time and each thing in its own proper turn; so I passed by the bank and branched off and started for the two lacking members of the Expedition. A cab lazied by, and I took it upon persuasion. I gained no speed by this, but it was a reposeful turnout and I liked reposefulness. The week-long jubilations over the six hundredth anniversary of the birth of Swiss liberty and the Signing of the Compact was at flood tide, and all the streets were clothed in fluttering flags.

The horse and the driver had been drunk three days and nights, and had known no stall nor bed meantime. They looked as I felt — dreamy and seedy. But we arrived in course of time. I went in and rang, and asked a housemaid to rush out the lacking members. She said something which I did not understand, and I returned to the chariot. The girl had probably told me that those people did not belong on her floor, and that it would be judicious for me to go higher, and ring from floor to floor till I found them; for in those Swiss flats there does not seem to be any way to find the right family but to be patient and guess your way along up. I calculated that I must wait fifteen minutes, there being three details inseparable from an occasion of this sort: 1, put on hats and come down and climb in: 2, return of one to get " my other glove;" 3, presently, return of the other one to fetch

" my *French Verbs at a Glance.*"   I would muse during the fifteen minutes and take it easy.

A very still and blank interval ensued, and then I
felt a hand on my shoulder and started.   The intruder
was a policeman.   I glanced up and perceived that
there was new scenery.   There was a good deal of a
crowd, and they had that pleased and interested look
which such a crowd wears when they see that somebody is out of luck.   The horse was asleep, and so
was the driver, and some boys had hung them and me
full of gaudy decorations stolen from the innumerable
banner poles.   It was a scandalous spectacle.   The
officer said:

" I'm sorry, but we can't have you sleeping here all
day."

I was wounded and said with dignity:

" I beg your pardon, I was not sleeping; I was
thinking."

" Well, you can think if you want to, but you've
got to think to yourself; you disturb the whole neighborhood."

It was a poor joke, and it made the crowd laugh.   I
snore at night sometimes, but it is not likely that I
would do such a thing in the daytime and in such a
place.   The officer undecorated us, and seemed sorry
for our friendlessness, and really tried to be humane,
but he said we mustn't stop there any longer or he
would have to charge us rent — it was the law, he said,
and he went on to say in a sociable way that I was
looking pretty mouldy, and he wished he knew —

I shut him off pretty austerely, and said I hoped one
might celebrate a little these days, especially when one
was personally concerned.

" Personally?" he asked.   How?"

" Because 600 years ago an ancestor of mine signed
the compact."

He reflected a moment, then looked me over and said:

" Ancestor! It's my opinion you signed it yourself. For of all the old ancient relics that ever I — but never mind about that. What is it you are waiting here for so long?"

I said:

" I'm not waiting here so long at all. I'm waiting fifteen minutes till they forget a glove and a book and go back and get them." Then I told him who they were that I had come for.

He was very obliging, and began to shout inquiries to the tiers of heads and shoulders projecting from the windows above us. Then a woman away up there sang out:

" Oh, they? Why I got them a cab and they left here long ago — half-past eight, I should say."

It was annoying. I glanced at my watch, but didn't say anything. The officer said:

" It is a quarter of twelve, you see. You should have inquired better. You have been asleep three-quarters of an hour, and in such a sun as this. You are baked — baked black. It is wonderful. And you will miss your train, perhaps. You interest me greatly. What is your occupation?"

I said I was a courier. It seemed to stun him, and before he could come to we were gone.

When I arrived in the third story of the hotel I found our quarters vacant. I was not surprised. The moment a courier takes his eye off his tribe they go shopping. The nearer it is to train time the surer they are to go. I sat down to try and think out what I had best do next, but presently the hall boy found me there, and said the Expedition had gone to the station half an hour before. It was the first time I had known them to do a rational thing, and it was very confusing.

This is one of the things that make a courier's life so difficult and uncertain. Just as matters are going the smoothest, his people will strike a lucid interval, and down go all his arrangements to wreck and ruin.

The train was to leave at twelve noon sharp. It was now ten minutes after twelve. I could be at the station in ten minutes. I saw I had no great amount of leeway, for this was the lightning express, and on the Continent the lightning expresses are pretty fastidious about getting away some time during the advertised day. My people were the only ones remaining in the waiting-room; everybody else had passed through and "mounted the train," as they say in those regions. They were exhausted with nervousness and fret, but I comforted them and heartened them up, and we made our rush.

But no; we were out of luck again. The door-keeper was not satisfied with the tickets. He examined them cautiously, deliberately, suspiciously; then glared at me a while, and after that he called another official. The two examined the tickets and called another official. These called others, and the convention discussed and discussed, and gesticulated and carried on, until I begged that they would consider how time was flying, and just pass a few resolutions and let us go. Then they said very courteously that there was a defect in the tickets, and asked me where I got them.

I judged I saw what the trouble was now. You see, I had bought the tickets in a cigar shop, and, of course, the tobacco smell was on them; without doubt, the thing they were up to was to work the tickets through the Custom House and to collect duty on that smell. So I resolved to be perfectly frank; it is sometimes the best way. I said:

"Gentlemen, I will not deceive you. These railway tickets —"

32***

" Ah, pardon, monsieur! These are not railway tickets."

" Oh," I said, " is that the defect?"

" Ah, truly yes, monsieur. These are lottery tickets, yes; and it is a lottery which has been drawn two years ago."

I affected to be greatly amused; it is all one can do in such circumstances; it is all one can do, and yet there is no value in it; it deceives nobody, and you can see that everybody around pities you and is ashamed of you. One of the hardest situations in life, I think, is to be full of grief and a sense of defeat and shabbiness that way, and yet have to put on an outside of archness and gayety, while all the time you know that your own Expedition, the treasures of your heart, and whose love and reverence you are by the custom of our civilization entitled to, are being consumed with humiliation before strangers to see you earning and getting a compassion which is a stigma, a brand — a brand which certifies you to be — oh, anything and everything which is fatal to human respect.

I said, cheerily, it was all right, just one of those little accidents that was likely to happen to anybody — I would have the right tickets in two minutes, and we would catch the train yet, and, moreover, have something to laugh about all through the journey. I did get the tickets in time, all stamped and complete, but then it turned out that I couldn't take them, because in taking so much pains about the two missing members, I had skipped the bank and hadn't the money. So then the train left, and there didn't seem to be anything to do but go back to the hotel, which we did; but it was kind of melancholy and not much said. I tried to start a few subjects, like scenery and transubstantiation, and those sorts of things, but they didn't seem to hit the weather right,

We had lost our good rooms, but we got some others which were pretty scattering, but would answer. I judged things would brighten now, but the Head of the Expedition said, " Send up the trunks." It made me feel pretty cold. There was a doubtful something about that trunk business. I was almost sure of it. I was going to suggest —

But a wave of the hand sufficiently restrained me, and I was informed that we would now camp for three days and see if we could rest up.

I said all right, never mind ringing; I would go down and attend to the trunks myself. I got a cab and went straight to Mr. Charles Natural's place, and asked what order it was I had left there.

" To send seven trunks to the hotel."

" And were you to bring any back?"

" No."

" You are sure I didn't tell you to bring back seven that would be found piled in the lobby?"

" Absolutely sure you didn't."

" Then the whole fourteen are gone to Zurich or Jericho or somewhere, and there is going to be more débris around that hotel when the Expedition —"

I didn't finish, because my mind was getting to be in a good deal of a whirl, and when you are that way you think you have finished a sentence when you haven't, and you go mooning and dreaming away, and the first thing you know you get run over by a dray or a cow or something.

I left the cab there — I forgot it — and on my way back I thought it all out and concluded to resign, because otherwise I should be nearly sure to be discharged. But I didn't believe it would be a good idea to resign in person; I could do it by message. So I sent for Mr. Ludi and explained that there was a courier going to resign on account of incompatibility

FF***

or fatigue or something, and as he had four or five vacant days, I would like to insert him into that vacancy if he thought he could fill it. When everything was arranged I got him to go up and say to the Expedition that, owing to an error made by Mr. Natural's people, we were out of trunks here, but would have plenty in Zurich, and we'd better take the first train, freight, gravel, or construction, and move right along.

He attended to that and came down with an **invitation** for me to go up — yes, certainly; and, while we walked along over to the bank to get money, and collect my cigars and tobacco, and to the cigar shop to trade back the lottery tickets and get my umbrella, and to Mr. Natural's to pay that cab and send it away, and to the county jail to get my rubbers and leave p. p. c. cards for the Mayor and Supreme Court, he described the weather to me that was prevailing on the upper levels there with the Expedition, and I saw that I was doing very well where I was.

I stayed out in the woods till four P. M., to let the weather moderate, and then turned up at the station just in time to take the three o'clock express for Zurich along with the Expedition, now in the hands of Ludi, who conducted its complex affairs with little apparent effort or inconvenience.

Well, I had worked like a slave while I was in office, and done the very best I knew how; yet all that these people dwelt upon or seemed to care to remember was the defects of my administration, not its creditable features. They would skip over a thousand creditable features to remark upon and reiterate and fuss about just one fact, till it seemed to me they would wear it out; and not much of a fact, either, taken by itself — the fact that I elected myself courier in Geneva, and put in work enough to carry a circus to Jerusalem, and

yet never even got my gang out of the town. I finally
said I didn't wish to hear any more about the subject,
it made me tired. And I told them to their faces that
I would never be a courier again to save anybody's
life. And if I live long enough I'll prove it. I think
it's a difficult, brain-racking, overworked, and thoroughly ungrateful office, and the main bulk of its
wages is a sore heart and a bruised spirit.

THE GERMAN CHICAGO

I FEEL lost in Berlin. It has no resemblance to the city I had supposed it was. There was once a Berlin which I would have known, from descriptions in books — the Berlin of the last century and the beginning of the present one: a dingy city in a marsh, with rough streets, muddy and lantern-lighted, dividing straight rows of ugly houses all alike, compacted into blocks as square and plain and uniform and monotonous and serious as so many dry-goods boxes. But that Berlin has disappeared. It seems to have disappeared totally, and left no sign. The bulk of the Berlin of to-day has about it no suggestion of a former period. The site it stands on has traditions and a history, but the city itself has no traditions and no history. It is a new city; the newest I have ever seen. Chicago would seem venerable beside it; for there are many old-looking districts in Chicago, but not many in Berlin. The main mass of the city looks as if it had been built last week, the rest of it has a just perceptibly graver tone, and looks as if it might be six or even eight months old.

The next feature that strikes one is the spaciousness, the roominess of the city. There is no other city, in any country, whose streets are so generally wide. Berlin is not merely *a* city of wide streets, it is *the* city of wide streets. As a wide-street city it has never had its equal, in any age of the world. " Unter den

Linden '' is three streets in one; the Potsdamerstrasse
is bordered on both sides by sidewalks which are themselves wider than some of the historic thoroughfares of
the old European capitals; there seem to be no lanes
or alleys; there are no short cuts; here and there,
where several important streets empty into a common
center, that center's circumference is of a magnitude
calculated to bring that word spaciousness into your
mind again. The park in the middle of the city is so
huge that it calls up that expression once more.

The next feature that strikes one is the straightness
of the streets. The short ones haven't so much as a
waver in them; the long ones stretch out to prodigious
distances and then tilt a little to the right or left, then
stretch out on another immense reach as straight as a
ray of light. A result of this arrangement is, that at
night Berlin is an inspiring sight to see. Gas and the
electric light are employed with a wasteful liberality,
and so, wherever one goes, he has always double ranks
of brilliant lights stretching far down into the night on
every hand, with here and there a wide and splendid
constellation of them spread out over an intervening
'' Platz ''; and between the interminable double procession of street lamps one has the swarming and darting cab lamps, a lively and pretty addition to the fine
spectacle, for they counterfeit the rush and confusion
and sparkle of an invasion of fire-flies.

There is one other noticeable feature — the absolutely
level surface of the site of Berlin. Berlin — to recapitu-
late — is newer to the eye than is any other city, and
also blonder of complexion and tidier; no other city
has such an air of roominess, freedom from crowding;
no other city has so many straight streets; and with
Chicago it contests the chromo for flatness of surface
and for phenomenal swiftness of growth. Berlin is the
European Chicago. The two cities have about the

same population — say a million and a half. I cannot speak in exact terms, because I only know what Chicago's population was week before last; but at that time it was about a million and a half. Fifteen years ago Berlin and Chicago were large cities, of course, but neither of them was the giant it now is.

But now the parallels fail. Only parts of Chicago are stately and beautiful, whereas all of Berlin is stately and substantial, and it is not merely in parts but uniformly beautiful. There are buildings in Chicago that are architecturally finer than any in Berlin, I think, but what I have just said above is still true. These two flat cities would lead the world for phenomenal good health if London were out of the way. As it is, London leads by a point or two. Berlin's death rate is only nineteen in the thousand. Fourteen years ago the rate was a third higher.

Berlin is a surprise in a great many ways — in a multitude of ways, to speak strongly and be exact. It seems to be the most governed city in the world, but one must admit that it also seems to be the best governed. Method and system are observable on every hand — in great things, in little things, in all details, of whatsoever size. And it is not method and system on paper, and there an end — it is method and system in practice. It has a rule for everything, and puts the rule in force; puts it in force against the poor and powerful alike, without favor or prejudice. It deals with great matters and minute particulars with equal faithfulness, and with a plodding and painstaking diligence and persistency which compel admiration — and sometimes regret. There are several taxes, and they are collected quarterly. Collected is the word; they are not merely levied, they are collected — every time. This makes light taxes. It is in cities and countries where a considerable part of the community shirk pay-

ment that taxes have to be lifted to a burdensome
rate. Here the police keep coming, calmly and
patiently, until you pay your tax. They charge you
five or ten cents per visit after the first call. By experiment you will find that they will presently collect
that money.

In one respect the million and a half of Berlin's
population are like a family: the head of this large
family knows the names of its several members, and
where the said members are located, and when and
where they were born, and what they do for a living,
and what their religious brand is. Whoever comes to
Berlin must furnish these particulars to the police immediately; moreover, if he knows how long he is
going to stay, he must say so. If he take a house he
will be taxed on the rent and taxed also on his income.
He will not be asked what his income is, and so he
may save some lies for home consumption. The
police will estimate his income from the house-rent he
pays, and tax him on that basis.

Duties on imported articles are collected with
inflexible fidelity, be the sum large or little; but the
methods are gentle, prompt, and full of the spirit of
accommodation. The postman attends to the whole
matter for you, in cases where the article comes by
mail, and you have no trouble and suffer no inconvenience. The other day a friend of mine was informed
that there was a package in the post-office for him,
containing a lady's silk belt with gold clasp, and a
gold chain to hang a bunch of keys on. In his first
agitation he was going to try to bribe the postman to
chalk it through, but acted upon his sober second
thought and allowed the matter to take its proper and
regular course. In a little while the postman brought
the package and made these several collections: duty
on the silk belt, 7½ cents; duty on the gold chain, 10

cents; charge for fetching the package, 5 cents. These devastating imposts are exacted for the protection of German home industries.

The calm, quiet, courteous, cussed persistence of the police is the most admirable thing I have encountered on this side. They undertook to persuade me to send and get a passport for a Swiss maid whom we had brought with us, and at the end of six weeks of patient, tranquil, angelic daily effort they succeeded. I was not intending to give them trouble, but I was lazy and I thought they would get tired. Meanwhile they probably thought I would be the one. It turned out just so.

One is not allowed to build unstable, unsafe, or unsightly houses in Berlin; the result is this comely and conspicuously stately city, with its security from conflagrations and breakdowns. It is built of architectural Gibraltars. The building commissioners inspect while the building is going up. It has been found that this is better than to wait till it falls down. These people are full of whims.

One is not allowed to cram poor folk into cramped and dirty tenement houses. Each individual must have just so many cubic feet of room-space, and sanitary inspections are systematic and frequent.

Everything is orderly. The fire brigade march in rank, curiously uniformed, and so grave is their demeanor that they look like a Salvation Army under conviction of sin. People tell me that when a fire alarm is sounded, the firemen assemble calmly, answer to their names when the roll is called, then proceed to the fire. There they are ranked up, military fashion, and told off in detachments by the chief, who parcels out to the detachments the several parts of the work which they are to undertake in putting out that fire. This is all done with low-voiced propriety, and strangers think these people are working a funeral. As a rule, the fire is confined to a single floor in these great masses of bricks and masonry, and consequently there is little or no interest attaching to a fire here for the rest of the occupants of the house.

There is abundance of newspapers in Berlin, and there was also a newsboy, but he died. At intervals of half a mile on the thoroughfares there are booths, and it is at these that you buy your papers. There are plenty of theaters, but they do not advertise in a loud way. There are no big posters of any kind, and the display of vast type and of pictures of actors and performance framed on a big scale and done in rainbow colors is a thing unknown. If the big show-bills existed there would be no place to exhibit them; for there are no poster-fences, and one would not be allowed to disfigure dead walls with them. Unsightly things are forbidden here; Berlin is a rest to the eye.

And yet the saunterer can easily find out what is going on at the theaters. All over the city, at short distances apart, there are neat round pillars eighteen feet high and about as thick as a hogshead, and on these the little black and white theater bills and other notices are posted. One generally finds a group around each pillar reading these things. There are plenty of things in Berlin worth importing to America. It is these that I have particularly wished to make a note of. When Buffalo Bill was here his biggest poster was probably not larger than the top of an ordinary trunk.

There is a multiplicity of clean and comfortable horse-cars, but whenever you think you know where a car is going to you would better stop ashore, because that car is not going to that place at all. The car routes are marvelously intricate, and often the drivers get lost and are not heard of for years. The signs on the cars furnish no details as to the course of the

journey; they name the end of it, and then experiment around to see how much territory they can cover
before they get there.   The conductor will collect your
fare over again every few miles, and give you a ticket
which he hasn't apparently kept any record of, and
you keep it till an inspector comes aboard by and by
and tears a corner off it (which he does not keep),
then you throw the ticket away and get ready to buy
another.   Brains are of no value when you are trying
to navigate Berlin in a horse-car.   When the ablest of
Brooklyn's editors was here on a visit he took a horse-
car in the early morning, and wore it out trying to go
to a point in the center of the city.   He was on board
all day and spent many dollars in fares, and then did
not arrive at the place which he had started to go to.
This is the most thorough way to see Berlin, but it is
also the most expensive.

But there are excellent features about the car system,
nevertheless.   The car will not stop for you to get on
or off, except at certain places a block or two apart
where there is a sign to indicate that that is a halting
station.   This system saves many bones.   There are
twenty places inside the car; when these seats are filled,
no more can enter.   Four or five persons may stand on
each platform — the law decrees the number — and
when these standing places are all occupied the next
applicant is refused.   As there is no crowding, and as
no rowdyism is allowed, women stand on the platforms
as well as the men; they often stand there when there
are vacant seats inside, for these places are comfortable, there being little or no jolting.   A native tells me
that when the first car was put on, thirty or forty years
ago, the public had such a terror of it that they didn't
feel safe inside of it or outside either.   They made the
company keep a man at every crossing with a red flag
in his hand.   Nobody would travel in the car except

convicts on the way to the gallows. This made business in only one direction, and the car had to go back
light.   To save the company, the city government
transferred the convict cemetery to the other end of
the line.   This made traffic in both directions and kept
the company from going under.   This sounds like
some of the information which traveling foreigners are
furnished with in America.   To my mind it has a
doubtful ring about it.

The first-class cab is neat and trim, and has leather-
cushion seats and a swift horse.   The second-class cab
is an ugly and lubberly vehicle, and is always old.   It
seems a strange thing that they have never built any
new ones.   Still, if such a thing were done everybody
that had time to flock would flock to see it, and that
would make a crowd, and the police do not like crowds
and disorder here.   If there were an earthquake in
Berlin the police would take charge of it and conduct it
in that sort of orderly way that would make you think
it was a prayer-meeting.   That is what an earthquake
generally ends in, but this one would be different from
those others; it would be kind of soft and self-
contained, like a republican praying for a mugwump.

For a course (a quarter of an hour or less), one
pays twenty-five cents in a first-class cab, and fifteen
cents in a second-class.   The first-class will take you
along faster, for the second-class horse is old — always
old — as old as his cab, some authorities say — and
ill-fed and weak.   He has been a first-class once, but
has been degraded to second-class for long and faithful
service.

Still, he must take you as *far* for fifteen cents as the
other horse takes you for twenty-five.   If he can't do
his fifteen-minute distance in fifteen minutes, he must
still do the distance for the fifteen cents.   Any stranger
can check the distance off — by means of the most

33ᴬ

curious map I am acquainted with. It is issued by
the city government and can be bought in any shop
for a trifle. In it every street is sectioned off like a
string of long beads of different colors. Each long
bead represents a minute's travel, and when you have
covered fifteen of the beads you have got your money's
worth. This map of Berlin is a gay-colored maze, and
looks like pictures of the circulation of the blood.

The streets are very clean. They are kept so — not
by prayer and talk and the other New York methods,
but by daily and hourly work with scrapers and
brooms; and when an asphalted street has been tidily
scraped after a rain or a light snowfall, they scatter
clean sand over it. This saves some of the horses from
falling down. In fact, this is a city government which
seems to stop at no expense where the public convenience, comfort, and health are concerned — except in
one detail. That is the naming of the streets and the
numbering of the houses. Sometimes the name of a
street will change in the middle of a block. You will
not find it out till you get to the next corner and discover the new name on the wall, and of course you
don't know just when the change happened.

The names are plainly marked on the corners — on
all the corners — there are no exceptions. But the
numbering of the houses — there has never been anything like it since original chaos. It is not possible
that it was done by this wise city government. At first
one thinks it was done by an idiot; but there is too
much variety about it for that; an idiot could not
think of so many different ways of making confusion
and propagating blasphemy. The numbers run up
one side the street and down the other. That is endurable, but the rest isn't. They often use one number
for three or four houses — and sometimes they put the
number on only one of the houses and let you guess at

the others. Sometimes they put a number on a house
— 4, for instance — then put 4*a*, 4*b*, 4*c*, on the succeeding houses, and one becomes old and decrepit
before he finally arrives at 5. A result of this system-
less system is that when you are at No. 1 in a street
you haven't any idea how far it may be to No. 150; it
may be only six or eight blocks, it may be a couple of
miles. Frederick street is long, and is one of the great
thoroughfares. The other day a man put up his money
behind the assertion that there were more refreshment
places in that street than numbers on the houses — and
he won. There were 254 numbers and 257 refreshment places. Yet as I have said, it is a long street.

But the worst feature of all this complex business is
that in Berlin the numbers do not travel in any one
direction; no, they travel along until they get to 50 or
60, perhaps, then suddenly you find yourself up in the
hundreds — 140, maybe; the next will be 139 — then
you perceive by that sign that the numbers are now
traveling towards you from the opposite direction.
They will keep that sort of insanity up as long as you
travel that street; every now and then the numbers will
turn and run the other way. As a rule, there is an
arrow under the number, to show by the direction of
its flight which way the numbers are proceeding.
There are a good many suicides in Berlin; I have seen
six reported in a single day. There is always a deal of
learned and laborious arguing and ciphering going on
as to the cause of this state of things. If they will set
to work and number their houses in a rational way perhaps they will find out what was the matter.

More than a month ago Berlin began to prepare
to celebrate Professor Virchow's seventieth birthday.
When the birthday arrived, the middle of October, it
seemed to me that all the world of science arrived with
it; deputation after deputation came, bringing the

homage and reverence of far cities and centers of learning, and during the whole of a long day the hero of it sat and received such witness of his greatness as has seldom been vouchsafed to any man in any walk of life in any time, ancient or modern.   These demonstrations were continued in one form or another day after day, and were presently merged in similar demonstrations to his twin in science and achievement, Professor Helmholtz, whose seventieth birthday is separated from Virchow's by only about three weeks; so nearly as this did these two extraordinary men come to being born together. Two such births have seldom signalized a single year in human history.

But perhaps the final and closing demonstration was peculiarly grateful to them. This was a Commers given in their honor the other night by 1,000 students. It was held in a huge hall, very long and very lofty, which had five galleries, far above everybody's head, which were crowded with ladies — four or five hundred, I judged.

It was beautifully decorated with clustered flags and various ornamental devices, and was brilliantly lighted. On the spacious floor of this place were ranged, in files, innumerable tables, seating twenty-four persons each, extending from one end of the great hall clear to the other, and with narrow aisles between the files.   In the center on one side was a high and tastefully decorated platform twenty or thirty feet long, with a long table on it behind which sat the half-dozen chiefs of the givers of the Commers in the rich mediæval costumes of as many different college corps. Behind these youths a band of musicians was concealed. On the floor directly in front of this platform were half a dozen tables which were distinguished from the outlying continent of tables by being covered instead of left naked.   Of these the central table was reserved for the two heroes of the occasion and twenty particularly eminent professors of the Berlin University, and the other covered tables were for the occupancy of a hundred less distinguished professors.

I was glad to be honored with a place at the table of the two heroes of the occasion, although I was not really learned enough to deserve it. Indeed, there was a pleasant strangeness in being in such company; to be thus associated with twenty-three men who forget more every day than I ever knew. Yet there was nothing embarrassing about it, because loaded men and empty ones look about alike, and I knew that to that multitude there I was a professor. It required but little art to catch the ways and attitude of those men and imitate them, and I had no difficulty in looking as much like a professor as anybody there.

We arrived early; so early that only Professors Virchow and Helmholtz and a dozen guests of the special tables were ahead of us, and 300 or 400 students. But people were arriving in floods now, and within fifteen minutes all but the special tables were occupied, and the great house was crammed, the aisles included. It was said that there were 4,000 men present. It was a most animated scene, there is no doubt about that; it was a stupendous beehive. At each end of each table stood a corps student in the uniform of his corps. These quaint costumes are of brilliant colored silks and velvets, with sometimes a high plumed hat, sometimes a broad Scotch cap, with a great plume wound about it, sometimes — oftenest — a little shallow silk cap on the tip of the crown, like an inverted saucer; sometimes the pantaloons are snow-white, sometimes of other colors; the boots in all cases come up well above the knee; and in all cases also white gauntlets are worn; the sword is a rapier with a bowl-shaped guard for the hand, painted in several colors. Each corps

33***

has a uniform of its own, and all are of rich material, brilliant in color, and exceedingly picturesque; for they are survivals of the vanished costumes of the Middle Ages, and they reproduce for us the time when men were beautiful to look at.   The student who stood guard at our end of the table was of grave countenance and great frame and grace of form, and he was doubtless an accurate reproduction, clothes and all, of some ancestor of his of two or three centuries ago — a reproduction as far as the outside, the animal man, goes, I mean.

As I say, the place was now crowded.   The nearest aisle was packed with students standing up, and they made a fence which shut off the rest of the house from view.   As far down this fence as you could see all these wholesome young faces were turned in one direction, all these intent and worshiping eyes were centered upon one spot — the place where Virchow and Helmholtz sat.   The boys seemed lost to everything, unconscious of their own existence; they devoured these two intellectual giants with their eyes, they feasted upon them, and the worship that was in their hearts shone in their faces.   It seemed to me that I would rather be flooded with a glory like that, instinct with sincerity, innocent of self-seeking, than win a hundred battles and break a million hearts.

There was a big mug of beer in front of each of us, and more to come when wanted.   There was also a quarto pamphlet containing the words of the songs to be sung.   After the names of the officers of the feast were these words in large type:

"*Während des Kommerses herrscht allgemeiner Burgfriede.*"

I was not able to translate this to my satisfaction, but a professor helped me out.   This was his explanation: The students in uniform belong to different college corps; not all students belong to corps; none join the corps except those who enjoy fighting. The corps students fight duels with swords every week, one corps challenging another corps to furnish a certain number of duelists for the occasion, and it is only on this battlefield that students of different corps exchange courtesies. In common life they do not drink with each other or speak. The above line now translates itself: there is truce during the Commers, war is laid aside and fellowship takes its place.

Now the performance began. The concealed band played a piece of martial music; then there was a pause. The students on the platform rose to their feet, the middle one gave a toast to the Emperor, then all the house rose, mugs in hand. At the call "One — two — three!" all glasses were drained and then brought down with a slam on the tables in unison. The result was as good an imitation of thunder as I have ever heard. From now on, during an hour, there was singing, in mighty chorus. During each interval between songs a number of the special guests — the professors — arrived. There seemed to be some signal whereby the students on the platform were made aware that a professor had arrived at the remote door of entrance; for you would see them suddenly rise to their feet, strike an erect military attitude, then draw their swords; the swords of all their brethren standing guard at the innumerable tables would flash from their scabbards and be held aloft — a handsome spectacle! Three clear bugle notes would ring out, then all these swords would come down with a crash, twice repeated, on the tables, and be uplifted and held aloft again; then in the distance you would see the gay uniforms and uplifted swords of a guard of honor clearing the way and conducting the guest down to his place. The

GG***

songs were stirring, the immense outpour from young life and young lungs, the crash of swords and the thunder of the beer mugs gradually worked a body up to what seemed the last possible summit of excitement. It surely seemed to me that I had reached that summit, that I had reached my limit, and that there was no higher lift desirable for me. When apparently the last eminent guest had long ago taken his place, again those three bugle blasts rang out and once more the swords leaped from their scabbards. Who might this late comer be? Nobody was interested to inquire. Still, indolent eyes were turned towards the distant entrance; we saw the silken gleam and the lifted swords of a guard of honor plowing through the remote crowds. Then we saw that end of the house rising to its feet; saw it rise abreast the advancing guard all along, like a wave. This supreme honor had been offered to no one before. Then there was an excited whisper at our table —'' MOMMSEN!'' and the whole house rose. Rose and shouted and stamped and clapped, and banged the beer mugs. Just simply a storm! Then the little man with his long hair and Emersonian face edged his way past us and took his seat. I could have touched him with my hand — Mommsen! — think of it!

This was one of those immense surprises that can happen only a few times in one's life. I was not dreaming of him, he was to me only a giant myth, a world-shadowing specter, not a reality. The surprise of it all can be only comparable to a man's suddenly coming upon Mont Blanc with its awful form towering into the sky, when he didn't suspect he was in its neighborhood. I would have walked a great many miles to get a sight of him, and here he was, without trouble or tramp or cost of any kind. Here he was, clothed in a Titanic deceptive modesty which made him look like

other men. Here he was, carrying the Roman world
and all the Cæsars in his hospitable skull, and doing it
as easily as that other luminous vault, the skull of the
universe, carries the Milky Way and the constellations.

One of the professors said that once upon a time an
American young lady was introduced to Mommsen,
and found herself badly scared and speechless. She
dreaded to see his mouth unclose, for she was expecting him to choose a subject several miles above her
comprehension, and didn't suppose he *could* get down
to the world that other people lived in; but when his
remark came, her terrors disappeared: " Well, how do
you do? Have you read Howells's last book? *I*
think it's his best."

The active ceremonies of the evening closed with the
speeches of welcome delivered by two students and the
replies made by Professors Virchow and Helmholtz.

Virchow has long been a member of the city government of Berlin. He works as hard for the city as does
any other Berlin alderman, and gets the same pay —
nothing. I don't know that we in America could
venture to ask our most illustrious citizen to serve in a
board of aldermen, and if we might venture it I am
not positively sure that we could elect him. But here
the municipal system is such that the best men in the
city consider it an honor to serve gratis as aldermen,
and the people have the good sense to prefer these
men and to elect them year after year. As a result,
Berlin is a thoroughly well-governed city. It is a free
city; its affairs are not meddled with by the State;
they are managed by its own citizens, and after methods of their own devising.

A PETITION TO THE QUEEN OF ENGLAND

HARTFORD, *Nov.* 6, 1887.

MADAM: You will remember that last May Mr. Edward Bright, the clerk of the Inland Revenue Office, wrote me about a tax which he said was due from me to the Government on books of mine published in London — that is to say, an income tax on the royalties. I do not know Mr. Bright, and it is embarrassing to me to correspond with strangers; for I was raised in the country and have always lived there, the early part in Marion County, Missouri, before the war, and this part in Hartford County, Connecticut, near Bloomfield and about eight miles this side of Farmington, though some call it nine, which it is impossible to be, for I have walked it many and many a time in considerably under three hours, and General Hawley says he has done it in two and a quarter, which is not likely; so it has seemed best that I write your Majesty. It is true that I do not know your Majesty personally, but I have met the Lord Mayor, and if the rest of the family are like him, it is but just that it should be named royal; and likewise plain that in a family matter like this, I cannot better forward my case than to frankly carry it to the head of the family itself. I have also met the Prince of Wales once in the fall of 1873, but it was not in any familiar way, but in a quite informal way, being casual, and was, of course, a surprise to us both. It was in Oxford street, just where

(518)

you come out of Oxford into Regent Circus, and just as he turned up one side of the circle at the head of a procession, I went down the other side on the top of an omnibus. He will remember me on account of a gray coat with flap pockets that I wore, as I was the only person on the omnibus that had on that kind of a coat; I remember him of course as easy as I would a comet. He looked quite proud and satisfied, but that is not to be wondered at, he has a good situation. And once I called on your Majesty, but you were out.

But that is no matter, it happens with everybody. However, I have wandered a little away from what I started about. It was this way. Young Bright wrote my London publishers, Chatto and Windus — their place is the one on the left as you come down Piccadilly, about a block and a half above where the minstrel show is — he wrote them that he wanted them to pay income tax on the royalties of some foreign authors, namely, "Miss De La Ramé (Ouida), Dr. Oliver Wendell Holmes, Mr. Francis Bret Harte, and Mr. Mark Twain." Well, Mr. Chatto diverted him from the others, and tried to divert him from me, but in this case he failed. So then young Bright wrote me. And not only that, but he sent me a printed document the size of a newspaper, for me to sign all over in different places. Well, it was that kind of a document that the more you study it the more it undermines you and makes everything seem uncertain to you; and so, while in that condition, and really not responsible for my acts, I wrote Mr. Chatto to pay the tax and charge to me. Of course my idea was, that it was for only one year, and that the tax would be only about one per cent. or along there somewhere, but last night I met Professor Sloane of Princeton — you may not know him, but you have probably seen him every now and then, for he goes to England a good deal, a large man and very handsome and absorbed in thought, and **if** you have noticed such a man on platforms after the train is gone, that is the one, he generally gets left, like all those specialists and other scholars who know everything but how to apply it — and he said it was a back tax for *three* years, and not one per cent., but two and a half!

That gave what had seemed a little matter a new aspect. I then began to study the printed document again, to see if I could find anything in it that might modify my case, and I had what seems to be a quite promising success. For instance, it opens thus — polite and courteous, the way those English government documents always are — I do not say that to hear myself talk, it is just the fact, and it is a credit:

"To Mr. Mark Twain: IN PURSUANCE of the Acts of Parliament for granting to Her Majesty Duties and Profits," etc.

I had not noticed that before. My idea had been that it was for the Government, and so I wrote *to* the Government; but now I saw that it was a private matter, a family matter, and that the proceeds went to yourself, not the Government. I would always rather treat with principals, and I am glad I noticed that clause. With a principal, one can always get at a fair and right understanding, whether it is about potatoes, or continents, or any of those things, or something entirely different; for the size or nature of the thing does not affect the fact; whereas, as a rule, a subordinate is more or less troublesome to satisfy. And yet this is not against them, but the other way. They have their duties to do, and must be harnessed to rules, and not allowed any discretion. Why, if your Majesty should equip young Bright with discretion — I mean his own discretion — it is an even guess that he would discretion you out of house and home in 2 or 3 years. He would not *mean* to get the family into straits, but that would be the upshot, just the same. Now then, with Bright out of the way, this is not going to be any Irish question; it is going to be settled pleasantly and satisfactorily for all of us, and when it is finished your Majesty is going to stand with the American people just as you have stood for fifty years, and surely no monarch can require better than that of an alien nation. They do not all pay a British income tax, but the most of them will in time, for we have shoals of new authors coming along every year; and of the population of your Canada, upwards of four-fifths are wealthy Americans, and more going there all the time.

Well, another thing which I noticed in the Document was an item about "Deductions." I will come to that presently, your Majesty. And another thing was this: that Authors are not mentioned in the Document at all. No, we have "Quarries, Mines, Iron Works, Salt Springs, Alum Mines, Water Works, Canals, Docks, Drains, Levels, Fishings, Fairs, Tolls, Bridges, Ferries," and so-forth and so-forth and so-on — well, as much as a yard or a yard and a half of them, I should think — anyway a very large quantity or number. I read along — down, and down, and down the list, further, and further, and further, and as I approached the bottom my hopes began to rise higher and higher, because I saw that everything in England *that* far was taxed by name and in detail, except perhaps the family, and maybe Parliament, and yet still no mention of Authors. Apparently they were going to be overlooked. And sure enough, they were! My heart gave a great bound. But I was too soon. There was a footnote, in Mr. Bright's hand, which said: "You are taxed under Schedule D, section 14." I turned to that place, and found these three things: "Trades, Offices, Gas Works."

Of course, after a moment's reflection, hope came up again, and then certainty: Mr. Bright was in error, and clear off the track; for Authorship is not a Trade, it is an inspiration; Authorship does not keep an Office, its habitation is all out under the sky, and everywhere where the winds are blowing and the sun is shining and the creatures of God are free. Now then, since I have no Trade and keep no Office, I am not taxable under Schedule D, section 14. Your Majesty sees that; so I will go on to that other thing that I spoke of, the " deductions "— deductions from my tax which I may get allowed, under conditions. Mr. Bright says all deductions to be claimed by me must be restricted to the provisions made in Paragraph No. 8, entitled " Wear and Tear of Machinery, or Plant." This is curious, and shows how far he has gotten away on his wrong course after once he has got started wrong: for Offices and Trades do not have Plant, they do not have Machinery, such a thing was never heard of; and, moreover, they do not wear and tear. You see that, your Majesty, and that it is true. Here is the Paragraph No. 8:

Amount claimed as a deduction for diminished value by reason of Wear and Tear, where the Machinery or Plant belongs to the Person or Company carrying on the Concern, or is let to such Person or Company so that the Lessee is bound to maintain and deliver over the same in good condition:—

*Amount £*_____

There it is — the very words.

I could answer Mr. Bright thus.

It is my pride to say that my Brain is my Plant; and I do not claim any deduction for diminished value by reason of Wear and Tear, for the reason that it does not wear and tear, but stays sound and whole all the time. Yes, I could say to him, my Brain is my Plant, my Skull is my Workshop, my Hand is my

Machinery, and I am the Person carrying on the Concern; it is not leased to anybody, and so there is no Lessee bound to maintain and deliver over the same in good condition. There. I do not wish to any way overrate this argument and answer, dashed off just so, and not a word of it altered from the way I first wrote it, your Majesty, but indeed it does seem to pulverize that young fellow, you can see that yourself. But that is all I say; I stop there; I never pursue a person after I have got him down.

Having thus shown your Majesty that I am not taxable, but am the victim of the error of a clerk who mistakes the nature of my commerce, it only remains for me to beg that you will of your justice annul my letter that I spoke of, so that my publisher can keep back that tax-money which, in the confusion and aberration caused by the Document, I ordered him to pay. You will not miss the sum, but this is a hard year for authors; and as for lectures, I do not suppose your Majesty ever saw such a dull season.

With always great and ever increasing respect, I beg to sign myself your Majesty's servant to command,

MARK TWAIN.

HER MAJESTY THE QUEEN, LONDON.

A MAJESTIC LITERARY FOSSIL

IF I were required to guess off-hand, and without collusion with higher minds, what is the bottom cause of the amazing material and intellectual advancement of the last fifty years, I should guess that it was the modern-born and previously non-existent disposition on the part of men to believe that a new idea can have value. With the long roll of the mighty names of history present in our minds, we are not privileged to doubt that for the past twenty or thirty centuries every conspicuous civilization in the world has produced intellects able to invent and create the things which make our day a wonder; perhaps we may be justified in inferring, then, that the reason they did not do it was that the public reverence for old ideas and hostility to new ones always stood in their way, and was a wall they could not break down or climb over. The prevailing tone of old books regarding new ideas is one of suspicion and uneasiness at times, and at other times contempt. By contrast, our day is indifferent to old ideas, and even considers that their age makes their value questionable, but jumps at a new idea with enthusiasm and high hope — a hope which is high because it has not been accustomed to being disappointed. I make no guess as to just when this disposition was born to us, but it certainly is ours, was not possessed by any century before us, is our peculiar mark and badge, and is doubtless the bottom reason why we are

a race of lightning-shod Mercuries, and proud of it —
instead of being, like our ancestors, a race of plodding
crabs, and proud of that.

So recent is this change from a three or four thousand year twilight to the flash and glare of open day
that I have walked in both, and yet am not old.
Nothing is to-day as it was when I was an urchin; but
when I was an urchin, nothing was much different from
what it had always been in this world. Take a single
detail, for example — medicine. Galen could have
come into my sick-room at any time during my first
seven years — I mean any day when it wasn't fishing
weather, and there wasn't any choice but school or
sickness — and he could have sat down there and stood
my doctor's watch without asking a question. He
would have smelt around among the wilderness of cups
and bottles and vials on the table and the shelves, and
missed not a stench that used to glad him two thousand
years before, nor discovered one that was of a later
date. He would have examined me, and run across
only one disappointment — I was already salivated; I
would have him there; for I was always salivated,
calomel was so cheap. He would get out his lancet
then; but I would have him again; our family doctor
didn't allow blood to accumulate in the system. However, he could take dipper and ladle, and freight me
up with old familiar doses that had come down from
Adam to his time and mine; and he could go out with
a wheelbarrow and gather weeds and offal, and build
some more, while those others were getting in their
work. And if our reverend doctor came and found
him there, he would be dumb with awe, and would get
down and worship him. Whereas if Galen should appear among us to-day, he could not stand anybody's
watch; he would inspire no awe; he would be told he
was a back number, and it would surprise him to see

34A

that that fact counted against him, instead of in his favor. He wouldn't know our medicines; he wouldn't know our practice; and the first time he tried to introduce his own we would hang him.

This introduction brings me to my literary relic. It is a *Dictionary of Medicine*, by Dr. James, of London, assisted by Mr. Boswell's Doctor Samuel Johnson, and is a hundred and fifty years old, it having been published at the time of the rebellion of '45. If it had been sent against the Pretender's troops there probably wouldn't have been a survivor. In 1861 this deadly book was still working the cemeteries — down in Virginia. For three generations and a half it had been going quietly along, enriching the earth with its slain. Up to its last free day it was trusted and believed in, and its devastating advice taken, as was shown by notes inserted between its leaves. But our troops captured it and brought it home, and it has been out of business since. These remarks from its preface are in the true spirit of the olden time, sodden with worship of the old, disdain of the new:

If we inquire into the Improvements which have been made by the Moderns, we shall be forced to confess that we have so little Reason to value ourselves beyond the Antients, or to be tempted to contemn them, that we cannot give stronger or more convincing Proofs of our own Ignorance, as well as our Pride.

Among all the systematical Writers, I think there are very few who refuse the Preference to *Hieron, Fabricius ab Aquapendente*, as a Person of unquestion'd Learning and Judgment; and yet is he not asham'd to let his Readers know that *Celsus* among the Latins, *Paulus Aegineta* among the Greeks, and *Albucasis* among the Arabians, whom I am unwilling to place among the Moderns, tho' he liv'd but six hundred Years since, are the Triumvirate to whom he principally stands indebted, for the Assistance he had receiv'd from them in composing his excellent Book.

[In a previous paragraph are puffs of Galen, Hippocrates, and other débris of the Old Silurian Period of Medicine.] How many Operations are there now in Use which were unknown to the Antients?

That is true. The surest way for a nation's scientific men to prove that they were proud and ignorant was to claim to have found out something fresh in the course of a thousand years or so. Evidently the peoples of this book's day regarded themselves as children, and their remote ancestors as the only grown-up people that had existed. Consider the contrast: without offense, without over-egotism, our own scientific men may and do regard themselves as grown people and their grandfathers as children. The change here presented is probably the most sweeping that has ever come over mankind in the history of the race. It is the utter reversal, in a couple of generations, of an attitude which had been maintained without challenge or interruption from the earliest antiquity. It amounts to creating man over again on a new plan; he was a canal-boat before, he is an ocean greyhound to-day. The change from reptile to bird was not more tremendous, and it took longer.

It is curious. If you read between the lines what this author says about Brer Albucasis, you detect that in venturing to compliment him he has to whistle a little to keep his courage up, because Albucasis " liv'd but six hundred Years since," and therefore came so uncomfortably near being a " modern " that one couldn't respect him without risk.

Phlebotomy, Venesection — terms to signify bleeding — are not often heard in our day, because we have ceased to believe that the best way to make a bank or a body healthy is to squander its capital; but in our author's time the physician went around with a hatful of lancets on his person all the time, and took a hack at every patient whom he found still alive. He robbed his man of pounds and pounds of blood at a single operation. The details of this sort in this book make terrific reading. Apparently even the healthy did not escape, but were bled twelve times a year, on a particular day of the month, and exhaustively purged besides. Here is a specimen of the vigorous old-time practice; it occurs in our author's adoring biography of a Doctor Aretæus, a licensed assassin of Homer's time, or thereabouts:

> In a Quinsey he used Venesection, and allow'd the Blood to flow till the Patient was ready to faint away.

There is no harm in trying to cure a headache — in our day. You can't do it, but you get more or less entertainment out of trying, and that is something; besides, you live to tell about it, and that is more. A century or so ago you could have had the first of these features in rich variety, but you might fail of the other once — and once would do. I quote:

> As Dissections of Persons who have died of severe Head-achs, which have been related by Authors, are too numerous to be inserted in this Place, we shall here abridge some of the most curious and important Observations relating to this Subject, collected by the celebrated *Bonetus*.

The celebrated Bonetus's " Observation No. 1 " seems to me a sufficient sample, all by itself, of what people used to have to stand any time between the creation of the world and the birth of your father and mine when they had the disastrous luck to get a " Head-ach ":

> A certain Merchant, about forty Years of Age, of a Melancholic Habit, and deeply involved in the Cares of the World, was, during the Dog-days, seiz'd with a violent pain of his Head, which some time after oblig'd him to keep his Bed.
>
> I, being call'd, order'd Venesection in the Arms, the Application of Leeches to the Vessels of his Nostrils, Forehead, and Temples, as also to those behind his Ears; I likewise prescrib'd the Application of Cupping-glasses, with Scarification, to his Back: But, notwithstanding these Precautions, he dy'd. If any Surgeon, skill'd in Arteriotomy, had been present, I should have also order'd that Operation.

I looked for " Arteriotomy " in this same Dictionary, and found this definition: " The opening of an
Artery with a View of taking away Blood." Here was
a person who was being bled in the arms, forehead,
nostrils, back, temples, and behind the ears, yet the
celebrated Bonetus was not satisfied, but wanted to
open an artery. " with a View " to insert a pump,
probably. " Notwithstanding these Precautions "—
he dy'd. No art of speech could more quaintly con-
vey this butcher's innocent surprise. Now that we
know what the celebrated Bonetus did when he wanted
to relieve a Head-ach, it is no trouble to infer that if
he wanted to comfort a man that had a Stomach-ach
he disemboweled him.

I have given one " Observation "— a single Head-
ach case; but the celebrated Bonetus follows it with
eleven more. Without enlarging upon the matter, I
merely note this coincidence — they all " dy'd." Not
one of these people got well; yet this obtuse hyena
sets down every little gory detail of the several assas-
sinations as complacently as if he imagined he was
doing a useful and meritorious work in perpetuating
the methods of his crimes. " Observations," indeed!
They are confessions.

According to this book, " the Ashes of an Ass's
hoof mix'd with Woman's milk cures chilblains."
Length of time required not stated. Another item:
" The constant Use of Milk is bad for the Teeth, and
causes them to rot, and loosens the Gums." Yet in
our day babies use it constantly without hurtful results.
This author thinks you ought to wash out your mouth
with wine before venturing to drink milk. Presently,
when we come to notice what fiendish decoctions those
people introduce into their stomachs by way of medicine, we shall wonder that they could have been afraid
of milk.

34***

It appears that they had false teeth in those days.
They were made of ivory sometimes, sometimes of
bone, and were thrust into the natural sockets, and
lashed to each other and to the neighboring teeth with
wires or with silk threads. They were not to eat with,
nor to laugh with, because they dropped out when not
in repose. You could smile with them, but you had
to practice first, or you would overdo it. They were
not for business, but just decoration. They filled the
bill according to their lights.

This author says " the Flesh of Swine nourishes
above all other eatables." In another place he mentions a number of things, and says " these are very
easy to be digested; so is Pork." This is probably a
lie. But he is pretty handy in that line; and when he
hasn't anything of the sort in stock himself he gives
some other expert an opening. For instance, under the
head of " Attractives " he introduces Paracelsus, who
tells of a nameless " Specific "— quantity of it not set
down — which is able to draw a hundred pounds of
flesh to itself — distance not stated — and then proceeds, " It happen'd in our own Days that an Attractive of this Kind drew a certain Man's Lungs up into
his Mouth, by which he had the Misfortune to be
suffocated." This is more than doubtful. In the first
place, his Mouth couldn't accommodate his Lungs —
in fact, his Hat couldn't; secondly, his Heart being
more eligibly Situated, it would have got the Start of
his Lungs, and, being a lighter Body, it would have
Sail'd in ahead and Occupied the Premises; thirdly,
you will Take Notice a Man with his Heart in his
Mouth hasn't any Room left for his Lungs — he has
got all he can Attend to; and finally, the Man must
have had the Attractive in his Hat, and when he saw
what was going to Happen he would have Remov'd it
and Sat Down on it. Indeed, he would; and then

how could it Choke him to Death? I don't believe the thing ever happened at all.

Paracelsus adds this effort: " I myself saw a Plaister which attracted as much Water as was sufficient to fill a Cistern; and by these very Attractives Branches may be torn from Trees; and, which is still more surprising, a Cow may be carried up into the Air." Paracelsus is dead now; he was always straining himself that way.

They liked a touch of mystery along with their medicine in the olden time; and the medicine-man of that day, like the medicine-man of our Indian tribes, did what he could to meet the requirement:

Arcanum. A Kind of Remedy whose Manner of Preparation, or singular Efficacy, is industriously concealed, in order to enchance its Value. By the Chymists it is generally defined a thing secret, incorporeal, and immortal, which cannot be Known by Man, unless by Experience; for it is the Virtue of every thing, which operates a thousand times more than the thing itself.

To me the butt end of this explanation is not altogether clear. A little of what they knew about natural history in the early times is exposed here and there in the Dictionary.

The Spider. It is more common than welcome in Houses. Both the Spider and its Web are used in Medicine: The Spider is said to avert the Paroxysms of Fevers, if it be apply'd to the Pulse of the Wrist, or the Temples; but it is peculiarly recommended against a Quartan, being enclosed in the Shell of a Hazlenut.

Among approved Remedies, I find that the distill'd Water of Black Spiders is an excellent Cure for Wounds, and that this was one of the choice Secrets of Sir Walter Raleigh.

The Spider which some call the Catcher, or Wolf, being beaten into a Plaister, then sew'd up in Linen, and apply'd to the Forehead or Temples, prevents the Returns of a Tertian.

There is another Kind of Spider, which spins a white, fine, and thick Web. One of this Sort, wrapp'd in Leather, and hung about the Arm, will avert the Fit of a Quartan. Boil'd in Oil of Roses, and instilled into the Ears, it eases Pains in those Parts. *Dioscorides, Lib.* 2, *Cap.* 68.

HH***

Thus we find that Spiders have in all Ages been celebrated for their febrifuge Virtues; and it is worthy of Remark, that a Spider is usually given to Monkeys, and is esteem'd a sovereign Remedy for the Disorders those Animals are principally subject to.

Then follows a long account of how a dying woman, who had suffered nine hours a day with an ague during eight weeks, and who had been bled dry some dozens of times meantime without apparent benefit, was at last forced to swallow several wads of " Spiders-web," whereupon she straightway mended, and promptly got well. So the sage is full of enthusiasm over the spider-webs, and mentions only in the most casual way the discontinuance of the daily bleedings, plainly never suspecting that this had anything to do with the cure.

As concerning the venomous Nature of Spiders, *Scaliger* takes notice of a certain Species of them (which he had forgotten) whose Poison was of so great Force as to affect one *Vincentinus* thro' the Sole of his Shoe, by only treading on it.

The sage takes that in without a strain, but the following case was a trifle too bulky for him, as his comment reveals:

In Gascony, observes *Scaliger*, there is a very small Spider, which, running over a Looking-glass, will crack the same by the Force of her Poison. (*A mere Fable.*)

But he finds no fault with the following facts:

Remarkable is the Enmity recorded between this Creature and the Serpent, as also the Toad: Of the former it is reported, That, lying (as he thinks securely) under the Shadow of some Tree, the Spider lets herself down by her Thread, and, striking her Proboscis or Sting into the Head, with that Force and Efficacy, injecting likewise her venomous Juice, that, wringing himself about, he immediately grows giddy, and quickly after dies.

When the Toad is bit or stung in Fight with this Creature, the Lizard, Adder, or other that is poisonous, she finds relief from Plantain, to which she resorts. In her Combat with the Toad, the Spider useth the same Stratagem as with the Serpent, hanging by her own Thread from the Bough of some Tree, and striking her Sting into her enemy's Head, upon which the other, enraged, swells up, and sometimes bursts.

To this Effect is the Relation of *Erasmus*, which he saith he had from one of the Spectators, of a Person lying along upon the Floor of his Chamber, in the Summer-time, to sleep in a supine Posture, when a Toad, creeping out of some green Rushes, brought just before in, to adorn the Chimney, gets upon his Face, and with his Feet sits across his Lips. To force off the Toad, says the Historian, would have been accounted sudden Death to the Sleeper; and to leave her there, very cruel and dangerous; so that upon Consultation it was concluded to find out a Spider, which, together with her Web, and the Window she was fasten'd to, was brought carefully, and so contrived as to be held perpendicularly to the Man's Face; which was no sooner done, but the Spider, discovering his Enemy, let himself down, and struck in his Dart, afterwards betaking himself up again to his Web; the Toad swell'd, but as yet kept his station: The second Wound is given quickly after by the Spider, upon which he swells yet more, but remain'd alive still.— The Spider, coming down again by his Thread, gives the third Blow; and the Toad, taking off his Feet from over the Man's Mouth, fell off dead.

To which the sage appends this grave remark, "And so much for the historical Part." Then he passes on to a consideration of " the Effects and Cure of the Poison."

One of the most interesting things about this tragedy is the double sex of the Toad, and also of the Spider.

Now the sage quotes from one Turner:

I remember, when a very young Practitioner, being sent for to a certain Woman, whose Custom was usually, when she went to the Cellar by Candle-light, to go also a Spider-hunting, setting Fire to their Webs, and burning them with the Flame of the Candle still as she pursued them. It happen'd at length, after this Whimsy had been follow'd a long time, one of them sold his Life much dearer than those Hundreds she had destroy'd; for, lighting upon the melting Tallow of her Candle, near the Flame, and his legs being entangled therein, so that he could not extricate himself, the Flame or Heat coming on, he was made a Sacrifice to his cruel Persecutor, who delighting her Eyes with the Spectacle, still waiting for the Flame to take hold of him, he presently burst with a great Crack, and threw his Liquor, some into her Eyes, but mostly upon her Lips; by means of which, flinging away her Candle, she cry'd out for Help, as fansying herself kill'd already with the Poison. However in the Night her Lips swell'd up excessively, and one of her Eyes was much inflam'd; also her Tongue and Gums were somewhat affected; and, whether from the Nausea excited by the Thoughts of the Liquor getting into her Mouth, or from the poisonous Impressions communicated by the nervous *Fibrillæ* of those Parts to those of the Ventricle, a continual Vomiting attended: To take off which, when I was call'd, I order'd a Glass of mull'd Sack, with a Scruple of Salt of Wormwood, and some hours after a Theriacal Bolus, which she flung up again. I embrocated the Lips with the Oil of Scorpions mix'd with the Oil of Roses; and, in Consideration of the Ophthalmy, tho' I was not certain but the Heat of the Liquor, rais'd by the Flame of the Candle before the Body of the Creature burst, might, as well as the Venom, excite the Disturbance, (altho' Mr. *Boyle's* Case of a Person blinded by this Liquor dropping from the living Spider, makes the latter sufficient;) yet observing the great Tumefaction of the Lips, together with the other Symptoms not likely to arise from simple Heat, I was inclin'd to believe a real Poison in the Case; and therefore not daring to let her Blood in the Arm [If a man's throat were cut in those old days, the doctor would come and bleed the other end of him], I did, however, with good Success, set Leeches to her Temples, which took off much of the Inflammation; and her Pain was likewise abated, by instilling into her Eyes a thin Mucilage of the Seeds of Quinces and white Poppies extracted with Rose-water; yet the Swelling on the Lips increased; upon which, in the Night, she wore a Cataplasm prepared by boiling the Leaves of Scordium, Rue, and Elder-flowers, and afterwards thicken'd with the Meal of Vetches. In the mean time, her Vomiting having left her, she had given her, between whiles, a little Draught of Distill'd Water of Carduus Benedictus and Scordium, with some of the Theriaca dissolved; and upon going off of the Symptoms, an old Woman came luckily in, who, with Assurance suitable to those People, (whose Ignorance and Poverty is their Safety and Protection,) took off the Dressings, promising to cure her in two Days time, altho' she made it as many Weeks, yet had the Reputation of the Cure; applying only Plantain Leaves bruis'd and mixed with Cobwebs, dropping the Juice into her Eye, and giving some Spoonfuls of the same inwardly, two or three times a day.

So ends the wonderful affair. Whereupon the sage gives Mr. Turner the following shot — strengthening it with italics — and passes calmly on:

"*I must remark upon this History, that the Plantain, as a Cooler, was much more likely to cure this Disorder than warmer Applications and Medicines."*

How strange that narrative sounds to-day, and how grotesque, when one reflects that it was a grave contribution to medical " science " by an old and reputable physician! Here was all this to-do — two weeks of it — over a woman who had scorched her eye and her lips with candle grease. The poor wench is as elaborately dosed, bled, embrocated, and otherwise harried and bedeviled as if there had been really something the matter with her; and when a sensible old woman comes along at last, and treats the trivial case in a sensible way, the educated ignoramus rails at her ignorance, serenely unconscious of his own. It is pretty suggestive of the former snail-pace of medical progress that the spider retained his terrors during three thousand years, and only lost them within the last thirty or forty.

Observe what imagination can do. " This same young Woman '' used to be so affected by the strong (imaginary) smell which emanated from the burning spiders that " the Objects about her seem'd to turn round; she grew faint also with cold Sweats, and sometimes a light Vomiting." There could have been Beer in that cellar as well as Spiders.

Here are some more of the effects of imagination: " *Sennertus* takes Notice of the Signs of the Bite or Sting of this Insect to be a Stupor or Numbness upon the Part, with a sense of Cold, Horror, or Swelling of the Abdomen, Paleness of the Face, involuntary Tears, Trembling, Contractions, a (****), Convulsions, cold Sweats; but these latter chiefly when the Poison has been received inwardly," whereas the modern physician holds that a few spiders taken inwardly, by a bird or a man, will do neither party any harm.

The above " Signs " are not restricted to spider

bites — often they merely indicate fright.   I have seen
a person with a hornet in his pantaloons exhibit them
all.

As to the Cure, not slighting the usual Alexipharmics taken internally,
the Place bitten must be immediately washed with Salt Water, or a Sponge
dipped in hot Vinegar, or fomented with a Decoction of Mallows, Origanum,
and Mother of Thyme; after which a Cataplasm must be laid on of the
Leaves of Bay, Rue, Leeks, and the Meal of Barley, boiled with Vinegar,
or of Garlick and Onions, contused with Goat's Dung and fat Figs.   Mean
time the Patient should eat Garlick and drink Wine freely.

As for me, I should prefer the spider bite.   Let us
close this review with a sample or two of the earthquakes which the old-time doctor used to introduce
into his patient when he could find room.   Under this
head we have "Alexander's Golden Antidote," which
is good for — well, pretty much everything.   It is
probably the old original first patent-medicine.   It is
built as follows:

Take of Afarabocca, Henbane, Carpobalsamum, each two Drams and a
half; of Cloves, Opium, Myrrh, Cyperus, each two Drams; of Opobalsamum,
Indian Leaf, Cinamon, Zedoary, Ginger, Coftus, Coral, Cassia, Euphorbium,
Gum Tragacanth, Frankincense, Styrax Calamita, Celtic, Nard, Spignel,
Hartwort, Mustard, Saxifrage, Dill, Anise, each one Dram; of Xylaloes,
Rheum, Ponticum, Alipta Moschata, Castor, Spikenard, Galangals, Opop-
onax, Anacardium, Mastich, Brimstone, Peony, Eringo, Pulp of Dates, red
and white Hermodactyls, Roses, Thyme, Acorns, Penyroyal, Gentian, the
Bark of the Root of Mandrake, Germander, Valerian, Bishops Weed, Bay-
Berries, long and white Pepper, Xylobalsamum, Carnabadium, Macodonian,
Parsley-seeds, Lovage, the Seeds of Rue, and Sinon, of each a Dram and a
half; of pure Gold, pure Silver, Pearls not perforated, the Blatta Byzantina,
the Bone of the Stag's Heart, of each the Quantity of fourteen Grains of
Wheat; of Sapphire, Emerald, and Jasper Stones, each one Dram; of Hasle-
nut, two Drams; of Pellitory of Spain, Shavings of Ivory, Calamus Odoratus,
each the Quantity of twenty-nine Grains of Wheat; of Honey or Sugar a
sufficient Quantity.

Serve with a shovel.   No; one might expect such

an injunction after such formidable preparation; but it is not so. The dose recommended is "the Quantity of an Hasle-nut." Only that; it is because there is so much jewelry in it, no doubt.

Aqua Limacum. Take a great Peck of Garden-snails, and wash them in a great deal of Beer, and make your Chimney very clean, and set a Bushel of Charcoal on Fire; and when they are thoroughly kindled, make a Hole in the Middle of the Fire, and put the Snails in, and scatter more Fire amongst them, and let them roast till they make a Noise; then take them out, and, with a Knife and coarse Cloth, pick and wipe away all the green froth: Then break them, Shells and all, in a Stone Mortar. Take also a Quart of Earth-worms, and scour them with Salt, divers times over. Then take two Handfuls of Angelica and lay them in the Bottom of the Still; next lay two Handfuls of Celandine; next a Quart of Rosemary-flowers; then two Handfuls of Bearsfoot and Agrimony; then Fenugreek; then Turmerick; of each one Ounce: Red Dock-root, Bark of Barberry-trees, Wood-sorrel, Betony, of each two Handfuls.—Then lay the Snails and Worms on the top of the Herbs; and then two Handfuls of Goose-dung, and two Handfuls of Sheep-dung. Then put in three Gallons of Strong Ale, and place the pot where you mean to set Fire under it: Let it stand all Night, or longer; in the Morning put in three Ounces of Cloves well beaten, and a small Quantity of Saffron, dry'd to Powder; then six Ounces of Shavings of Hartshorn, which must be uppermost. Fix on the Head and Refrigeratory, and distil according to Art.

There. The book does not say whether this is all one dose, or whether you have a right to split it and take a second chance at it, in case you live. Also, the book does not seem to specify what ailment it was for; but it is of no consequence, for of course that would come out on the inquest.

Upon looking further, I find that this formidable nostrum is "good for raising Flatulencies in the Stomach"— meaning *from* the stomach, no doubt. So it would appear that when our progenitors chanced to swallow a sigh, they emptied a sewer down their throats to expel it. It is like dislodging skippers from cheese with artillery.

When you reflect that your own father had to take such medicines as the above, and that you would be taking them to-day yourself but for the introduction of homœopathy, which forced the old-school doctor to stir around and learn something of a rational nature about his business, you may honestly feel grateful that homœopathy survived the attempts of the allopathists to destroy it, even though you may never employ any physician but an allopathist while you live.

THE END.

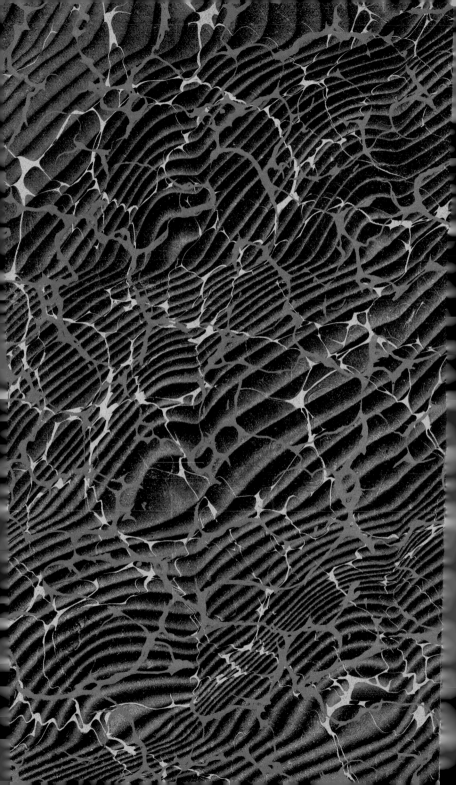